CHAIR SEATING

Dedication
To our families, with our thanks for their patience and support

CHAIR SEATING

Techniques in Cane, Rush, Willow and Cords

Kay Johnson
Olivia Elton Barratt
Mary Butcher

Acknowledgments

We would like to thank the many friends who have helped and encouraged us: Bill Crawforth for the drawings in the cane section and hours of help with the complicated frames and patterns; Susan Colman for coming to the rescue with her graphic expertise; Rev. Philip Spence for the cartoons; Barry Westwood for advice and for developing many of the photographs; Mick Duff and Mike Waterman for photography; Meg Tapley, Enid Ellis and Viviene Jones for helpful reading of the text; Andrew Butcher and Hilda Butcher for assistance in preparation of part of the manuscript; Mark Buxton for his patient explanations of 'quick methods' and other useful hints and tips; Margaret Bradbury of Much Cowarne; Harriet Bisson; Mr and Mrs Peter Gilbert of the Wycombe Cane and Rush Works; Robert Towers, the Orkney Chair maker of Kirkwall; the Ulster Folk and Transport Museum (all for information and advice); B. D. Cotton for historical information on rush-seated chairs; John Mayes of High Wycombe for historical information on rush and straw matting and skeined willow seats; members of the Basketmakers' Association.

Thanks also to the following for the loan of their chairs and for being so helpful: Hilbre Anderson, Dail Behannah, John Boardman, Mary Connell, Felicity Crawforth, Nancy Furlong, Jonathan Gordon, Simon Gordon Clark, M. B. Holliday, Jacob, Young & Westbury, Caroline James, Tom Kealy, Marian Murray, John Mayes, Capt R. Maynard, Hilary Mimpriss, Sue Nash, Peggy Pertwee, Nellie Pilcher, Linda Potter, Iorwerth Pritchard, Mary Shuldham, Ivan Sparkes, Trading Places of Ware, Robert Walton, Janet Watson, Shirley Westwood, Joy Viall.

Photographs 3.10, 3.11, 3.12, 3.16, 3.17, 3.18, 3.19, 3.20, 3.21, 3.22, 3.23, 3.24, 3.25 and 3.29 are reproduced with permission from the Institute of Agricultural History and the Museum of English Rural Life, University of Reading. Photographs in the cane and rush sections are by Kay Johnson.

The cover photograph shows, from left: a bolt of rushes, a bolt of willow, a chair caned in the five-way standard pattern by Jervis Johnson, a rush chair by Susan Torino, an open skeined willow chair by Mary Butcher, a stool seated in sea-grass, a bodkin, a rush smoother, a rapping iron, a shell bodkin. Photograph by Mick Duff.

First published 1988
by Dryad Press Ltd,
a division of B. T. Batsford

Reprinted 1990

All rights reserved.
No part of this publication may
be reproduced, in any form or
by any means, without written
permission from the Publishers.

This edition published by
Kay Johnson, Olivia Elton Barratt
& Mary Butcher

November 2000

Printed by
Mickle Print Ltd, Canterbury CT1 1YY

ISBN 0 952 5541 1 9
(This ISBN number belongs to Mary Butcher)

© Kay Johnson, Olivia Elton Barratt
& Mary Butcher

Contents

Introduction 8

Part I **CANE 9**

1. Introducing cane seating 10
Chair caning in England 10
Introduction to cane seating 11
Rattan 11

2. Caning simple shapes 12
Preparation of the chair 12
Tools useful for cane seating 12
Cutting out the old seat 13
The six-way standard pattern 13
Preparation of the cane 15
Selecting the correct size of cane 15
Seating square and rectangular shapes 16
Seating a rectangular stool 27
Alternative methods of beading and couching 28

3. Angles, circles and medallions 29
Victorian chamber chair 29
Bow-fronted chair 34
Circular chair seats 37
Oval shapes 41
Rising sun pattern 42
Medallions 47

4. Curved frames, blind caning and double caning 51
Saddle curves and curves generally 51
Antique armchair with a curved back 53
Blind or 'Continental' caning 54
Chairs with the cane hidden in a groove 55
Double caning 56
Bergère chairs 58
Chairs with curves below the arms 58

5. Loom cane and different patterns 59
Loom cane (or cane webbing) seats 59
Hexagonal or 'Star of David' 60
Double Victoria pattern 61
Single Victoria pattern 62
Five-way standard 62
Four-way standard 63

6. Quick methods and renovating   64
   Quick methods of weaving   64
   Methods of colouring cane   65
   Simple renovating and repairs   66
   Checklist   66

Part II   **RUSH   67**

7. Historical background   68

8. Materials and tools   70

9. English traditional methods   72

10. Simple shapes   74
   Basic methods for square, rectangular and trapezium shapes   74
   Alternative techniques   79
   Drop-in seats   87

11. Continental methods   88
   Methods of working on square, rectangular and trapezium shapes   89
   Variations of pattern   90
   Chair backs   93
   Drop-in seats   94

12. Problem shapes   98
   Chairs with long side-rails   98
   Widely-curved rails   100
   Awkward arms   100
   Triangular seats   103
   Circular stools   104
   Sofas   106

13. Straw-wrapped rush seating   108
   Materials   109
   Preparing and dyeing straw   109
   Methods of working   109

14. Orkney chairs   112
   Techniques   113
   Making a chair back   115
   Repairing   116

15. Irish straw rope chairs   118

16. Using artificial rush   121

Part III **WILLOW, CLOSE CANING AND CORDS 123**

17. Willow seating 124
Willow and its preparation 124
Tools 125

18. Whole willow seating 126

19. Skeined willow chairs 137
Tools 137
How to make willow skeins 138

20. Close skeining 140
The traditional method 141
Leslie Maltby's method 149

21. Open-skeined seats 158
Barbara Maynard's method 159
The Campaign chair method 162
Leslie Maltby's method 164

22. Close caning 168
Chairs with drop-in seats 169

23. Danish cord chairs 173
Chairs with single side-rails 175
Chairs with double side-rails 176

24. Stools and seats in seagrass and cord 177
Woven methods 178
Open weaving method 184
The rush pattern used on stools 186
The false rush pattern 187
Knotted seating 188

Recommended reading 189
Suppliers 190
Index 191

Introduction

In this book we have sought to describe many of the existing kinds of woven and wrapped seating. Our aim has been to provide detailed and explicit accounts of as wide a variety as possible of methods of seating restoration and replacement. From our instructions we hope that even beginners will be able to achieve a high standard of seating.

In setting down basic methods of work, and variations upon them, many of which we believe have never been described in print before, we have had two main purposes in mind. The first was to record techniques so that they might be preserved and passed on. The second was to respond to a surge of interest in chair seating which has taken place in recent years.

As more and more people have become enthusiastic about furniture restoration and want to learn the skills of yesterday's craftsmen, so the work for amateur and professional chair seaters has grown rapidly. We hope this book will be useful to students, teachers and professionals alike, to support Adult Educational or Vocational courses, and to assist people working on their own. We have tried to indicate places where problems may arise and ways to solve them, and we have described various tools and aids which make the tasks simpler.

We owe it to furniture makers, past and present, to make possible the achievement of high standards, and we realise that whenever chair seaters get together they argue about the best methods to use. What we have written, therefore, is not meant to be rigidly prescriptive, but to enable you to discover the methods you prefer. We hope that it will encourage the development of new techniques, and will further work in collecting and recording the skills of past craftsmen.

Part I
CANE

Introducing cane seating **10**
Caning simple shapes **12**
Angles, circles and medallions **29**
Curved frames, blind caning and double caning **51**
Loom cane and different patterns **59**
Quick methods and renovation **64**

Kay Johnson

1. Introducing cane seating

Chair caning in England

Caning seems to have been introduced into England when Charles II was given an elaborately carved ebony chair with a cane seat. This was of Indian origin and had been imported into Europe. This, and other chairs from Europe, particularly Holland, inspired English furniture makers to copy them in expensive walnut, and in much cheaper uncarved versions in beechwood. These new lighter, more elegant chairs were like the others in having caned panels in the back and seat. Their popularity increased rapidly in the 1670s, and sets of six plus two armchairs were introduced. These beechwood chairs slowly became more elaborate again. They appeared in the King's palaces and were introduced into the royal apartments by William and Mary in 1689. Cane started to be used for table tops, day beds and other luxury goods with caning of very high quality.

In the first half of the eighteenth century the Chippendale chair styles were unsuitable for caning and so it ceased to be fashionable. The process was revived in the late eighteenth century with the introduction of chairs of beech covered with Japanese lacquer and which had caned seats. These were made by a number of small firms in London, some of which moved out of the city. Many went to High Wycombe to be near the source of the wood, in the Chilterns. Bergère or library chairs with caned backs and arms were also made in large numbers. Nursery furniture, such as high chairs and elegant cradles which had hoods with mahogany frames and caned panels, were popular in the Regency period.

Although most Victorian furniture was heavily upholstered, a great variety of bedroom chairs were made and caned in High Wycombe. In 1851 Michael Thonet in Austria perfected his technique of wood steaming, making possible the production of the first Bentwood chairs, which had cane seats. These were exported worldwide and could be seen everywhere in shops and cafés.

The Edwardians produced rather heavy versions of the Bergère chair, but did not use caning much elsewhere. Its popularity declined, although itinerant menders could be heard with their call 'chairs to mend!' After the First World War some disabled veterans were trained as chair caners and repaired chairs, but by the end of the Second World War there were very few people left who were skilled at the craft.

In Charles II's reign caned chair seats had large holes in the rails which were far apart and the cane woven through these was very coarse. This gradually changed as cane producers and caning workers became more skilful. The long strands of cane were produced from imported whole round cane, which had to be split and shaved down (skeined) until only a fine strip of bark of an even width was produced. This was a skilled job, as the whole cane comes in very long lengths and the cut edges are very sharp. This job was done by men known as 'Makers off'. The seating was done by the women and children of a family.

By the end of the seventeenth century very fine and beautiful caning was introduced from France and Germany. In the eighteenth century holes in chair-frames were smaller and closer. Finer, better-prepared cane was used, but in Victorian times the work became less delicate. At the end of the nineteenth century cane preparation was carried out with machinery in factories and later it was imported, ready prepared, from Indonesia and Malaysia via Europe. Today cane can be woven into the standard cane patterns by machine, and can be bought by the square metre. Modern chairs for caning do not all have the traditional holes but some have a groove round the seat frame into which the machined cane is fitted.

Until about 1850 all caning was in the six-way traditional pattern and chairs were not beaded. In the mid-nineteenth century other patterns such as the single and double Victoria were introduced, partly for their speed of working. Many chairs were then finished with a beaded edge.

In the last twenty years there has been a revival of interest in caning, and as a result Victorian chairs which once had very little value are now sought after. There is an increasing number of people with the skills to repair chairs of any age and small chair-caning businesses are now flourishing.

Introduction to cane seating

The first chapters in this section are concerned with chairs which are hand-caned. You may already have one in need of repair. If, on the other hand, you do not and are looking for one, the following points may help when rummaging through antique shops on the trail of a chair needing to be recaned.

Cane-seated chairs have holes drilled in the frame, and the cane is threaded through these. They are not always apparent, as quite often the seats have been upholstered instead of recaned, or a piece of shaped and moulded plywood may have been nailed on top of the old cane seat. Look at the underside of the seat; if it was originally seated with cane you will probably be able to see the holes, which may still have some strands of cane woven through them.

If the holes in the frame are few and very widely spaced, perhaps as much as 5 cm (2 in), and the seat frame has raised corners similar to a rush chair, it will have been designed for close caning. Instructions for this can be found in Part III.

Chair backs are often 'blind' caned, in which case the holes are not drilled right through the frame (see page 55). Holes can also be hidden underneath the seat or behind a caned back by putting them into a groove which is then covered by a spline of wood. This can often be quite difficult to detect if the match is good.

Modern chairs may be seated with factory-woven 'loom' cane, in which case the seats will have been constructed with a groove round the frame into which the cane is glued. (See page 59.)

Rattan

Chair-seating cane is imported from the Far East. The best varieties grow in Indonesia and Malaysia. The cane comes from the hard, shiny inner bark of the rattan or cane palm (also known as *Asalan Rattan*). This is a climbing palm which grows to a great length in tropical rain forests.

The outer bark of the rattan is thorny, as are the tendrils with which it attaches itself to the tree tops. This is stripped before it is cut into manageable lengths and graded for size and quality. The sorting is a very skilled job, as only a very small amount is of high enough quality for chair-caning, and much that is cut is spoiled.

After being washed in chemicals which remove any insects or fungus, it is then fumigated in a sulphur chamber, which highlights the colour.

The shiny surface is smoothed to remove the leaf ridges, and then passed through precision machines which strip the outer surfaces of the cane. This is then split into the fine narrow strips used for chair seating. Today, the highest grade of cane stripping is done in Indonesia.

Like all palm, the rattan stem is solid (bamboo is hollow) and once the outer surface is removed the stem is split into rounds of various thicknesses, known as 'centre' or 'pith' cane, used for basketry.

2. Caning simple shapes

Preparation of the chair

Once you have found a chair to re-cane, look at the old seat, if there is enough of it left. It may be helpful to retain it for reference, so cut it out carefully. Do be sure that it *is* correct before copying, as it might be one of those badly-caned seats that you will come across from time to time. In this case you might keep it as an example of how *not* to cane your seat!

A checklist of points to look out for (see page 66) will be of help in assessing how a chair has previously been caned, and will act as a guide to the beginner as well as to the more experienced caner.

Tools useful for cane seating

1. Knife: for trimming the ends of the cane and cutting plugs.
2. Sidecutters: used for cutting plugs and trimming cane, etc. (not shown).
3. Thin bodkin: very useful for lifting cane in awkward corners and compressing the cane in small holes.
4. Clearing tool: for removing plugs.
5. Hammer: used in conjunction with clearing tool, etc.
6. Shell bodkins: these come in various sizes and are very useful particularly in weaving the crossing stages.
7. Drawing-through tool: used mainly in the weaving stage.
8. Golf tees: two dozen in various sizes for pegging.
9. Tape measure (not shown).
10. Toenail cutters: the kind with curved tips are ideal for cutting ends of cane within holes under the seat.
11. Scissors.

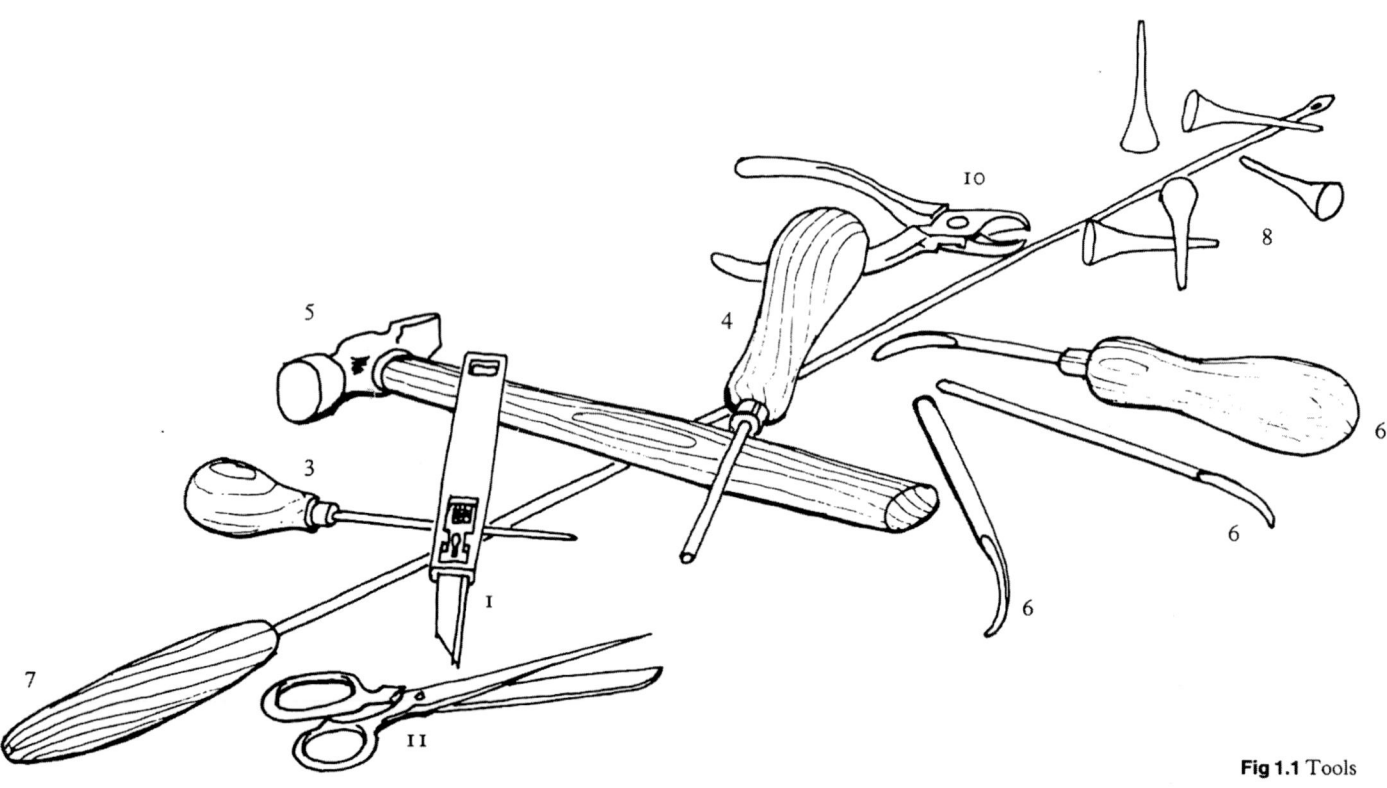

Fig 1.1 Tools

Cutting out the old seat

METHOD

1. Using a sharp knife, cut through the old cane, removing it as close to the edge of the frame as possible.
2. Turn the chair upside-down and, using a strong penknife, slip the blade under the loops of cane and lever up. If the loop does not lift out, twist the blade so that the loop is cut. Work all round the underside of the seat.
3. Turn the chair right-side up, lift the beading (if there is any) and many of the cut ends will come away too.
4. Now turn it upside-down again, use a clearing tool (Fig. 1.1) or a nail which is slightly smaller than the diameter of the hole to push out the plug (having first removed the point of the nail with a hacksaw). You may need to use a hammer, and if the plug still refuses to move, drill it out using a bit of the same diameter as the hole. **Note:** Do not try to push out the plugs from the *top* of the seat. It is much easier to push them up from below. Often plugs have been tapered and they are always pushed in from the top of the seat.

   If the holes are 'blind', which is often the case in the corner over a chair leg, the plugs will probably need to be drilled out very carefully.
5. Having removed the cane, check the chair for loose joints, woodworm holes etc. All repairs must be dealt with before starting to re-cane.
6. Any cleaning up and polishing should also be done at this stage, as once the caning is started it will not be possible to polish the seat. Clean off surface dirt with warm water or a rag soaked in turpentine, or use one of the recipes on page 66. Dry with an old cotton cloth and finish with a little polish.

Instructions for stripping down and repolishing and how to go about minor repairs are given at the end of the section on cane seating (page 66).

The six-way standard pattern

There are several different patterns which can be woven onto a seat, but the most widely used, and the strongest, is the six-way. This is considered the standard pattern for cane seating and the one which will be used in the following chapters. In a later chapter the other patterns will be described and most can be used on uncomplicated shapes.

The six stages in this pattern are known as:

1. The two *settings*
2. The two *weavings*
3. The two *crossings*

The *settings* usually run from back to front of the seat.

The *weavings* usually run from side to side.

The *crossings* cross the seat from left front to right back and from right front to left back.

These stages were probably so called because the settings were often set in place first. Then the weavings were both woven across in and out of the settings. Finally the crossings were woven diagonally across the seat.

The build-up of the six-way pattern can be achieved this way and in some later chapters this method is used. However, the following instructions are more suitable for a beginner, as they require less weaving.

METHOD

Fig 1.2 The first setting
Fig 1.3 The first weaving

The first *setting* is placed from the back to the front of the seat (Fig. 1.2).

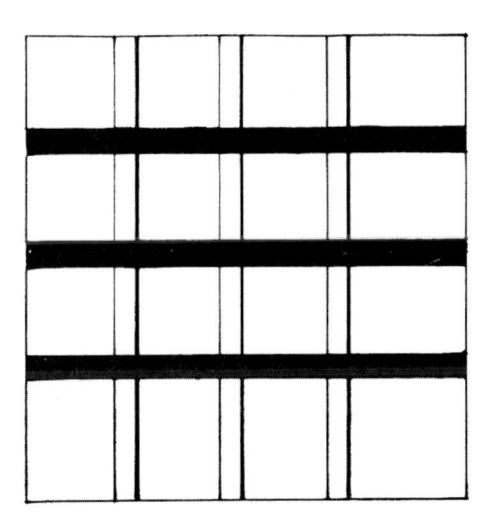

The first *weaving* is placed on top of the first setting and lies across it from one side of the seat to the other (Fig. 1.3).

13

Fig 1.4 The second setting
Fig 1.5 The second weaving

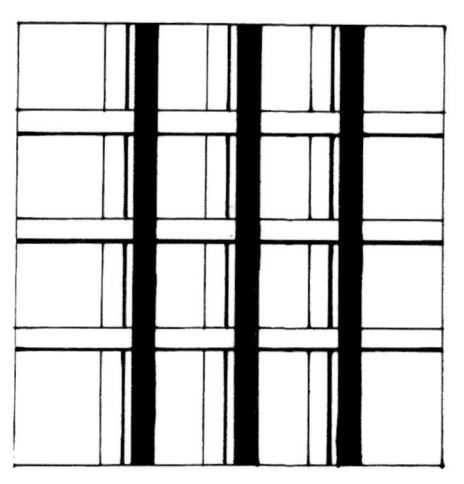

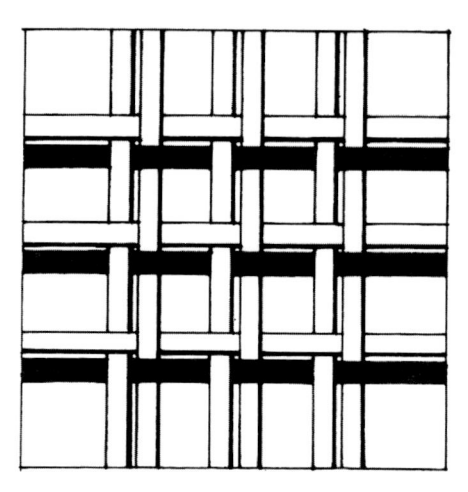

The second *setting* is threaded through the same holes as the first and is placed to the *right* of it (Fig. 1.4).

The second *weaving* is threaded through the same holes as the first weaving and its position is in *front* of the first weaving. It is woven over the second setting and under the first setting, causing all four canes to interlock (Fig. 1.5).

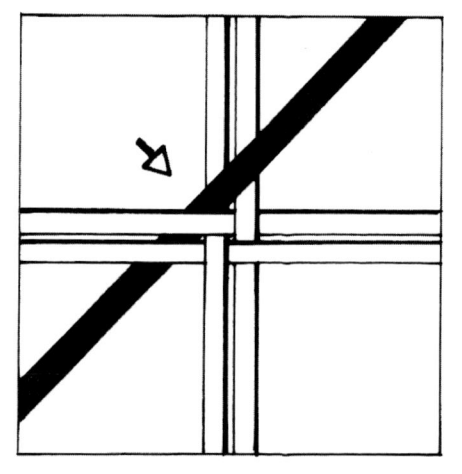

Fig 1.6 (a & b) The first crossing

The first *crossing* is woven diagonally from the left front corner to the right back corner. The diagram shows how it is woven over the settings and under the weavings, slipping neatly in the corner between the first weaving and the first setting (Fig. 1.6a and b).

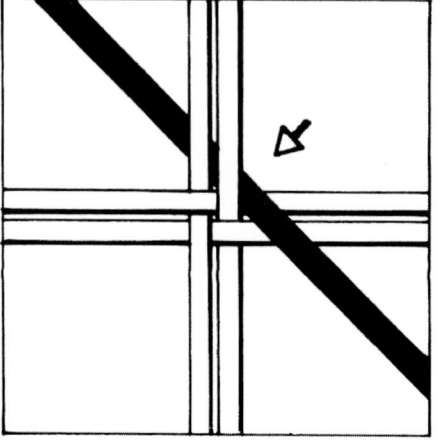

Fig 1.7 (a & b) The second crossing

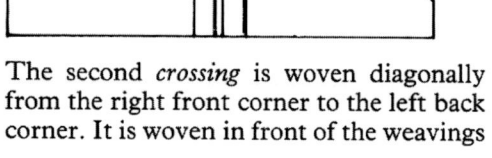

The second *crossing* is woven diagonally from the right front corner to the left back corner. It is woven in front of the weavings and behind the settings, slipping neatly in the corner between the first weaving and the second setting (Fig. 1.7a and b).

These six stages make up the six-way pattern. After the sixth stage has been completed, the chair can be finished off by plugging each hole, or, as is most usual with square, rectangular and trapezium-shaped seats, every second hole is plugged and a length of wide cane known as the *beading*, usually No. 6, is applied to all four sides over the holes. This is held in place with a smaller size of cane (the *couching*) which is 'sewn' through the unplugged holes.

The following need to be taken into consideration when deciding which cane to use:

1. Availability of the cane.
2. Is the chair one of a set? If so, which size cane is used on the others?
3. Is the chair in heavy daily use? If so, it might be better to use all No. 3 cane instead of Nos. 2 and 3.
4. How large an area does the seat cover? If the holes are close together and Nos. 1 and 2 are indicated, perhaps it would be better to use No. 2 cane for all the six stages to give added strength.

If the cane used is too thin for the chair seat, the result will look fragile and not last very well. Alternatively, if too thick a size is used the crossings (diagonal weaves) will be very difficult to thread into place and the finished seat will look clumsy. With the help of the size guide (page 16), your finished six-way pattern should be strong, long-lasting and attractive.

Preparation of the cane

METHODS

1. The cane can be worked dry as long as it is possible to keep the tension tight and the cane does not crack or split.
2. Otherwise, it can be soaked for a minute or two and then kept wrapped in a damp cloth to mellow while the seat is being worked. Do not wet more than can be used up, as cane deteriorates if it is soaked and dried too many times.
3. Other methods include drawing the lengths of cane through water immediately before using them, or simply damping a sponge and stroking the absorbent side of the cane.
4. Drawing the underside of the cane across a piece of beeswax or candlewax helps the cane to slide smoothly through in the weaving stages, as well as making it supple.

Note: If the cane is wound in tight coils when bought, soak it in cold water for a few minutes and hang it up to dry. This will make it straighten out. Store it in a place that is not too hot and dry.

Choose long lengths of cane for the first three stages (the two settings and the first weaving). Inspect each strand carefully for faults, cracks, and blemishes. Reject imperfect pieces. There are small nodes on most lengths of cane where the leaves were attached. Avoid these coinciding with the edge of a hole, as they may catch and break. The best cane has long spaces between the leaf nodes.

Selecting the correct size of cane

Cane is available in the UK in seven sizes, numbered 0–6. Size 0, the narrowest, is rather more difficult to obtain, as is size 5. These two sizes are not very often used, however. Size 6, the widest, is used mainly for beading (the edging often applied round the cane seat to cover the holes).

Cane is mostly sold in 0.25 kg (½ lb) hanks. **Important note:** Choose the best quality cane, as cheaper cane may have splits, frayed edges and possibly uneven widths. There may be some variation in size, according to where the cane was manufactured.

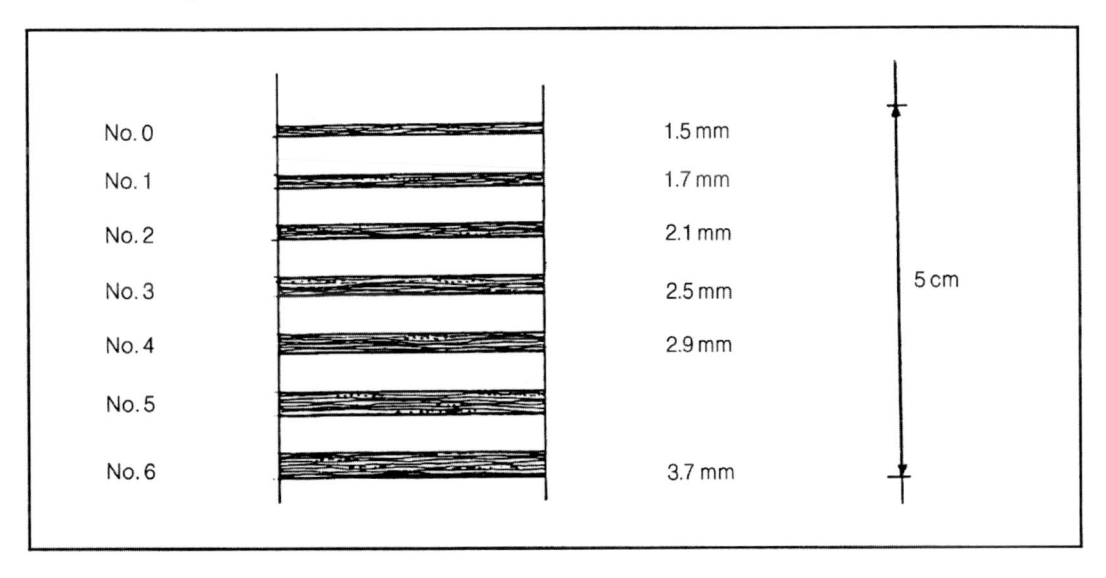

No. 0	1.5 mm
No. 1	1.7 mm
No. 2	2.1 mm
No. 3	2.5 mm
No. 4	2.9 mm
No. 5	
No. 6	3.7 mm

(5 cm overall)

Fig 1.8 Cane sizes

SIZE TO USE

The size used depends mainly on the distance between the holes in the chair seat. This is measured either from the centre of one hole to the centre of the next, or perhaps more accurately (as the holes are often unevenly drilled) by the number of holes within a given distance.

Usually the diameter of the holes is about 0.5 cm ($\frac{3}{16}$ in). The size of the holes, if they were drilled larger or smaller, could be a deciding factor as to whether to use 2 and 3 or 2 and 4, for instance.

Generally the appearance of the cane seat is more attractive if two sizes of cane are used: a smaller size for the first four stages (two settings and two weavings) and cane a size larger for the two crossings (diagonal weaves).

SIZE GUIDE

Number of holes per 15 cm (6 in)	Cane Nos.
16–17	0 & 1
15	1 & 2
14	1 & 2, or all 2
13–14	2 & 3, or all 2
12	2 & 3, 2 & 4, or all 3
9–11	3 & 4, 2 & 4, or all 4

Seating square and rectangular shapes

First measure how many holes occur within 15 cm (6 in) (see above). The stool illustrated has 11 holes. Two sizes of cane were used, No. 3 on the first four stages (the settings and weavings), and No. 4 for the last two stages (the crossings). No beading was required.

No. 3 cane could have been used for all six stages if No. 4 cane had not been available.

TOOLS

Most of those illustrated on page 12 will be helpful, and about two dozen golf tees will be needed for pegging.

MATERIALS

75 g (3 oz) of No. 3 cane (or whatever size is appropriate)

50 g (2 oz) of No. 4 cane (or whatever size is appropriate)

A good length of the right size of centre cane for plugging: 1.5 m ($4\frac{1}{2}$ feet).

Photo 1.1a Rectangular stool

THE FIRST SETTING (Fig. 1.2)
1. Select a long, strong strand of cane and either work with it dry, or choose one of the methods of preparation explained on page 15.
2. Thread the end down into the back left hole (*not* the corner, as the corner holes must be left empty until the crossings are woven). Leave an end about 10 cm (4 in) underneath for threading away afterwards. Peg with a golf tee (Fig. 1.9).
3. Keeping the shiny side of the cane uppermost and the tension tight, thread the cane down through the opposite hole in the front rail. Push in another golf tee so the tension does not slacken. Being very careful not to have a twist underneath the frame, thread the cane up the next hole to the right (Fig. 1.10).
   Note: Just before putting in the second peg, give the cane a quarter turn towards the next hole. This will help the cane to lie flatter underneath the seat. Be sure the cane does not become twisted between holes and that the shiny side remains outwards. It will help if every time you pick up the cane you pull the whole length through your fingers.
4. Now take the cane across the seat to the back rail, down through the appropriate hole, twist it slightly so that it is directed towards the next hole to the right and peg with a golf tee. Then take the cane up through this hole and peg it before working across to the front rail again (Fig. 1.11).
5. Continue in this manner until all the holes (except the corners) are used. The tension should be as tight as you can manage.
   Note: The two pegs marked black in Fig. 1.11 are moved to the right as the work progresses, keeping the tension from slackening. The first peg, which holds the starting end, remains in position until the stool seat is completed. A peg is also left securing the last end. Remember to leave a 10 cm (4 in) end.

JOINING
When it is necessary to join in a new piece the end is pegged, being sure to leave a long enough end. Peg the new end in the hole *next* to the old end so that the loops between the holes on the underside of the chair/stool are evenly spaced.

THE FIRST WEAVING (Fig. 1.3)
1. Select another strand of No. 3 cane. Check to make sure it has no blemishes or weaknesses. Give the cane a little tug to test its strength.
2. Thread the end down into the back hole on the right side of the frame (leaving the corner hole free). Make sure an end of at

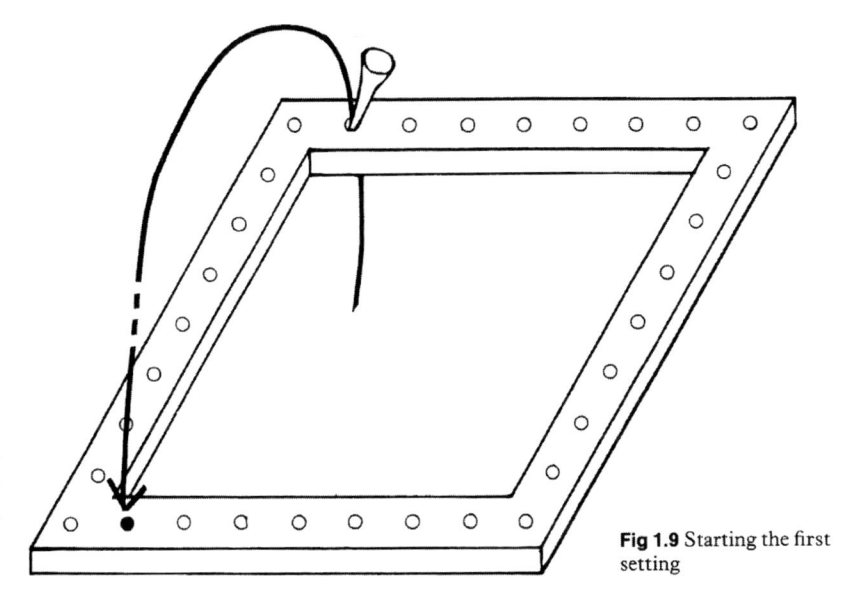

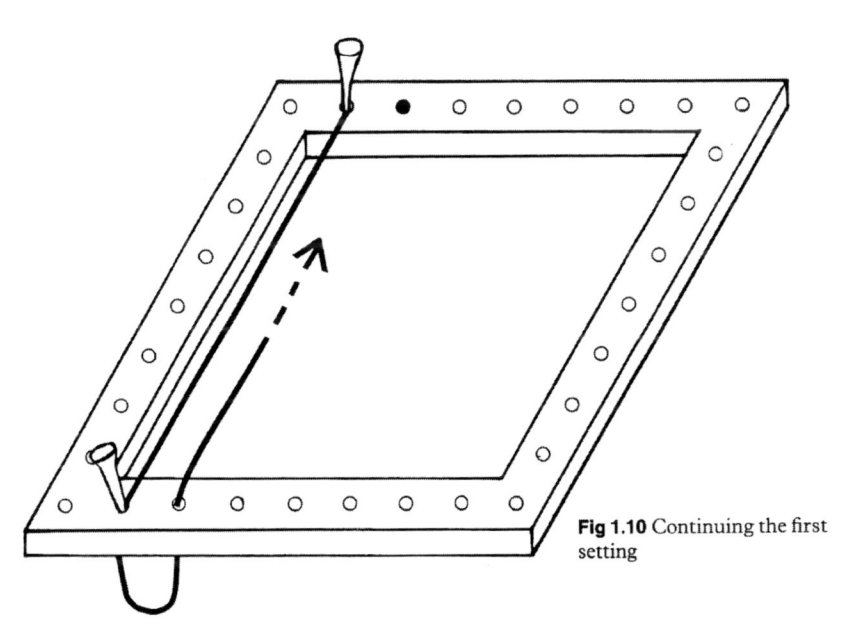

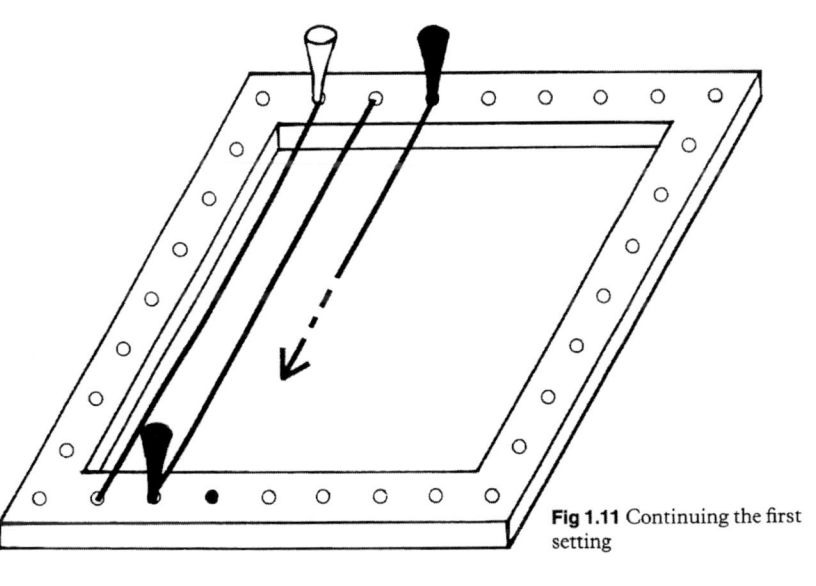

Fig 1.9 Starting the first setting

Fig 1.10 Continuing the first setting

Fig 1.11 Continuing the first setting

17

Fig 1.12 Starting the first weaving

Fig 1.13 Continuing the first weaving

Fig 1.14 The second setting

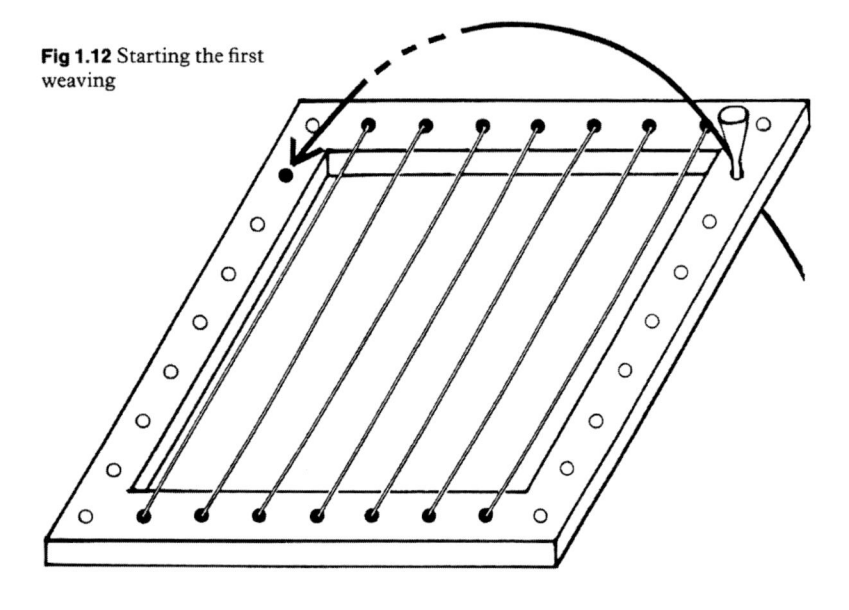

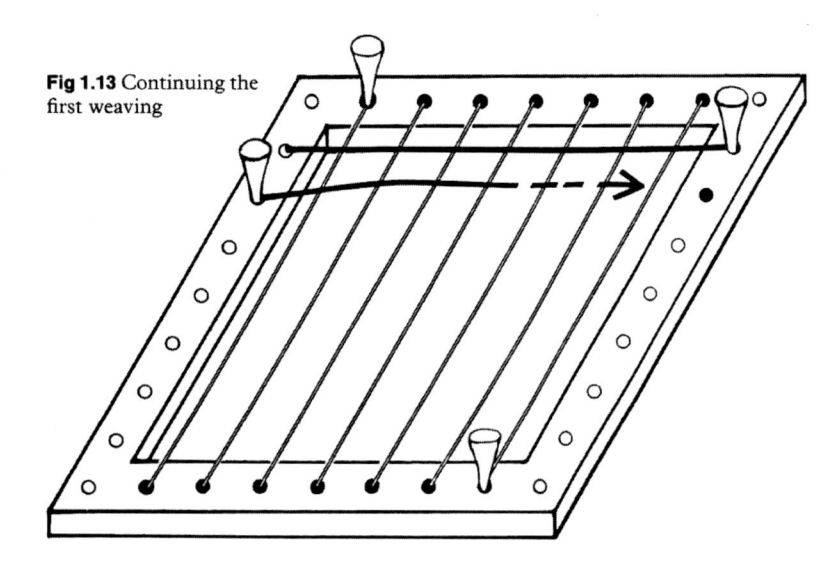

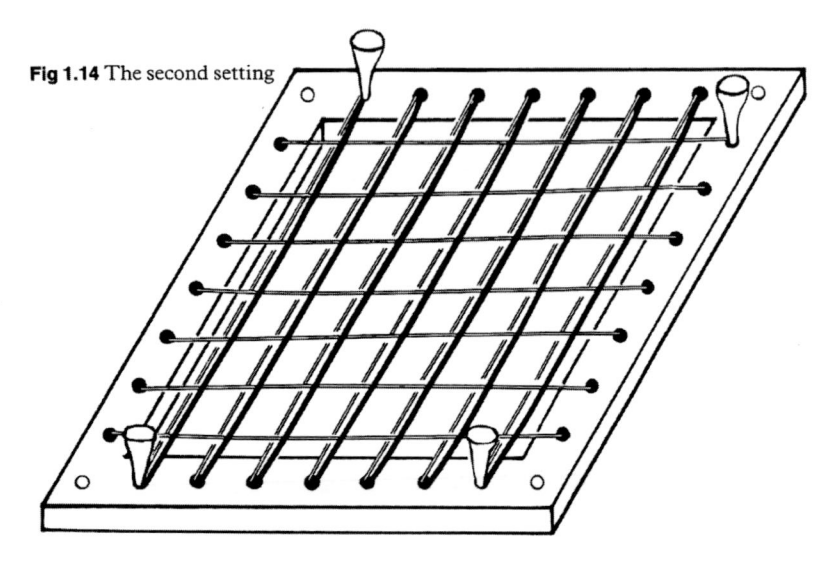

least 10 cm (4 in) is left after pegging (Fig. 1.12).

3. Now take the cane across to the left side-rail, laying it across the top of the first setting, down the correct hole (directly opposite the hole on the right rail). Make sure it is tight, turn it slightly towards the next hole it is to be threaded up through and peg firmly.

    Note: Continually check that the cane is not twisted and that the shiny side is outwards underneath the seat as well as on top.

4. Thread up through this next hole and move the peg into the hole to prevent the tension from slackening (Fig. 1.13).

5. Continue weaving with this cane until it runs out, joining in a new piece as above. Move the pegs to keep the tension and finish by pegging the end.

THE SECOND SETTING (Fig. 1.4).

This setting is threaded through the same holes as the first, but is laid to the *right of the first* and on top of the first weaving.

1. Thread the end of the cane down through the right back hole or the left front hole (not the corner) in whichever position allows the loops underneath the seat to cover the spaces between the holes not already covered by the first setting.

2. Bring the (untwisted) cane across to the appropriate hole in the front or back rail, keeping the tension and pegging firmly.

3. Continue as previously described, but making sure the cane lies to the right of the first setting (Fig. 1.14).

THE SECOND WEAVING (Fig. 1.5).

This is the first stage of the six-way pattern to be actually *woven*. The first weaving is laid in place, but when this second weaving is in place you will see that the result is that all four stages become interwoven.

Note: Before starting to weave with a piece of cane, look at it carefully. You will notice little bumps (leaf nodes) on the shiny side. These are slightly rough. Run your thumb nail along the length of the cane. In one direction it will catch – this is the *wrong* way and will snag on the settings as you pull it through. Be sure to weave the *right* way of the cane, so that it runs through smoothly.

1. Start a piece of cane by pegging the end in a front or back hole (next to the corner) either on the right or left side, whichever covers the spaces between the holes under the seat. *Keep to the front of the first weaving* (see Fig. 1.15).

    Note: It is easier, when you are a beginner, to work with a short piece of cane; use just enough to cross the seat twice. Later, as you

Fig 1.15 The second weaving

Fig 1.16 How to use the shell bodkin, showing its use in the crossing stage

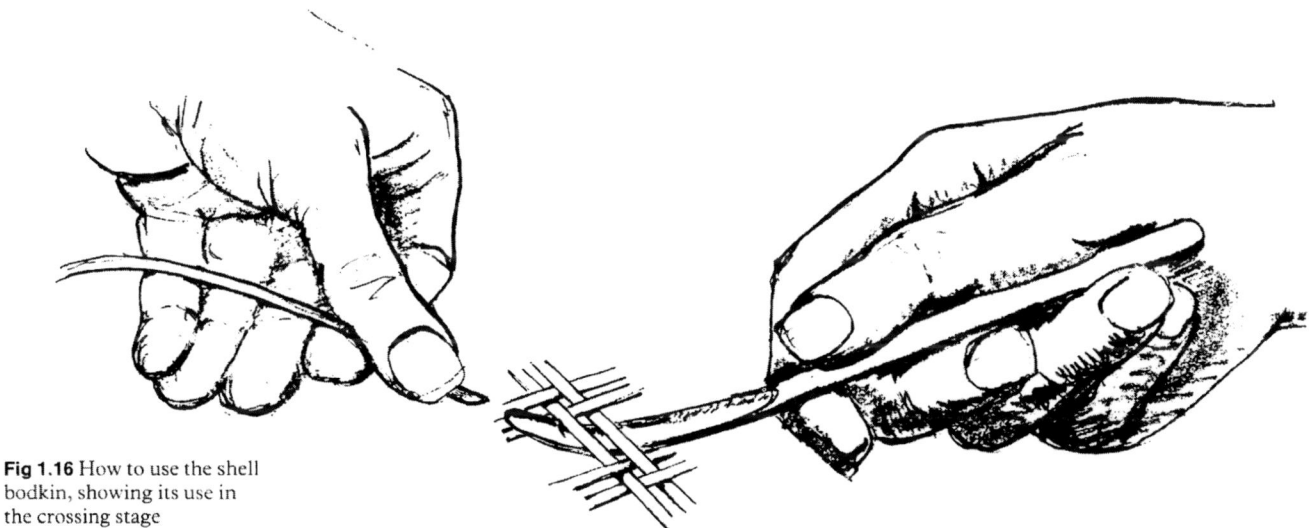

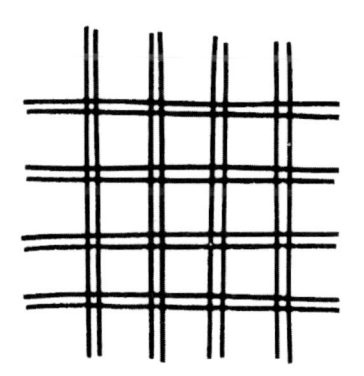

Fig 1.17 How the lines of cane should lie

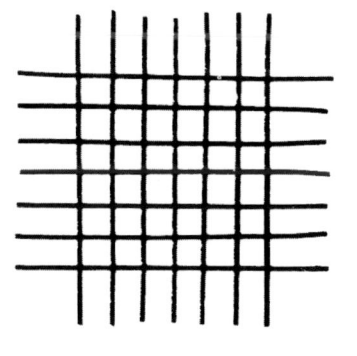

Fig 1.18 How the lines of cane should *not* lie

become more experienced, you will be able to work with a full length of cane without it becoming twisted.

2. Work with one hand under the seat and one on top. Handling only the first few centimetres of the piece of cane, thread it *under* the first setting and *over* the second, passing it down with one hand and threading it up again with the other. Do this four or five times and then pull the whole length through.

   Note: Be very careful the cane is not twisted before starting to pull it through.

3. If preferred, a shell bodkin can be used. The curved channel in the tool directs the cane back up so it is unnecessary to work with one hand under the chair

4. Continue weaving across the seat until all the holes at the sides of the frame contain two weaving canes, always keeping the second weaving to the front of the first, threading *under* the second setting and *over* the first.

5. Keep the tension using pegs. See that the lines of weaving lie straight from one side of the chair to the other.

   Note: It is often necessary to straighten the rows as you work by pushing back the completed pairs of weavings, which have a tendency to bow. A ruler or straight edge of some sort placed across the chair from time to time may help to show whether the lines are straight.

6. When the last weaving is in place, straighten all the rows and pinch the weavings and settings together into pairs so the seat looks like Fig. 1.17 rather than Fig. 1.18!

Fig 1.19 The first crossing *wrongly* woven

Fig 1.20 Starting the first crossing

Fig 1.21 Continuing the first crossing over the settings and under the weavings

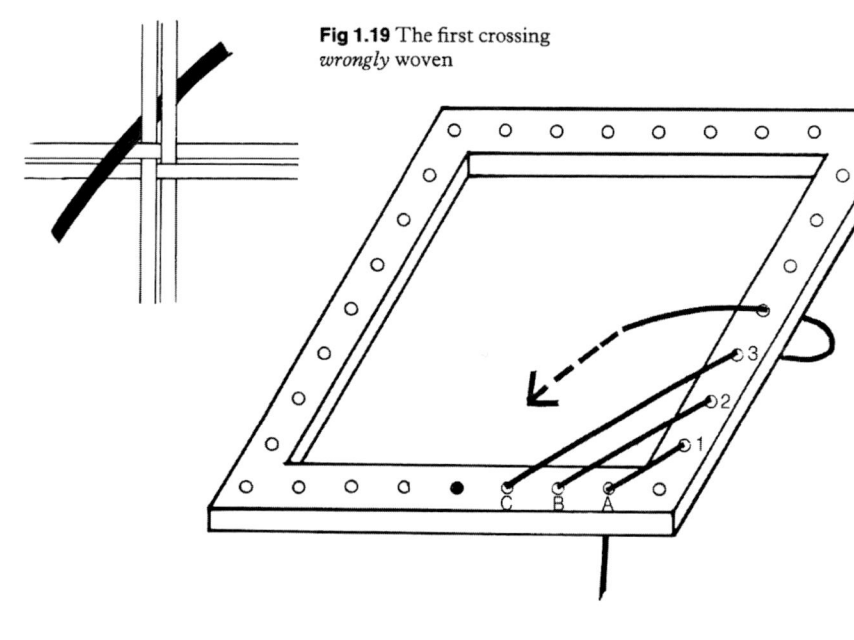

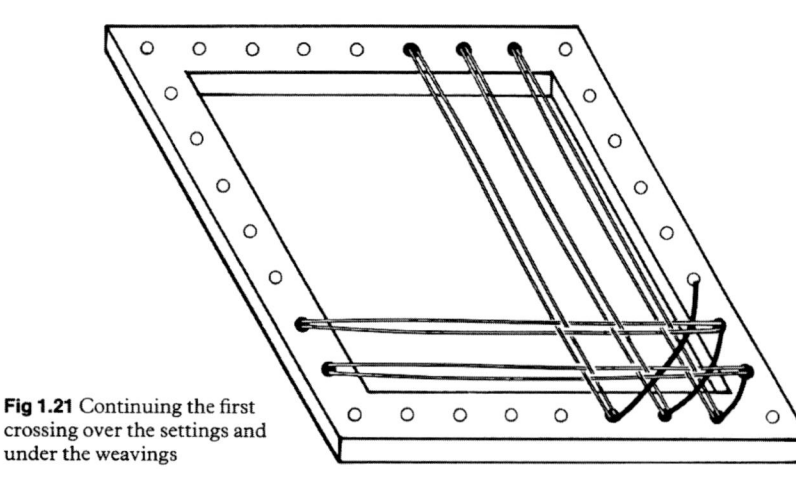

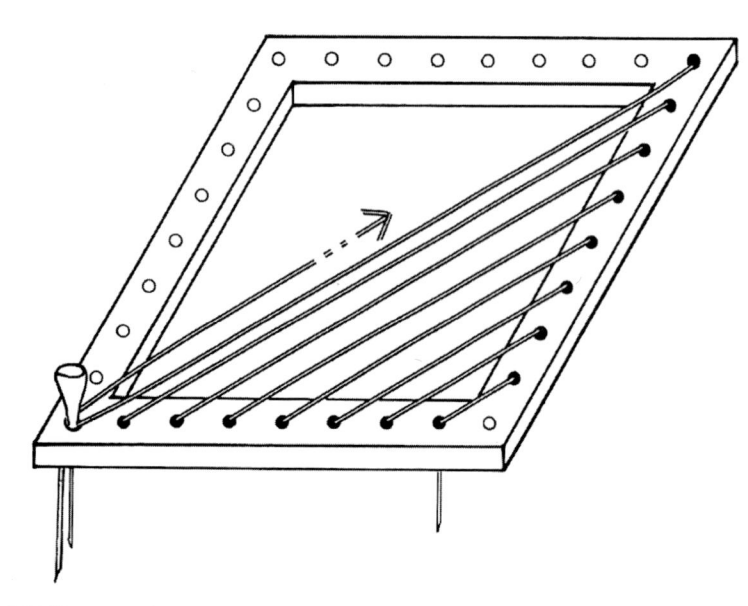

Fig 1.22 Two canes in a corner hole

THE FIRST CROSSING (Fig. 1.6a and b)
It is very important to get this correctly woven so that the crossing from left to right slides in *under* the first weaving and *over* the first setting (see Fig. 1.6)
Note: If this was woven over the weavings and under the settings by mistake, it would be difficult to pull through and would probably not lie straight. It would not slide into place at the arrowed corner (Fig. 1.19). Instead it would dig in, causing the seat to be rough rather than smooth. Consequently it would soon become worn, as well as looking untidy and obviously wrongly woven (Fig. 1.19).

1. Start by pegging a piece of No. 4 cane (or whichever size is appropriate for the seat being woven) in the hole next to the front right corner. This is marked **A** in the diagram.
2. Take the cane across to the hole on the other side of the corner marked **1** (Fig. 1.20).
3. From **1** up through **2** and from there back to **B** (threading under the weavings and over the settings).
4. From **B** to **C**, from **C** to **3**, threading over and under as you go.
   Note: You will notice that after the first crossing you should be threading under the ends of a pair of weavings on the side of the frame and over the ends of the settings on the front of the frame.
5. Continue in this way, weaving under the pairs of weavings, over the pairs of settings and into every hole in the front and side of the seat until you reach either the top right corner hole or the bottom left corner hole.
   Note: Each corner hole must have two crossings woven through it, as otherwise the pattern will not work out correctly. If the seat is completely square, with the same number of holes front and back as well as on each side, the crossings will run directly from one corner to another. It will therefore be necessary to start a new piece of cane from one of the two corner holes in order to achieve two crossings in each one.
   Note: Photograph 1.1 shows a rectangular shape with no 'corner' holes. For caning a similar shape refer to Fig. 1.37.
   Note: Two crossings woven into one hole are known as a 'double' or 'fisheye'.
6. Weave diagonally across the frame until each hole is filled (except the top left and bottom right corners).

Fig 1.23 Starting the second crossing, over the weavings and under the settings

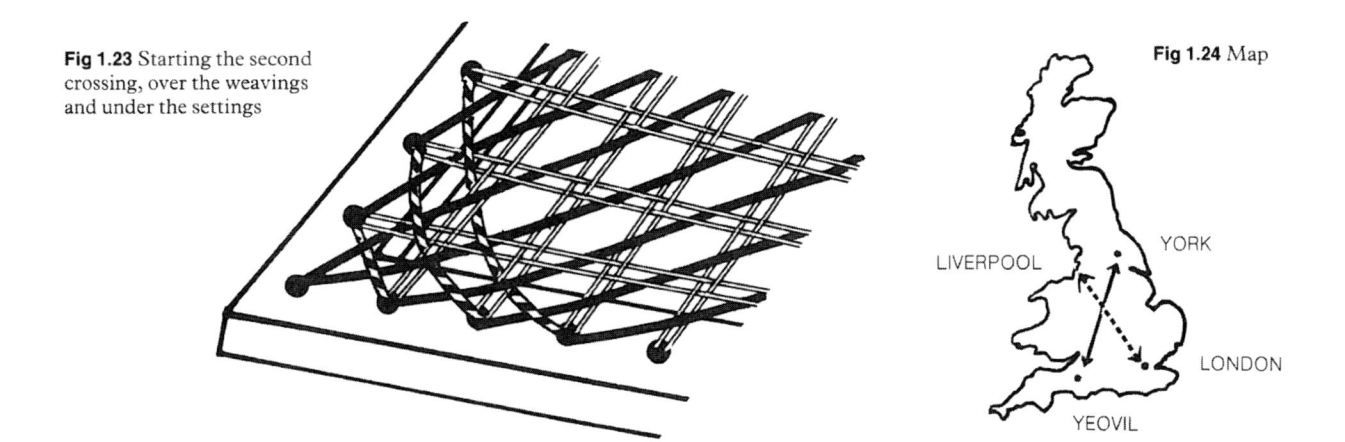

Fig 1.24 Map

THE SECOND CROSSING (Fig. 1.7a and b)
1. This time start in the bottom left hole next to the corner in the front rail, and work across to the hole next to the corner on the left side rail (Fig. 1.23).
   Note: This first stroke across the corner goes *over* a crossing and then *under* a crossing.
2. Throughout the second crossing the cane is woven *over* the pairs of weavings and *under* the pairs of settings, slipping into the corner where these four canes interlock.
3. Be sure to have two crossings in each corner hole and notice that as you weave across the seat you are continually going over and then under a cane or pair of canes. Be careful to always follow the rule: 'After weaving *over*, the next stroke *must* be woven *under*' (after weaving under, the next stroke must be woven over). It is important to see that this is also carried out at the edges of the seat, and that the crossing is woven *as far as possible*, following the above rule. This will ensure that the correct pattern is formed on the rails: Crosses (or kisses!) (Photo 1.2a) and not 'Clusters' (Photo 1.2b).
   Note: Fig. 1.24 shows another term to describe the crossings (diagonals):
   SE–NW (London to Liverpool)
   SW–NE (Yeovil to York)
   The origin of these terms is hazy, but may have originated in Victorian times, when cane chairs were very much in fashion and itinerant chair repairers used to call at houses and offer to repair a broken seat, often sitting in the street outside while mending the chair. Alternatively, it may have been used when teaching the blind.
4. When the second crossing is finished there should be two crossings in every hole round the frame.

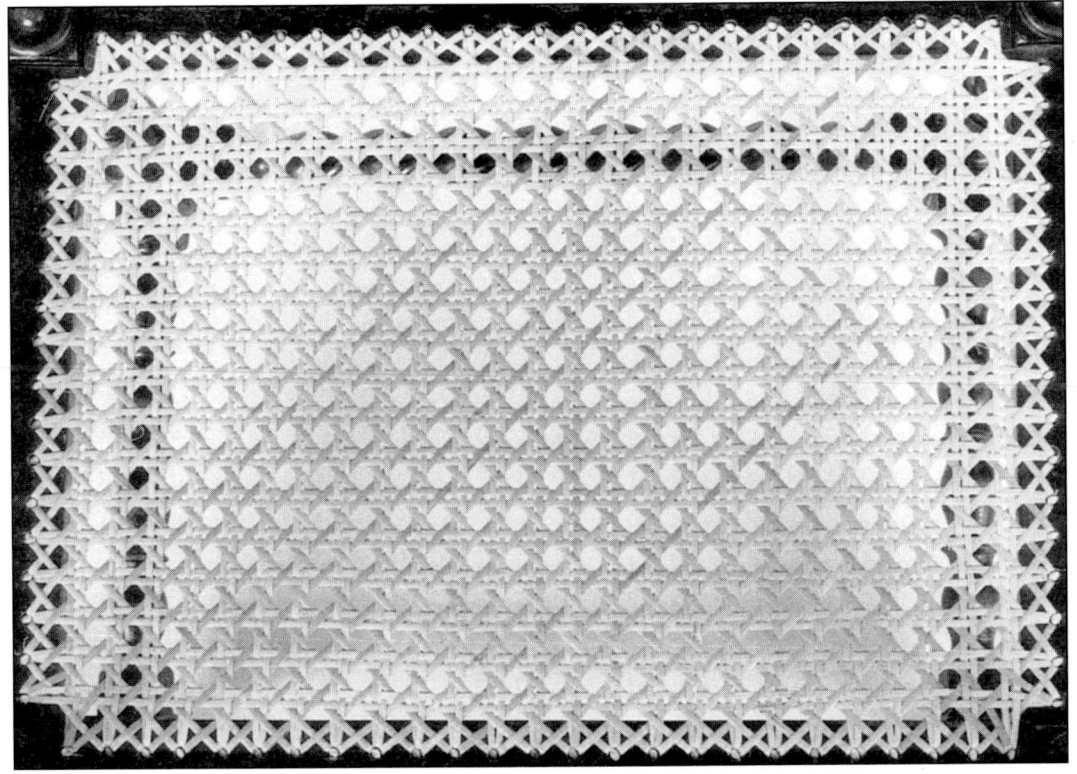

Photo 1.1b Rectangular stool close up

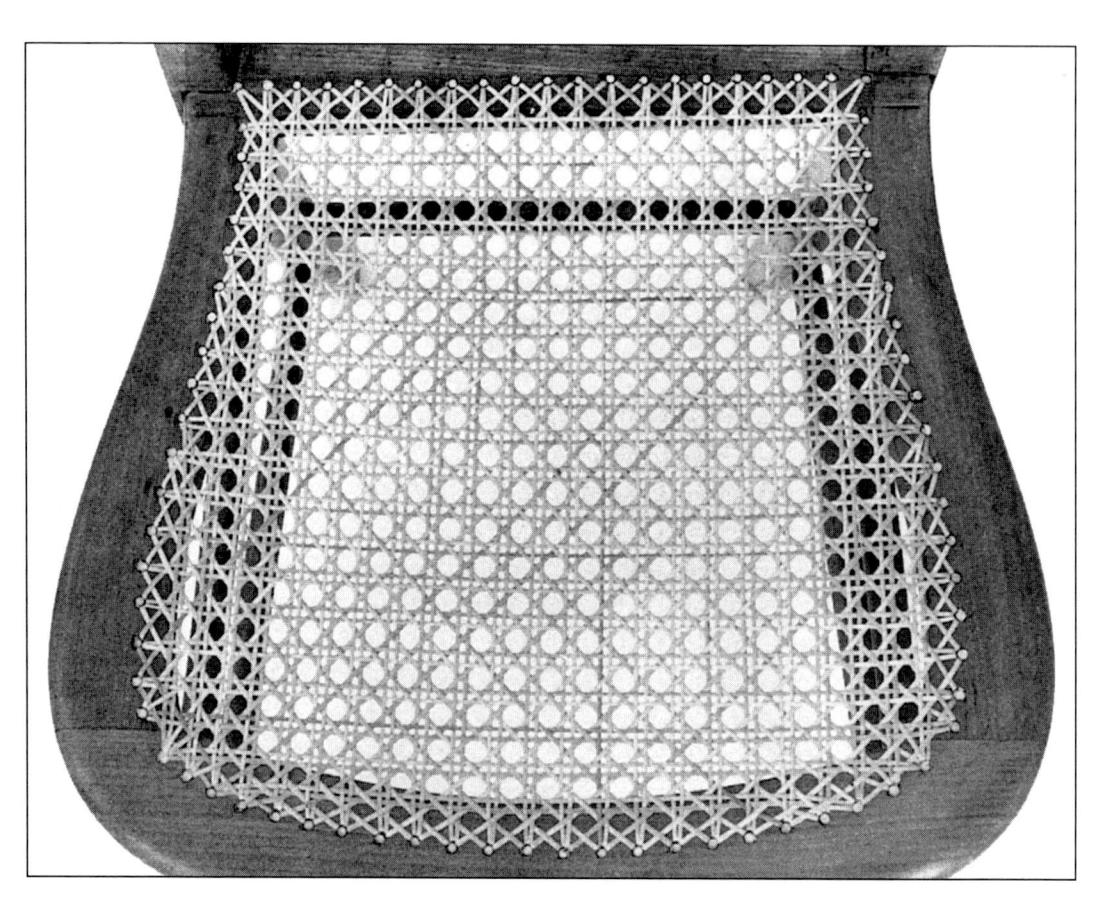

Photo 1.2a Correct crosses

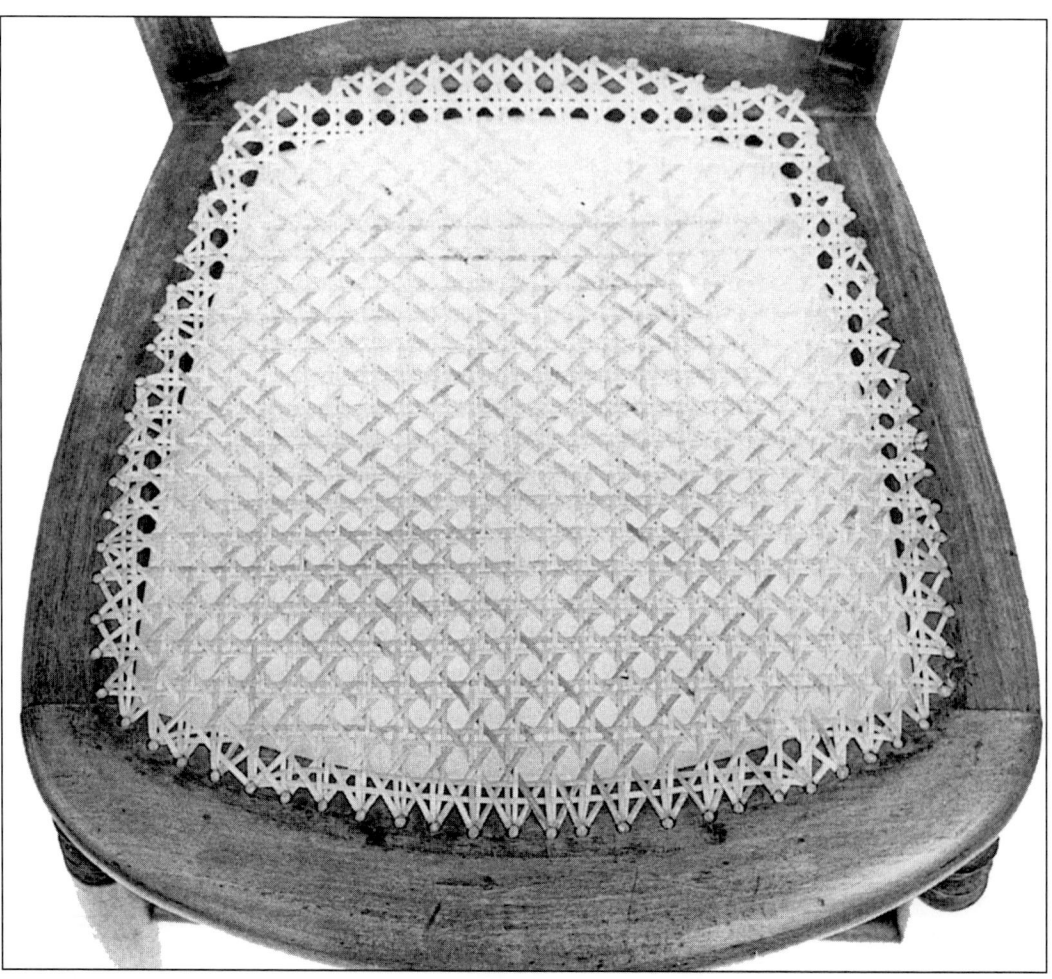

Photo 1.2b Incorrect crosses

22

FINISHING THE STOOL SEAT

Before about 1850 chair seats were not beaded. 'Beading' refers to the wider cane, usually No. 6, which is sometimes applied round the edge of the seat to cover the holes and neaten the appearance of the finished work. It is a comparatively 'modern' idea and probably came into fashion with the trapezium-shaped Victorian bedroom chair. Because of the position and the size of the holes, it looked neater if they were covered with a wide piece of cane – the beading.

TO FINISH WITHOUT BEADING

Every hole will now require a plug to keep the cane firmly in place and secure the loose ends. This can be done with centre cane. Choose a size which fits tightly into the holes.

Before starting the plugging, turn the chair upside-down to make sure that every hole has a tight loop of cane between it and the next hole. If you have missed some spaces, thread one of the ends (from a 'join') across the gap and push it up through the appropriate hole so that the end protrudes through to the top of the seat. Put a golf tee in this hole so the cane does not slip down while you are driving the other plugs home (Fig. 1.25).

The cleaner the plugs are cut, the better the finish looks. Use of sharp secateurs or a craft knife to cut the individual plugs before inserting is worth the time spent.

However, for those in a hurry:

1. Push the end of a length of centre cane of the right size firmly into one of the holes and cut it close to the seat with a pair of side cutters.
2. Press the plug home with the nose of the cutters, or tap into place with a clearing tool and mallet. The plug should be quite flush, or pushed just below the surface of the seat. It should not protrude below the seat. If it does, you are probably not using a large enough size of cane, or you may have cut the plug too long.

   Note: A 7–8 cm (3 in) nail makes a good tool. If you cut off the tip with a hacksaw, the head of the nail is useful for tapping down the plug, which can then be *slightly* countersunk with the tip.

3. When plugging a hole where there is a 'tail' threaded up from below, be careful to hold on to the end when driving the plug into place, so that it is not pushed down, causing a loop under the seat (Fig. 1.26).

   Note: Never try to drive a plug home with a hammer, as you may damage the surface of the chair or even split the cane you have so laboriously woven!

4. Put a plug into every hole. When you have finished and *before* cutting off the ends, turn the chair upside-down and check there are no loops from the ends which were threaded up and no gaps between holes. If there *are* any loops or gaps these must be attended to now, before the ends are trimmed. It is not difficult to remove and replace plugs at this stage.

5. Now cut off all the ends as short as possible, so that no rough bits can be felt. It is safer to pull the end of the cane on to the point of the knife than to cut down on to the cane, which might result in the wrong cane being cut.

   Note: Toenail cutters are excellent for safe trimming of ends. The downward curving points go right into the holes, so no jagged ends are left protruding.

6. Underneath the chair (if you have no toenail cutters!) the point of a slim knife can be inserted into the hole and the end of the cane pulled towards the blade so the cut end is inside the hole and cannot be felt.

   Note: When sitting on a finished chair or stool, you should be able to run your hand round under the edge of the seat and not feel any rough ends. These are sometimes referred to disparagingly as 'dragon's teeth'!

Fig 1.25 Threading ends up

Fig 1.26 Holding the ends

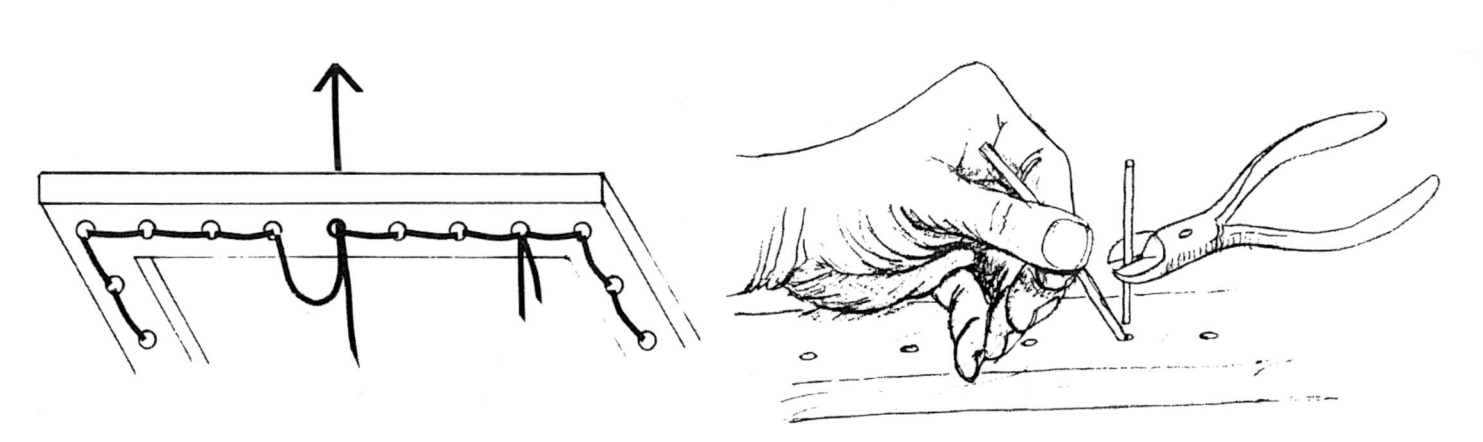

TO FINISH USING BEADING

There is more than one way of beading a stool or chair seat, but this is the one used most and is perhaps the strongest.

The beading surrounds the edge of the caned seat and covers the holes. It is usually applied in four separate lengths which are plugged at each corner and held in place along the length by a thinner strand of cane, usually No. 2, 'sewn' through the holes. The sewing of the beading is known as 'couching'. This is probably taken from the use of the term in embroidery to describe a stitch which holds down another longer stitch.

1. Place a golf tee in each corner hole. These four holes must *not* be plugged at this stage. You could use all red golf tees, keeping this colour just for the corners to remind you.
2. Now put a golf tee (of another colour) in every other hole across the front rail to indicate the holes to be plugged. Ideally the holes on each side of all four corners should be 'left open' to couch through, so that the beading at the corners is kept tight (Fig. 1.27).

Note: If there is an even number of holes across the front, back, or sides, there will be two plugged holes together (or two open holes next to each other). These are often placed at the centre of the rail (Fig. 1.28a,b). However, two plugged holes together means a longer uncouched stretch of beading, which would be especially undesirable on the front rail where most wear occurs. Fig. 1.28c shows how to avoid this by plugging next to the corner holes.

Another method is to leave two holes open for couching at one end of a rail with an even number of holes, but for appearance sake it is best to avoid this on the front or back rails (Fig. 1.28d). Try to keep the plugged and couched holes matching, front to back and side to side.

3. Any loose ends which are in the holes to be couched must be threaded up into one of the neighbouring holes which has been temporarily pegged with a golf tee (avoid the corners if possible). Choose the direction which will give the neatest finish under the seat and which covers any gaps between holes (Fig. 1.29).

Note: Any loose ends that are in the holes to be plugged (the ones with the golf tees) remain where they are and do not need to be threaded away.

4. Now plug the holes containing the tees, one at a time, holding any 'tails' which have been threaded up from below so that they are not pushed down, causing a loose loop under the seat.

Do not plug the corner holes (red golf tees!).

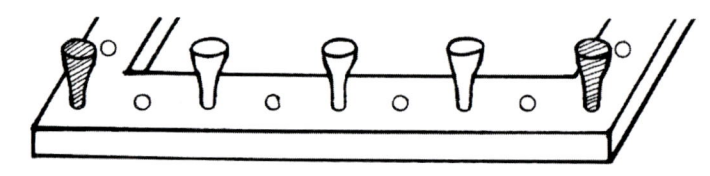

Fig 1.27 Pegs in every other hole

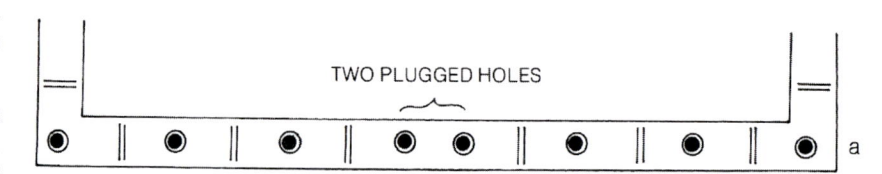

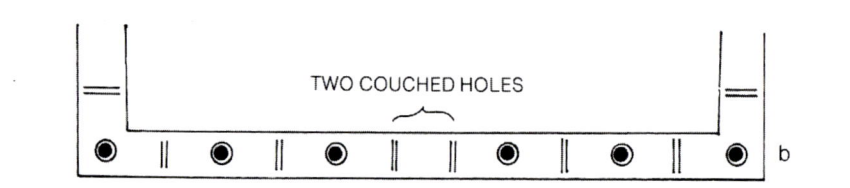

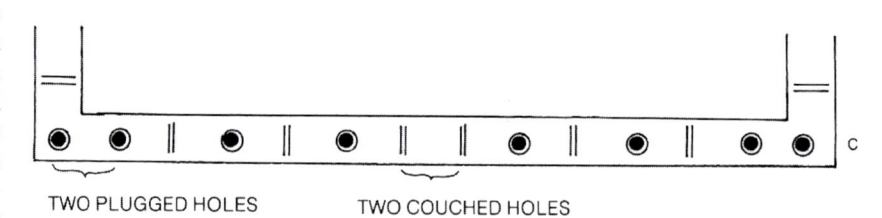

Fig 1.28 (a,b,c & d) Couching and plugging holes

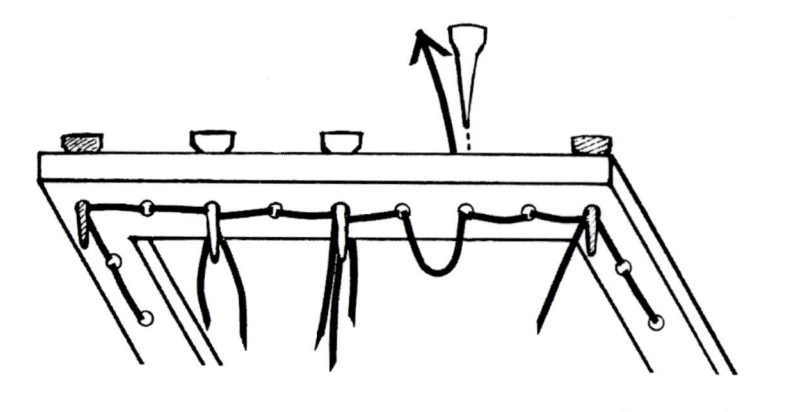

Fig 1.29 Loose end threaded up

5. Complete one side-rail in the same way, with a golf tee in each of the holes to be plugged, threading up through a 'next door' hole any ends which lie in the holes through which the couching will pass.
6. Repeat with the other side and then the back rail.
7. Now check that you have plugged the right holes and that all the ends have been threaded away correctly.
8. Cut the ends off very short (see page 23).

BEADING AND COUCHING

Start along the back rail, so that the finishing plug will be furthest from view.

1. Cut a piece of No. 6 cane long enough to cover the holes on the back rail with at least an extra 10 cm (4 in) on each end for threading down the two back corner holes.
2. Select a piece of strong No. 2 for the couching. This should be $2\frac{1}{2}$–3 times the length of the side to be couched.
   Note: Work with enough cane to couch one side at a time. It is easier to start a new piece on each side than to try to work with too long a length, as it may become twisted and break.
3. Push the end of the No. 2 cane which will be used for the couching up through the right-hand corner hole. Leave an end which will be long enough to cover the next hole to the left, so that it is held in place by the first strand of couching.
4. Now push the end of the beading cane (No. 6) down beside the couching cane and peg the two with a golf tee. Pull tight and push the other end down through the left-hand corner hole.
5. Thread the long end of the couching cane up the first hole to the left, over the top of the beading and down into the same hole, making sure everything is tight and there are no loose loops underneath the frame.
6. Now place a temporary golf tee underneath in this hole to keep the cane from slackening while you are couching through the next hole.
7. Move the tee along as each successive hole is couched. The couching should be very tight between the holes underneath the frame as well as on top. The beading should lie flat and be tightly fixed into place.

   Note: It is easier to manage the couching if when you thread it up from underneath the frame, it comes up on the outside of the beading cane, over the top and down through the same hole on the inside; then on to the next hole, up on the outside again, and so on.

   Couching in this way may produce a slightly slanting stroke on the underside of the frame.

   You may, however, prefer to thread up on the inside and down on the outside, then up on the outside and down on the inside, continuing to couch in this manner produces a stroke that lies straighter.

   The most important thing is to get the couching firm and tidy both on top and underneath the frame, so the beading is held tightly in place over the top of the holes.

8. When the last hole before the corner has been couched, peg this hole (from below) to keep the couching tight and bring the end of the couching cane up through the corner hole to be laid under the beading of the next side.
9. A second piece of No. 6 beading cane is cut to size and placed in the top left corner hole, at a right angle to the first piece.
10. Another length of No. 2 cane, $2\frac{1}{2}$–3 times the length of the side-rail, is pushed up through this hole. The short end should be long enough to cover the first hole, as before.

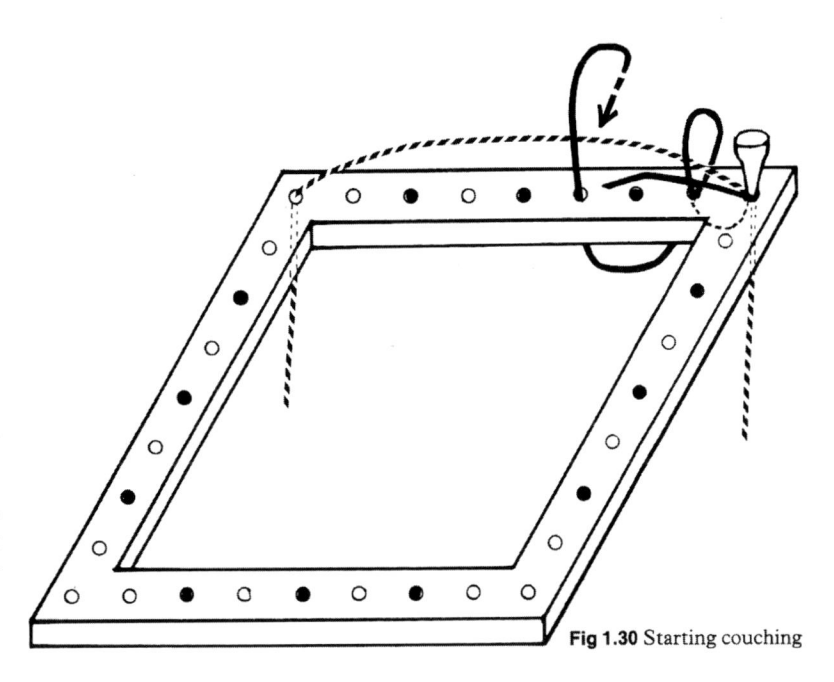

Fig 1.30 Starting couching

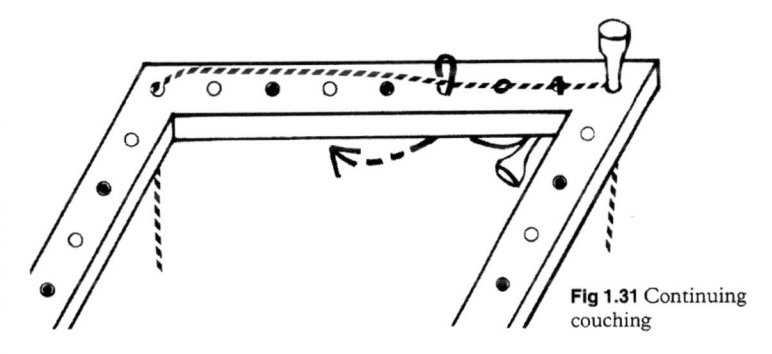

Fig 1.31 Continuing couching

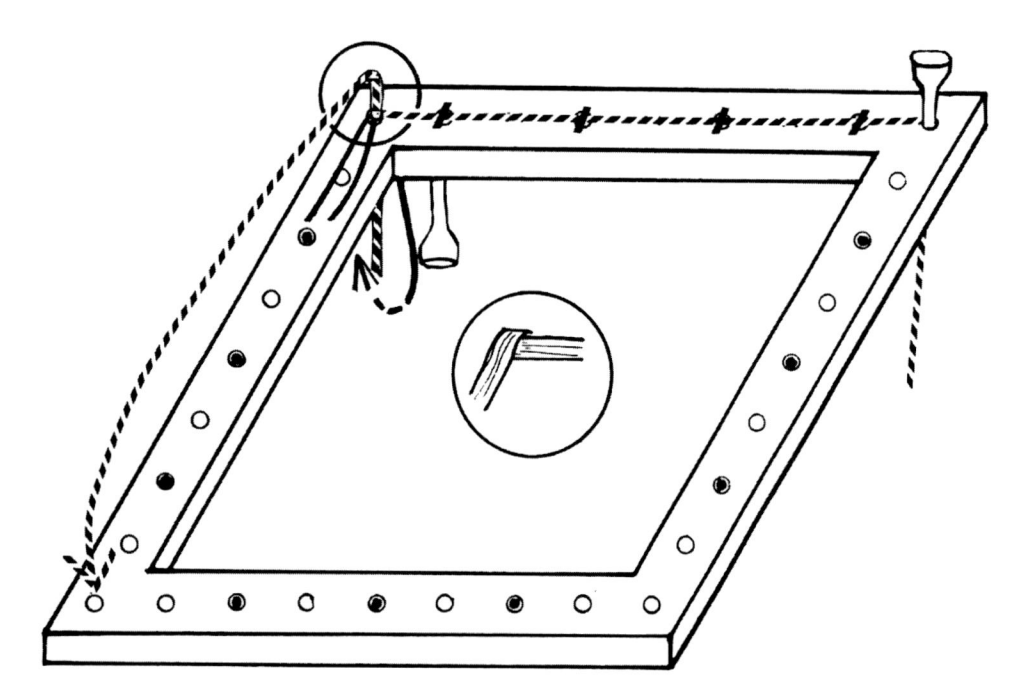

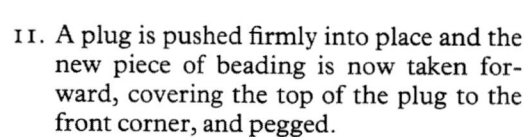

Fig 1.32 New piece of beading taken forward over plug

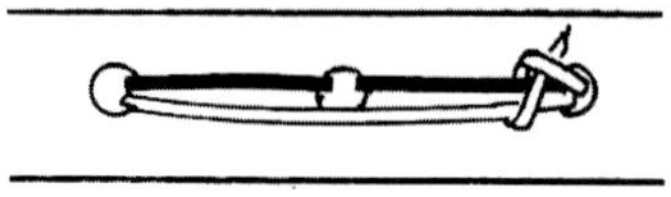

Fig 1.33 Joining beading

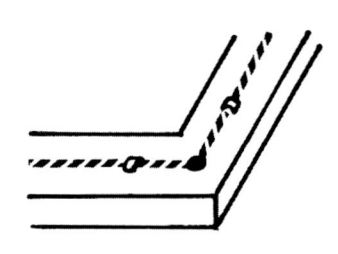

Fig 1.34 Finishing beading with plug showing

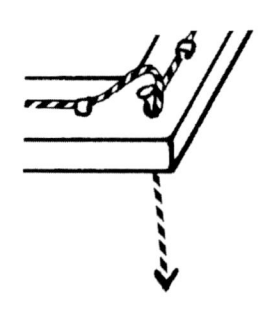

Fig 1.35 Finishing beading with plug hidden

11. A plug is pushed firmly into place and the new piece of beading is now taken forward, covering the top of the plug to the front corner, and pegged.
    Note: It may be necessary to join in the middle of a side if the cane breaks or the piece chosen is not long enough. This can be done with a simple half hitch round an adjacent loop on the underside of the frame. The 'old' end is threaded up through the next hole with the new cane (it lies underneath the new cane) and is placed under the beading and is secured by the next 'stitch'.
12. Complete the other two sides. The last corner can have the plug either showing or covered.
13. If you do not mind the plug showing, simply push the piece of centre cane down between the ends of the first and last lengths of beading cane in the same way as in normal plugging (Fig. 1.34).
14. If you do not want the plug to be seen, cut a piece of centre cane the right length and thickness for the final hole. Thread the end of the beading down the hole, leaving a loop on top and enough underneath to hold. Ease the plug in under the loop, and pull down the end while applying some pressure above with your thumb. If you have judged the size of plug correctly, everything should slip into place and the seat will be securely and tidily beaded.
15. Cut all the ends off neatly.

FINAL INSPECTION!

You could now have a look at the finished work and ask yourself the following:

1. Are the lines of weaving reasonably straight? If not, apply gentle pressure with a golf tee to the settings, weavings or crossings where adjustment is needed and you will find you can soon improve and straighten a wavy line.
2. If the seat is pegged and not beaded, is it neat on top and underneath with no ends showing?
3. If beaded, is the beading sitting flat on top of the holes and is the couching tight with no loose loops under the seat?
4. Are the loops evenly distributed between the holes, not bulky in some places and with gaps in others?

If you can answer 'yes' to the above questions and the tension of the work is firm as well, the seat has obviously been woven correctly and you can start on the more complicated shapes, many of which are described in the following chapters.

Seating a rectangular stool

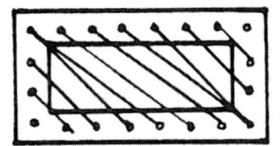

Fig 1.36 Rectangular shape showing position of doubles

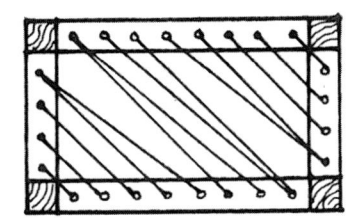

Fig 1.37 Rectangular shape with no corner holes

This is woven in the same sequence as a square stool or chair, the only difference being that the corners are not directly opposite each other, so the 'Doubles' are not at opposite ends of the same strands of cane. Sometimes the top of the leg of a stool or chair is so placed that there is no corner hole. In this case the holes on either side of the leg have double crossings. (This applies to square as well as rectangular seats.)

Alternative sequences – six-way standard pattern

The pattern described with the first crossing travelling *under* the pairs of weavings and over the pairs of settings (Fig. 1.6a and b) can be achieved in two different ways. This can be done either as already explained or as follows:

1. The first setting (from the back to the front of the seat).
2. The first weaving (from side to side on top of the first setting).
3. Second setting to the *left* of the first, instead of to the right (Fig. 1.38).
4. Second weaving threaded in *behind* the first weaving, instead of in front (Fig. 1.39).

Note: It is useful to understand how the sequence of the crossings changes according to the position of the *second* setting and *second* weaving in relation to the first setting and weaving. It may be necessary to repair one of a set of chairs, when the pattern of the others should be matched exactly.

In order to achieve the sequence shown in the diagram below, with the first crossing, travelling *over* the weavings and *under* the settings (Fig. 1.40) it is necessary to place

1. The second setting to the right of the first, and
2. the second weaving behind the first,

or

1. The second setting to the left of the first, and
2. the second weaving in front of the first.

To help demonstrate how the crossings slip into the mesh (see Fig. 1.40) cut six pieces of No. 6 cane (or something wider, such as lapping cane) about 30 cm (1 foot) long. Straighten by dipping in water if they are curved. Now lie them down one after the other:

1. The first setting
2. The first weaving
3. The second setting
4. The second weaving

Now take the first crossing and fit it into the four interlocking canes. It will be seen that it slips neatly into the corner (Fig. 1.6a), when the sequence is one of the first two explained.

Fig. 1.40 will demonstrate the position of the first crossing when the sequence used is one of the last two explained. The first crossing will *not* slip into place in the second two methods unless it travels *over* the weavings and *under* the settings.

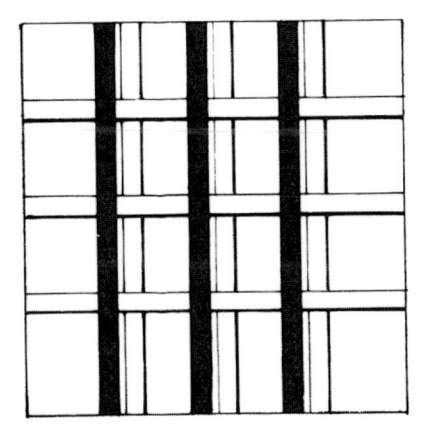

Fig 1.38 Second setting to *left* of the first

Fig 1.39 Second weaving *behind* the first

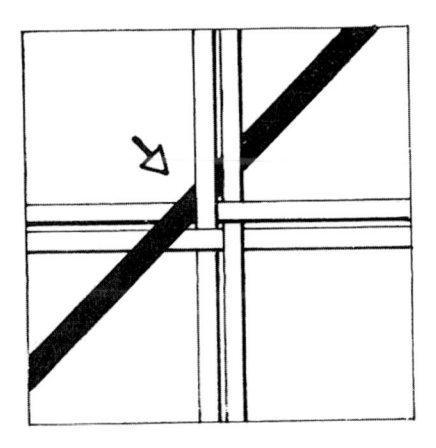

Fig 1.40 First crossing over the weavings and under the settings

Alternative methods of beading and couching

IORWERTH'S QUICK METHOD

Prepare the seat for beading and couching by plugging every other hole as on page 24.

1. Take a piece of beading cane and peg it in the back right corner hole.
2. Cut several pieces of No. 2 cane for couching into about 12 cm (6 in) lengths, or use any scrap pieces about this size.
3. Take a piece of centre cane and try it into one of the holes not already plugged. This must be a *snug* fit, *not* loose and not *too* tight. Cut as many pieces as you have unplugged holes in the seat. They must not be too long, or else they will protrude underneath the chair when in place.
4. Place the beading along the back rail, take one of the 12 cm lengths of No. 2 cane and fold it in two (like a hairpin). Put it over the beading and down the first unplugged hole.
5. Take one of the small pieces of centre cane and put it under the beading and between the two 'arms' of the hairpin. Pull the hairpin into place (Fig. 1.41). The hairpin and the plug should be so tight in the hole as to make it impossible to pull it into place with the fingers. It should require additional leverage from a pair of pliers to pull it down.
6. Continue to the end of the chair.
7. Cut off the ends under the chair as close as possible. (The toenail cutters come in very handy here.)

Note: This is probably not as secure as the traditional method.

BEADING HELD IN PLACE WITH PEGS

Occasionally the beading is held down by pegs, rather than couching. The size of the beading used will be critical. It must be wide enough to cover the holes, but narrow enough to be looped down into every other hole.

Prepare the chair for Beading in the usual way, plugging every other hole.

1. Soak the cane well and mellow in a damp cloth for about 15 minutes.
2. Peg one end in a corner hole.
3. Ease a loop of cane down into the first unplugged hole and push in a tightly fitting piece of centre cane, cut it off to the right length (Fig. 1.42).
4. If necessary, tap the plug into place using a short piece of stout centre cane or willow between the plug and the hammer so the beading is not damaged (Fig. 1.43).

Note: The centre cane must fit very tightly indeed, so that there is no chance of the beading coming adrift later on.

5. Continue round the chair seat and finish as in the instructions for beading and couching on page 25.

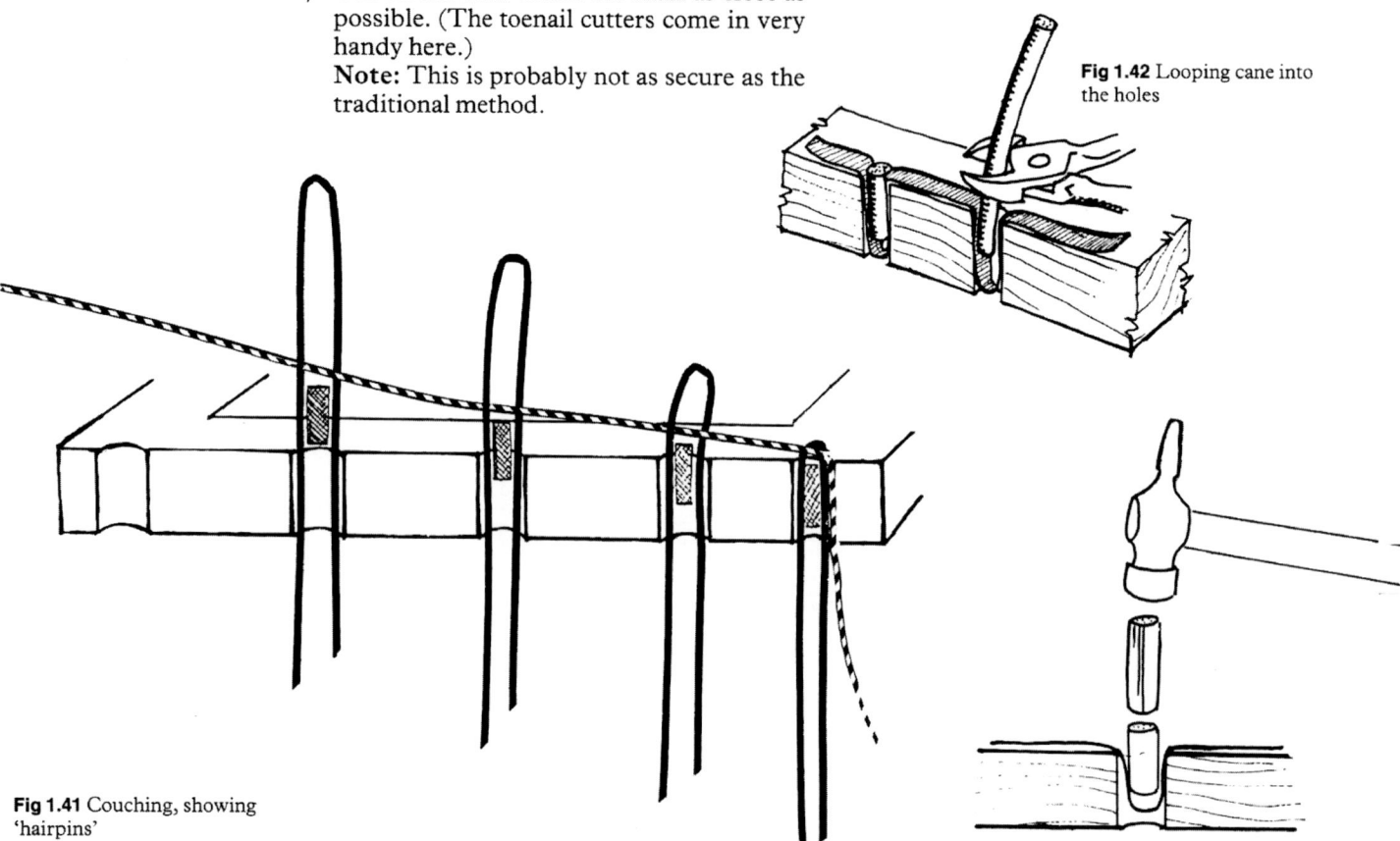

Fig 1.42 Looping cane into the holes

Fig 1.41 Couching, showing 'hairpins'

Fig 1.43 Tapping home the plug

3.
Angles, circles and medallions

Victorian chamber or bedroom chair

High Wycombe in Buckinghamshire was one of the centres where many of these little beechwood chairs were made. In 1900 the price for caning a seat like this would have been about twopence three farthings (1½p!).

You will notice that this shape of seat probably has more holes at the front than at the back. Occasionally there are the same number on each, and in this case those on the back rail will be closer together, making the crossing stage a little more difficult to weave.

THE FIRST SETTING

1. Having removed the old seat and any plugs and completed any cleaning up or repairs (page 13), decide what sizes of cane you are going to use.
2. Count the holes in the front and back rails. If the number is uneven, there will be one middle hole. Peg these, front and back, to mark the centre of both rails.
3. If the holes are even in number, place a golf tee in each of the two middle holes, front and back.
4. Select a long, strong, unblemished piece of No. 2 cane (if that is the size you have decided to use for the first four stages).
5. Remove the peg and thread half the length through the middle hole at the back of the frame, or the right-hand one if there are two middle holes. Peg firmly. Half the length will now lie on the top of the seat and half underneath.
6. Take the top length and thread it down through the opposite hole in the front rail, pull tight and peg (Fig. 1.45).

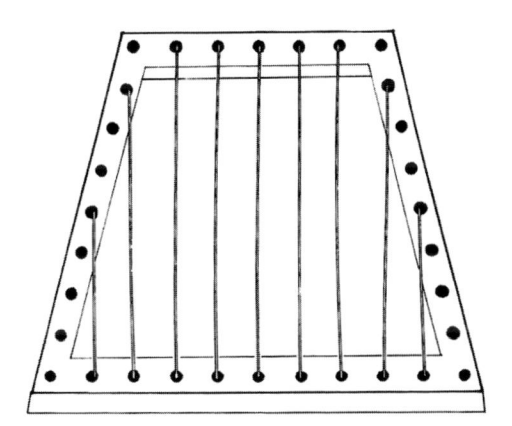

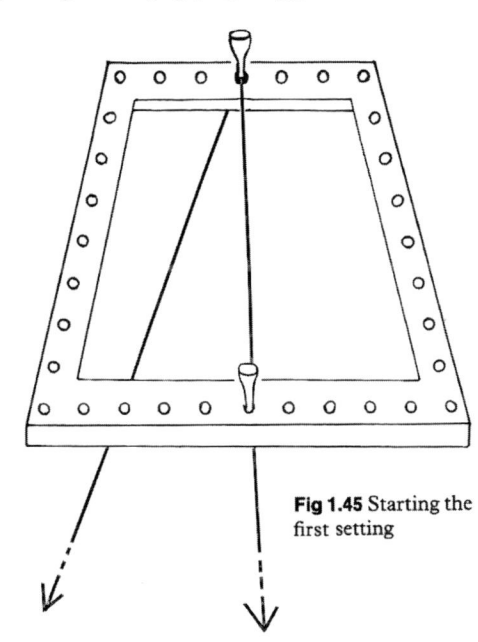

Fig 1.44a Trapezium shape, more holes in the front

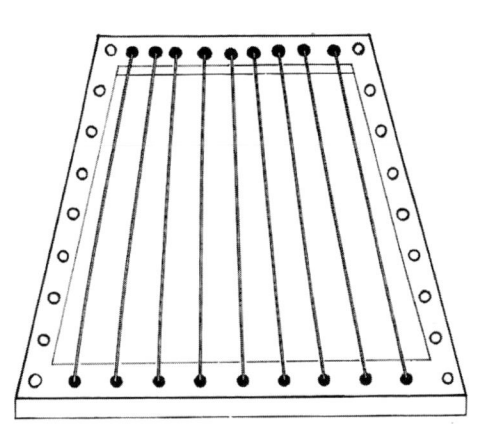

Fig 1.44b Trapezium shape, same number of holes front and back

Fig 1.45 Starting the first setting

Photo 1.3a Trapezium shape with more holes at the front

Photo 1.3b Trapezium shape with more holes at the front close up

Photo 1.4a Trapezium shape with same number of holes, front and back

Photo 1.4b Trapezium shape with same number of holes, front and back close up

7. Now continue to work across the seat to the right, following the instructions for the first setting. For joining, refer to page 17 – and remember to join in a new piece of cane in the *next door* hole, *not* on the opposite side of the frame.

8. Return to the other half of the cane which was left pegged in the middle and work to the left side of the frame using all the holes in the back rail except the corner holes.
   Note: Assuming that there are more holes at the front than the back, a 'short' setting will be needed to fill the gaps on either side. A 'short' setting is one which does not reach the whole width of the chair seat.

9. Add as many short settings as necessary, so all the holes in the front rail are used (except the corners). These short settings must be kept as parallel to each other and to the rest of the settings as possible. It will be necessary to miss some holes in the side rails to achieve this. If possible, the position of the short settings on one side should be mirrored on the other (Fig. 1.46).

   Note – odd holes!
   The reason for starting in the middle will probably be understood by now. If you had started at one side you might end up with a chair seat like Fig. 1.47! Occasionally you will come across a chair that has been unevenly drilled, and has an odd number of holes at the back, or even number in the front, or more holes one side than the other. In the first case you will need to have an extra short setting on one side (Fig. 1.48). In the case of an extra hole at one side you will need to skip one unless there is room to drill a new hole. Either way the aim should be to keep the strands of cane as parallel and equidistant as possible.

Fig 1.46 Mirroring the first settings

Fig 1.47 Wrongly woven

Fig 1.48 Extra short setting on one side

Fig 1.49 Extra hole on one side

THE FIRST WEAVING
This is laid on top of the first setting. A short weaving may be necessary if the frame is curved at the back. (See the chapter on Bow Fronted Chairs.)

THE SECOND SETTING
As on page 18, this is woven through the same holes as the first setting (there is no need to start in the middle this time). It must be placed slightly to the *right* of the first setting.

Before you start, look under the seat – check there are no twists in the cane and that the shiny side is outwards. Consider the place to *start* the second setting, so the loops under the chair become continuous.

When the second setting is complete and there is a second cane beside each of the first settings you can begin the second weaving.

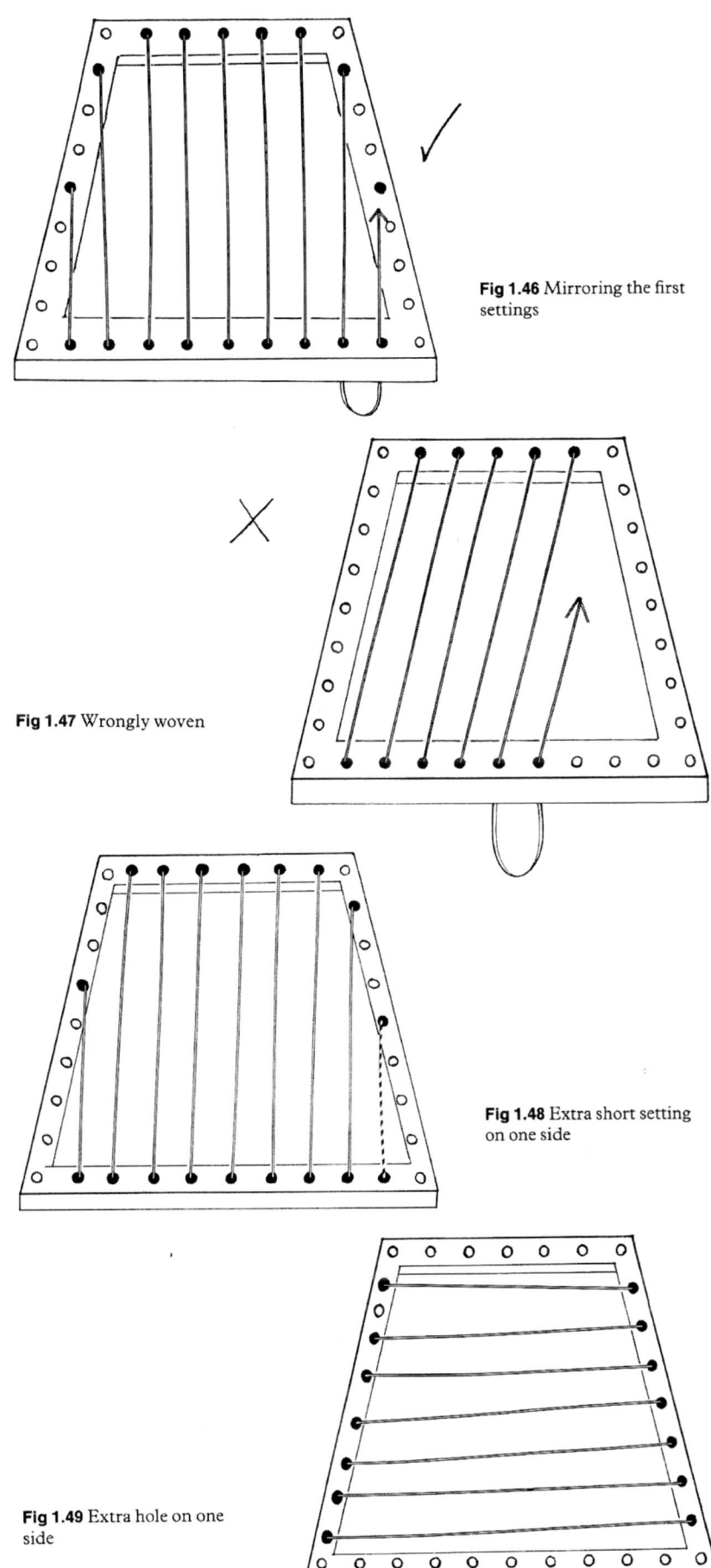

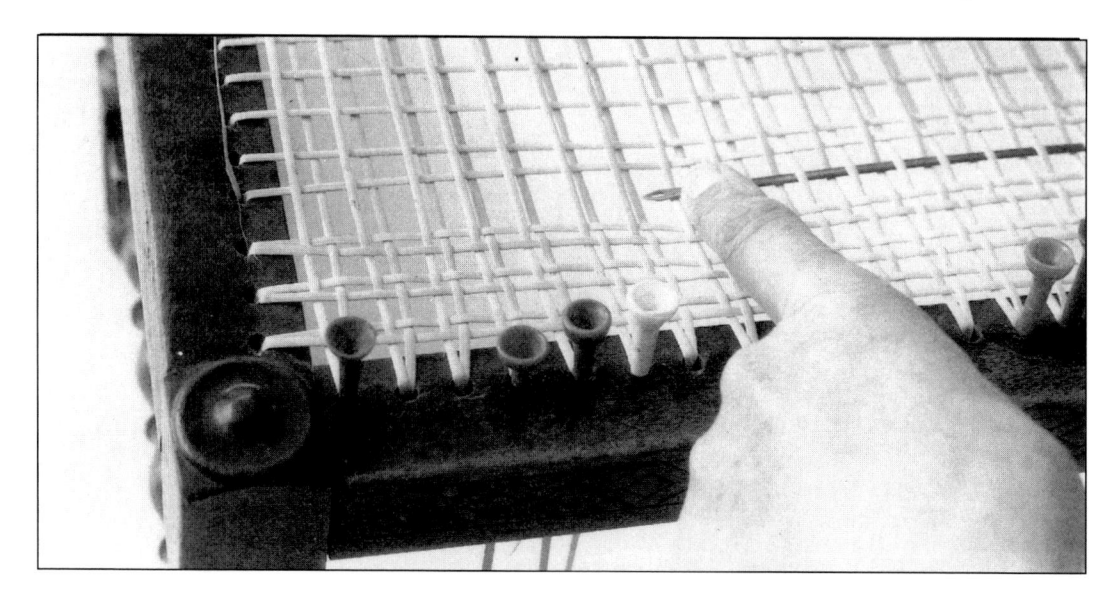

Photo 1.5a Using the drawing-through tool

Photo 1.5b Using the drawing-through tool

THE SECOND WEAVING

Follow the method on page 18. Be *very* careful to keep the second, 'short' settings to the *right* and weave *over* them. Sometimes these have a tendency to slip to the left. If not corrected, this will cause frightful confusion later on.

Note: You may wish to use a drawing-through tool here (see illustration of tools, Fig. 1.1). It speeds things a lot. When we first started chair caning it used to take about four hours to complete the second weaving on an average size chair: tedious indeed. Once this tool was discovered the job was speeded up enormously.

TO USE THE DRAWING-THROUGH TOOL

1. Weave the tool across the seat between the settings, depressing the strand of cane when going across the second setting, and pushing down on the tip of the tool when weaving under the first setting.
2. Now thread about 1 cm ($\frac{1}{2}$ in) of the weaving cane through the eye of the tool, pinch sharply to flatten the bend, and draw it back through the settings. Unthread the cane (after the pull through) and cut off the bent end, as it will probably break the next time.
3. Thread the cane down the appropriate hole and up the next, thread the tool through from the opposite direction, pass a short end through the eye as before and draw it back through the settings, repeating until the last one or two rows are reached.

You may find that you can only weave half a row at a time with the tool at this point (according to the tension of the weaving so far). You may prefer to finish off using a shell bodkin (see Fig. 1.1) or simply weave the last row or two with your fingers.

Note: Another, possibly quicker, method of setting and weaving is on page 64.

The first crossing – Yeovil to York

This can be woven starting across the right front and side corners (see Fig. 1.21), being careful to weave over the settings and under the weavings. Alternatively, start weaving from the front left corner or back right corner and weave diagonally across the seat, over the settings and under the weavings.

There are a few snags to weaving the crossings on a seat which is not square:

1. There must be two crossings in each corner hole. If there is *no* corner *hole*, there will be double crossings in the holes on either side of the corner (see Fig. 1.37)
2. Two crossings from the same direction, called a 'double' or 'fisheye', will be woven through the same hole for *each* short setting (Fig. 1.50). If possible these should be placed in the hole directly below the end of the short setting.
3. 'Misses' are holes that are missed, obviously! They are missed by the crossings from one direction, but contain the doubles from the other. In the weaving of the first crossing (Yeovil to York) the doubles will occur on the *right* side rail, and the misses on the *left*, in the holes directly opposite the doubles.

In weaving the second crossing (London to Liverpool) the doubles will be woven into the holes previously missed on the left and of course, the misses should occur in the holes containing doubles on the right. The aim is to have two crossings in every hole when the seat is finished.

4. This is the point which shows the exceptions to the last two points! Because of the shape of the frame and position of the holes, it may, in some cases, be difficult to 'miss' the hole containing a double from the other direction. The crossing which should have been threaded through the hole *below* the double may not be able to reach this hole easily and in this case it can be threaded through the hole *with* the double. Three in a bed!

There is another exception. Although every attempt should be made to place doubles in one hole below the short setting, again the shape and position of the holes may mean that this is not always possible, and the doubles will then be placed in the second or third hole down. Doubles are necessary to keep a good diagonal line and to avoid gaps on the frame in a chair of this shape.

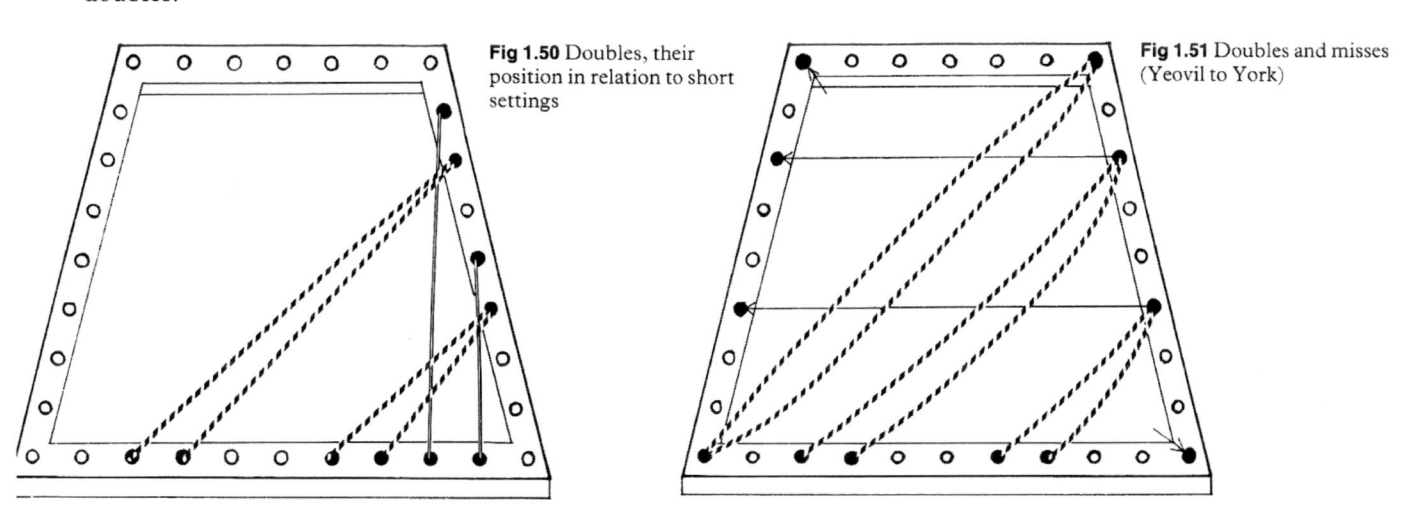

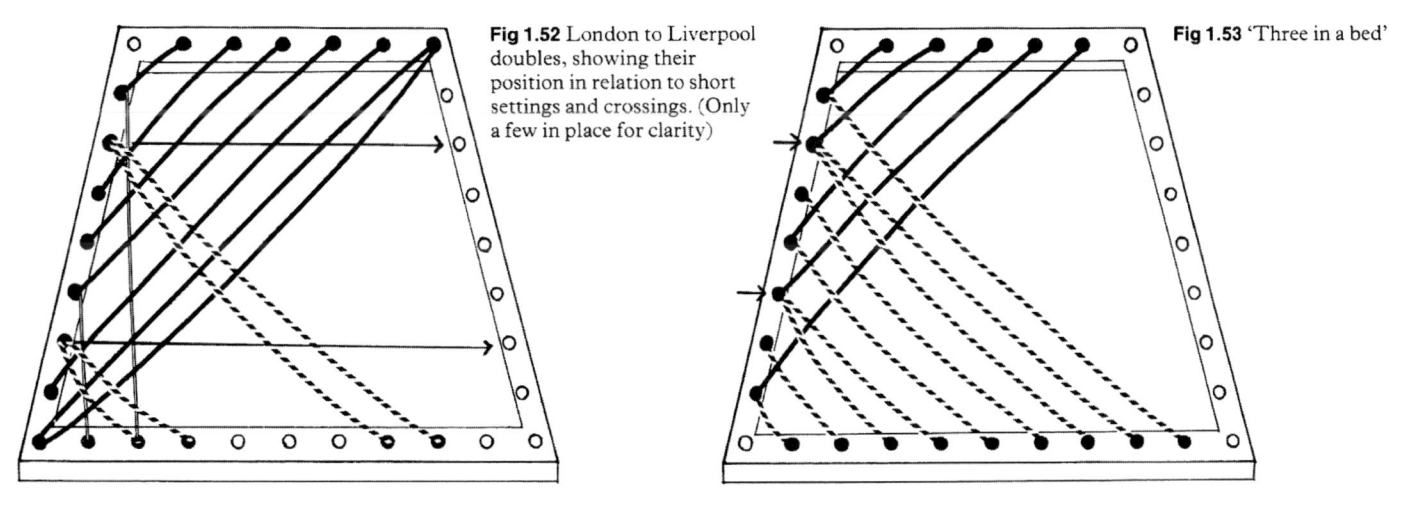

Fig 1.50 Doubles, their position in relation to short settings

Fig 1.51 Doubles and misses (Yeovil to York)

Fig 1.52 London to Liverpool doubles, showing their position in relation to short settings and crossings. (Only a few in place for clarity)

Fig 1.53 'Three in a bed'

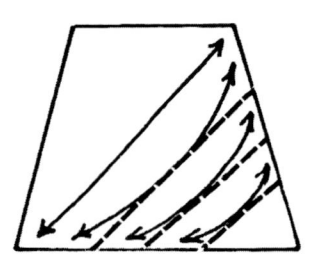

Fig 1.54 Crossings travelling as far as they can go

Fig 1.55 (a, b & c) Diagrams to show when the crossings double at each end and when they do not

Golden rule: the crossings must travel as *far* as they possibly can, before being threaded down a hole (Fig. 1.54), *but they must not cross over two pairs of settings one after the other or under two pairs of weavings one after the other* (or vice versa) before being threaded down the hole in the frame.

If these crossings are taken as far as they can go without breaking the 'golden rule', crosses (or 'kisses') will be formed on the front, back and side rails, instead of ugly 'clusters' and gaps.

The second crossing – London to Liverpool
This is now woven into place, under the settings and over the weavings, starting across from corner to corner on the left front rail (Fig. 1.53), or from the right front corner across the middle of the seat. This time the doubles will be on the left side rail, the misses on the right.

Beading and pegging
Decide whether you wish to bead or simply peg. Usually these trapezium-shaped Victorian chairs (often known in those days as chamber chairs) are beaded. Refer to instructions on page 24.

Point of interest
When dealing with chair frames which are wider at the front than the back rail, if the *increase* in the number of holes from the back to the side and from the side to the front rail *is the same*, then irrespective of the size of the frame and whether there are odd or even numbers of holes, the two crossings which started out from the front right-hand corner hole, will *both go down* the back left-hand corner hole. If the increase is not the same then they will *not* do so.

Corner holes
Although generally the corner holes are only used in the crossing stages, occasionally the angle of the side-rails makes it essential to use the back corner holes to keep the settings parallel.

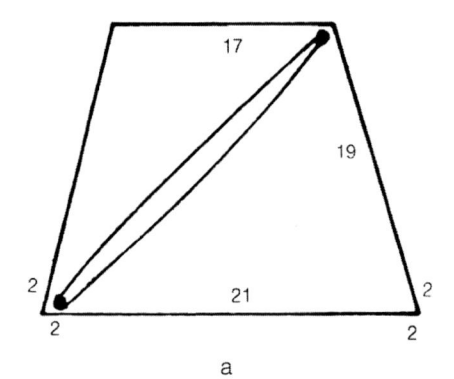

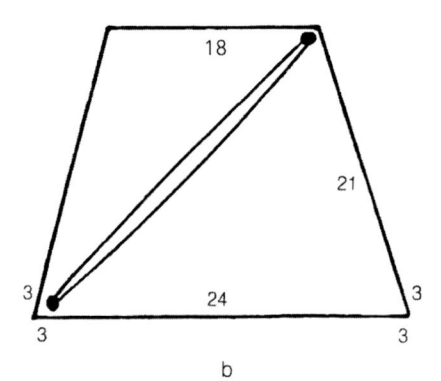

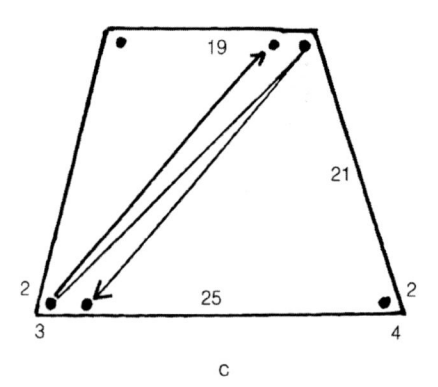

Bow-fronted or fancy Wycombe chair

These slender chairs in beech and birch were made with a cane seat from about the 1820s onwards.

The sequence of building up the six-way standard pattern will be the same as on pages 13–14. However, this shape will need extra short settings at the sides and short weavings will be required to fill the bow front. If the chair is curved across the back, another short weaving will also be required there (Fig. 1.56).
Note: A 'short' setting or weaving is one which does not reach the *full* width of the seat. On curves it will be 'short' at both ends (this means it will require a double for *each* end, one hole short of the ends).

The aim is to keep these short settings and weavings as parallel as possible to the other weavings and settings, with equal spacing between them. This may mean leaving out some holes on the sides.
Note: *No* holes should be missed along the 'front' rail when placing the settings in position. The 'front' is the part of the rail in front of the 'corner' hole (see Fig. 1.58). No holes should be missed in the back rail except the corner holes, at this stage. In most cases the back corner holes will not be used until the crossing stage.

FRONT 'CORNER' HOLES
For this shape of chair it works best to consider the 'corner' to be the hole in which the shortest short setting is threaded through the front of the frame. (All *weavings* in front of this are short strokes.)

1. The first setting will be started in the middle of the back of the chair as in the trapezium shape (see page 29).
2. The next three stages, two weavings and the second setting, are as on pages 31 and 32.

Fig 1.56 Short settings and weavings

Fig 1.58 Doubles required

CORNER

CORNER

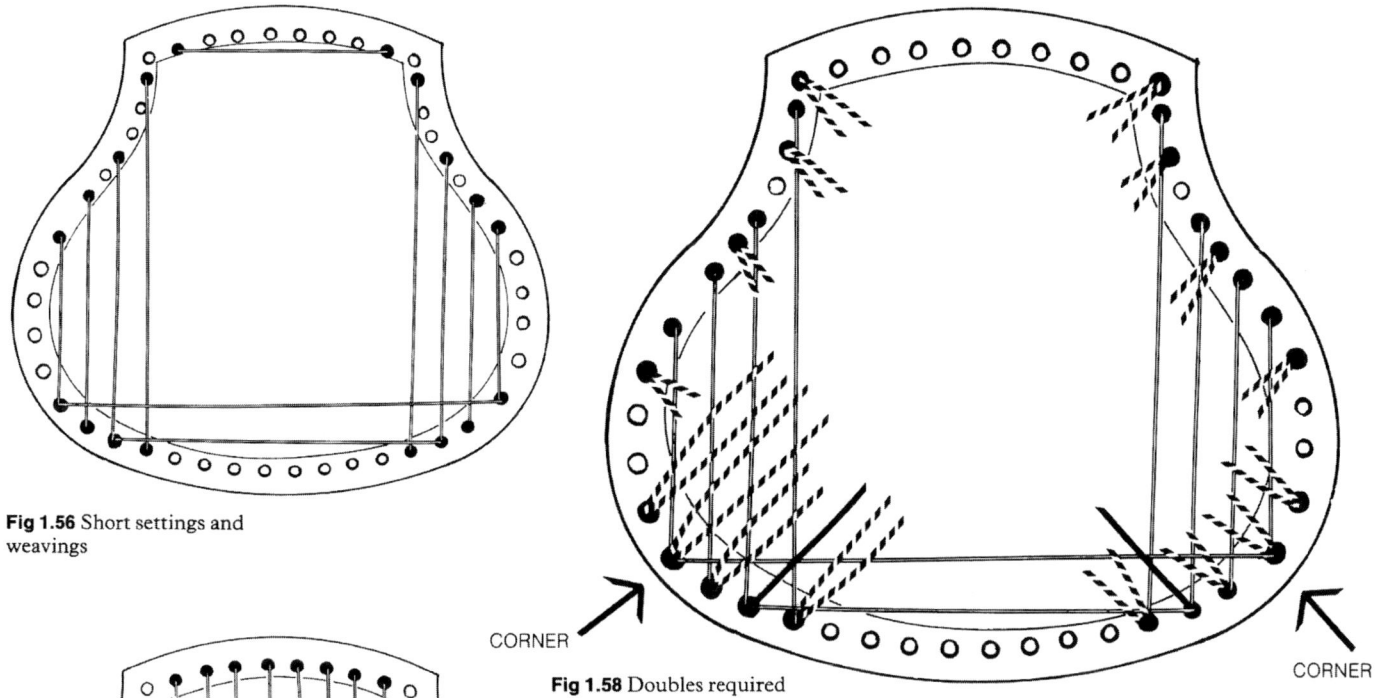

Fig 1.57 Settings in position

THE CROSSINGS

It is important to remember that on a curved frame:

1. Every short setting will require a double for either end and,
2. Every short weaving will require a double for either end.

    These will be in the hole *one short* of the end if possible. This will help to avoid a gap on the frame (Photo 1.2b).
3. Corner holes will also require doubles.
4. Missed holes are the ones opposite the doubles and are the holes where the crossing from the *other direction* will double.

The aim is to finish with two crossings in each hole. However, as explained in the chapter on trapezium shapes, this is by no means *always* possible (Fig 1.53).

Photo 1.6 Bow-fronted chair

35

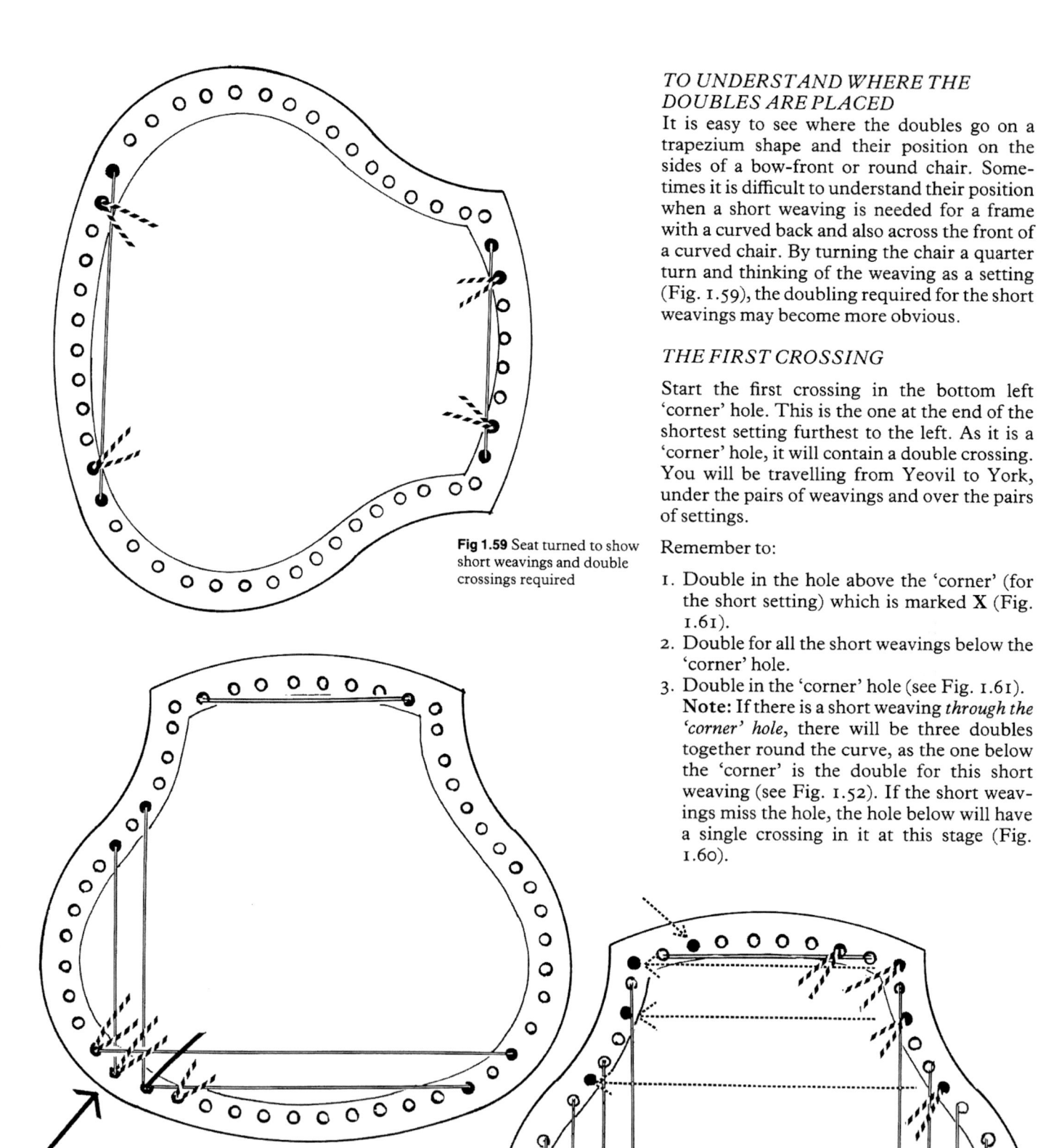

Fig 1.59 Seat turned to show short weavings and double crossings required

Fig 1.60 First crossing (Yeovil to York)

Fig 1.61 Showing doubles required for short settings and short weavings

TO UNDERSTAND WHERE THE DOUBLES ARE PLACED

It is easy to see where the doubles go on a trapezium shape and their position on the sides of a bow-front or round chair. Sometimes it is difficult to understand their position when a short weaving is needed for a frame with a curved back and also across the front of a curved chair. By turning the chair a quarter turn and thinking of the weaving as a setting (Fig. 1.59), the doubling required for the short weavings may become more obvious.

THE FIRST CROSSING

Start the first crossing in the bottom left 'corner' hole. This is the one at the end of the shortest setting furthest to the left. As it is a 'corner' hole, it will contain a double crossing. You will be travelling from Yeovil to York, under the pairs of weavings and over the pairs of settings.

Remember to:

1. Double in the hole above the 'corner' (for the short setting) which is marked **X** (Fig. 1.61).
2. Double for all the short weavings below the 'corner' hole.
3. Double in the 'corner' hole (see Fig. 1.61).
   Note: If there is a short weaving *through the 'corner' hole*, there will be three doubles together round the curve, as the one below the 'corner' is the double for this short weaving (see Fig. 1.52). If the short weavings miss the hole, the hole below will have a single crossing in it at this stage (Fig. 1.60).

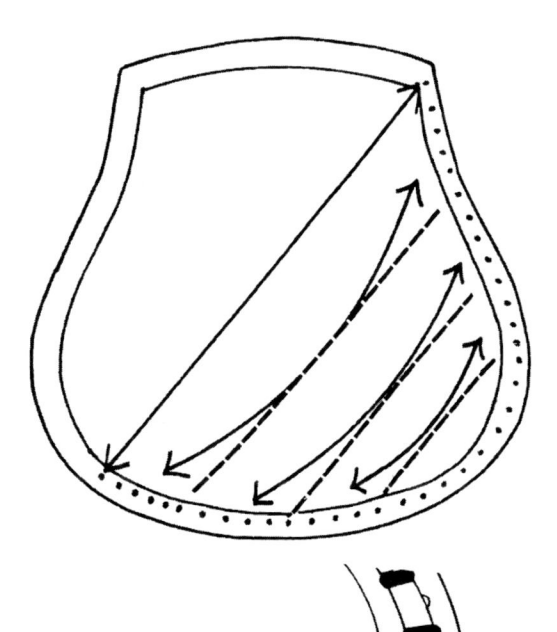

Fig 1.62 Taking the crossings as far as they will go

Fig 1.63 Three couched holes in a 'corner'

THE SECOND CROSSING
Complete the second crossing, travelling from London to Liverpool (bottom right to top left), threading over the pairs of weavings and under the pairs of settings as described on page 14. Be sure it mirrors the first crossing, with doubles in the holes exactly opposite each other and misses, if possible, in the holes where the first crossing doubled.
Note: If the holes in the chair have been unevenly drilled, it may not always be possible to follow the 'rules' for doubles and misses (page 33), so take the crossings *as far as they will go* before threading down a hole in the frame. Remember the 'over and under' golden rule (page 34) and follow the curve of the chair.

PLUGGING AND BEADING
This shape of chair can be simply plugged in every hole and left without a beading as on page 23.

If beading is required it is applied by the method described on page 25. Alternative methods of beading are on page 28.
Note: Round the curve on the two sides of a bow front it is often advisable to couch through two or three successive holes in order to keep the beading flat (Fig. 1.63). This must be remembered when putting the plugs in place. If you thread the couching up on the *inside* and then down on the *outside* of the beading each time, it will counteract the tendency of the beading to tip inwards on curved shapes.

Two lengths of beading cane will be needed: one length across the back of the frame, and the second, longer piece, which starts from the back left corner hole, round the front and finishes in the back right corner hole.
Note: If you wet the beading and then allow it to mellow in a damp towel for about 15 minutes, this will help to shape the beading smoothly round the curves. Stretching the edge which will be on the outside also helps the beading to stay flat round the curve.

Circular chair seats

This type of beechwood chair, known as Bentwood, was devised by an Austrian, Michael Thonet. He exhibited his new designs at the Great Exhibition of 1851 and won prizes in international exhibitions all over the world. At his home in Vienna he enjoyed the royal patronage of the Emperor of Austria.

By steam bending the beechwood he was able to meet the big demand for light, mass-produced chairs. These were then either polished in their natural colour or stained to appear like Rosewood, Walnut or Mahogany.

Although furniture of this kind is still made today, occasionally you may come across a chair which still has an original Thonet label on the inside of the seat frame. If so, you may have a valuable antique! Treat it with the care it deserves.

THE FIRST SETTING
Find the middle hole or holes and work out to the sides, first to the right and then to the left.
Note: It may be necessary to miss a hole between the last one or two settings on both

Photo 1.7 Circular chair

sides to keep the spacing even, but try to mirror on the left the spacing you have chosen on the right (Fig. 1.64). Occasionally this may not be possible if the holes have been unevenly drilled. In this case try to keep the lines of settings as parallel to each other as possible, rather than worrying about the position of the holes.

THE FIRST WEAVING

Find the middle hole (side to side) and work first one half and then the other. Try to repeat the spacings of the short settings when putting in the shorter weavings at the back and front of the chair.

THE SECOND SETTING

Repeat the first setting, using the same holes but placing the cane slightly to the right of the first setting.

THE SECOND WEAVING

This is threaded through the same holes as the first weaving and woven to the front of the first.

THE FIRST CROSSING

1. First find your 'corner' holes. These lie midway between the shortest setting and the shortest weaving (Fig. 1.65).

   Note: If the number of holes between the shortest weaving and the shortest setting are even, there will be two 'corner' holes. These corner holes will contain doubles and those on either side up to the end of the shortest weaving and shortest setting will also probably contain doubles.

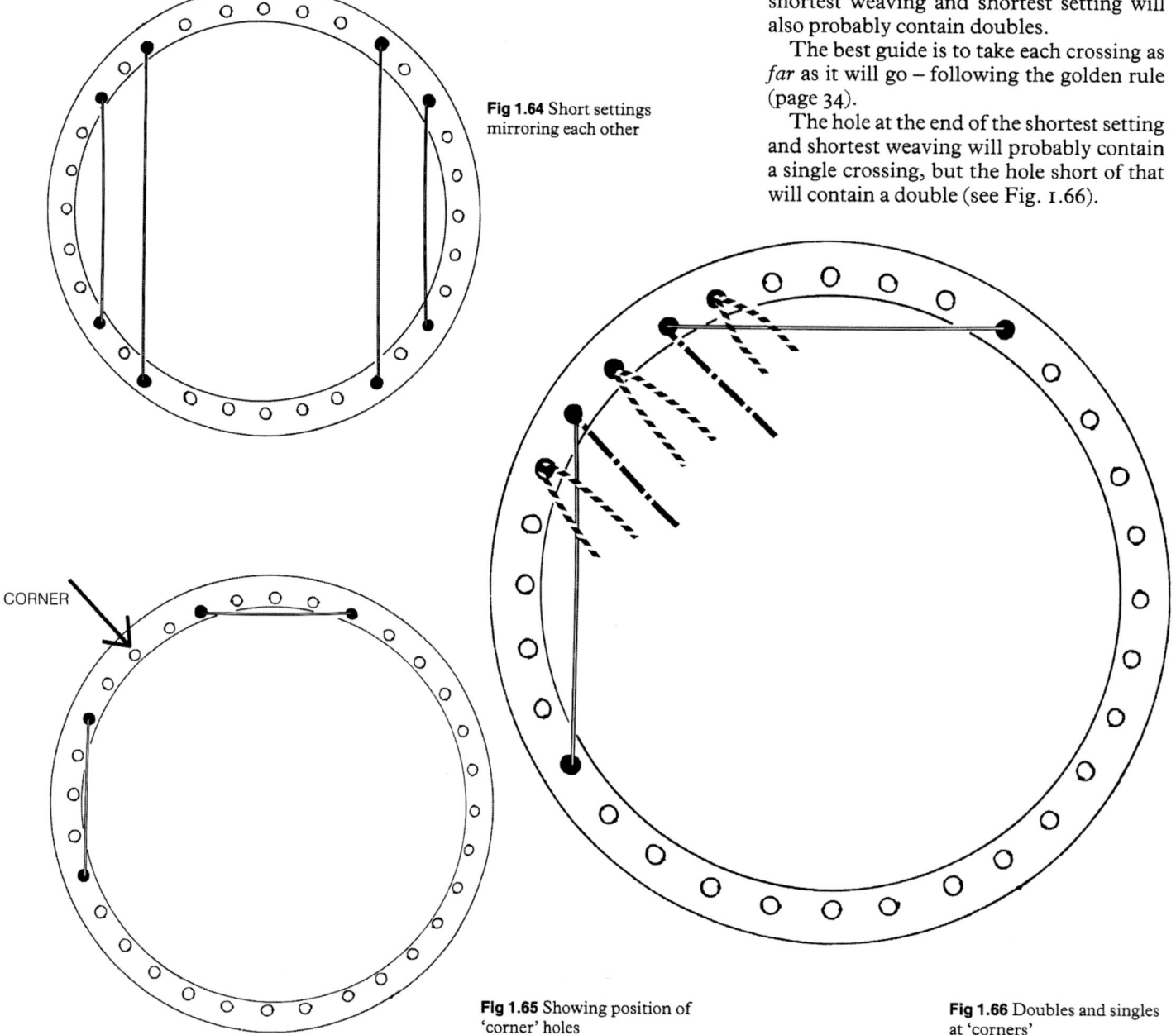

   The best guide is to take each crossing as *far* as it will go – following the golden rule (page 34).

   The hole at the end of the shortest setting and shortest weaving will probably contain a single crossing, but the hole short of that will contain a double (see Fig. 1.66).

Fig 1.64 Short settings mirroring each other

Fig 1.65 Showing position of 'corner' holes

Fig 1.66 Doubles and singles at 'corners'

2. Start in the bottom left 'corner' hole and weave across over the settings and under the weavings, to the top right 'corner' hole (Yeovil to York) (Fig. 1.67).

   Note: According to the number of holes in the frame, the doubles will either double again on the opposite side (Fig. 1.68a) or will separate (as in Fig. 1.68b).

3. Continue working across the seat, travelling over the settings and under the weavings, doubling for each end of every short setting and weaving *in one hole short* of its end (see Fig. 1.69).

   Note: The 'short' settings and weavings are those short of the 'corner' hole on the sides, back and front.

4. The four shortest crossings (two from each direction) to be woven will probably travel between the shortest weaving and the shortest setting (Fig. 1.70).

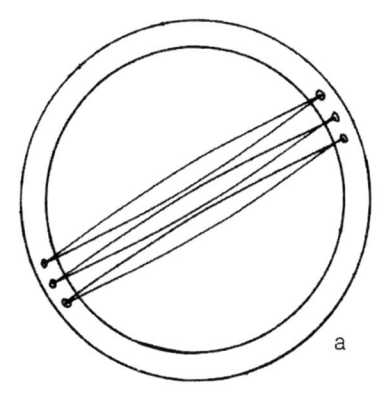

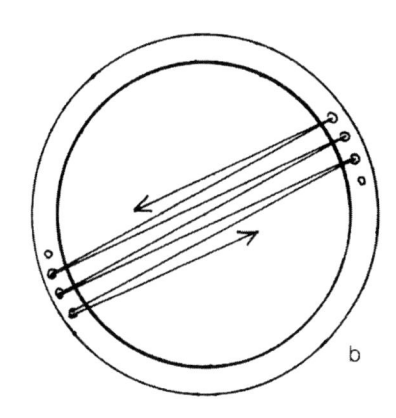

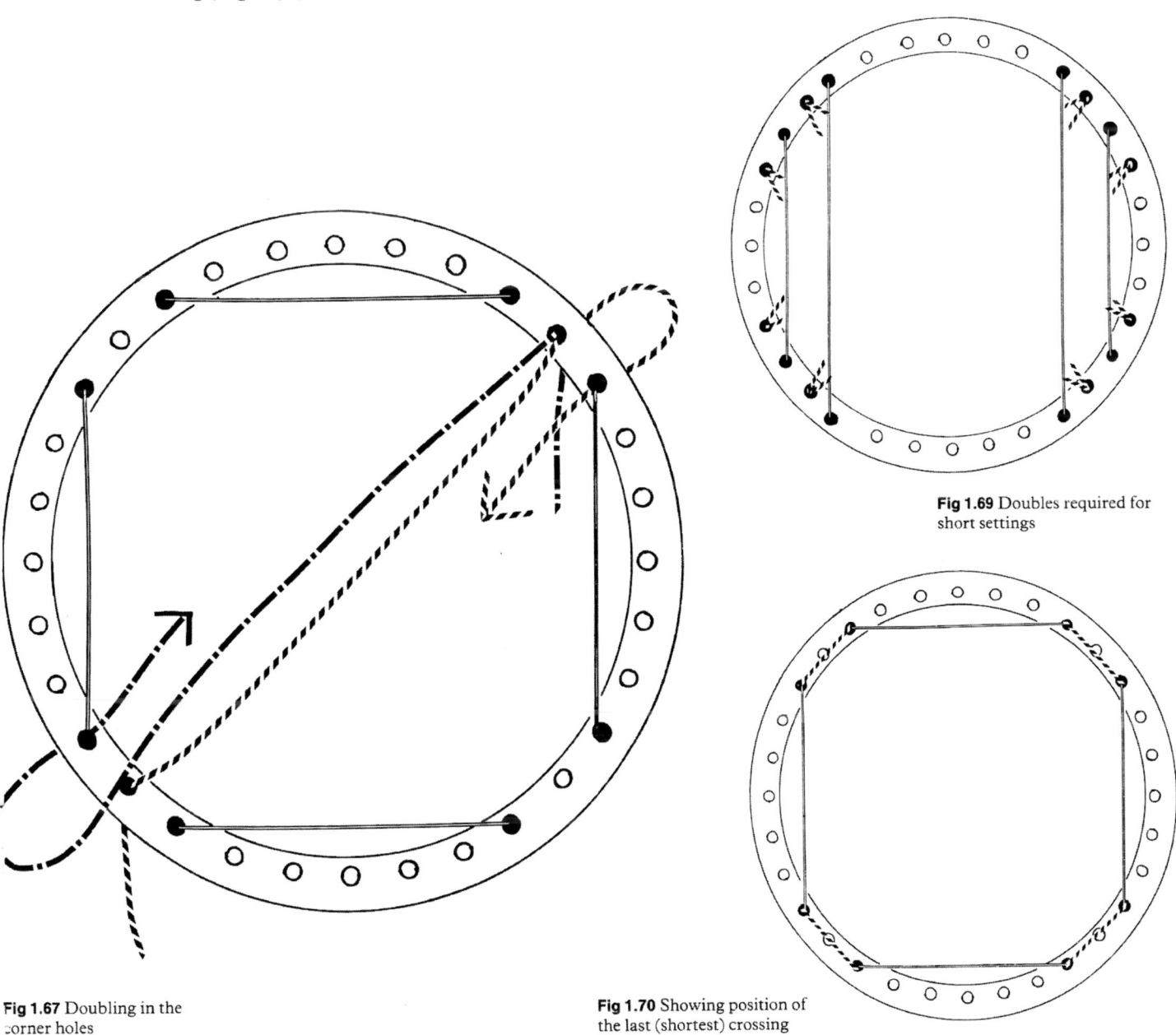

Fig 1.68 (a & b) Showing when the crossings double at each end and when they do not

Fig 1.67 Doubling in the corner holes

Fig 1.69 Doubles required for short settings

Fig 1.70 Showing position of the last (shortest) crossing

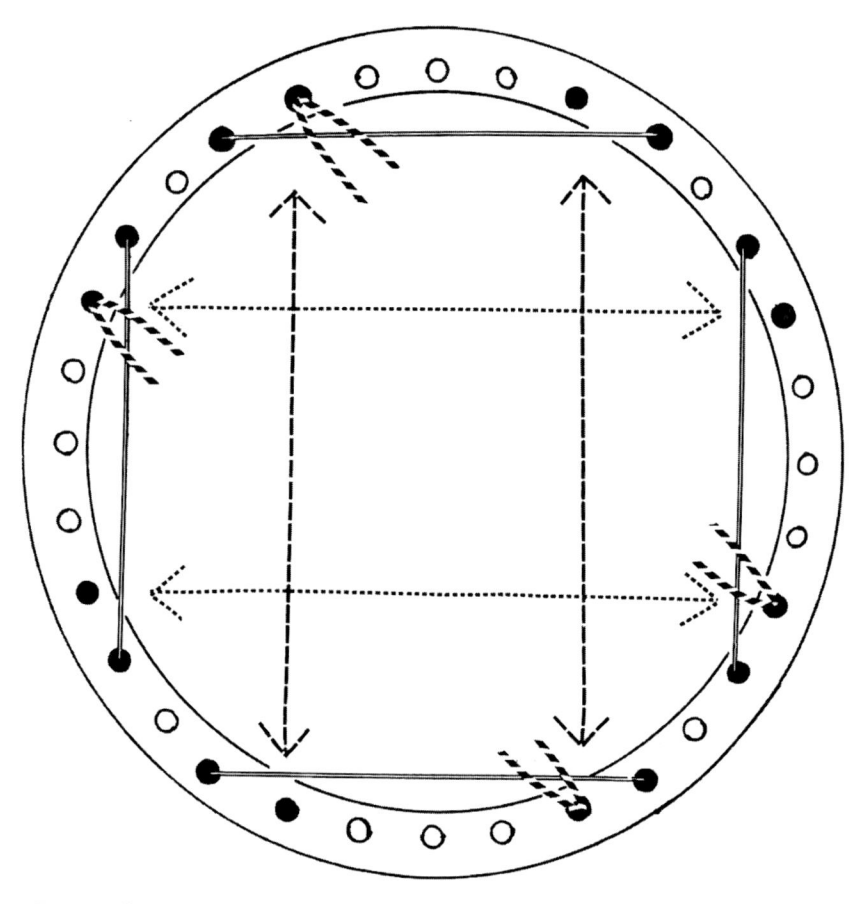

Fig 1.71a Doubles and misses

Fig 1.71b Circular pattern

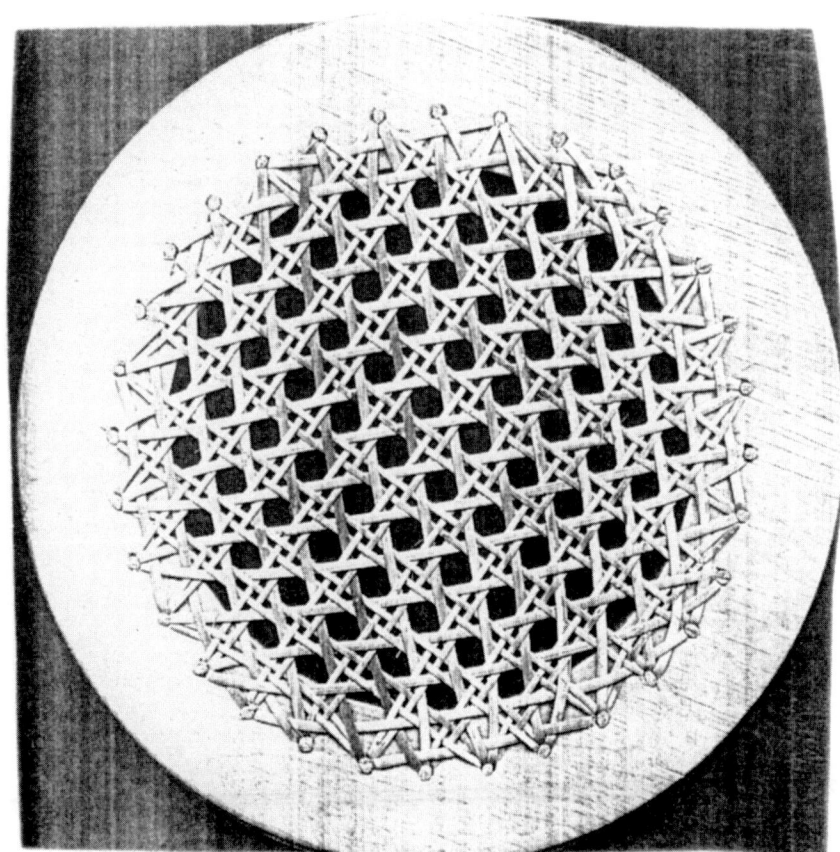

Remember to 'miss' the holes which will contain a double from the second crossing (Fig. 1.71a indicates a London to Liverpool crossing).

You should *aim* to have two crossings in every hole when the seat is finished. Sometimes, however, this is not possible (see page 33).

THE SECOND CROSSING
This mirrors the first, but travels over the weavings and under the settings (London to Liverpool). Follow the rule, taking each end as far as it will go, 'over and under', before threading down the correct hole.

PLUGGING
(See page 23 and 24). Every hole will be plugged if beading is not going to be applied, every other if beading is used.

BEADING AND COUCHING
If there is an uneven number of holes, it might be better to leave two consecutive holes unplugged (centre back) for couching. The alternative would be two plugged holes next to each other. This is undesirable on a curve, where the beading is less likely to stay flat.

One continuous piece of No. 6 beading cane is used. Damp the cane well so that it can be moulded to the curve of the chair (see page 37). Start with a temporary peg holding the end at the centre back of the seat. Couch through the unplugged holes and finish as in g. 1.34 or 1.35.

Ovals

This shape, found occasionally on a chair seat and often on a chair back, is worked in much the same manner as a circle. The curve (or 'corner') contains a number of doubles, but because of the elongated sides the double crossings from the area of the 'corner' will be woven across to the opposite side, rather than the opposite corner (Fig. 1.72b).

1. Settings are as in the round shape.
2. Weavings are as in the round shape.
   Note: If necessary, miss holes between the short settings and weavings to keep the rows evenly spaced. This is not usual with long oval caned insets on chair backs, however (see Fig. 1.72b).
3. Crossings are woven as in the round shape, taking each as far as it will go following the golden rule, before threading down the hole.

Plugging, beading and couching
Follow the directions for the round chair (page 40).

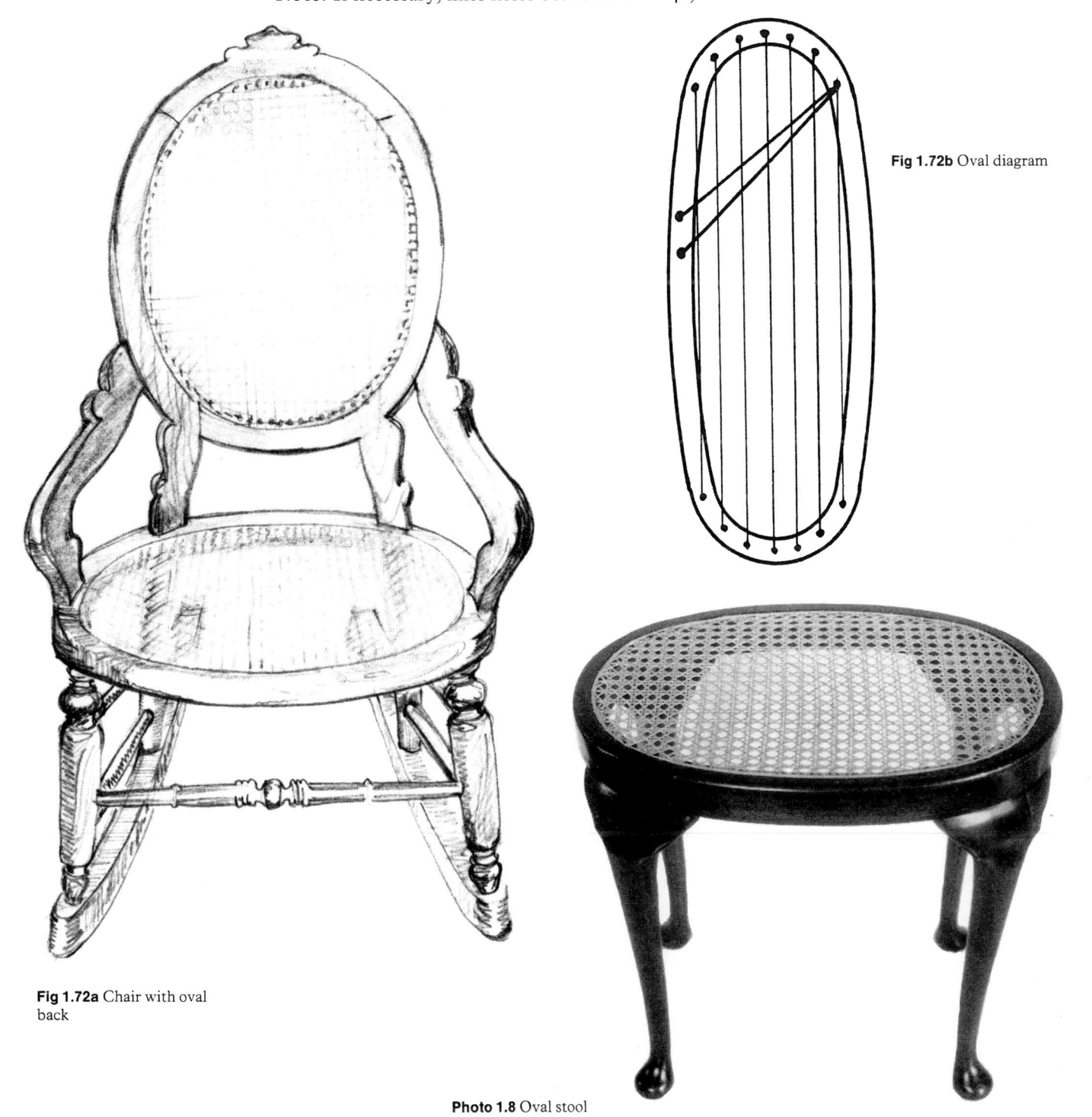

Fig 1.72b Oval diagram

Fig 1.72a Chair with oval back

Photo 1.8 Oval stool

41

Rising sun pattern

Photo 1.9a Rising sun chair

Photo 1.9b Rising sun chair close up

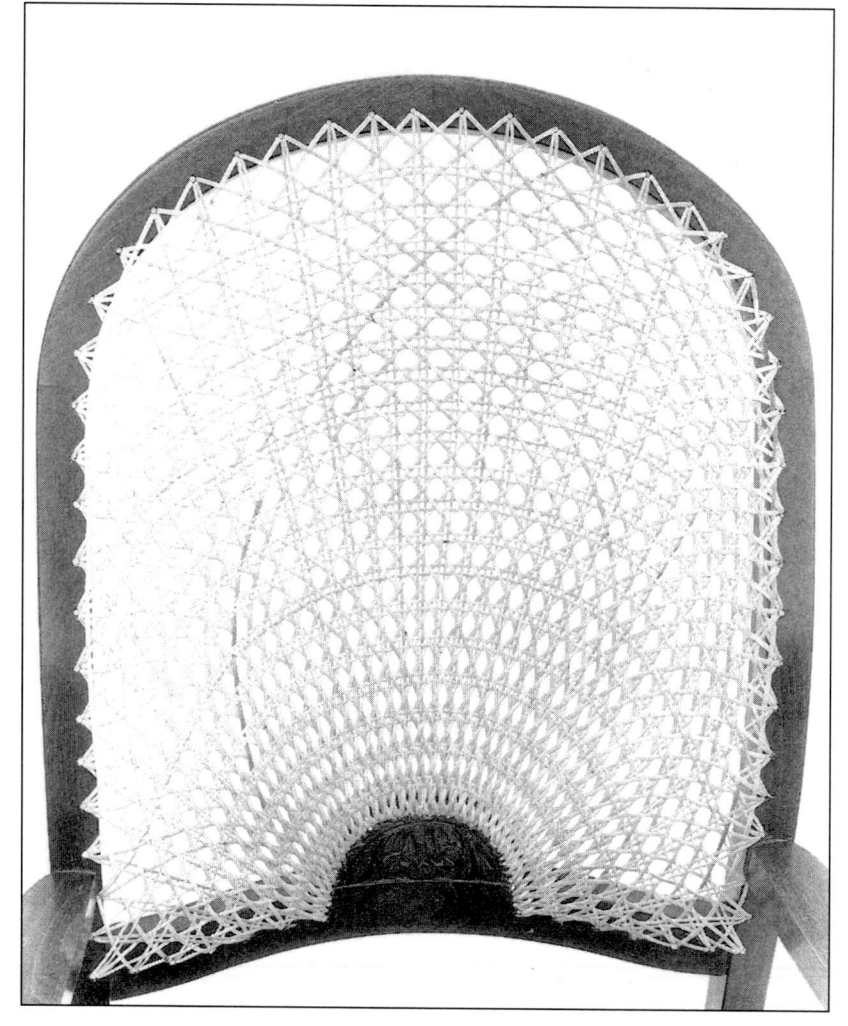

If the old cane is not too broken, remove it carefully as it may be useful for reference later on. Notice what size cane was used previously and whether it was right for the chair. If you think the cane used was a bit thin and spidery and are contemplating using a larger size, make sure that four canes (the two settings and the two larger sized canes which will probably be used for the crossings) will fit into the small holes in the 'sun' (the semi-circular block). The size previously used will probably have been Nos 2 and 3.

The sun may be at either the top or the bottom of the frame. Great care must be taken when clearing out any remaining old cane and pegs, as the holes in the sun are drilled very close together and can easily be damaged.

The sequence of weaving is different from the basic build-up of the six-way standard pattern described on pages 13 and 14. Both settings are placed in position first, and when finished they resemble the rays of the sun. The settings will be woven into every hole in the sun, but some holes in the frame may have to be missed in order to keep the pattern even. Short settings will be required across the corners next to the sun (Fig. 1.73).

1. Count the number of holes in the sun and find the middle one, or two, and mark with a peg of centre cane. A golf tee may be too big for the tiny holes, though it is possible to trim the shank of the tee to size with a sharp knife.
2. Find the corresponding hole or holes in the outer frame and mark. (Fig. 1.74).

THE FIRST SETTING

Start in the middle of the frame, in one of the marked holes, with a good long length of sound cane. Peg an end leaving at least 10 cm (4 in) for threading away afterwards. Work across to the sun, keeping the cane as tight as possible. Peg and work back across to the frame. Continue until all the holes on one side of the sun are filled.

JOINING

1. If it is necessary to join in a new piece of cane, this should be done on the frame, not the sun. Peg the new end in the next hole so that by the time the second setting is finished there will be tight loops across every other space between the holes (except where the old end finishes and the new one is started).
2. Now start again from the middle of the frame and work across to the other side, filling all the holes in the sun and appropriate holes in the frame.
3. Finally weave any short settings required in

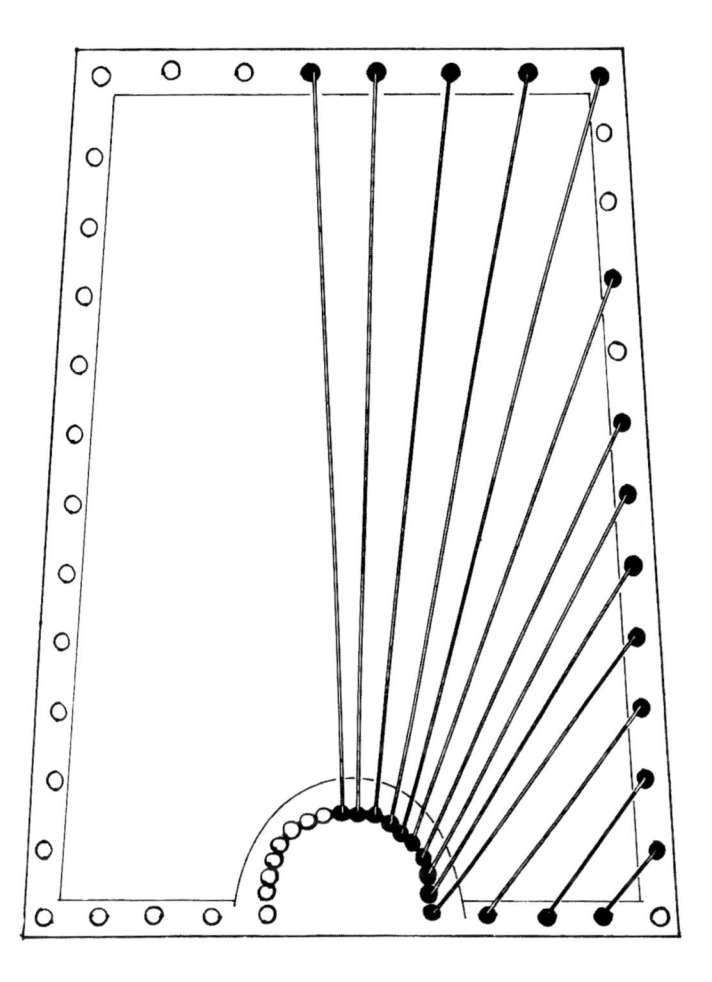

Fig 1.73 Settings in place

Fig 1.74 Pegs in the sun and the frame

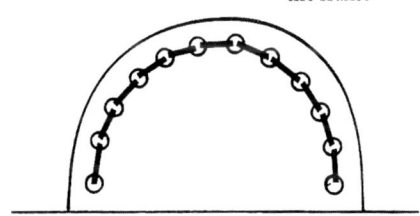

Fig 1.75 Loops of cane behind the sun

the holes on either side of the sun to complete the pattern (see Fig. 1.73).

THE SECOND SETTING

1. The second setting is now threaded into place, through the same holes as the first setting, but lying slightly to the right of it. Choose the starting place carefully (see below).

   Note: It is important, *mainly* from a cosmetic point of view, that there should be a continuous line of tight loops between the holes at the back of the *sun* by the time the second setting is finished. Make *sure* the loops of the second setting cross the unfilled spaces left by the first setting. The holes in the sun are very small and it may not be possible to loop the thicker cane, used in the two crossings through these holes to cover any gaps.

2. Work and complete the second setting as described above, keeping the cane as tight as possible and making sure all loose ends are pegged at the edge of the frame, not in the sun.

THE WEAVINGS

These are woven in pairs, one after the other, starting from the hole in the frame on the right of the sun and following the curve of the sun to the hole on the left (Fig 1.76).

Note: Do not position the first pair of weavings too close to the sun, or you will have difficulty fitting the crossings in later.

1. Weave from the hole on the right side of the sun, over the 'second' setting, under the 'first' and across to the left (see Fig. 1.76). Use a length of cane long enough to cover the distance with several inches of 'tail' left at each end. The starting and finishing hole on each side of the sun will act as a guide, indicating the distance that should lie between the sun and the first weaving. Keep this distance even right round the sun.

   Note: By using single strands for each weaving, you will be able to tighten them up after the first crossing. This stage tends to pull them into their correct position, and may alter the tension.

2. Now thread a second strand of cane through the same hole on the right of the

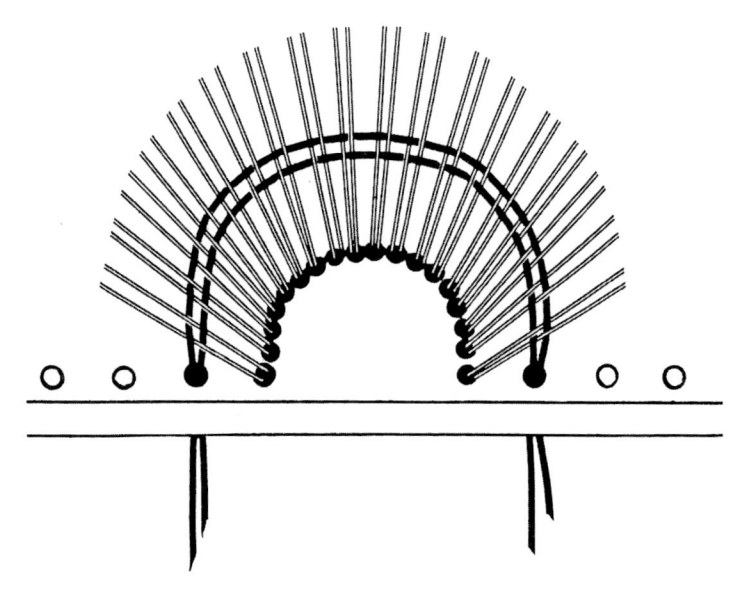

Fig 1.76 Weavings round the sun

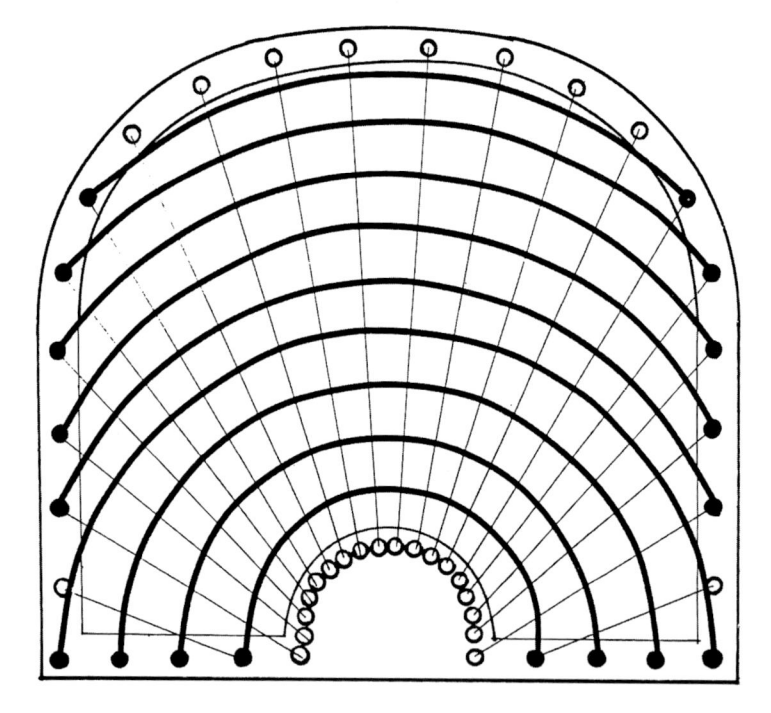

Fig 1.77 Rows of weavings

weavings to fill the frame and complete the pattern. (Fig. 1.78).

Important note: Make sure you peg every hole as the weavings are threaded, to keep the tension tight.

5. When all the weavings are in place, tighten any which appear slack, adjust the semi-circles and pinch the settings and weavings into pairs ready to take the crossings.

Note: Check at this point that you have put in *enough* rows of weaving, as the crossings tend to pull the last row slightly away from the top of the frame, possibly making a larger gap than you may have expected. You *cannot* add another row of weaving after the crossings are in place, as this would mean every one of the first crossings would have to be moved one hole further to the right and each of the second crossings one hole to the left. If they were not moved, clusters would be formed on the edge of the frame instead of crosses (See photos 2a and b).

THE CROSSINGS

Two different ways of threading the crossings are suggested. The first is for frames where the holes in the sun are very small and it can be difficult to fit the four canes – two settings and two crossings – through the holes.

The second method can be used where the holes are larger and all four pieces of cane are easily threaded through the sun.

METHOD 1

1. Choose a length of cane which is long enough to run from the frame to the sun twice, allowing a 'tail' at each end which will be threaded through the sun and left at the back.

   Mary's hint: The ends *can* be cut quite short, so there is enough to be plugged firmly into the hole, but not enough to come through to the back. This avoids the difficult job of trimming the ends neatly afterwards.

2. Starting through a hole in the back of the frame near the middle of the top, pull through enough cane to run to the sun. Choose the starting place keeping in mind the neatness at the back of the frame. Endeavour to have not more than two loops between each hole. Work the crossings which are going to travel *over the settings* and *under the weavings* first, as this makes it much easier to weave the second crossings (marked black in Fig. 1.79) at the sun where the canes become rather congested.

3. Take the other end of the cane and thread it through the frame to the front, across the adjacent settings, under the weavings, across the next pair of settings and continue

sun, this time travelling under the 'second' setting and over the 'first' in the usual way (see Fig. 1.76). Remember to leave a tail of about 10 cm (4 in) at each end.

3. The weavings continue to be woven in pairs, following the curve of the sun. First fill the holes on either side of the sun and then work up the side of the frame, usually into every hole, though sometimes one or two are missed to keep the spacing between the rows of weavings even. Try to keep the curves correct in relation to one another, and see that the rows of weavings do not flatten off too much.

4. If the top of the chair is square rather than rounded, it may be necessary to use short

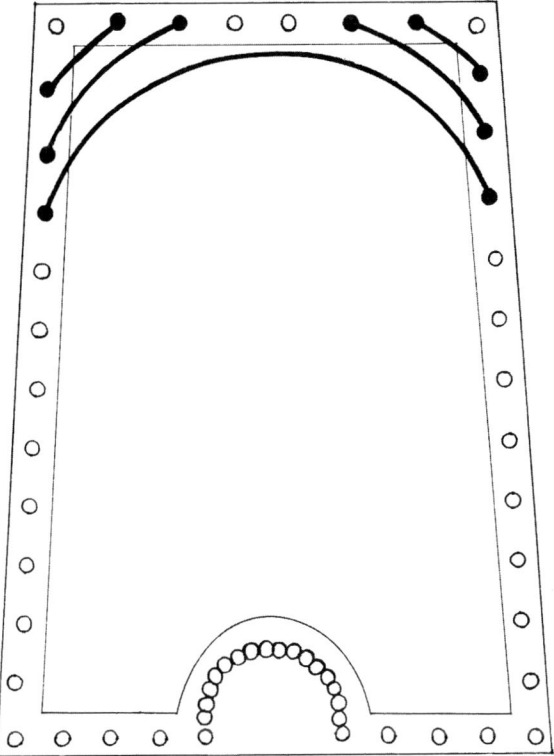

Fig 1.78 Short weavings across the top of the frame

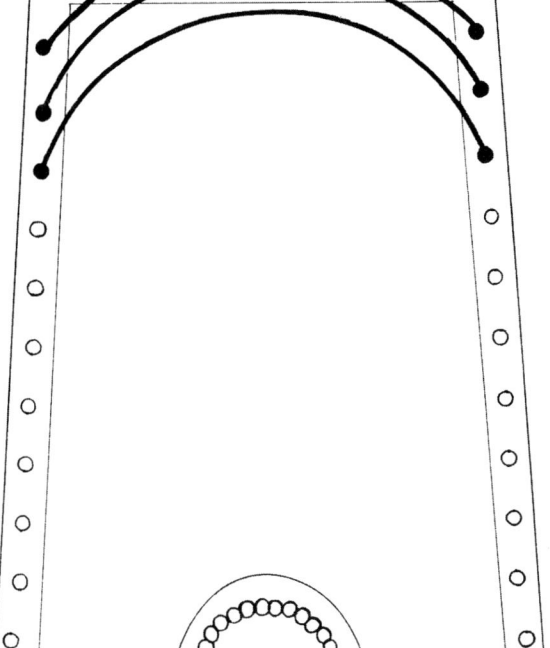

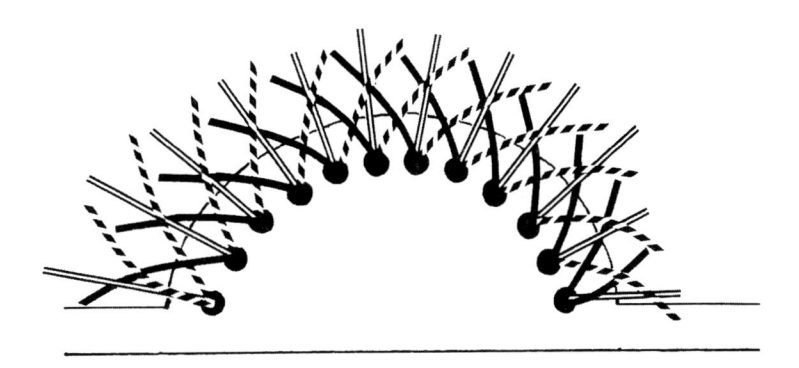

Fig 1.79 Congestion round the sun

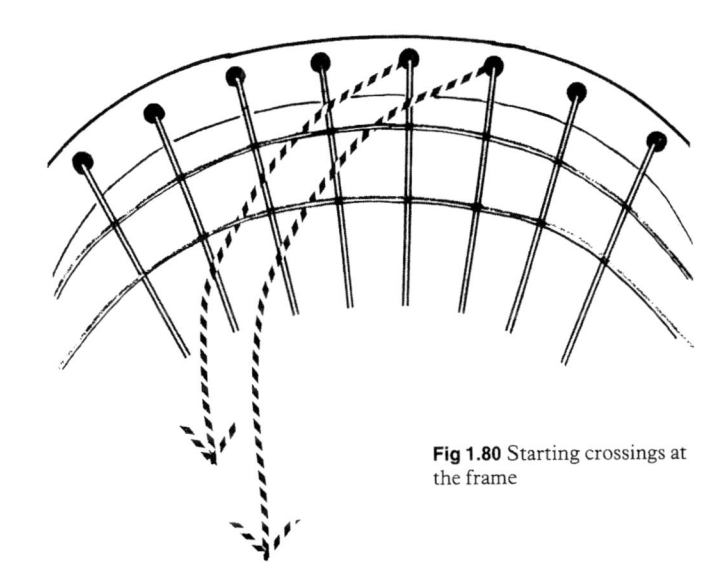

Fig 1.80 Starting crossings at the frame

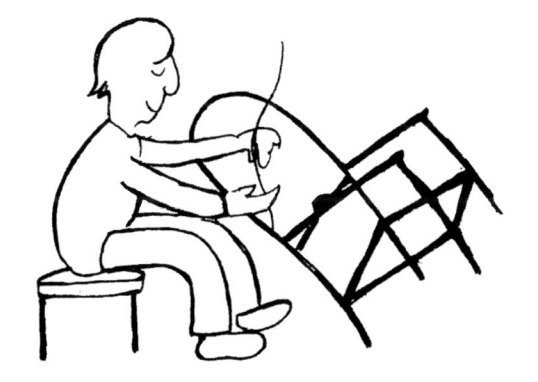

Fig 1.81 Chair back in lap

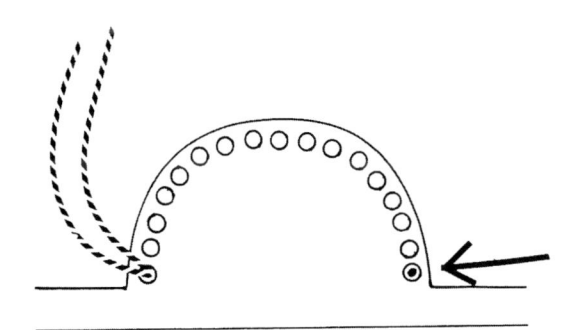

Fig 1.82 'Corner' hole with two crossings

following the line to the sun and observing the golden rule.

Hint: Having woven the first two crossings into place to establish the correct line to follow, I find it easiest to sit on a chair or stool and work with the back of the chair resting on my lap (Fig. 1.81). I use a shell bodkin (see Fig. 1.1) so there is no need to work with one hand under the back of the chair as this would be an awful stretch!

You will note that the holes in the sun are probably becoming quite difficult to thread the cane through, as each one already holds two settings. By easing a thin bodkin or stiletto into the hole and gently compressing the cane, the space can be enlarged slightly and they can be threaded through more easily.

Note: The last hole in the sun on the left-hand side will be treated as a 'corner' and will hold two crossings when travelling from top right to bottom left (York to Yeovil) over the settings and under the weavings (Fig. 1.82). The hole on the right (arrowed) will remain empty until the second crossing is woven, when it will contain two crossings.

45

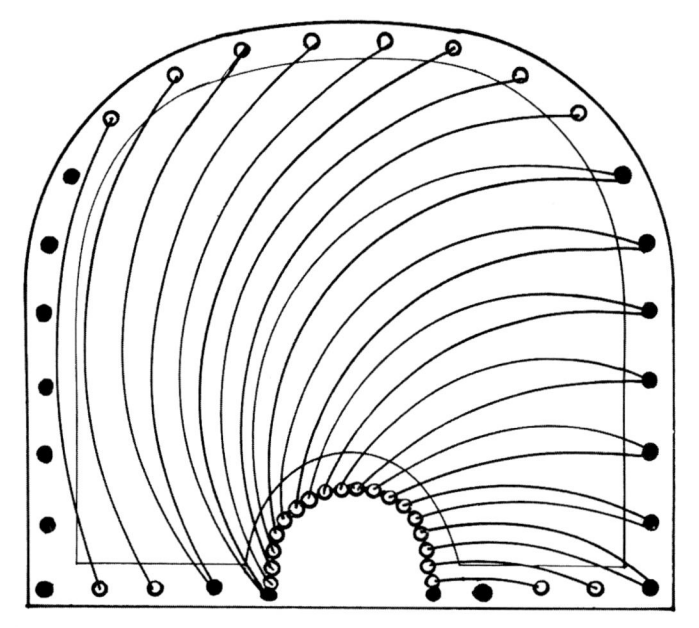

Fig 1.83 Showing York to Yeovil crossings only

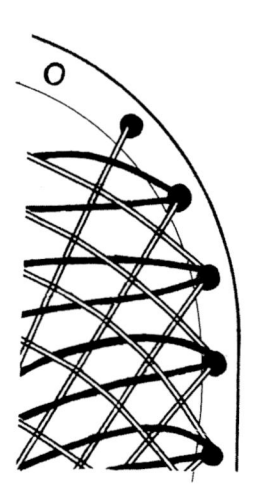

Fig 1.84 The golden rule; crossings travelling under, then over, etc

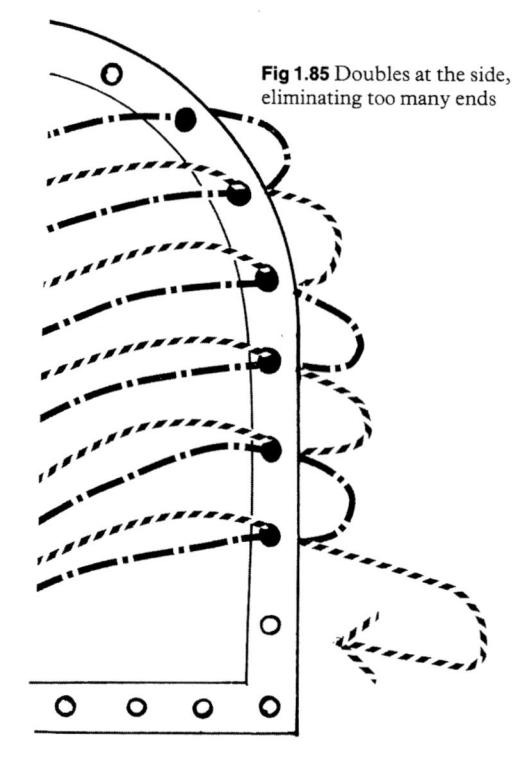

Fig 1.85 Doubles at the side, eliminating too many ends

4. Further crossings will be taken to the right and left side of the sun to complete the final pattern. Remember that when both crossings are finished every hole should contain two crossings, either two from one direction (the shaded holes) a double or one from each direction – the unshaded holes.

Note: As you work round the frame, weaving in the first crossing, you will notice how it becomes necessary to double on the right-hand side. Remember to take each end as *far* as it will go following the curve of the rail and the pattern. Again the golden rule must be applied. Never weave over two settings one after the other, or two weavings one after the other. It is important to keep every hole which contains loose ends pegged.

Hint: Work two crossings with one length of cane, frame to sun twice. When placing the doubles it is possible to continue to work in this way so the back of the frame is neat and without too many ends to thread away (see Fig. 1.85). Be sure the loops at the back of the frame are tight, shiny side out and untwisted. Check this continually.

The second crossing

1. Start at the middle of the back with a long enough piece of cane to run from the frame to the sun twice. Loop the middle of the cane between two holes in the frame. Choose a place where there is a single strand of cane crossing the space, rather than two, in order to keep the back of the frame as neat as possible, with not more than two tight loops between holes.
2. Work down to the sun, first with one end and then with the other. If the holes in the sun are very small, you may need to taper the ends of the cane with a knife so you are able to insert them into the cramped holes. Either just push the tapered end into the hole, and peg, or pull the end through to the back. A pair of pliers may be useful here.
3. Continue working the second crossing, mirroring the position of the first. Two crossings go into the 'corner' hole on the right side of the sun this time (Fig. 1.82).

   Hint: It will be necessary to use a fine shell bodkin or stiletto when weaving the crossings over and under the settings next to the sun. Great care must be taken to get the weaving sequence correct so that all the crossings bed in snugly.
4. When the second crossing is finished, check the work carefully.
   a) Do any of the weavings need further tightening?
   b) Is the sequence correct throughout?
   c) Does each side mirror the other?
   d) Are there two crossings in every hole?
   e) Is the back neat, with not more than two strands between each hole?

METHOD 2: IN WHICH THE CROSSINGS ARE WORKED OUTWARDS FROM THE SUN

In some Rising Sun patterns, the holes in the sun may be large enough to allow both the settings and the crossings to be looped through the holes. In this case the lengths of cane can be threaded through the back of the *sun* and both ends woven out to the edge of the frame where they are pegged. Working outwards from the sun may help to hold the correct curve on the weavings.

Plugging

Beading is not usually applied to rising sun patterns as there would not be enough room to couch through the sun. All holes are carefully plugged using a very small size of centre cane (or matchsticks) on the sun, a larger size on the frame. The plugging must be neatly and carefully done so the finished appearance of the chair is not spoiled.

Trim any ends neatly with side cutters (or toenail clippers if you can find some sharp ones!).

Note: After plugging firmly, some strands may be cut out between holes at the back of the frame *if there are too many* in one or two places.

Chair back with a medallion

Photo 1.10a Medallion chair

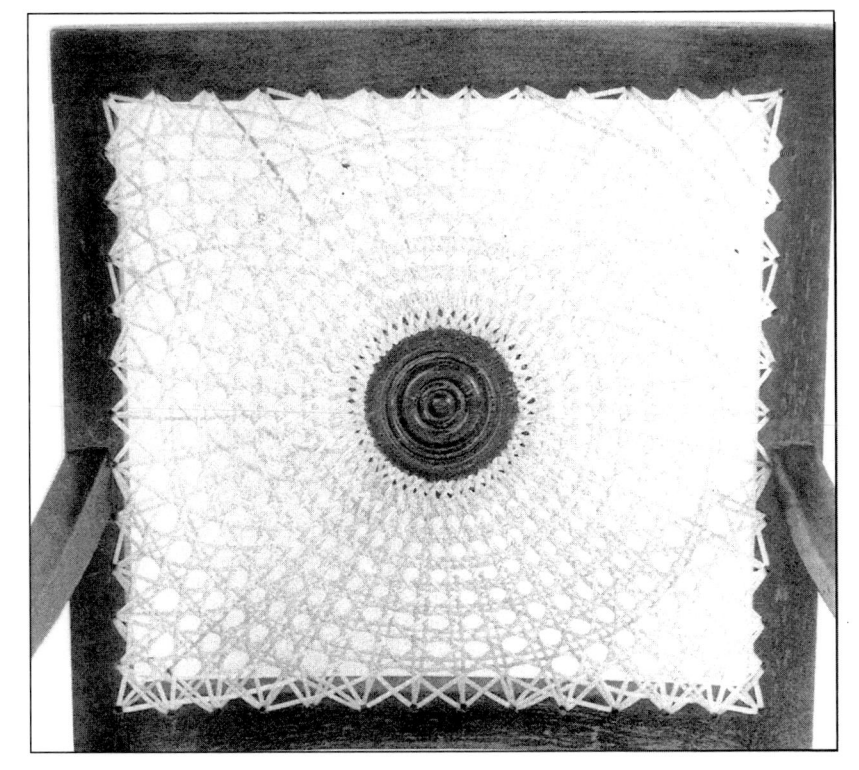

Photo 1.10b Medallion chair close up

These are not really as difficult as they look. Anyone who has a bit of experience of seating different shapes with the six-way standard pattern should be able to manage with the help of the following instructions.

The first thing to do is to look at the remaining old cane carefully before removing it. If you consider that it has been properly done, you may like to keep the cane for reference, so be careful how you cut it from the frame. It might be a good idea to make a sketch of the back, holes, doubles etc., particularly if the frame is square, which makes the crossing stage slightly more complicated so that quite a lot of doubles will be necessary.

Look carefully at the wooden block in the middle. Are the holes 'blind'? If they are, you will probably have to drill out the cane. This is a very delicate job, so be sure to use the correct size bit and a depth gauge. Great care must be taken when clearing the holes as they will be small and very close together. Sometimes it may appear that the holes are blind, but on closer inspection you may find a piece of veneer stuck over the back or else a fillet of wood glued into a groove on top of the ends of the cane. These will have to be carefully removed (see both instructions on page 55).

Note that there *should* be the same number of holes in the frame as in the medallion.

You will need:

A piece of soft wood about 2 cm (1 in) square, and long enough to reach across the frame.

Four screws slightly smaller in diameter than the holes in the frame and the medallion. The screws must be long enough to go through the holes and screw into the batten.

1. Count the holes in the medallion and mark the middle of the top, bottom and sides with golf tees or centre cane pegs.
2. Do the same with the frame.
3. Screw the medallion to the middle of the piece of wood, placing it whichever way fits best (Fig. 1.86).
4. Measuring carefully to make sure the medallion is placed exactly in the middle of the frame and that it is the right way up, put two screws through the centre hole on either side of the front of the frame to hold the strip of wood. Fasten in place.

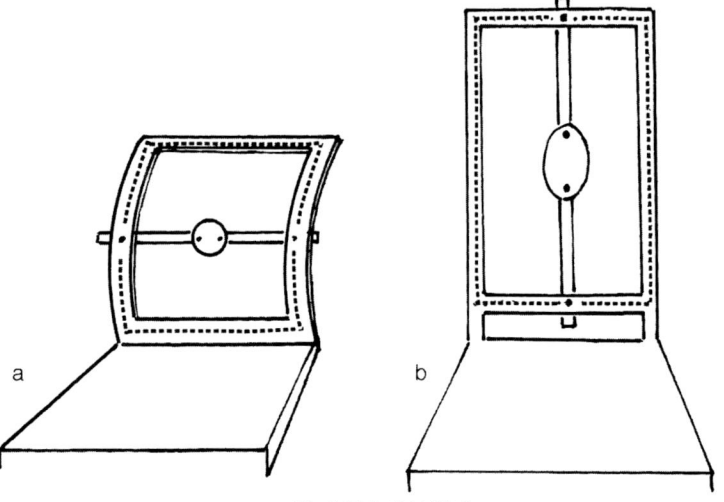

Fig 1.86 (a & b) Fixing medallion to chair back

Fig 1.87 Reaching the Bar!

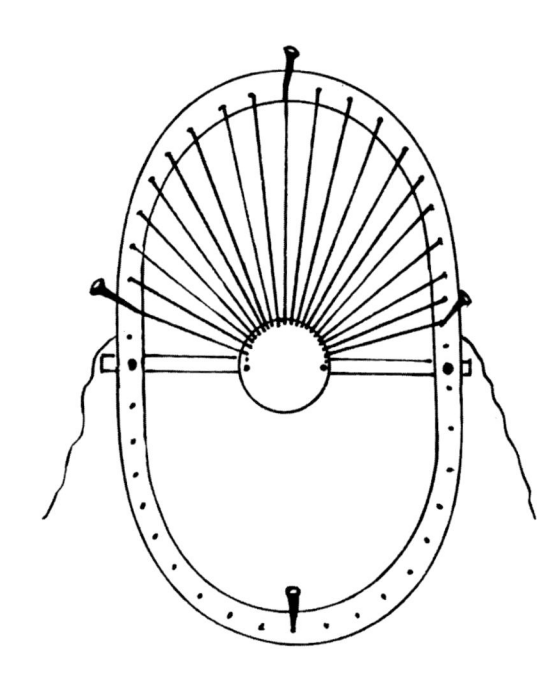

5. If the holes in the medallion and/or the frame are blind, use clamps to attach the batten to the frame and then clamp the medallion in exactly the right position. Protect the wood by putting paper or cloth in the clamps.

   Important note: Make sure that the marked holes on the medallion marry up exactly with the marked holes on the frame.

THE FIRST SETTING

If the holes are blind refer to instructions for blind caning on page 54. The settings must be placed in position first, however, so follow the sequence given here.

1. Choose a long perfect length of cane and start in one of the pegged middle holes in the frame removing the peg and threading half the length through the hole. Replace the peg.
2. Take the length lying on top of the frame and thread it across to the medallion, down through the appropriate hole and up through the next hole, keeping the cane as tight as possible and pegging with tees or centre cane to keep the tension.
3. Work round the frame until the batten holding the medallion in place is reached. Peg the end firmly, but do *not* cut off any remaining length of cane.
4. Return to the other half of the cane pegged in the first hole. Work round to the batten on the other side to complete the first half.
5. Now place the settings in the other half of the frame in the same way, pegging the ends which are left over when the batten is reached on both sides (Fig. 1.87).

THE SECOND SETTING

1. Repeat as for the first setting, but make sure that this time the loops cover the opposite spaces on the back of the medallion and frame, so all the gaps are covered. *All joins should be made on the frame.* By the time the second setting is finished, the holes at the back of the medallion should have a continuous line of tight loops between them and *no* ends!
2. Make sure all ends are tightly pegged, then unscrew the batten.
3. The medallion will now be firmly and accurately fixed in the middle of the frame. The pegged ends of the unfinished settings can be threaded through the remaining holes (which were obscured by the batten) to complete the first and second settings.

   Note: This last threading away of the ends of the first and second settings can sometimes be tricky, as you will have four loose ends at each side to choose from. Make sure the tight loops at the back of the medallion are continuous and that all ends are finally pegged on the frame.

THE WEAVINGS

There are two methods:

1. This uses two long pieces of cane. The first and second weaving are woven alongside each other in an ever-widening circle from the medallion to the frame. The strand nearest the medallion travels under the first setting and then over the 'second' setting and the second strand does the opposite (Fig. 1.88).

   Note: This first method avoids the necessity of numerous joins needed in the second method, but it is more difficult to get the tension exactly right. If joins are needed they are made by overlapping the old and new ends for about three pairs of settings.

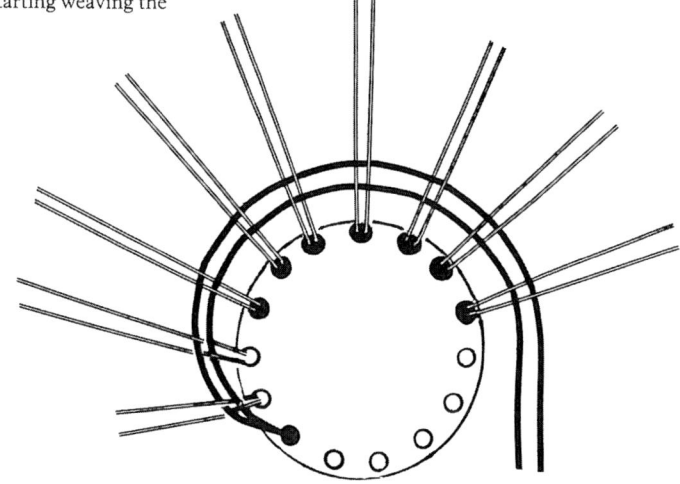

Fig 1.88 Starting weaving the 'snail'

Whichever method you use, work the pairs of weavings following the shape of the medallion until the frame is reached. The spaces between the pairs of weavings will gradually increase. See that the spaces between the settings and weavings equal each other as in Fig. 1.90.

Using a shell bodkin you can weave under and over about four pairs of settings at a time while the weaving is near the medallion. As you get closer to the frame and the settings are further apart, you will probably only be able to manage three pairs and then two.

Note: The weavings are not *always* spaced further and further apart as above. You may prefer to space them at regular intervals, or perhaps you are repairing one of a matching pair. It may be helpful to have 'wedges' of the right size to tuck in between the rows while they are being woven to ensure the spaces are regular.

THE CROSSINGS

If the frame is not round or oval mirroring the shape of the medallion, some of the crossings will be doubles. This will be no problem if each one is taken *as far as it will go* following the golden rule.

Note: If the first method of weaving is being used, hole **A** must contain a double crossing and will be missed by the crossing from the other direction.

THE FIRST CROSSING

Weave the crossing which travels over the settings and under the weavings first, as this makes the weaving easier near the medallion where the canes tend to become very congested (Fig. 1.79).

A little difficulty may be experienced when weaving over and under the overlapping ends in Method 2, but care and patience will win through!

2. The second method uses separate lengths of cane for each circle, and the ends are overlapped as before. Leave a long enough 'tail' on each end of the overlapping canes (one of which will lie at the back of the work and one at the front) so that the weavings can be tightened up later if they should become wrinkled after the crossings are woven into place.

Note: Some people advocate spacing the joins in different places round the medallion, while others keep them all in a vertical line in the bottom half of the panel where they are not so noticeable. Staggering the joins slightly, first to the right and then to the left, helps to hold them in place as they will lie against a weaving strand rather than another join. It may also be helpful to secure the overlapping ends with a twist tie (the kind used to secure plastic bags) until the weaving stage is finished.

Extra weavings will be needed across the corners in a square or rectangular frame (Fig. 1.89).

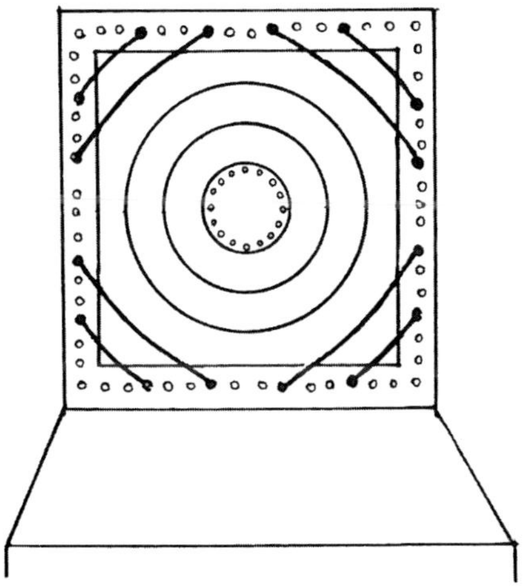

Fig 1.89 Extra weavings across square corners

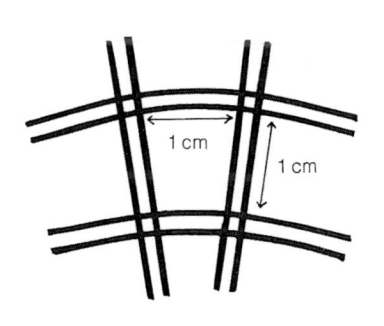

Fig 1.90 Equal spaces between the settings and weavings

Fig 1.91 Showing double at start of 'snail'

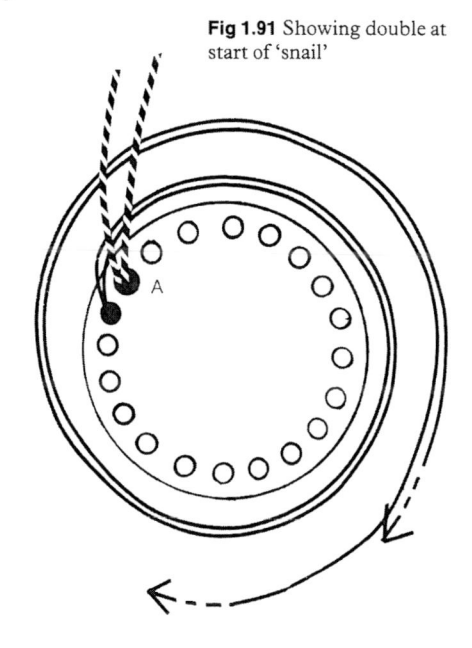

THE SECOND CROSSING

This is woven under the settings and over the weavings, each end being taken as far as possible 'over and under the pairs of settings and pairs of weavings', before being threaded down into the appropriate hole.

Note: The two different ways suggested for weaving the crossings in the Rising Sun pattern also apply to the pattern with a medallion. It would be a good idea to read Methods 1 and 2 under 'Crossings' (pages 44–47).

FINISHING

Pull up any weavings which may be wrinkled and glue the overlapping ends if necessary. Check that all holes in the frame have loops between them. A 'hairpin' of cane can be plugged into place if there is a gap at the back of the frame between two holes and no loose end available to cover the gap.

PLUGGING

Plug each hole (page 23).

VARIATIONS

The crossings do not always start close to the medallion. This helps to avoid congestion at the centre where 'buckling' can occur. Fig. 1.92 shows one way of achieving this. Try to repeat the pattern used previously. This will be essential if there are a pair of chairs and only one is to be repaired.

OPTIONAL EXTRA!

A friend of mine tells how someone she knows sent a chair with a medallion to be recaned. The chair was eventually returned to her, the back caned as normal and the medallion, threaded on a piece of string, hung from one arm. So, if you cannot understand the instructions...!

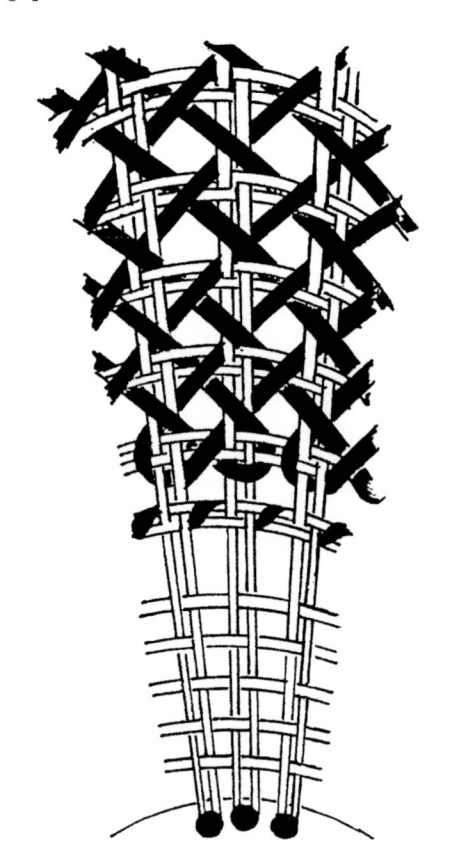

Fig 1.92 Variations at the sun

4.
Curved frames, blind caning and double caning

Saddle curved stools and curves generally

Photo 1.11 Tub chair

There are several ways of weaving curves, but the two main ones are as follows:

1. Work the two settings first across the curve to define it, and then thread in the two weavings one after the other.
2. Work the first setting across the curve. The first weaving is laid underneath it and the second setting is then passed under both the first setting and the first weaving.

Note: Do not pull these last two stages too tight or you may distort the curve formed by the first setting. The second weaving is threaded through in the usual manner as are the two crossings.

51

Fig 1.94 Showing the strap or 'steamer'

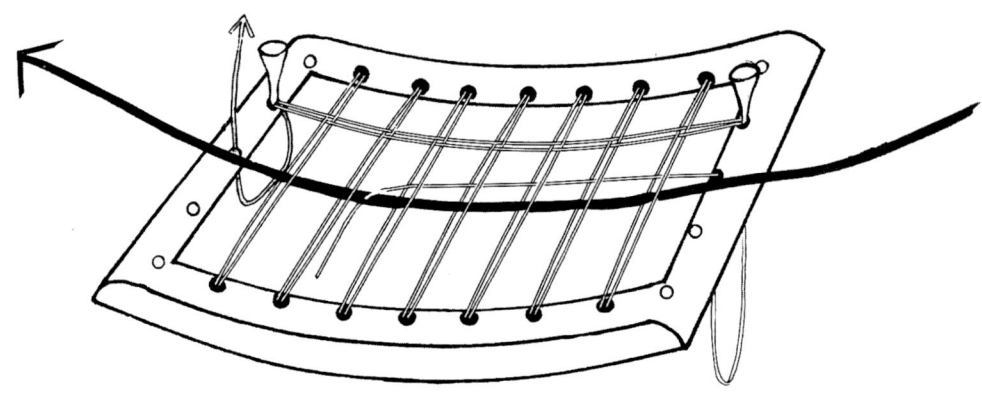

METHOD 1

1. The two settings are worked firmly first to establish the curve.
2. The two weavings are worked between the settings, one after the other.
   Note: A simple way to speed up this operation is to weave a length of plastic strapping (the kind used to fasten parcels is ideal), or else a length of lapping cane, over and under the first and second settings. This 'strap', or 'steamer' as it is sometimes called, should be a little longer than three times the width to be woven and should have a hole punched in the middle large enough to take the piece of cane which is being woven.
3. Start two lengths of cane in opposite holes on each side of the frame. Peg them securely.
4. Take the long end on the left. Thread down through the hole in the strap and pull it across through the settings to the right.
5. Take the cane out of the strap and thread it down the hole on the right-hand side of the frame where the second cane is pegged and then up through the next hole where *it* is pegged. Now pull the strap towards you slightly, so you have room for the next weaving to be threaded.
6. Take the second weaving cane on the right and thread it across the seat using your fingers, a shell bodkin or a drawing-through tool. Thread it down the hole where the first weaving cane is pegged and up the next on the left of the frame.
   Note: These two movements, first weaving with the strap back across the seat to the left and then threading the second weaving back to the right side, are alternated until the weavings are complete. It is essential to begin the two lengths of cane on opposite sides of the seat so that the tight loops between the holes underneath the frame are continuous.

   This method is very quick and can be applied to many different shapes, not only curved, but also ordinary seats. Some people prefer this method for most of their work.
7. The crossings are woven in the usual way.

   The sequence of building up the six-way standard pattern is different, but the end result is the same.

METHOD 2

1. The first setting is woven into place across the curve.
2. The first weaving is woven through the holes in the usual way but is then *threaded under* the settings so that it takes on the curve. This should not be threaded *too* tightly.
3. The second setting is woven through the same holes as the first but lies slightly to the right of the first and is then taken *under* the first weaving and first setting, but not too tightly so the curve is not lost.
4. The second weaving is threaded through the settings in the normal way, in front of the first weaving.
5. The two crossings are woven as usual.
   Note: Fig. 1.95 shows other shapes which would be caned using one of the two methods described.

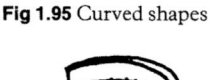

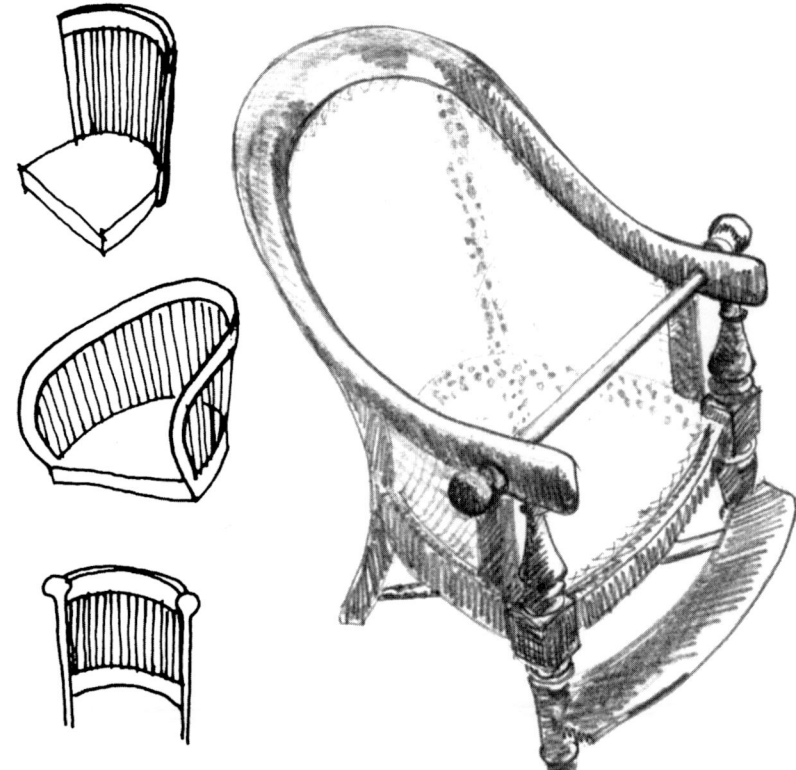

Fig 1.95 Curved shapes

Antique armchair with a curved back

Occasionally you may come across a chair with more than just a simple curve in one direction, as in the chair back illustrated in Photo 1.12.

There are several ways of working this, two of which are described below.

METHOD 1

Foundation canes
Place three or four single pieces of strong cane (No. 4) from top to bottom of the frame and peg firmly. These are temporary strands and will help to establish the curve in the horizontal rails (Fig. 1.96).

The first setting
Settings are the canes usually placed across chair seats from front to back. On curved shapes they are often set in place before the weavings to define the curve (see Saddle-Curved Stool, page 52).

In this chair back, which has curves on two planes, temporary foundation canes are put in first from top to bottom to define the horizontal bow. The settings are then put in one after the other from *side to side* and will lie in front or behind the vertical foundation canes, according to the curve of the side-rails.

1. Using a smaller size of cane, probably No. 2 (see guide, page 16) thread the first setting (horizontal strands) in place, either in front or behind the No. 4 cane as the curves in the vertical rails dictate (Fig. 1.97). The tension of the settings should be adjusted so the horizontal curve is maintained. Don't pull too tight, as the curve is lost.

Note: The strands of No. 4 may have to be slacked off slightly, so that all three curves are correctly established by the time the first setting is in place.

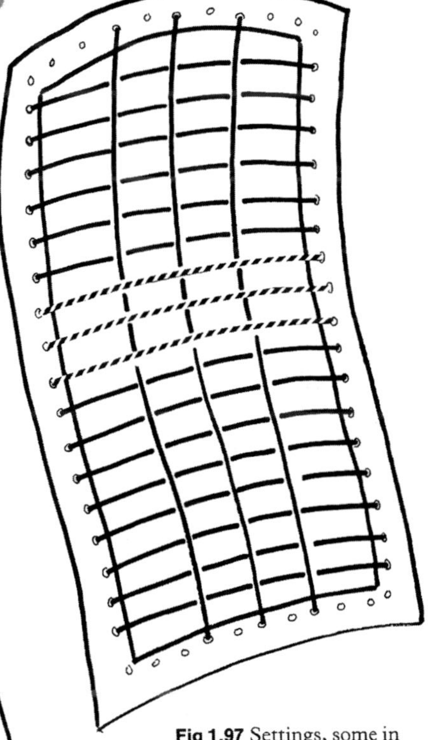

Photo 1.12 Antique armchair, curved back

Fig 1.97 Settings, some in front, some behind

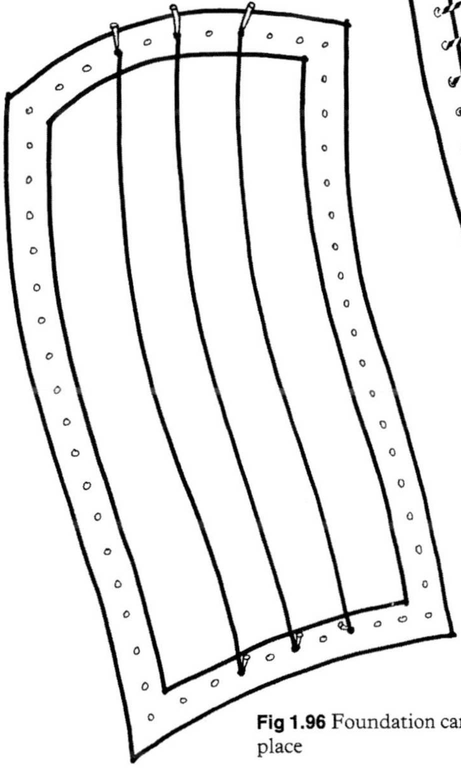

Fig 1.96 Foundation canes in place

53

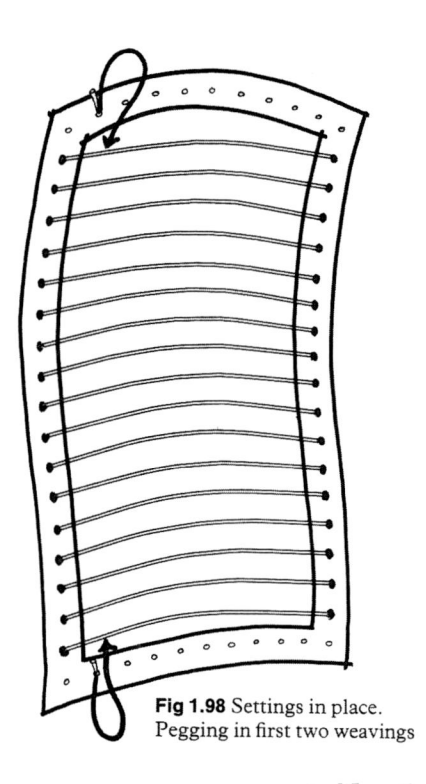

Fig 1.98 Settings in place. Pegging in first two weavings

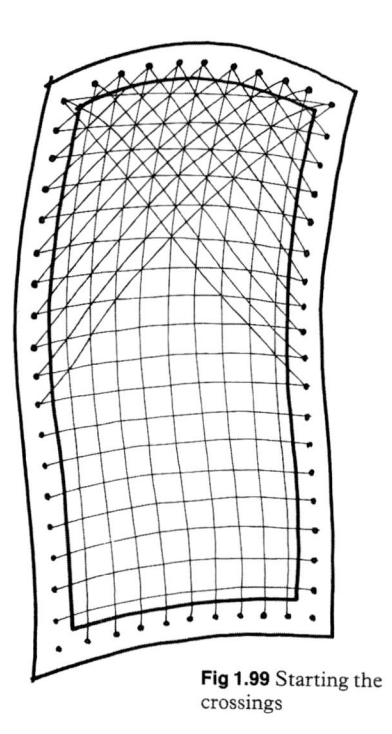

Fig 1.99 Starting the crossings

'York to Yeovil' and then some from 'Liverpool to London' (Fig. 1.99). This helps to maintain the correct curves. Complete these crossings, taking each as far as it will go before threading it down through a hole in the frame. Finish with two crossings in every hole.
Note: Watch the loops between the holes on the back of the frame, make sure they are tight and placed evenly between the holes.

Plugging
As on page 23. Plug every hole if beading is not required.

Beading and couching
Follow instructions on page 25.

JERVIS'S METHOD FOR THE MORE EXPERIENCED CANER

This method may be slightly quicker, as only three stages are woven instead of four as in the last method and the second setting can be woven with the drawing-through tool. Unless you are fairly experienced, however, you may find it difficult to keep the tension correct so that the right curves are formed. (No foundation canes needed).

1. Thread the first setting in place from the *top to the bottom of the frame* (and bottom to top).
2. Thread the first weaving in *behind* the first setting.
3. Place the second weaving in *front*, smoothing each strand down with your hand before it is pegged, so that it is the same tension as the first weaving which lies at the back.
4. The second setting is woven from the bottom of the frame to the top, using a drawing-through tool. Long 'hairpins' of cane are used and looped through the holes at the bottom of the frame. Each arm of the hairpin needs to be long enough to reach to the top of the frame with enough to spare for pegging, and a bit over.
Note: It may not be possible to weave the whole length of the back at once, as the tool blade may not be long enough and the 'S'-shaped curve may make it a little difficult, so two threadings and two pulls through will be required for each setting – work from the bottom of the frame to the middle and then middle to the top.
5. The crossings are woven as usual.
6. Pegging, beading and couching are worked as required.

2. Now thread the second setting through the same holes, but be careful to see that the tight loops at the back of the chair frame cover the spaces between the holes left by the first setting. This second setting should lie slightly below (to the front) of the first, rather than directly on top.

The weavings
First count the number of holes in the top and bottom rails. If the numbers are unequal, refer to page 29.
1. Following the instructions on page 52, weave a strap through the settings.
2. Peg a length of cane in the top left hole (not corner) and another in the bottom left hole. Weave these alternately through the settings, one with the strap (see Fig. 1.94) and one with your fingers or a shell bodkin. Remove the temporary framework as it is reached.
Note: It is not essential to use the 'strap' method: you may prefer to weave the cane using your fingers and perhaps a bodkin. Whichever way you choose, be careful not to pull the cane so tight that the curves are lost.

The crossings
It may be found helpful to weave these across the *top* of the back first, a few crossings from

Blind or 'Continental' caning

In blind caning, known also as French or 'Continental' caning, the holes do not go right through the frame. It is mostly found on the arms and backs of chairs. As the holes do not go right through the frame, each length of cane must be cut off short at each end and fixed in place individually. You will need wood adhesive and *plastic* golf tees or nails of a suitable size to hold the cane tightly in the holes while the glue sets.

PREPARATION

First the holes will have to be cleared of the old cane and any plugs. It is safest to use a hand-drill with a depth marked by an elastic band on the bit. Only use a power drill if you have a proper depth gauge.

Each stage is worked in the usual order (see Figs 1.2–1.7).

THE FIRST SETTING

1. Apply a little wood adhesive to the underside of a piece of cane. Insert it in the hole and peg firmly.
2. Pull tight and cut to the right length. This should not be too long, but on the other hand long enough for security and short enough so that it will fit snugly into the hole keeping the tension as firm as possible. Glue and peg the other end.
3. Finish all the settings in this way and leave to set before removing the pegs. This should be overnight if possible.

THE FIRST WEAVING

This can be done straight after the first setting if it does not mean moving any of the pegs.

Use the same procedure as for the first settings. If you put a little wood adhesive on a saucer it will not dry out for quite some time and it is easy to dip the underside of each new length of cane into the glue. When the first end has been fixed, apply the glue to the other end of the piece of cane with the tip of a penknife blade or other suitable instrument and peg firmly.

THE SECOND SETTING

When the glue has dried completely, remove the pegs and place the second settings in position, remembering to lay each piece slightly to the right of the first. Glue and peg tightly as before.

THE SECOND WEAVING

1. Pull all the lengths of cane through with a drawing-through tool.
2. Glue one side and peg.
3. Pull up tight, and glue and peg the other side.

FIRST AND SECOND CROSSING

1. Weave all the strands in place, leaving ends a little longer than the depth of the hole.
2. Glue and plug or peg one side, using centre cane (see below).
3. Pull the opposite side tight, cut all the canes *exactly* the right length and glue and plug or peg with centre cane.
4. Do the same with the other two sides.

PLUGGING

If no beading is required, each hole is firmly plugged with centre cane.

BEADING AND COUCHING

The beading is usually 'couched' into every other hole, though occasionally you will come across beading which is held in place by 'hairpins' of cane into *every* hole.

In the first case, plug alternate holes round the panel and fix the beading in place with 'hairpins' of No. 2 cane. These can be held in place by very small pieces of centre cane or matchsticks which have a touch of glue to hold everything tight.

Note: If every hole is to be couched, no plugging is done initially and the 'hairpins' of cane are glued into place over the top of the beading. Small plugs can then be pushed into the holes if there is enough space. If these are placed first on one side of the beading and then on the other, it will help the beading to stay flat.

Chairs with the cane hidden in a groove

Some chairs are caned in the normal way, but with the cane loops lying in a groove at the back of the frame which is then filled in with a fillet of wood to hide the cane.

It is not always possible to remove this fillet for recaning and replace it afterwards without damaging the chair. In the case of a valuable antique chair it will probably be wiser to drill or scrape out the old cane very carefully and then follow the directions for blind caning.

If, however, you think you can remove it, run the blade of a sharp knife round the edge of the fillet, cutting down to the bottom of the groove. Find a join in the fillet and try to lever it up very carefully, with a suitable sized screwdriver. If the fillet will not come out, squirt in some water to loosen the glue, and leave it for some time to penetrate before trying to lever it up again. Continue soaking and levering until the fillet comes out. Using a clearing tool (as below) may also help.

Replace the fillet after re-caning. If it is too badly damaged, a piece of suitable-sized centre cane can be used as in the loom cane method (see page 60).

JOHN'S METHOD FOR REMOVING A SPLINE

Using a hot-air paint stripper, *very* carefully heat a small portion of the back of the panel and the spline – this will soften the glue. By inserting a clearing tool through the holes on the front of the cane panel, the spline can be forced out bit by bit.

Note: Great care must be taken not to overheat the frame and blister the polish or, worse, burn up the chair!

Double caning

Photo 1.13 Double caning

This is most often found on large armchairs and sofas. If the holes are blind, each panel will be worked quite separately following the directions for blind caning.

If the holes go right through the frame the method will be as follows.

1. Work the settings and weavings on the inside of the frame in the usual way. Make sure the loops alternate between the holes on the outside, so by the time these stages are completed there will be a continuous line of tight loops between every hole.
   Note: There will not be a loop between the hole next to the corner and the corner hole (Fig. 1.100). Leave a long enough 'tail' when you start and finish, so an end can be taken across this space and into the corner hole where it will be pegged at the finish (Fig. 1.101).
2. Now work the settings and weavings on the outside of the frame, again making sure that all the holes, this time on the *inside* have tight loops between them.
   Note: Any 'short strokes' required must start and finish in the same holes, both inside and outside the frame.

THE CROSSINGS

These are worked in unison, inside and outside, using one length of cane.

1. Thread the cane through the hole in the top rail next to the front corner hole. Pull it through so half its length is on the inside and half on the outside of the frame (Fig. 1.102). Peg.
2. Take the length on the inside, through the hole below this corner **B** so that it now lies on the outside.
3. The length of cane which is on the outside is now taken through the same hole, so that it is on the inside. Now peg, so both these canes are secured (Fig. 1.103).
4. Now weave the cane on the inside over the settings and under the weavings across the frame from top right to the appropriate hole in the bottom of the frame, and through this hole to the outside.
5. Weave the cane on the outside (from hole **B**) in the same manner, except that it travels under the settings and over the weavings (as long as the basic pattern has been built up correctly) (Fig. 1.104).
6. The end of the cane is threaded through the same hole at the bottom of the frame as the first cane (Fig. 1.105).
7. Continue working in this way until the bottom corner is reached. Two crossings must be woven into this hole. This is quite straightforward if you remember that all ends should finish at the bottom of the frame as this gives added strength to the top

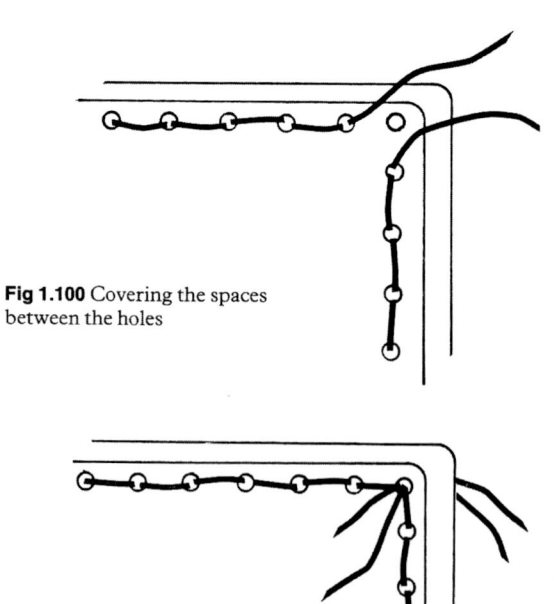

Fig 1.100 Covering the spaces between the holes

Fig 1.101 Threading the ends through the corner holes

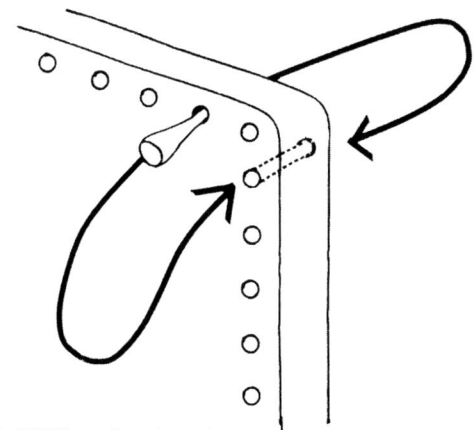

Fig 1.102 Threading through the holes next to the corner

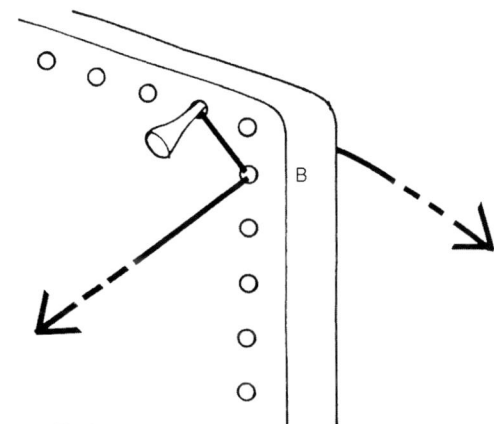

Fig 1.103 Both canes through hole **B**

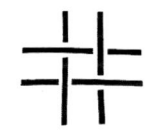

Fig 1.104 Basic pattern build-up

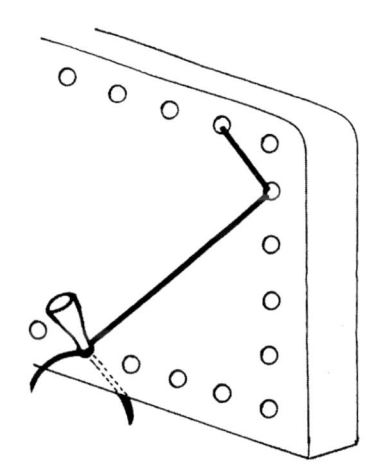

Fig 1.105 Both crossings pegged at the bottom

of the cane panel where the most wear will be (Fig. 1.106).

Note: This diagram shows that **A** and **B** are two separate canes starting at the top and finishing in the same corner hole.

8. The rest of the crossings start at the top and finish at the bottom in the same manner. Remember to start two (a double) from the top left corner hole.
9. When the first stage of the crossings is complete, start from the top back and reverse the procedure as described in stages 1–9 (Fig. 1.107). Remember to double for all short settings or short weavings.

Note: Thread away the 'tails' into the corner holes to complete the uninterrupted line of tight loops round the inside and outside of the cane panels.

Beading and couching
If this is required, plug every other hole. The method described in the chapter on blind caning is used on both sides (page 55).

Plugging
Each hole is firmly plugged and the ends are then cut off as short as possible.

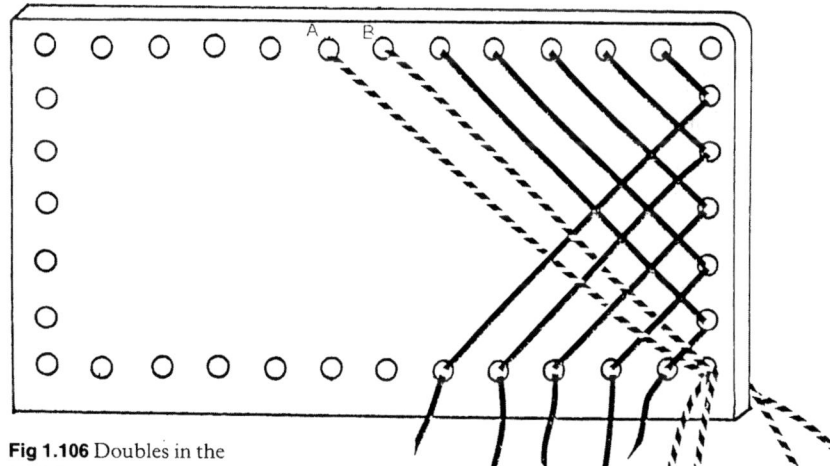

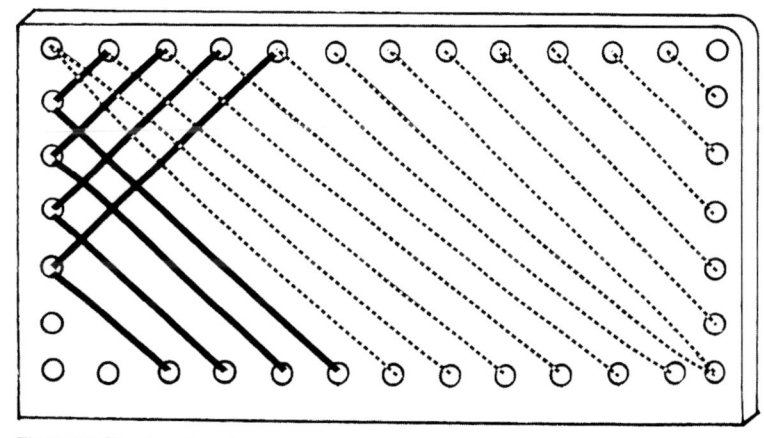

Fig 1.106 Doubles in the corner

Fig 1.107 Starting the other corner

57

Bergère chairs

The Bergère chair was introduced to this country from France in about 1725 and in those days it was a wide upholstered armchair. The word *Bergère* was anglicised by cabinet makers to Burjair, Bargair and Birjair. These names were also applied to couches.

Sheraton, in the *Cabinet Dictionary* of 1803, describes a Bergère as 'having a caned back and arms. Sometimes the seats are caned, having loose covers'. One of the characteristics of eighteenth-century Bergère chairs was a long seat and a comfortable rake to the back.

The backs, arms and seats of these low-backed chairs and sofas are either caned or upholstered, or combine both with cushions.

Photo 1.14 Bergère chair

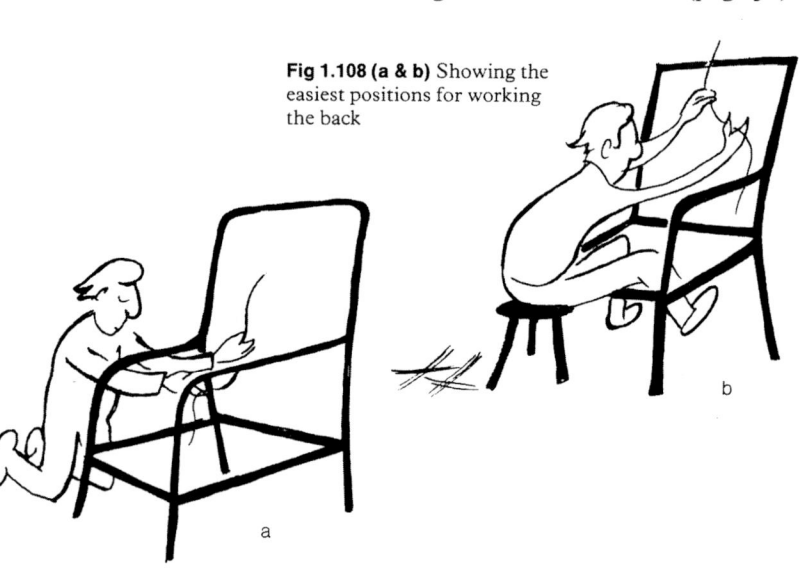

Fig 1.109 Bergère chair with curved panels below the arms

METHOD USING THE SIX-WAY STANDARD PATTERN

If the back, arms and seats are all caned, many holes will be common to all three areas of caning. As the seat usually needs to be re-caned before the arms and back, it is as well to cane this last as it will be easier to remove it at a later date if the canes in the common holes lie on top of those from the other two areas.

1. Work on the back panel first. Sitting with your feet through seat frame (as long as the chair seat is not upholstered!) will help you to reach the back (Fig. 1.108a). Being able to reach under the arms can also be a help (Fig. 1.108b).
2. Cane the arms next. You will probably need to insert a very thin bodkin (or knitting needle) into some of the common holes which already hold canes from the back, in order to gently compress the cane and widen the space.
   Note: Be very careful to keep the loops tight at the back and the sides of the frame, and neat, with no gaps between holes.
3. The seat is caned last and is usually straight forward, although it does take quite a long time and involves a lot of stretching.

Beading
This is not usually applied, but if it is used it is placed across the front rail, round the front and top of the arms and back, but not usually around the inside of the seat.

Plugging
Follow the instructions on page 23.
Note: Photo 1.13 shows a Bergère chair with double caning underneath the arms (page 56).

Fig 1.108 (a & b) Showing the easiest positions for working the back

CHAIR WITH CURVES BELOW THE ARMS

The armchair illustrated was caned in the following way:

1. The two settings were woven into position first, from the top to the bottom of the panel.
2. The weavings were woven using *long* 'hairpins' of cane which ran from the back of the frame to the front and then to the back again, leaving the ends projecting at the back where they were all pegged temporarily and then tightened as necessary after the crossings were finished (Fig. 1.109).

5.
Loom cane and different patterns

Loom cane seats

Loom cane refers to machine-made sheet cane, which is also known as chair cane webbing. This is used on modern chair seats, and cannot be used on chairs designed for hand caning. Most craft suppliers stock this pre-woven cane.

TOOLS

1. Hammer or mallet
2. Wood adhesive (*Evo-Stik* or other good brand)
3. A dozen hardwood wedges (easily made from a strip of wood 2 cm ($\frac{3}{4}$ in) wide and 7 mm ($\frac{1}{4}$ in) thick. Cut pieces 6 cm ($2\frac{1}{2}$ in) long and taper one end to 3 mm ($\frac{1}{4}$ in) thick. This is quite simple to do with an electric sander (Fig. 1.110).

MATERIALS

1. A piece of loom cane large enough to cover the seat with approximately 5 cm (2 in) to spare all the way round.
2. A length of centre cane which is the right size to be forced into the groove round the edge of the seat. It is possible to buy a wedge-shaped spline which is specially manufactured for this job, but a piece of centre cane, usually No. 12 or No. 15, works just as well.

METHOD

1. Remove the spline, old cane and glue using a small chisel and hammer. Clean the channel right out.
2. Cut the sheet cane about 6 cm (2 in) larger than the outer edge of the groove round the chair seat.
3. Soak the cane for 10–15 minutes in *warm* water. Remove and either allow to drain or mop it with a dry cloth.
4. Run the adhesive into the groove and place the cane on the seat, aligning the horizontal lines with the front of the chair frame.

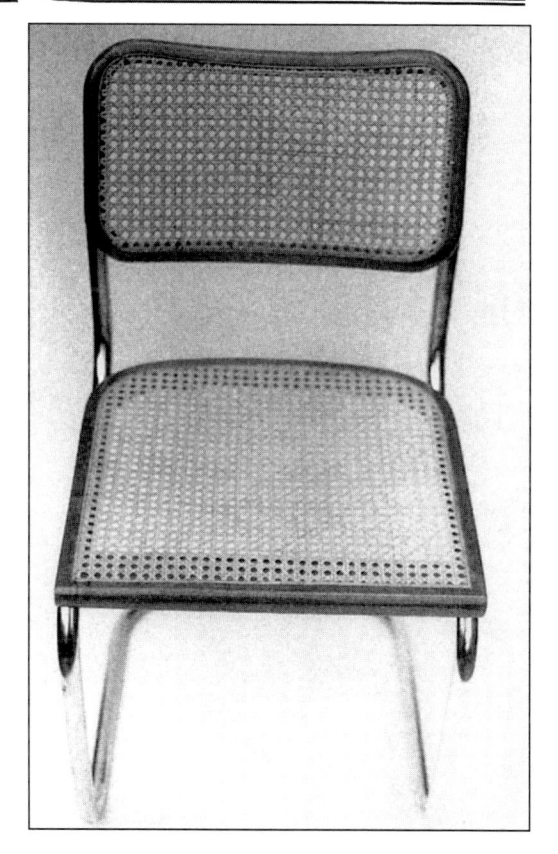

Photo 1.15 Loom cane chair

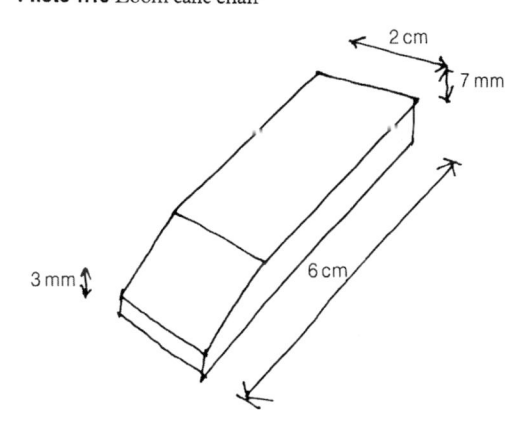

Fig 1.110 Wedges

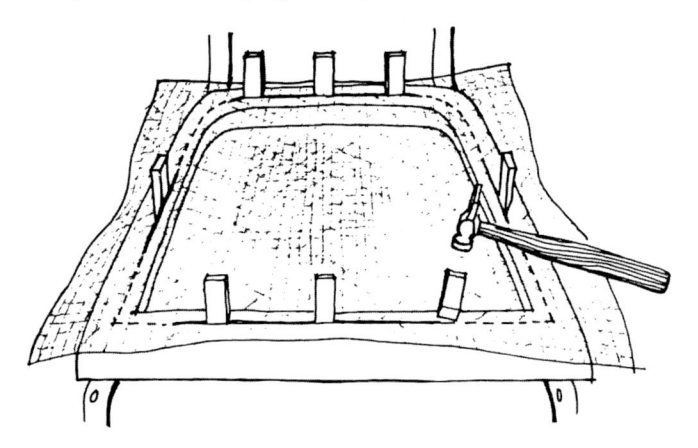

Fig 1.111 Loom cane in place

5. Force the cane into the groove using the wedges. Do the centre back and front first, leaving a wedge in the middle to keep the cane in place. Work round the chair, driving a wedge into the groove in the middle of each side and stretching the cane over the seat (Fig. 1.111).

6. Now position the other wedges on each side of the four that are already in place, making sure the cane is really tightly in position.

GLUING THE SPLINE IN PLACE AND FINISHING

Measure the groove and cut the centre cane to exactly the right length to fit tightly in place. For a rectangular seat cut four separate pieces and for a curved seat use a continuous piece, joining at the centre back.

1. Remove the wedges and run more glue in all round the groove. Tap the centre cane into position using a mallet or hammer and one of the little wedges, inverted this time so that the thicker end is placed against the spline. As the wedges are made of hardwood they will not be damaged when tapped by the hammer on the thin edge.
2. Cut round the *outside* edge of the spline to remove the surplus cane.
3. Stand back and admire your work!

Hexagonal or 'Star of David' pattern

This is a very attractive decorative pattern, also known as Spider weave (or Spider web), Étoile and Marguerite. It is not suitable for a chair which is going to have heavy use, and is best kept for the bedroom, to support clothes rather than people.

1. Use No. 3 cane for the first setting. Weave this into every hole except the corners, from front to back, as *tightly* as possible.
2. Use No. 4 cane for the first weaving. This is woven through every *other* hole from side to side, travelling over the top of the settings.
3. Use No. 4 cane and weave the first 'steep' crossing from left to right (Liverpool to London), starting in the left back corner hole, and threading through every other hole on the front and back of the frame. These 'steep' crossings travel over the weavings and under the settings. Some adjustments may be needed (holes missed) on the side rails to keep the crossings as diagonal as possible.
4. Use No. 4 cane and weave the second 'steep' crossing from York to Yeovil. This will use the same holes in the front and back

Photo 1.16a Chair caned in hexagonal pattern

Phot 1.16b Close-up of hexagonal pattern

60

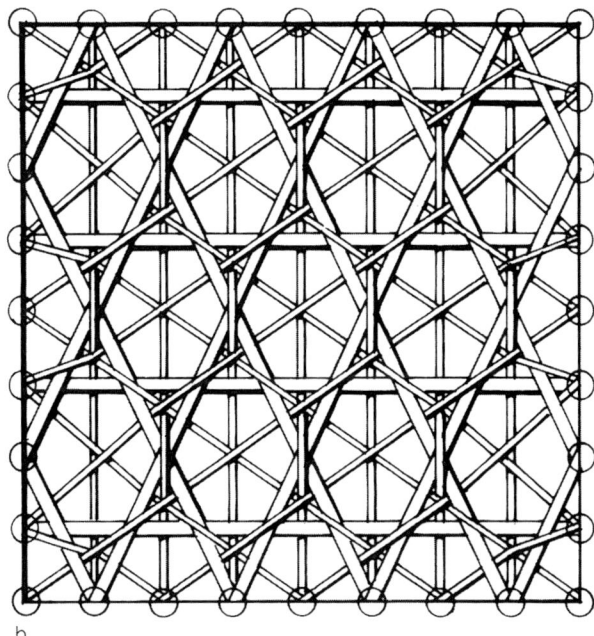

Fig 1.112 (a & b) Hexagonal patterns

of the frame as the first steep crossing and will travel over the weavings and under the settings in the same way as the first. Again adjustments may be needed on the sides.

5. Use No. 3 cane and weave the first 'shallow' crossing. Weave through alternate holes, avoiding those used by the 'steep' crossings and travel from York to Yeovil (top right to bottom left). Keep the lines as parallel to each other as possible and go over everything except the London to Liverpool 'steep' crossings. Repeat this sequence for each 'shallow' crossing, and you will soon see that you are threading down into one triangle, across a space and up into the next triangle.

6. Use No. 3 cane and weave the second 'shallow' crossing from Liverpool to London (top left to bottom right), starting at a corner if possible. Again keep these crossings as parallel to each other as you can, and this time travel over everything except the York to Yeovil steep crossings. Finish in the most convenient hole.

Note: There are many variations of this pattern, some following as many as nine different directions.

PROBLEMS OF SHAPING

Fitting this pattern into a shaped seat does present some difficulty. However, the first setting and the first weaving are quite straightforward.

When weaving the crossings, start out from the back rail and work across to the front and sides, keeping the crossings as parallel to each other as possible and trying to maintain a good diagonal line. Choosing the appropriate hole to finish each strand of cane sometimes takes lengthy deliberation! Round the corners of a bow-fronted chair the positioning of the crossings in the holes becomes irregular. A good guide is to watch the shape of the middle of the 'star' and try not to get it too elongated.

Note: Fig. 1.112b shows a slight variation. The London to Liverpool 'shallow' crossing was woven before the Yeovil to York one.

Other cane patterns

DOUBLE VICTORIA (DOUBLE DIAMOND OR STAR)

This is quicker to weave than the six-way standard pattern, but not as strong, as only one crossing is interwoven. The other five strands used to make up the pattern are all laid one on top of the other (Fig. 1.113).

1. Two settings are laid side by side in No. 2 cane.
2. Two weavings are laid side by side in No. 2 cane on top of the settings.
3. One crossing (London to Liverpool) is laid on top using No. 3 cane.
4. One crossing (Yeovil to York) is woven using No. 3 cane, over a single crossing and then under the intersection of settings, weavings and crossings. This is sometimes known as 'Over the bars and under the stars'.

Note: Double Victoria *never* doubles in the corner holes!

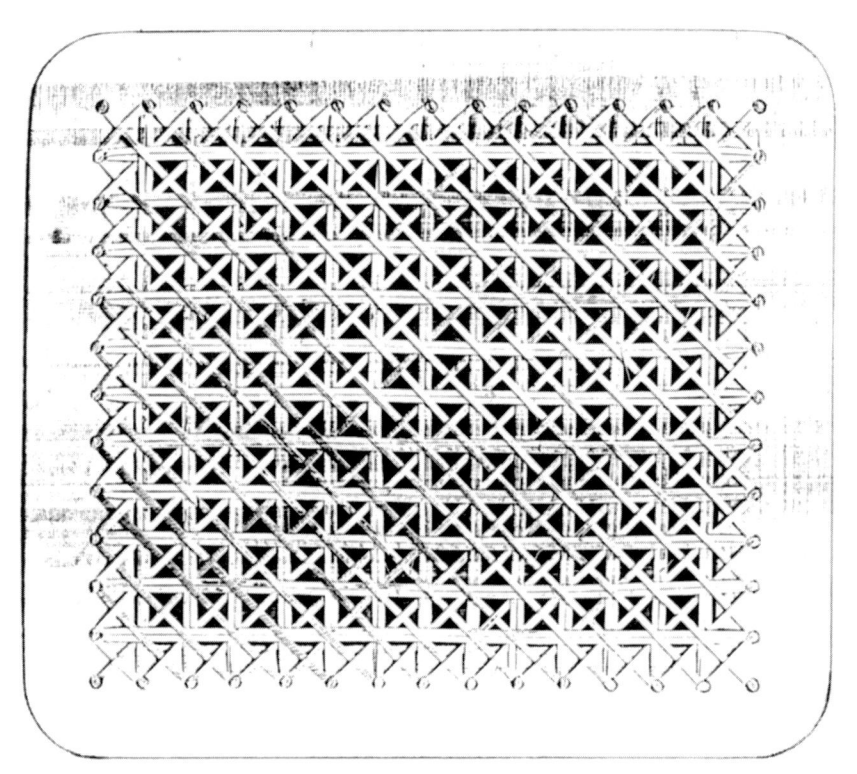

Fig 1.113 Double Victoria

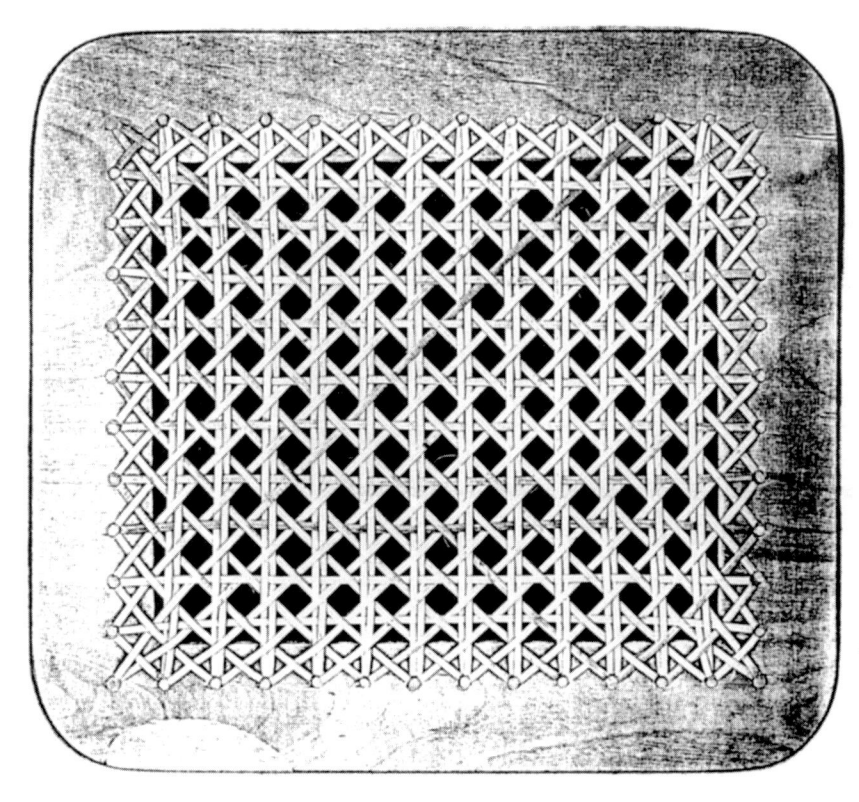

Fig 1.114 Five-way standard pattern

Shaped seats
Always double in the hole one short of the 'short stroke'. (See chapter on trapezium shapes, page 33.) Leave these double crossings slightly slack so that there is room to weave the crossing from the other direction between them.

Double Victoria is not a very suitable pattern for a bow-fronted chair.

Curved shapes
Work as for curved shapes (page 51).

1. The two settings are laid in place.
2. The two weavings are woven *underneath* the settings.
3. The first crossing is laid underneath the weavings and settings.
4. The second crossing is woven the opposite way from before, this time it travels 'Under the bars and over the stars'.

SINGLE VICTORIA

1. One setting in No. 4 cane.
2. One weaving in No. 4 cane, over the setting.
3. One crossing in No. 3 cane, over the weaving.
4. One crossing woven over the bars and under the stars as above.

FIVE-WAY STANDARD PATTERN

This pattern looks quite different from the six-way standard. It is both attractive and slightly quicker to weave. It is useful for chair frames with very close-set holes. (The curved cane chair on the jacket of this book was woven in the five-way standard pattern.)

1. Two settings laid side by side in No. 2 cane.
2. One weaving interwoven using No. 2 cane (see Fig. 1.114).
3. One crossing woven under the weaving and over the settings.
4. The second crossing woven over the weavings and under the settings.

Unlike the double and single Victorias, the four and five-way patterns double in the corner holes. They also double and miss for every 'short stroke' (see page 36).

Curved shapes (see the cane chair shown on the jacket)
Two methods are suggested. The first is quite straightforward, and the second makes it possible to use the drawing-through tool and so speeds up the work. It is recommended for the more experienced worker.

Method 1

1. Both settings are laid in place first.
2. The weaving is then woven between the two settings.
3. The crossings are woven into place as above.

Method 2

1. The first setting is threaded into place, using long lengths of cane and keeping it very tight.
2. Peg an end of cane on the left hand side of the frame and lay the first weaving *behind* the first setting, down the hole on the opposite side and up through the next hole. Peg (very important).
3. Now take the cane across in *front*, leaving this weaving slack enough to follow the curve of the first setting and first weaving, smoothing it with your hand.
4. Now thread it down the appropriate hole and peg. Up the next, peg and across *behind* again.
5. Continue laying the weavings in place, one after the other until the panel is complete.
6. The second setting is woven into place using the drawing-through tool, over one weaving and under the next.
7. The two crossings are woven as before, making sure they interlock.

FOUR-WAY STANDARD PATTERN

This is a very quick pattern, but not really strong enough for a chair seat and should be used for decorative panels only.

1. One setting in No. 4 cane.
2. One weaving laid on top in No. 4 cane.
3. The first crossing and second crossing are woven into place one after the other in No. 3 cane. Double in the corner holes.

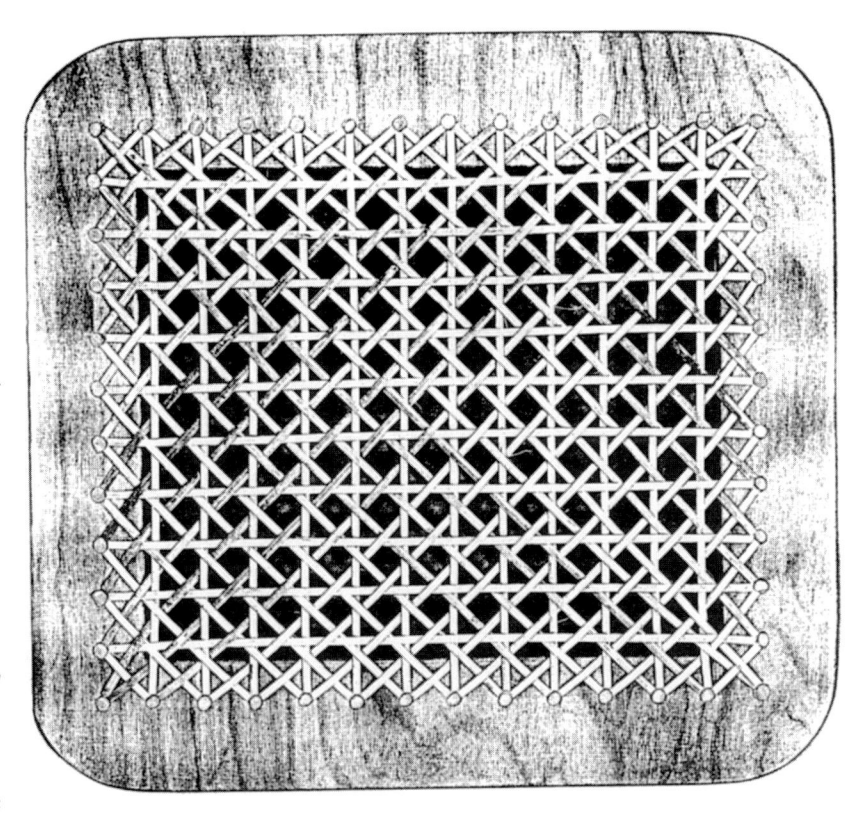

EXTRA-QUICK FOUR-WAY (OR 'GYPSY') PATTERN

1. The first setting.
2. The first crossing laid on top (doubling in the corners for both crossings).
3. The first weaving laid on top of the setting and crossing.
4. The second crossing woven into place, travelling over a weaving and the first crossing and then under a setting and first crossing.

There are many variations to these weaves, and it can be interesting to work out your own.

Fig 1.115 Four-way pattern

6. Quick methods and renovating

Quick method of weaving

Fig 1.116 Metal comb

Instead of weaving the first setting and then the first weaving, the second setting and then the second weaving, both settings can be woven first (as in the saddle stool, page 52) and then the first and second weavings are threaded into place one after the other.

1. Thread the first setting in place.
2. Thread the second settings in place, slightly to the right of the first settings.
3. Using a strap (or 'steamer'), weave it through the settings at the back of the frame and draw the first weaving through into position.
   Note: This strap can also be made of spring steel, 6 mm wide, but be careful the edges have been well rubbed with emery paper so that they do not cut the cane. The length should be slightly more than twice the width to be woven, and there must be a hole in the middle to pass the cane through. This works very well, as it can also be used to push the row straight after the cane is woven into place.
4. Pull the strap forward and weave the second weaving into place in front of the first weaving, using a drawing-through tool or a shell bodkin.
5. Push the two rows into place using your fingers, a golf tee or a metal comb made of mild steel (Fig. 1.116). These combs are used in France, usually in five different sizes. The measurement is the distance between the teeth: 10 mm, 11 mm, 12 mm, 13 mm, ($\frac{1}{2}$ in) and 14 mm. They are not readily available but you could have one made by a metal worker.

Continue weaving as in stages 3–5 until the last row or two is reached. These will probably have to be woven without the strap, as the weaving becomes tight.
Note: On a shaped chair, when the short settings are reached, just slide the end of the strap between the appropriate settings and then carry on weaving!

The French method

This is another quick method of weaving two canes at a time, which is especially valuable for closely spaced holes, as the weaving starts at the sides and finishes in the middle where the canes are more 'elastic'.
Note: If the seat is shaped, the short strokes are placed into position first on either side of the seat.

1. Place the settings in position first, *from side to side* of the frame, one slightly in front of the other (Fig. 1.117).
2. Peg a length of cane in the front left hole, **A**, next to the corner (shown striped).
3. Weave this across the chair to the back, over and under the settings and down the appropriate hole, up the next to the right and peg.
4. Start two new pieces of cane, one in hole **B** and one in **C** at the back of the frame (shown black).
5. Weave a needle or drawing-through tool across from the front to the back through the *opposite settings to the first weaving*.
6. Thread the two new canes through the eye of the needle and pull through to the front of the frame. Remove the canes from the needle and thread one down the left front hole with the first Weaving **A** and the other down the right front hole next to the corner **D**. Now thread them up the next hole on the left and right.
7. Thread the needle again from front to back over the opposite settings to the last two weavings.
8. Start a new length of cane in hole **C** (right back). Peg one end and thread the other end through the needle together with the end of the *first* weaving. Pull these two (striped) ends through the settings to the front of the chair (Fig. 1.117).
9. Now the first pair of weavings is threaded

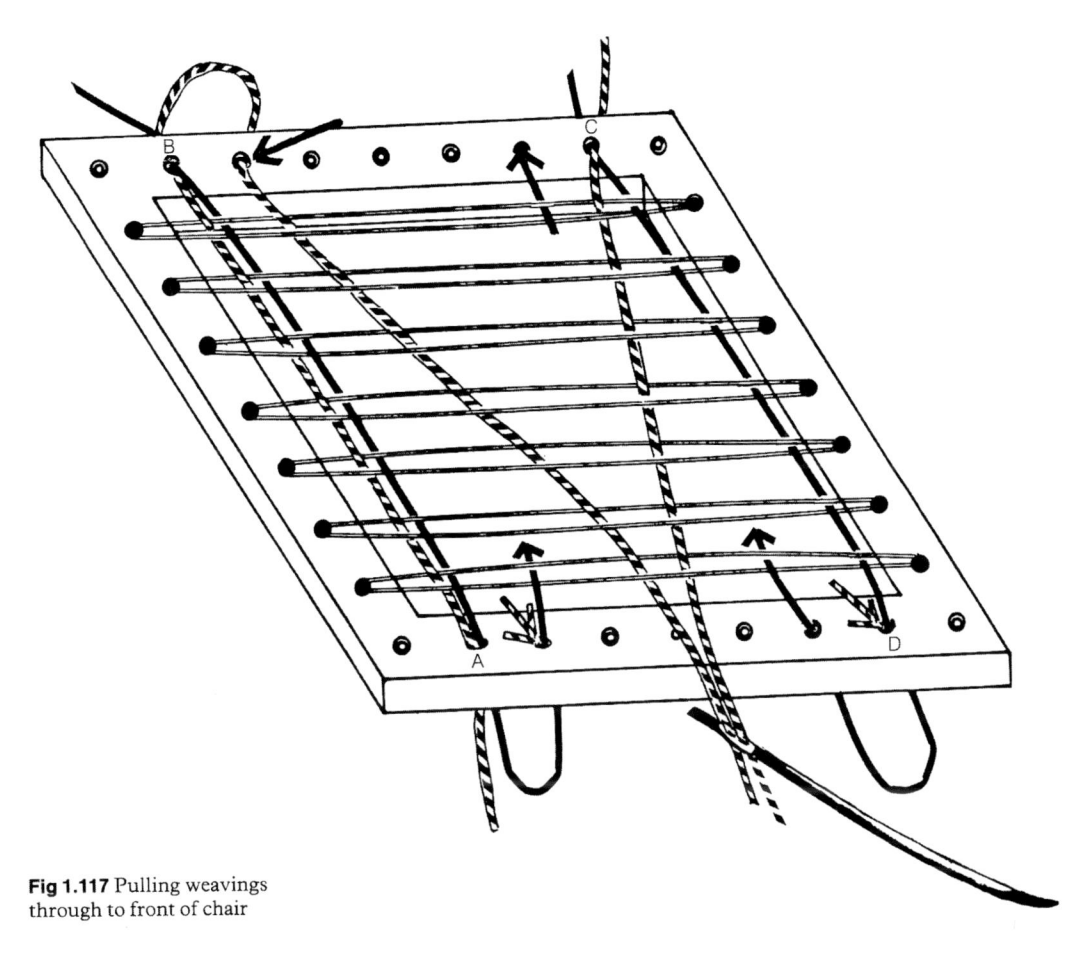

Fig 1.117 Pulling weavings through to front of chair

to the back of the frame and through the opposite settings to the last weavings.
10. These weavings with two canes at a time, each in the same 'shed' but threaded down holes on opposite sides of the frame, continue until one cane is left to be woven in the middle. This is done by hand to complete the first four stages.
11. Wet the canes with a damp cloth (this helps to keep them together) and either pinch them into pairs or use the right-sized combs.
12. Weave the crossings as usual.

Point of interest: In France, chairs for re-caning are often priced according to the distance between holes. The combs are used to gauge this price, so much for 10 mm, etc.

Methods of colouring cane

Spirit-based stains may soak into the cane better than water or oil-based stains, but with these it is important to get the colour right the first time, as further coats make very little difference to the shade. Try out the stain on a spare piece of loom cane. This *may* make the stain look a little paler than it would on a newly-woven seat, especially if the prewoven cane has been finished with a sealer, so be careful. Do not use acrylic-based stains, as these are inclined to chip.

It is possible to buy dyes in powder form from some specialist firms which supply the french polish trade. These should be spirit-soluble. After mixing to a fairly strong solution with methylated spirit and straining to remove sediment, they are then mixed with french polish in a 50/50 proportion. Apply with a stiff brush to work the polish well in to the corners and immediately wipe over with a french polisher's rubber. The advantage of these dyes is that by mixing your own you can obtain the colour you want. There are also ready-mixed tins available in walnut and other colours, which you also mix with french polish and apply.

Another way of colouring is to use Van Dyck Crystals. These are dissolved in water and applied with a brush to give a rich brown colour, varying from a deep tone to a light shade. A dash of ammonia added to the mixture may help the dye to penetrate.

Permanganate of potash is often recommended. This is also dissolved in water. Several coats will be needed and the cane will gradually become darker with each one. This stain fades quite quickly, however.

There are a number of brands of wood-dye on the market in a wide range of colours. These can be applied with a brush or cloth. More than one coat may be needed.

After using any of the above methods, the

cane on panels can be enhanced with either coloured or clear wax polish. These can be thinned with *pure* turpentine. When quite dry, a coat of surface equaliser can be applied to seal the surface. Be cautious in using this on chairs, just in case the polish *should* come off on clothing.

Simple renovating and repairs

If there is heavy or badly-flaked varnish you want to remove from a chair, scrape it off with a blunt knife. Difficult bits can be removed using a paint stripper and size 00 steel wool. Finish with very fine grade (0000). Working with the grain, dip the steel wool in methylated spirit, rub and immediately wipe off with a soft cloth and repeat until the surface is smooth.

If you clean down to the bare wood, you may want to apply a stain. French polish can be used on top to give a hard finish and this is waxed over the top when dry.

Colron Antique Oil gives a natural finish if you wish to leave the chair unstained. Coat after coat can be built up to give a hard satin finish. Linseed oil can also be used for a natural finish (the raw oil penetrates better than the boiled).

MENDING A SPLIT RAIL

The rails should be checked very carefully. The slightest crack must be reinforced with screws, as the new canework will put considerable strain on the frame. It is annoying, to say the least, if the whole thing collapses after you have finished reseating!

If part of the rail is split down the line of holes, insert some glue, if possible, and put in some countersunk screws, being *very* careful that they are *between* every few holes. Plastic golf tees inserted in the holes keeps them free of glue while the repair is drying.

CLEANING THE CHAIR FRAME
Rose's recipe:
  1 part pure turpentine (not white spirit)
  1 part methylated spirit
  1 part raw linseed oil

Rub on and buff off with a clean cloth. Alternatively:
  1 part linseed oil
  1 part vinegar
  1 part methylated spirit

Both these will help to clean off the old grime and revive the polish.

Note: For repairs such as loose joints or broken rails, refer to the section on *Further reading*.

Checklist for assessment of completed chair in six-way standard pattern

1. Have the appropriate sizes of cane been used?
2. Is the sequence of weaving correct on the main body of the seat?
3. Are the lines of weaving reasonably straight, and appropriately spaced?
4. Are the short settings and weavings suitably positioned?
5. Is the tension correct?
6. Is there no damaged, split and badly discoloured cane?
7. Are the doubles and misses in the correct places, allowing crosses on the rails to extend as far as possible to the ends of short settings and weavings?
8. Do the crossings run smoothly across the seat?
9. If the chair has a pegged finish, is the chair neat, top and bottom, with no ends showing?
10. If the chair is beaded, is the beading sitting flat and evenly on top of the holes? Is the couching neat and tight, with no loose loops on the underside?
11. Are the tight loops under the chair evenly distributed and neat, not bulky in some places and gaps in others?
12. Is the total appearance of the finished chair generally pleasing?

Part II
RUSH

Historical background **68**
Materials and tools **70**
English traditional methods **72**
Simple shapes **74**
Continental methods **88**
Problem shapes **98**
Straw-wrapped rush seating **108**
Orkney chairs **112**
Irish straw rope chairs **118**
Using artificial rush **121**

Olivia Elton Barratt

7. Historical background to rush-seated chairs

The very earliest examples of rush seating are to be found on stools in the Pyramids of Ancient Egypt, but rushes have been in general use for the seating of stools and chairs since the Middle Ages. The earliest reference to a rush-seated chair I have been able to find is in a set of household accounts dated 1578. Seventeenth-century inventories of property show many such chairs in households both in England and on the Continent, although Continental chairs were probably seated in straw, straw-wrapped rushes, sedge or marram grass. Photographs of rush-seated chairs made as early as 1660 can be found in books on furniture in both England and America.

Rushes, a locally available material, were used to make a seat more comfortable than the earlier, solid wooden stools and chairs, and in many parts of the country, chairmakers produced different forms of simple rush-seated spindle and ladder-back chairs. Particular styles have become associated with particular regions. Details such as the number of rows of spindles, the shape of the ladders, the turning of the stretchers and the shape of the front legs are all features which help the expert to determine the age and area of origin of the chair. Such areas as Lincolnshire, Buckinghamshire, Worcestershire, North Cheshire and Lancashire all have their own traditions of chairmaking. The techniques used varied from area to area, as did the names given to the workers. In Lincolnshire and the North they were called 'Rush Bottomers', whereas in Buckinghamshire they were always called 'Rush Matters'.

The wood used for chair frames was often ash, with elm or beech. Alder was also used (particularly in the North). In the eighteenth and early nineteenth centuries the wood was often painted red, blue, green, reddish brown or black. The rush seats were painted too, in the same colours as the frames. This was as much a form of decoration as a way of preserving the wood and rushes. Painted seats were widespread in the North-West. In the Victoria and Albert Museum there is a chair dated 1775, which belonged to David Garrick the actor. It has a beech frame turned to resemble bamboo, and painted in white with green and black splashes. The rush seat is painted in green and white stripes of variable widths. Sheraton's *Cabinet Dictionary* of 1803 gives directions for painting rush seats with no less than three coats. The first and second primer coats, to preserve and harden, were of ground white lead, linseed oil, and spirits of turpentine. The third was of white lead and turpentine mixed with hard varnish so that it would dry quickly and make a hard finish that would not turn soft with the heat of the body! Later in the nineteenth century, painted seats and frames were less popular and frames were stained to imitate woods such as the fashionable mahogany.

The size of coil seems to have varied with the style of chair, and possibly also with the rushes available in a particular area. The simple early chairs appear to have had quite thick coils, perhaps as few as four coils per 2.5 cm (1 in), whereas on chairs where the style was influenced by classical or fashionable design, the coils were extremely fine. David Garrick's chair, with its elaborately interlaced back and its curved drop-in seat, has as many as ten coils per 2.5 cm (1 in), the finest I have seen. Many of the simple shapes used in the nineteenth century also had quite thick coils, but in the last years of the century designers such as Voysey and William Morris used fine coils, about 7 per 2.5 cm (1 in).

Apart from those of some designers in the Edwardian era, there seem to be few really finely-coiled rush-seated chairs made in the twentieth century, but five or six coils per 2.5 cm (1 in) are found on many mass-produced institutional type chairs, such as those found in schools or chapels. The modern pine kitchen chair looks good with quite thick coils, as do imported Continental or Scandinavian chairs, with their different seat patterns.

Although the seating pattern used throughout the chapter on basic rush-seating methods is generally accepted as that used traditionally in England, there is some evidence that other patterns may have been used on early chairs. Continental patterns, found on many Scandinavian chairs, vary considerably in appearance from the English, and in France both English and Continental patterns were used.

In the 1930s writers on rush seating were again advocating a coat of varnish to protect the rushes, but this is not used today. The beautiful colour and texture of the rush needs no enhancing, and a single coat of varnish forms a brittle top layer to the coils which can flake off, taking the skin of the rush with it.

In the nineteenth century the price for rush seating a chair was 6d. The work was dirty and unpleasant, and it was said that 'you could smell a rush matter a mile off'. Nowadays, commercially available rushes are clean and free from mud, we no longer work on earth floors, and the workshop (and worker) need no longer smell like a cowshed. The soft texture of mellowed rushes makes them a delight to handle, and the rewards for your skill are, quite rightly, rather more than 6d!

8.
Materials and tools

Rushes

The material generally used for chair seating is the bulrush, *Scirpus lacustris*, which grows in many countries of the world. In England and on the Continent it is harvested as a commercial crop, and can be bought from suppliers. It grows in rivers, streams, and ponds, and varies in size, quality and texture with the area, and often with the season. The round, pithy stem is emerald green when growing, but paler when dried, and has no leaf, just a silvery sheath at the butt, or root end, and a cluster of reddish brown flowers at the tip (Fig. 2.1a). Lengths between 1.8 m (6 feet) and 2.75 m (9 feet) are usual, although in some areas rushes grow taller, possibly because of the amount of lime in the water.

Rushes are harvested when green, and in England this was traditionally between the hay and the corn harvest. The rushes are at their best from late June and throughout July, depending on the weather during the growing time. The clumps, or 'stands', are harvested in alternate years to encourage growth, and are cut as close to the roots as possible. The sap is dried out either under cover, in an open shed, or out in the open. This takes from a few days to about three weeks, and the rushes are then best stored in a dry, dark shed. They can be kept for several seasons, but may go mouldy if stored in damp conditions. Commercial harvesting is generally done from boats or punts, but the amateur harvester can manage very well by paddling, or even swimming! If you know where rushes grow, and can get permission to harvest them, handle them carefully, as they are very brittle when green. Tie them into bundles for drying and storage.

English rushes are a beautiful material for seating, but European rush is also excellent for the purpose. It tends to be thinner and more even in size, which can be an advantage. Freshwater rushes from Portugal and Holland are long and soft, and an attractive greeny-gold colour. Dutch saltwater rushes are shorter and tend to be brown and hard, while Yugoslavian rush can be very hard indeed. Hard textured rushes can be difficult to mellow and to use.

Fig 2.1a *Scirpus lacustris* – the bulrush

Other materials

The European flat rush, or reedmace, is also good for seating. It is greenish-fawn in colour, semi-circular rather than round, and hard in texture. The leaves of the English reedmace *Typha lattifolia*, can also be used successfully. They are wide and flat, and have a fleshy area at the base where they join the hard stem carrying the long brown velvety seed head (see Fig. 2.1b). They give a nice rustic appearance to the seat, and wear very well, but are difficult to use for very fine coils. The reedmace can often be a free material, as it is very prolific and swamps other vegetation. I have had pond owners begging me to come and cut it!

The wild iris, or yellow flag, can also be used, although it is rather fibrous and untidy when coiled. It has lovely silvery stripes when dry, but I use it for interest rather than commercially.

These materials are harvested and dried in the same way as rushes, and they store well. Don't forget to ask for permission before cutting any materials which are not in your own garden.

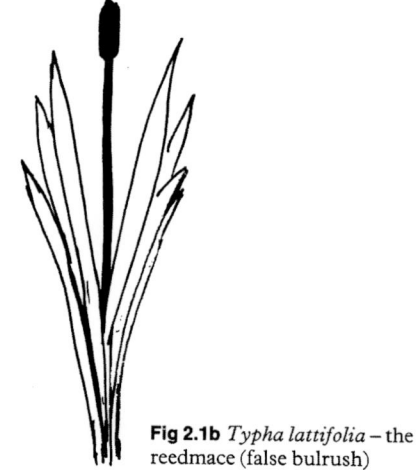

Fig 2.1b *Typha lattifolia* – the reedmace (false bulrush)

Quantities

Rushes are sold in 'bolts' (bundles) or by weight. (See list of Suppliers, page 190.) It is difficult to estimate quantities exactly, as chairs and workers differ. Here, however, is a rough estimate:

30 cm (12 in) square stool	up to 700 g (1½ lbs) dry rush
61 cm (24 in) by 30 cm (12 in) stool	up to 1.25 kg (2½ lbs) dry rush
38 cm (15 in) by 41 cm (16 in) chair	up to 1.5 kg (3 lbs) dry rush

These weights include the rushes used for stuffing.

Preparation and selection of materials

The rushes must be dampened and mellowed before use, to make them supple. Lay the amount of material to be used on the ground, and water it on both sides with a hose or watering can. Then wrap it tightly in a thick damp cloth to mellow for about three hours. It needs to absorb the water slowly. Don't ever soak rushes, as they will break easily if too wet, and then shrink when dry. If you have nowhere to use a hose or can, lay the rushes in the bath with the plug out, and spray them with a shampoo hose. The amount of mellowing time needed varies with the rushes. Some can be used almost immediately, while others must be left overnight. Try not to prepare more than you need for a working session. If necessary, the materials can be kept damp for a couple of days without spoiling, and they can be dried out and re-damped once without damage. Too long in the damp bundle, or too much re-damping, however, will weaken and discolour them, and cause them to smell bad.

For the majority of chairs there is no need to sort the material into sizes before damping it down. However, if the chair is to have very fine coils it would be sensible to take out any very fat rushes which would make them too bulky.

Tools

THREADING TOOL
for helping the rushes through small spaces in the final stages. A football lacer is ideal for this if you can find one (Fig. 2.2a). They don't lace up footballs these days, so you might have to make do with a large sacking needle (Fig. 2.2b). A wire coathanger can be cut and bent into an eye, with the ends bound to form the shaft, or a skewer eye can be hammered flat.

STUFFING STICK
for pushing stuffing into the seat and for packing the coils together. This is a flat, wedge-shaped piece of wood about 25 cm (10 in) long by 4 cm (1½ in), tapering to a smooth end (Fig. 2.3a). A kitchen spatula is excellent, particularly if it has a slight curve to it. An excellent stuffing stick I saw at the Cane and Rush Works in High Wycombe looks as if it was made from the arm of a wooden chair, about 30 cm (12 in) long, curved, tapering and very strong (Fig. 2.3b).

DOLLY (SMOOTHER)
for 'ironing down' the completed seat to give it a good finish. It is like a rather flat wooden doorknob with a smaller knob at the back for a handle (Fig. 2.3c). The rush matters in the High Wycombe area used these. A wooden doorknob from a DIY shop does very well.

OTHER REQUIREMENTS
Sharp knife for cutting out old seats
Tack remover ⎫
Hammer ⎬ for removing
Pliers ⎭ protective wooden slats
Metal hacksaw blade

Fig 2.2a Football lacer

Fig 2.2b Sacking needle

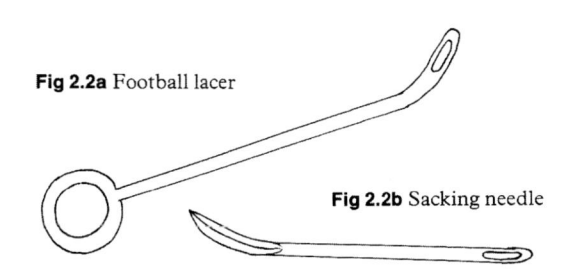

Fig 2.3a Stuffing stick – kitchen spatula

Fig 2.3b Stuffing stick made from the arm of a chair

Fig 2.3c Dolly

9. English traditional methods

How to recognise a chair for rushing

The frame for a rush seat has four rails joined by raised corner posts, and an open space in the centre. The rails are unpolished, and may be rounded or square. The seat will be formed by wrapping coils of rush over the rails in a regular pattern round the seat frame, gradually filling the open space, and finishing in the centre.

How the seat is formed

THE COILS

These are formed by twisting several rushes smoothly together, adding more as the work progresses, to maintain length and thickness. The number of rushes in the coil varies with the size of the rushes available and the thickness of the coil required for the chair (see page 69). It is the size of the coil which is important, not the number of rushes in the coil, so decide the size you consider most suitable for the chair. Very fine coils are more difficult for a beginner to handle.

The coils are wrapped around the seat rails from one corner to the next, moving anti-clockwise. They cross each other at right angles on each corner (Fig. 2.4). The crosses will form diagonal lines running towards the centre. On a square seat these diagonal lines meet in the centre (Fig. 2.5a). On a rectangle, or on most trapezium-shaped chairs (wider front than back), they meet two on each side, and form a bridge, a straight line across the centre from side to side (Fig. 2.5b and c). This happens because the side rails on such seats are filled in completely before the front and back rails, leaving a central section to be filled in with coils over the front and back rails only.

Fig 2.4 Sequence of coiling round the seat

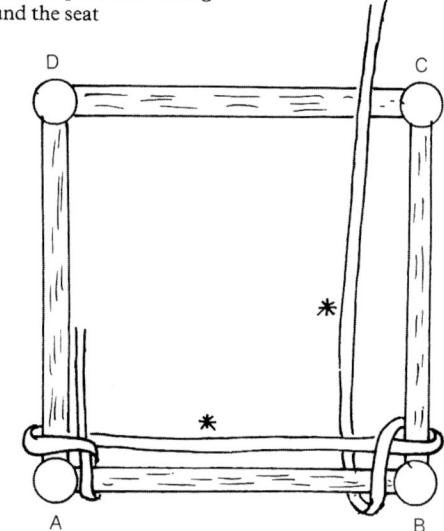

Fig 2.5 Square, rectangular and trapezium shapes, showing lines formed by the corner angles

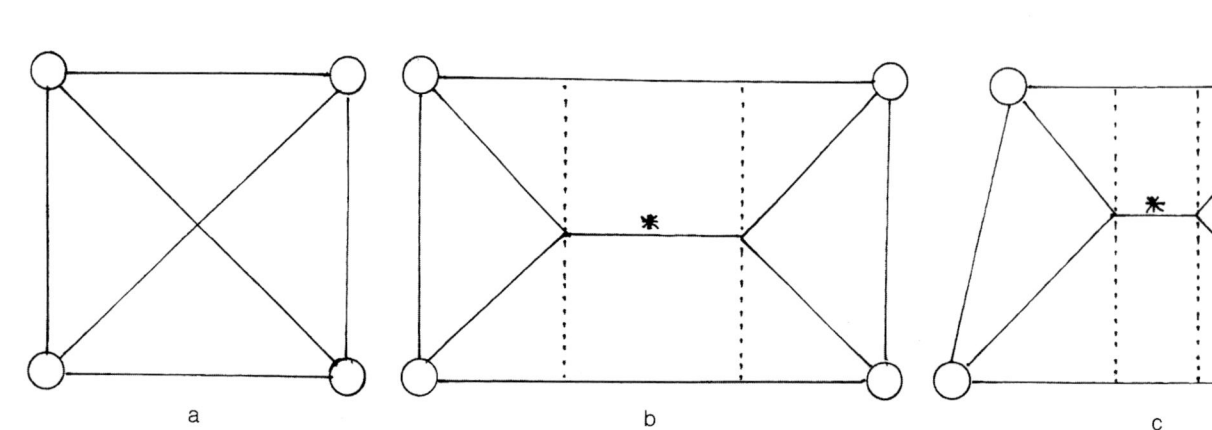

a   b   c

STUFFING

The coils form a top *and* bottom layer, and the space between them is firmly stuffed from the underneath only, with waste rushes saved as you work. Good firm stuffing pushes the top coils upwards, making a rounded, comfortable seat, and protecting them from wear caused by the rails.

In the English method, the rushes are coiled on top of the seat and left flat and uncoiled underneath, so that they bed in to one another, holding the stuffing well. On Continental and Scandinavian seats, where finer materials, such as sedges, straw or a fine reedmace are often used, the coils are twisted underneath the seat as well as on top, to hold the material together. These twisted coils under the seat do not retain the stuffing quite so well. As you will see later, all the Continental patterns can be followed using the English method, leaving the coils untwisted underneath.

DIRECTION OF COILS

They may either be twisted away from the corner on each side of the corner post, which gives an 'arrowhead' finish where they meet in the centre of the rail (Fig. 2.6a; Photo 2.1), or all twisted in the same right-handed (clockwise) direction, which means they all slant in the same direction across the seat (Fig. 2.6b; Photo 2.2). This is the 'straight across' finish. In England, older chairs seem mostly to have had an arrowhead finish, although many chair seaters now prefer the straight across. On the Continent most chairs are worked straight across, with the coil remaining twisted in the same direction as it goes over the rail, under the seat, and up in the centre again to complete the corner.

There is no reason why the coils should not be twisted in a left-handed (anti-clockwise) direction throughout, or wrapped round the frame in a clockwise direction. A left-handed worker might find this easier. On the whole, though, both hands do the same amount of work, and the methods described below seem to suit left- or right-handed workers.

TERMINOLOGY

Where names are given to the corners of the chair, **A** = front left, **B** = front right, **C** = back right, and **D** = back left (Fig. 2.4), these apply to the seat as you look down on it with the back furthest away. The same names are used when the chair is turned round during work.

Interior coils are the rushes running across the space between opposite rails. They will be covered up by the top and bottom coils as the work progresses (* on Fig. 2.4).

Bridge: the straight line running from side to side of a rectangular or trapezoid seat, where the central section is filled in by working from front to back only. Where the rushes cross in this figure of eight, a line is formed (* on Fig. 2.5).

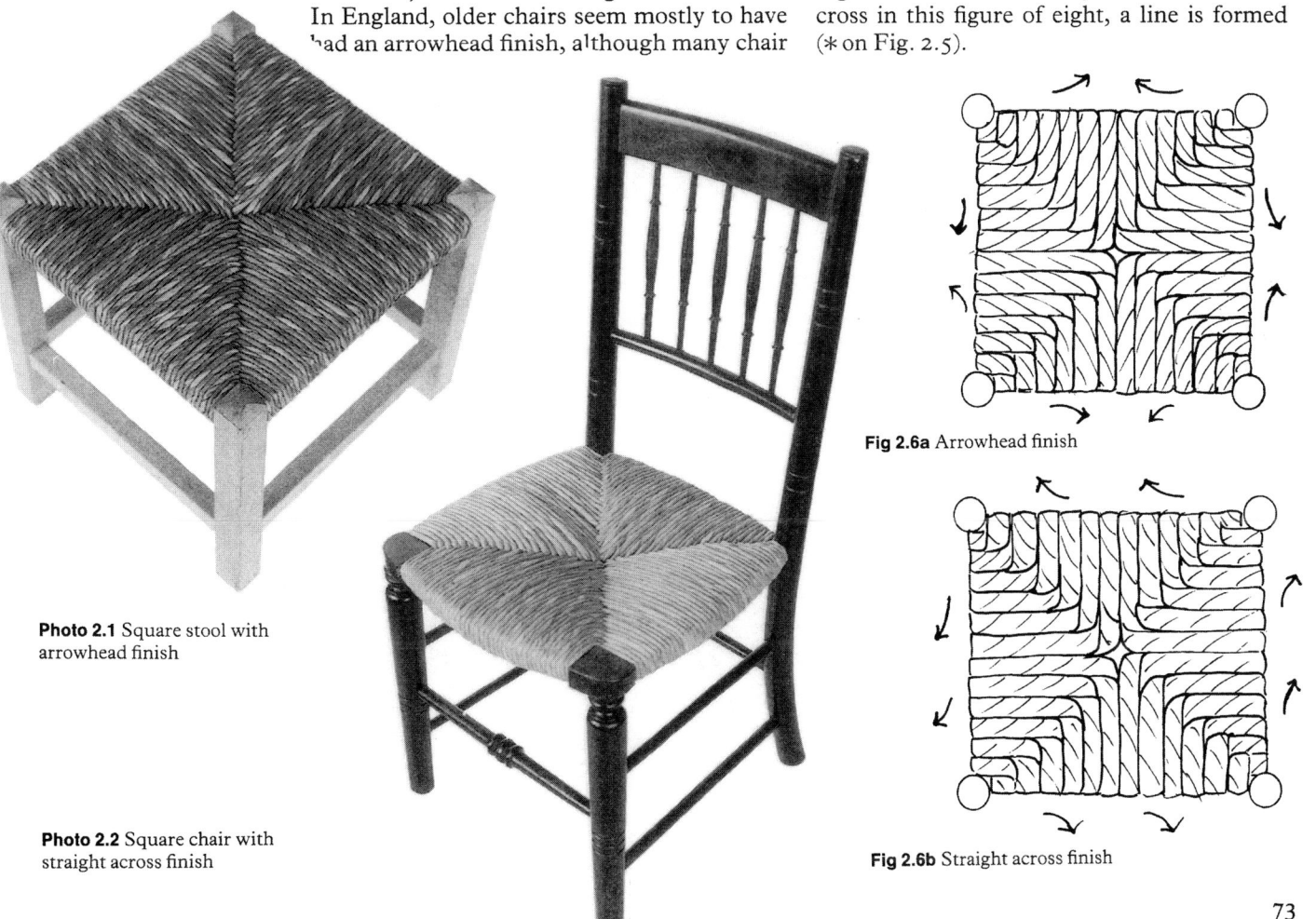

Photo 2.1 Square stool with arrowhead finish

Photo 2.2 Square chair with straight across finish

Fig 2.6a Arrowhead finish

Fig 2.6b Straight across finish

73

10. Simple shapes

Photo 2.3 Miniature chairs with square seats and arrowhead finish

Basic method for seating a square chair or stool

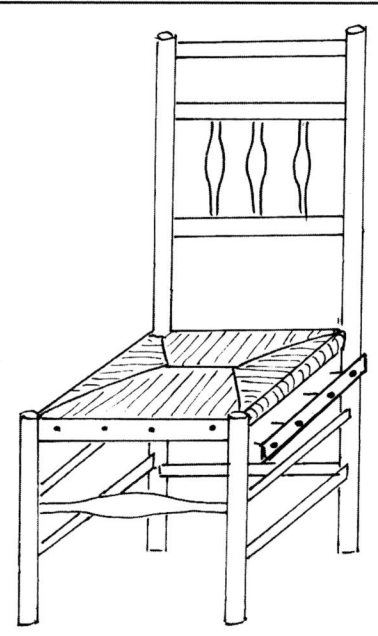

Fig 2.7 Rush seated chair with protective slats

PREPARATION OF THE CHAIR
Make a note of the pattern and thickness of coils used, if you want to restore it to its original appearance. Keep a few of the coils for reference, or note the number of coils per cm (or inch).

Old chairs often have protective wooden slats nailed over the rush on the rails (Fig. 2.7; Photo 2.15). If you want to replace these after re-rushing, try not to damage them when taking them off, as the nails may be rusted in, and the wood can easily be split.

To remove slats
1. Cut through the rush coils above or below the slats with a sharp knife, and pull the rushes away from between slats and chair rails.
2. Tap the slats gently between the nails with a padded hammer, to knock them against the

rail. If the nails are not too rusty, this will loosen them. Pull out the nails with pliers.
3. If the nails are really rusted in, the slats will not move. Slip a metal hacksaw blade between slats and rails, and saw through the nails. The stubs can then be pulled out with pliers, or hammered flat into the rails. (Very often they disintegrate when hammered.)
4. Sometimes the slats are sprung into grooves on the chair legs on either side. Remove by levering outwards gently at the centre of the rail.

Repairs

Do any repairs or renovations to the frame that are needed, such as stripping and repolishing, or re-glueing the frame. For hints on wood finishes, see page 66. Check that the seat rails are sound and firm, and treat any woodworm.

TO START THE WORK

Prepare the rushes as described on page 71. Find yourself a comfortable position to work in. I like to sit on a stool with the chair in front of me, so that I can grip it with my legs. This leaves both hands free for keeping a good tension on the work. If you work standing, with the chair on a table, be careful to tilt it towards you every so often so that you can look at the appearance of your work from a distance. It cannot be properly assessed close up. Some workers use a turntable at lower than table height, to which the chair is fixed. We shall be twisting the coils in one direction only, for a straight across finish (Photo 2.2).

1. On a stool, tie a piece of string round the left front leg to mark the beginning of a round. This saves you from losing your way in the sequence of work.
2. Loop a rush round the back rail, beside the back left corner as you look down on the seat. Bring both ends towards the front rail. (This loop will be hidden later by the first coil over the back left rail.)
3. Join on by the butts or thick ends, enough rushes for the size of coil required, using a half hitch (see Fig. 2.8a). Have confidence in this knot; it really will stay put if you pull it tight. Pull on all the long ends with your right hand, and on the short butts with your left. Leave the butts pointing downwards. Make the knot half-way along the side rail.
4. With your right hand twist this group of rushes together in a right-handed, clockwise direction, with a rounding smoothing movement. The right hand slides down the coil with each twist, and the left hand follows, keeping up the tension and smoothing and compressing the coil.
   Note: The coil should look like one smoothly twisted rush, not one wound round another (Fig. 2.8b). All the air should be pressed out as you work. Some workers prefer a very tight twist, some less so, but it must always be firm and smooth.
   Make the coil the right size for the chair (see page 69), and maintain this size from now on.
5. Coil enough to go over the front rail, and underneath for about 2½ cm (1 in), and lay it close against the front corner (Fig. 2.9a). The direction of this twist is away from the corner. Don't allow any short rushes to drop out of the coil at the edge.
6. Bring the coil under the rail and up in the centre, and with the left hand twist the rushes towards the corner. (This is in fact the same direction as before.)
7. Lay it at right angles over the first coil and the left side rail, and close against the corner (Fig. 2.9b). Bring it under the rail and up in the centre.

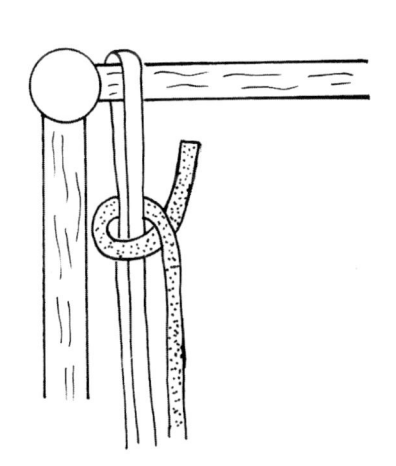

Fig 2.8a Half hitch knot

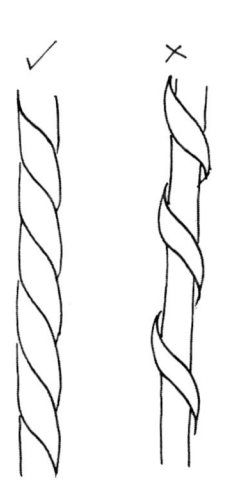

Fig 2.8b Rush coils, showing correct and incorrect appearance

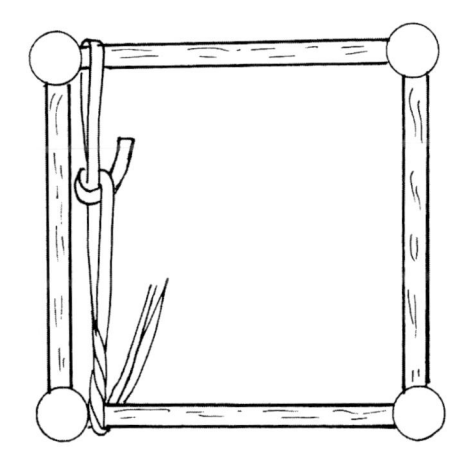

Fig 2.9a First half of corner

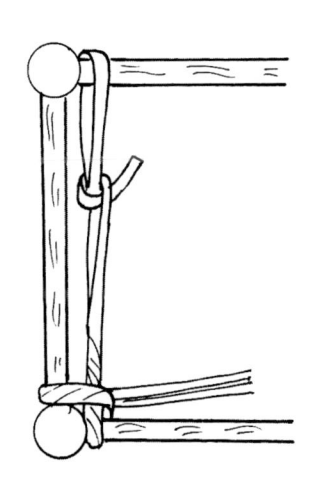

Fig 2.9b Second half of corner

8. Take it across to the opposite side rail, hitching in a new rush (by the butt) if needed to maintain the thickness. Keep the knot in the middle of the open space, out of the way of the corners (Fig. 2.10).
9. Twisting it as before, wrap the coil over the right side rail, up in the centre, and out over the front rail. Then bring it up in the centre again.
10. Complete the two back corners as for the front, covering up the initial loop over the left back rail.
11. Repeat steps 5 to 10 continuously to build up the seat.
    Note: I like to work the first half of each corner with the coil running from left to right, twisting with the right hand. I then turn the chair clockwise, and complete the second half of the corner with the coil running from right to left, twisting with the left hand (Fig. 2.11). You may prefer to use your right hand for both steps, turning the chair after you have completed the corner.

Work really tightly, stretching each coil as you pass over the rail, and laying it very close to its predecessor. Pull it up tightly in the centre, and use your other hand to press upwards on the underneath of the chair to tighten and flatten it. Tension is all important for a good result.

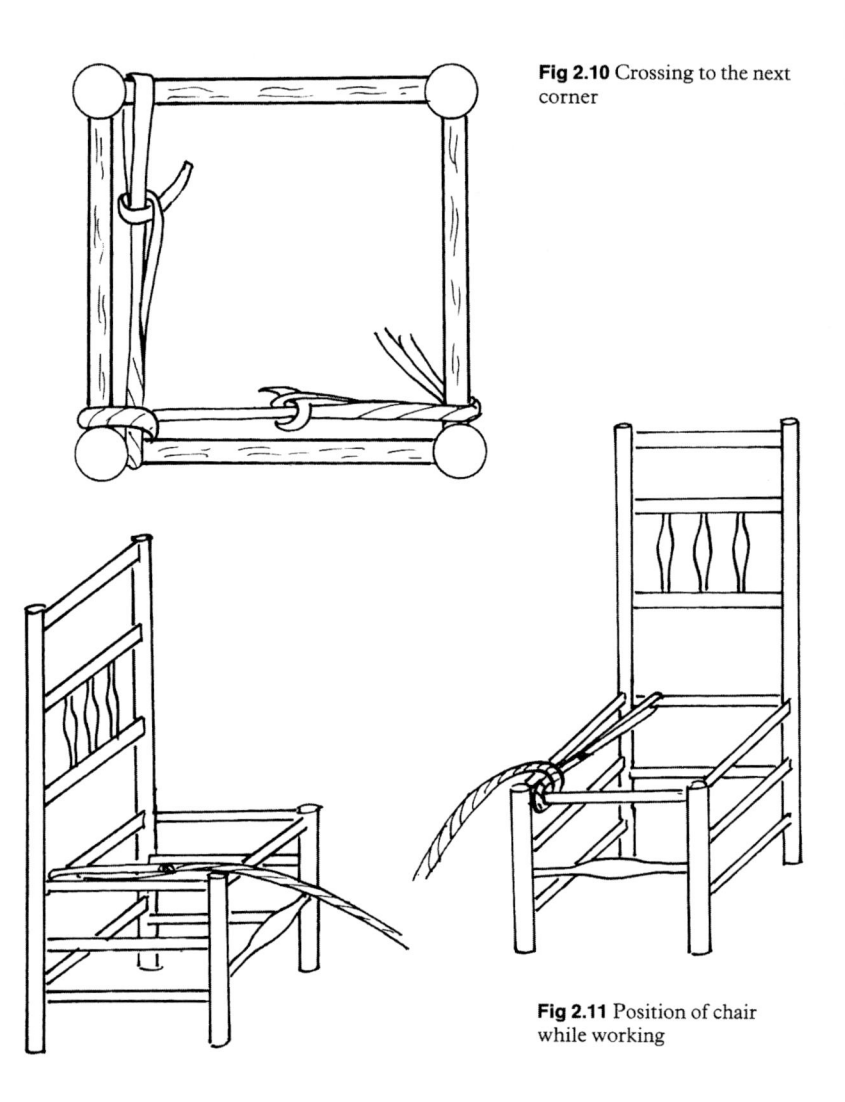

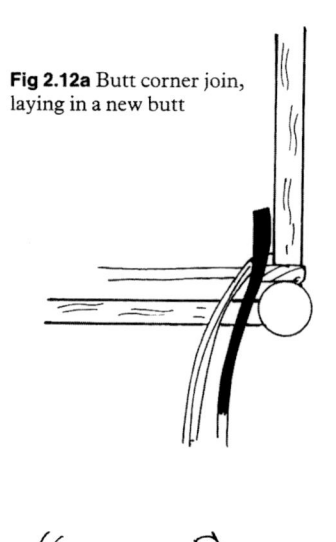

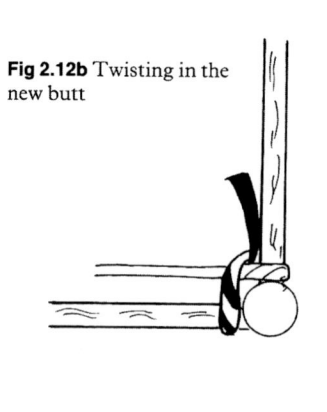

Fig 2.10 Crossing to the next corner

Fig 2.11 Position of chair while working

Fig 2.12a Butt corner join, laying in a new butt

Fig 2.12b Twisting in the new butt

Fig 2.13 Reef knot

Butt corner joins

You will often need to add rushes on the corners as well as halfway between corners, to ensure that the thickness of the coil is maintained. The following is my favourite method for doing this.

1. Complete the first half of the corner, and bring the coil up in the centre.
2. Lay a new butt to the right of and partly under the working coil, with about 8 cm ($3\frac{1}{4}$ in) of the butt lying along the rail (Fig. 2.12a).
3. Twist the new rush in with the working coil as invisibly as possible. The butt will be hidden by the top and bottom layers (Fig. 2.12b).

For another method for corner joins, see pages 79, 80, *Alternative methods*.

Note: Use the full length of each rush, but discard tips in the centre if they are too short to go over the rail. If the whole coil breaks in the centre, use a reef knot to join in new rushes (Fig. 2.13). Don't allow cracks or breaks in the rush to show on top of the coil. Give them an extra twist to hide them underneath, or replace the damaged rush.

Fig 2.14 Importance of correct angles on the corners

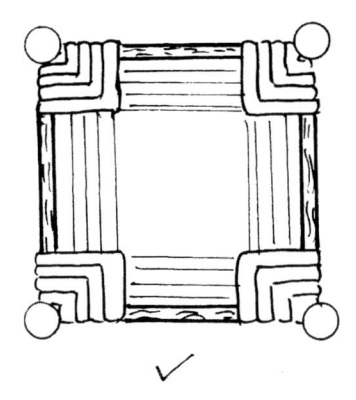

Corner angles

Good right angles at the corners are vital. The coils must be parallel with each other and approach the rails at a right angle, otherwise there will be gaps later on. Obtuse angles fill up the rails more quickly, leaving gaps in the centre; acute angles fill up the centre more quickly, leaving gaps on the rails (Fig. 2.14).

After several rounds, use the stuffing stick to pack the coils really hard against both sides of each corner. Use the edge of the stick to press the coils straight on top of the seat. Then check the corner angles.

Obtuse angles

These are generally caused by insufficient tension, and coils spaced too widely. Frequent hard packing in towards the corners may correct this. Otherwise, when completing the second half of the next corner, lift the coil up vertically and give it an extra twist as it emerges from the centre, pushing out the right angle as you lay it in place. Hold the coil which forms the first half of the corner straight with your right hand, so that you can pull the second half really tight as you lay it over the rail without rounding off the corner again (Fig. 2.15). Use the stuffing stick to press the coils straight on top of the seat.

Acute angles

These may appear when you have packed the coils in towards the corners. When you bring the coil up in the centre for the second half of the corner, pull it forwards against the interior coils and then lay it in very close to the previous right angle, allowing it to round off a little (Fig. 2.16).

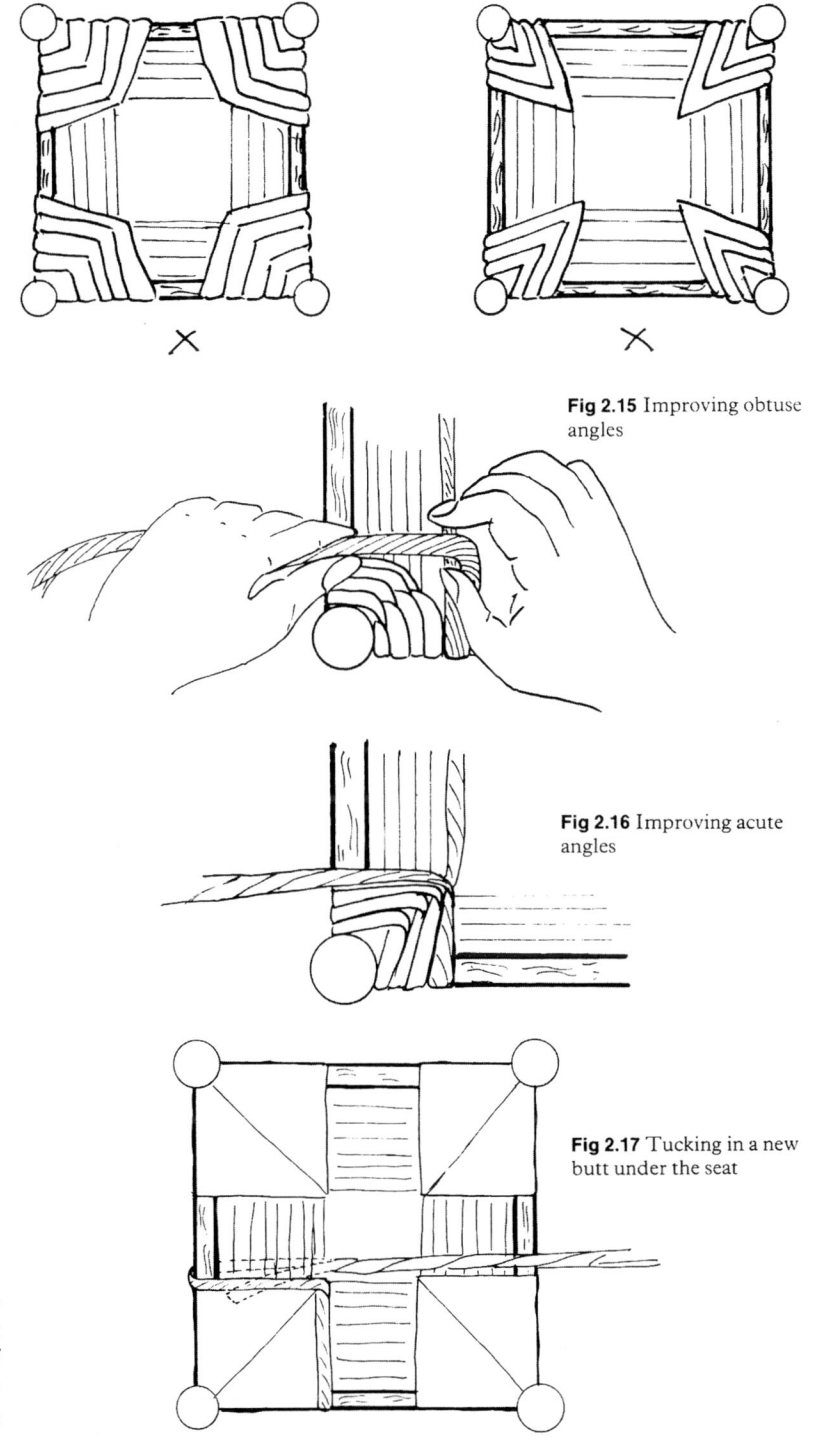

BUILDING UP THE SEAT

Continue to work around the chair as in steps 5 to 10 of the basic method. If you need to have long gaps between work sessions, wrap a damp cloth round the end of the working coil for a couple of hours before starting work again, to make it supple.

As the gap in the centre gets smaller, there will eventually be no room for half hitches between corners. Add new rushes by tucking the butts into the underneath pocket to the left of the centre hole. Hold them in place with the left hand and start twisting the coil with the right, just where it emerges from under the seat (Fig. 2.17).

Keep the underneath tidy, tucking away any ends. There should be no knots visible under the chair at this stage. Lay all the butt-join ends flat under the coil as you complete the second half of each corner.

Fig 2.15 Improving obtuse angles

Fig 2.16 Improving acute angles

Fig 2.17 Tucking in a new butt under the seat

STUFFING

Some workers prefer to stuff the seat when it is completed, and this is a method suitable for more experienced workers (see page 80).

For the beginner, who may be working slowly, (which means that the coils have time to dry out and become looser between sessions) and whose tension may not be very tight, it is easier to stuff as you go along.

1. Turn the chair upside down and stuff all the eight pockets underneath, packing dry rushes well in using the stuffing stick. Use dry rush to avoid mould. It is easier to pack really tightly if you work towards you (Fig. 2.18). Use the rush just as it comes; don't cut it into pieces.
2. When the gaps on the rails are about 3 cm (1½ in) wide, allow the chair to dry out overnight and stuff again.
3. Lodge extra stuffing across the central gaps, tucking it under the coils to hold it in place. This provides the stuffing for the central part (yet to be worked).

FINISHING THE SEAT

Fill up the remaining gaps on the rails as tightly as you can with coils. You must pack in as many rounds as you can, forcing the coils towards the corners with the stuffing stick to make room. Each coil must lie on the wood where it passes over the rail.

Use the threader to help the coils through the diminishing hole, and be careful not to lose your way in the sequence.

Keep the rushes really tight under the seat, and running straight from the rail to the centre. Don't allow them to overlap each other too much, as this will make them loose.

Finish at the end of a round.

1. Bring the last coil over the back rail, and turn the chair upside down.
2. Divide the coil into two groups, and thread them under the opposite coil coming from the front, one from each side (Fig. 2.19a).
3. Pull them well down into the centre and tie a reef knot. Tuck away the ends close to the knot (Fig. 2.19b).
4. Tuck any ends left showing away into the coils.
5. On the top, bed in any overcrowded coils by sliding the stuffing stick between them and easing them sideways. If you have packed the coils in really tightly, you may have one or two overlapping on top of the seat. Start at the corners, and gradually work inwards toward the centre, easing the coils outwards to make room for each other.
6. Iron down the top of the chair by pressing firmly towards the centre, using the dolly, the stuffing stick, or the flat of your hand. Press really hard, as this makes a great difference to the appearance.

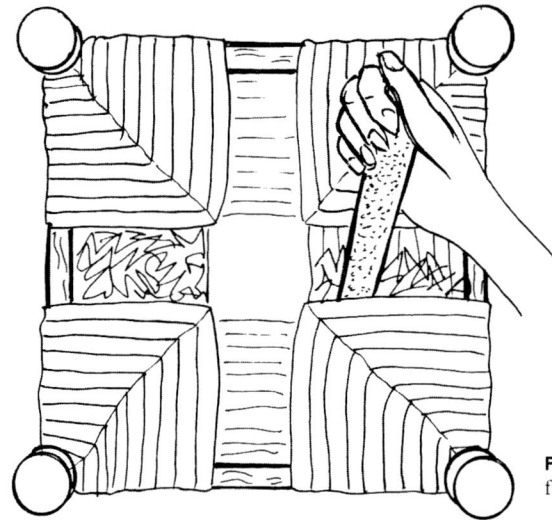

Fig 2.18 Stuffing the seat from underneath

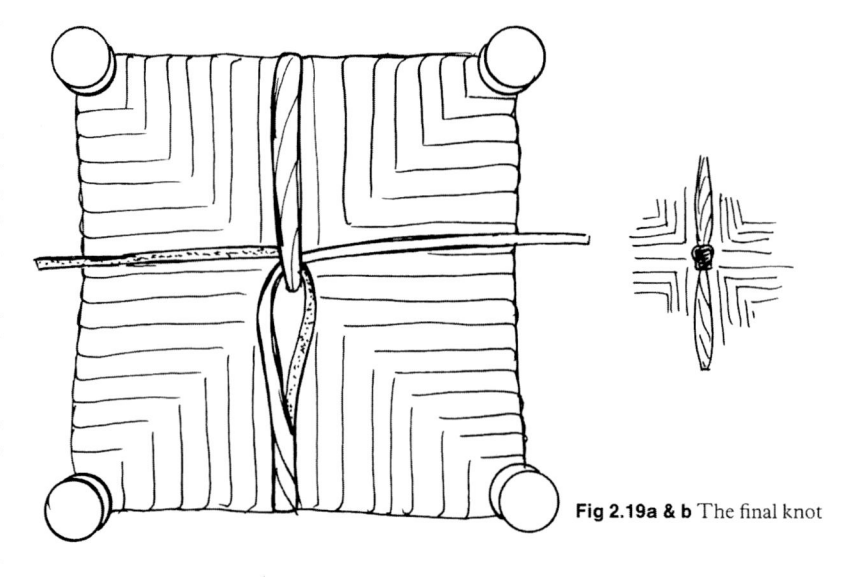

Fig 2.19a & b The final knot

For an alternative method of finishing the seat, see page 80.

HINTS FOR A GOOD FINISH

1. No cracks or breaks in the rush should show on top of the seat.
2. In the later stages, rushes can be added by the tips if you seem to have too large a gap on the frame. The long coils in the centre can get thin as they approach the rail.
3. To correct a seat with a gap in the centre after the final round, see page 80, Finishing Methods No. 3 and Fig. 2.24.
4. A single loose coil standing up from the others is caused by too loose a tension. Sometimes it can be tightened up by adding a little more stuffing, or by poking it under some of the other coils underneath the seat to tighten it on the top.

Alternative methods

You may find that some of these suit you better than those described above.

DIRECTION OF COILS
If you want the coils to meet in the centre of each rail in an arrowhead, the method of working is a little different. Work the first half of the corner as usual. For the second half, twist the coil to the left (anticlockwise), away from the corner post on the left-hand side. For butt corner joins, lay the new butt to the left of the working coil, instead of the right.

STARTING THE WORK

Method 1
Tie a piece of fine string tightly round the butt ends of the rushes, enough to make a coil, and then tie them tightly to the centre of the side rail. The string is hidden by subsequent coils, and can even be cut away just before it would be covered by coils.

Method 2
Tie the butt ends tightly as before, and use a large headed tack, or a staple, to secure them to the inside edge of the left-side rail.

JOINING IN NEW RUSHES
In the basic method above, page 75, rushes are always added by the butt to an existing coil, using a half hitch, and each rush is worked out to the tip. Here are some variations.

Method 1
This was the method I was first taught, and it was advocated in a number of early books on rushwork.

Add new rushes butt to butt and tip to tip using reef knots and cut the discarded ends short. Try to have a butt and a tip in each coil, to distribute the thickness evenly. Make the knots halfway along the rails. This method can produce an even-sized coil, and reduce the need for butt corner joins. It is slower, as a reef knot takes longer to tie than a half hitch, and more of the rush is wasted by not working out each one to the tip. It is hard to maintain tension while knotting, and the knots must be very neat, otherwise the work will be lumpy.

Method 2
This was much used in the North of England. No knots are used at all. When joining in new rushes after completing a corner, the new butts are laid between the working coil and the previous work, under the rail, before twisting them into the coil as you cross the seat. It is a very quick method, but wastes more of the butts than using half hitches.

Ordinary butt corner joins are used when necessary.

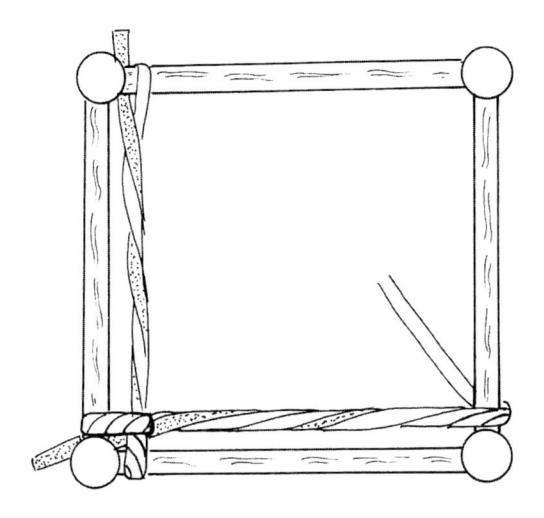

Fig 2.20 North Country method of joining in new rushes

1. To start the seat, loop a rush over the left back rail. Make it up to size by poking a new butt through the loop and under the back rail, before incorporating it into the twist (Fig. 2.20).
2. For joining after completing a corner, keep the coil tight with the left hand, and hold it down away from the underneath of the seat.
3. With the right hand, push the new butt under the rail and over the top of the working coil from right to left, with the butt end poking down under the seat. Leave an inch or so of butt protruding (Fig. 2.20).
4. Bring the working coil up tightly into the centre of the seat, trapping the new butt end firmly, and then twist the new rush into the coil.

Note: This method leaves rows of butt ends protruding from under the seat between the coils. Trim them all off short with a sharp knife or scissors.

If you prefer, the short ends can be tucked out of sight using the threader, for a smooth finish. However, the whole point of this method is speed, so the short ends can be left showing.

For a trapezium seat without any knots, use the first Continuous Doubling Method on page 83 with the above joining method.

The seat should be stuffed after completion.

Method 3
This is something I discovered for myself, as no doubt many other workers have! When the central hole is beginning to fill up, it can be helpful to add a new rush by the tip, laying it

over the side rail and covering it with the working coil. Twist the new tip into the coil underneath the seat (Fig. 2.21a and b).

BUTT CORNER JOINS

Method 1
This is Kay's favourite method.

As you complete the first half of the corner, and bring the working coil under the seat towards the centre, put the new butt end down between the first and second interior coils, and between the working coil and the first half of the corner. When the working coil is pulled forwards and upwards, the butt is firmly trapped, and the new rush can be twisted smoothly into the working coil (Fig. 2.22). This method can be used whichever way you are twisting the coils.

The projecting butt ends can either be tucked out of sight, or trimmed off short afterwards, to form rows of short ends under the chair, running in towards the centre.

Method 2
Use the Basic Method described on page 76, but leave the butt-ends projecting straight downwards, to be trimmed off later. Many old chairs have these projecting butts.

Method 3
A neat, firm method, but slower.

Tuck the new butt end well under the working coil, and into the right-hand pocket under the seat, before you bring the coil up in the centre. Twist in the new rush as usual (Fig. 2.23).

FINISHING METHODS

Method 1
A method much used in rush workshops.

Take the final coil over the back rail, and tuck it well down into the coils underneath the seat. A little stuffing can be pushed in on top for extra security.

Method 2
Take the final coil to the centre under the seat, and thread it under a coil from the opposite side. Then half hitch to itself before tucking away the ends.

Method 3
Take the final coil to the centre under the seat, and thread it under the opposite coil from the front rail, then under a coil on its own side, and tuck the ends down into the work on the front half of the chair, close to the centre.

Note: If the seat has a slight gap in the centre, run the final coil under coils from all four sides in turn. Draw this ring tight to close the gap, before tucking away the ends (Fig. 2.24).

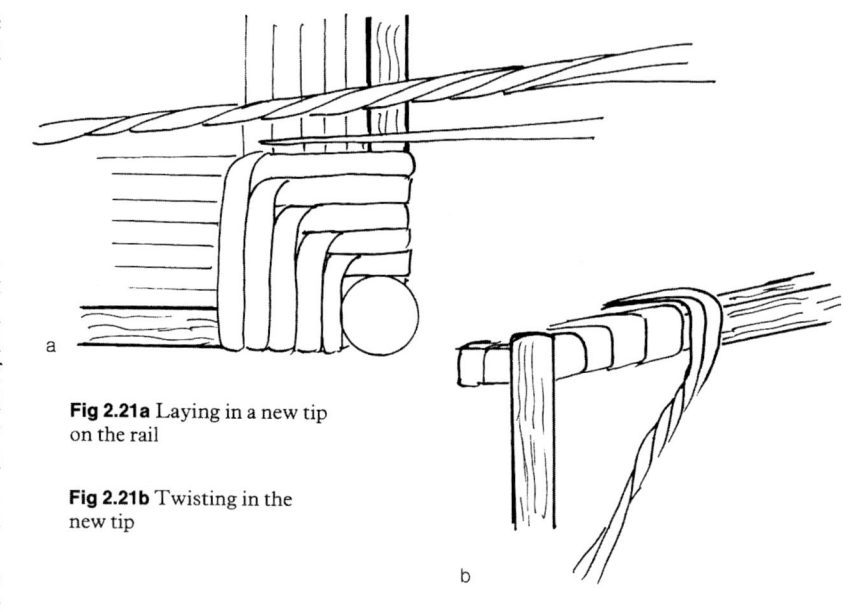

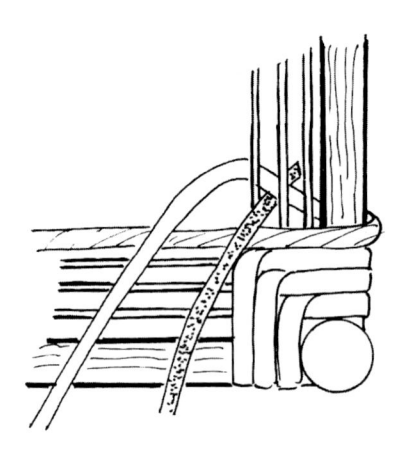

Fig 2.21a Laying in a new tip on the rail

Fig 2.21b Twisting in the new tip

Fig 2.22 First alternative butt corner join

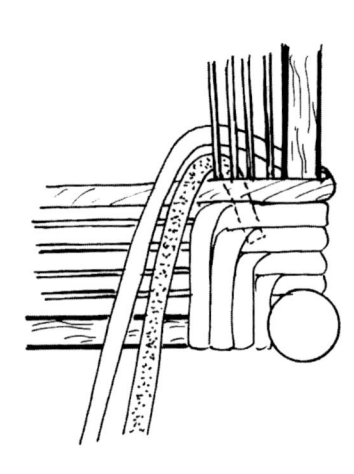

Fig 2.23 Second alternative butt corner join

STUFFING AFTER COMPLETING THE SEAT

Many professionals prefer to stuff the seat after it has been completed, and before it has dried. (Dry coils could be damaged with this method, and do not bed down so well on top of the seat.)

If you are going to use this method, your work must be very tight indeed, and the coils tightly packed together, or you will stretch the coils during stuffing, and your work will be loose when it dries out. It is a very quick method, and gives a tight seat with no bulges underneath.

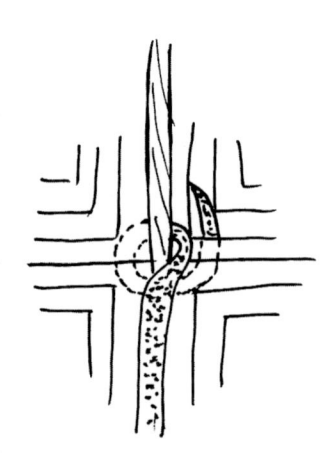

Fig 2.24 Closing a central gap with the final knot

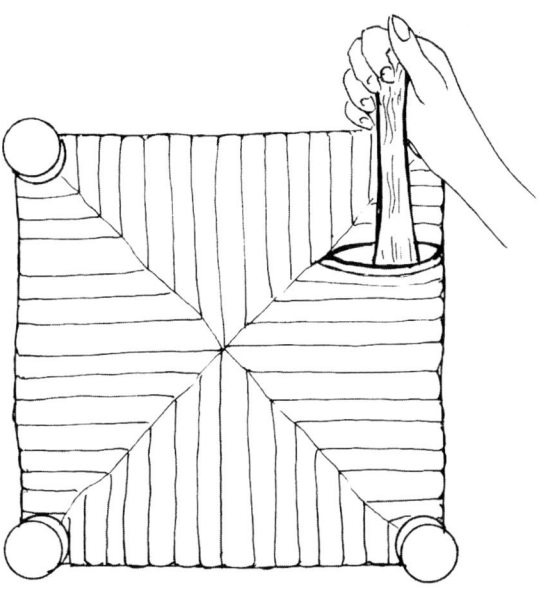

Fig 2.25 Stuffing the seat after completion

1. Turn the seat upside down.
2. Push the stuffing stick in between the coils about 7 cm (3 in) in from the corner, and pack in dry rush across the centre two thirds of each triangular section (Fig. 2.25).
   Note: The corners need not be stuffed with this method. (Many workers consider it unnecessary.) You can turn the chair on its side, and pack downwards, if you find this easier. Use dry rush to avoid mould.
3. Pack in as much stuffing as you can along the rail and towards the centre of each section. The seat must be very hard and firm.
4. When each section of the seat is stuffed, complete steps 4 to 6 of *Finishing the seat*, page 78.

Note: A good worker will have so little waste that there may be difficulty in finding enough waste rush for stuffing. Some workers use the broken up contents of old seats, but the results of this can be very lumpy if you are not careful. Straw is another candidate. I would prefer to use new rushes if there is no waste.

NOW ASSESS YOUR WORK

Now compare your first rush seat with the following check-list. If you can answer 'yes' to all these questions, you have done a good job, and are ready to tackle rectangular and trapezium shapes. If the result is not quite so good, you know what to watch out for in your next piece of work!

Check-list
1. Is the general appearance good?
2. Is the tension tight, with no excessive movement of the coils on the rails?
3. Is it firmly stuffed, with no sagging underneath?
4. Do the coils bed in neatly on top and underneath?
5. Are the coils an appropriate size for the chair?
6. Are the coils even in size throughout, smooth, and with no breaks on the surface?
7. Does the seat finish correctly at the end of a round?
8. Are the lines made by the corners straight as they run to the centre?
9. Are there any gaps where the coils meet in the centre?
10. Is the underneath free of visible joins, except for a final knot if used, and projecting butt ends if worked in this way?

Rectangular seats

Photo 2.4 Rectangular stool with long bridge and straight across finish

DIRECTION OF COILS

If you are using the arrowhead finish (page 79), you must decide whether you prefer the arrowheads to meet in the centre of the longest rails, or at one end of the bridge. If in the centre, then mark the rails with a pencil at this point.

Note: It can be difficult to make sure the change of direction comes exactly in the centre. If it shifts along as you pack the coils, it can look untidy. Pack the first half of the bridge well before changing direction. Some workers prefer to work the whole bridge in the same direction, so that the arrowheads meet at the end of the bridge.

METHOD

1. Work as for square seats until the gaps on the shortest rails are 3 cm (1½ in) wide, then allow to dry overnight and stuff. Lodge

81

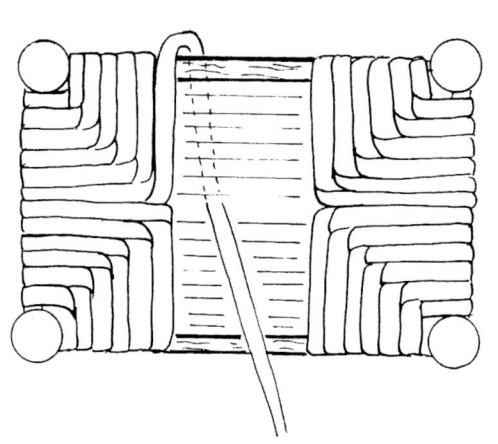

Fig 2.26a Starting the bridge on a rectangular seat

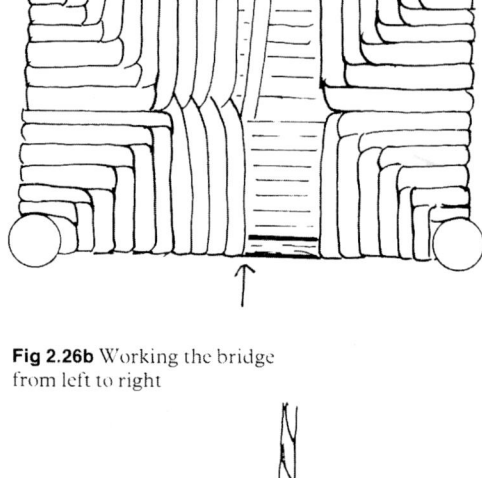

Fig 2.26b Working the bridge from left to right

extra stuffing across the gaps on the shortest rails, and across the bridge as well if it is short enough for the stuffing to stay in place.

2. Work until the side rails are tightly filled with coils, finishing at the end of a round (Fig. 2.26a).
3. With the left side rail toward you, work in a figure of eight over the front and back rails, coming up in the centre and out over the rail each time. Fill up the gap on the rails from left to right (Fig. 2.26b). Finish as in *Basic method* page 78.
4. With an arrowhead finish, change the twist at the marked point. Back and front now twist towards you (Fig. 2.27), still filling in the bridge from left to right.
5. If the bridge is a long one, work till the gaps on the rails are 3 cm (1½ in) wide, then dry, stuff, and finish as above.

Note: For a really long bridge, stuff the work as it progresses, as otherwise it will be difficult to get the stuffing right down it. Work really tightly, and try not to stretch the damp coils. Compress the coils where they cross in the centre, to prevent them bowing outwards, and make room for as many as possible. Tuck away the ends as you go to keep the centre tidy.

If you prefer, complete the seat before stuffing as on page 81.

EMERGENCY MEASURES

1. At step 2 above you may find it impossible to fill in the side rails with a complete final round without overcrowding. If this happens, on the final round work the two front corners only, and start the figure of eight from the right side of the bridge. Finish over the back rail. This gives two extra coils on the front rail, but it is easy to compress these without overcrowding (Fig. 2.28).

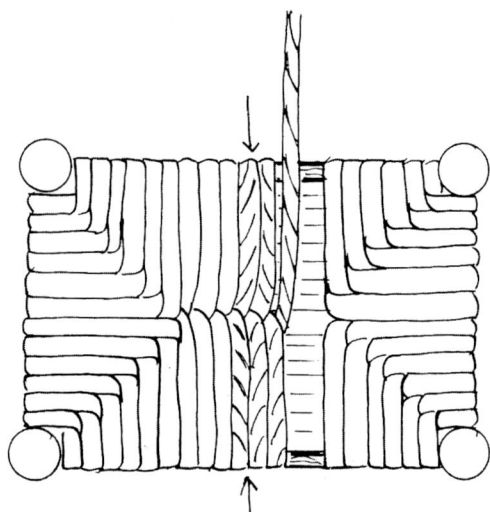

Fig 2.27 Working the bridge with an arrowhead finish

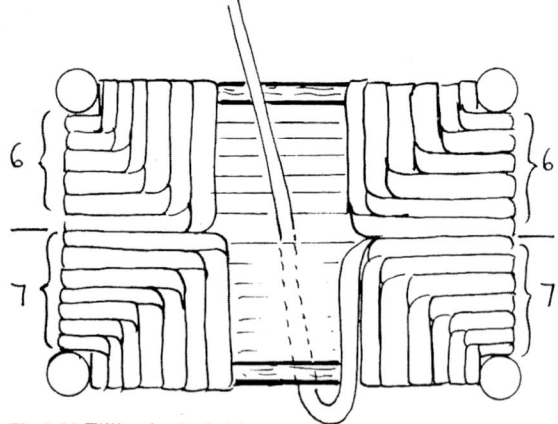

Fig 2.28 Filling in the bridge from right to left

2. If wedge-shaped gaps appear in the centre when you are filling in the side rails, because your right angles were too obtuse, lay an extra wrap on both side rails in the final round as follows:
   a Complete the back right corner, and turn the coil back again to lay an extra wrap on the right side rail, keeping it flattish at the centre to hide the gap (Fig. 2.29a).

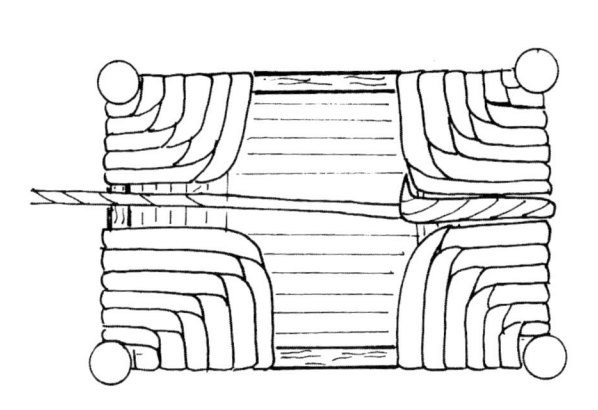

Fig 2.29a An extra wrap over the right side rail

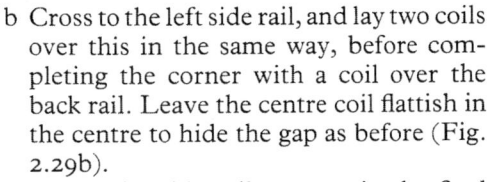

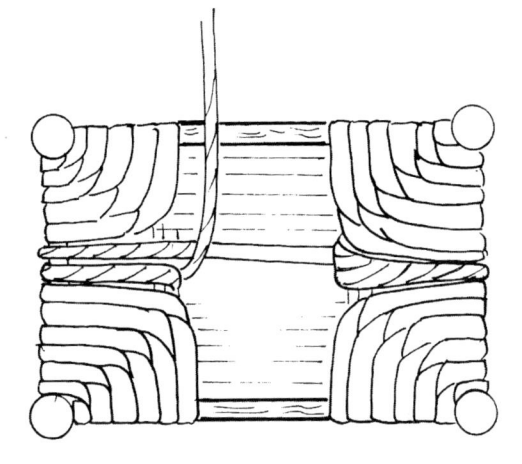

Fig 2.29b An extra wrap over the left side rail

   b Cross to the left side rail, and lay two coils over this in the same way, before completing the corner with a coil over the back rail. Leave the centre coil flattish in the centre to hide the gap as before (Fig. 2.29b).

3. Gaps on the side rails appear in the final stages if your angles have become too acute. Add new rushes by the tips so that the coils become thicker as they approach the rails. Cut off the butts under the seat when they are too short to make the next coil. (This prevents them muddling up the centre.)
4. If the coils do not cross each other in a straight line along the bridge, poke them into place with the threader.

Trapezium-shaped chairs

These are chairs whose fronts are wider than their backs. If the side rails are fairly short in comparison with the front rail, they will have a bridge (Fig. 2.5c). Because of the longer front rail they require a process called 'doubling'. This means working more coils over the front rail than over the back until the uncovered part of both rails measures the same.

DOUBLING

This is my favourite method. It is worked continuously round the chair, and is very quick to do. Start by looping a rush over the back rail.

1. Work the two front corners, and then tie the working coil temporarily to the right side rail (Fig. 2.30).

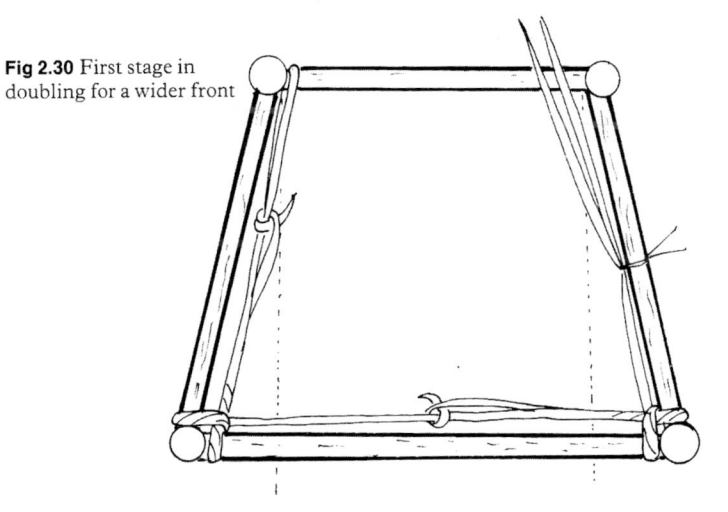

Photo 2.5 Trapezium-shaped ladderback chair, seated with reedmace in a straight across finish

Fig 2.30 First stage in doubling for a wider front

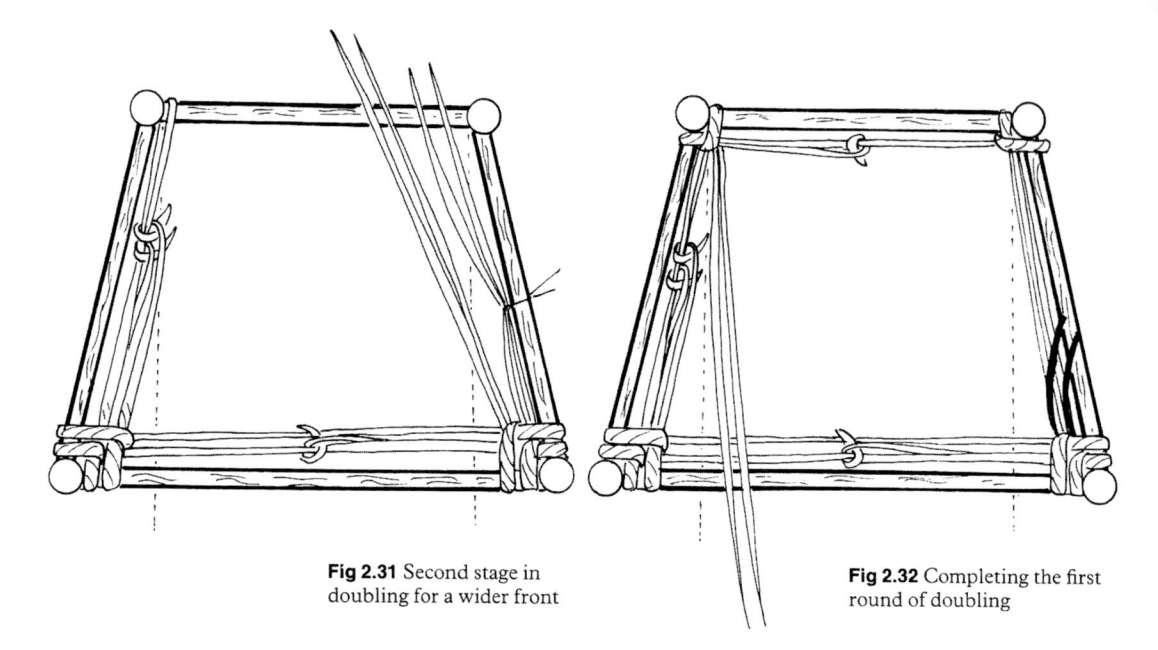

Fig 2.31 Second stage in doubling for a wider front

Fig 2.32 Completing the first round of doubling

2. Half-way along the left side rail, half-hitch enough rushes to the first coil to make a new one. Pull the knot very tight to stop it slipping.
3. Work the two front corners again with this second coil (Fig. 2.31).
4. Untie the first coil from the right side rail and use enough rushes from both coils to make a single one, leaving out unwanted rushes. Work the two back corners with this. There will now be two coils over the front corners, and one over the back corners (Fig. 2.32).
   Note: Trim off any unwanted rushes at step 4. The short ends lie flat over the interior coils.
5. Repeat steps 1 to 4 until the gaps on the front and back rails are equal (Fig. 2.33). At step 1, tuck the coil temporarily into the interior coils to hold it, or hitch it over the back rail.
6. When the gaps on the front and back rails are equal, continue to work round the chair without doubling.
7. Push the coils tightly in towards the corners, and complete the seat as for a square or a rectangle, depending on whether there is a bridge.
   Note: Take care that the first working of the right front corner does not become loose while you are completing steps 2 and 3. Pull it tight again at step 4. Make good right angles, and keep the coils straight.

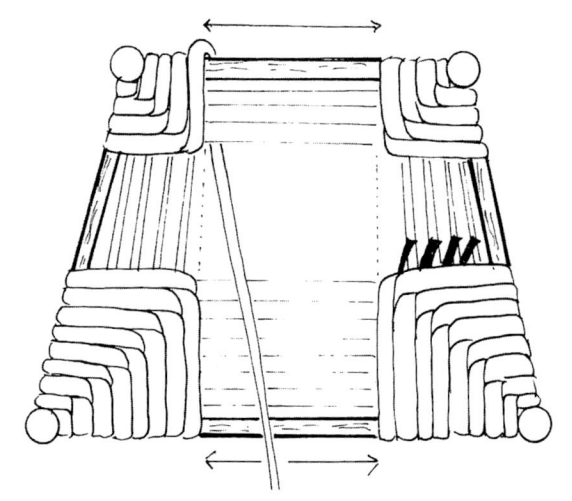

Fig 2.33 Doubling stage completed

Alternative methods of doubling

FURTHER CONTINUOUS METHODS

Method 1
This is the way I was first taught, 25 years ago.

1. Put a complete round of coils on the chair.
2. At the start of the second round, divide the coil into 2 groups. Make one group up to size, leaving the other till later.
3. Work the two front corners with the first group, and tuck the coil temporarily into the work (Fig. 2.34).
4. Make the second group up to size and work the two front corners again.
5. Join the two groups together for a single coil over the two back corners, as in the previous method, Step 4 (above).
6. Repeat on each round until the extra space on the front rail is filled, and the gaps on front and back rails are equal.

Method 2
This entails working twice round the two front corners on alternate rounds.

1. Complete the first corner as usual.

Fig 2.34 An alternative continuous method of doubling

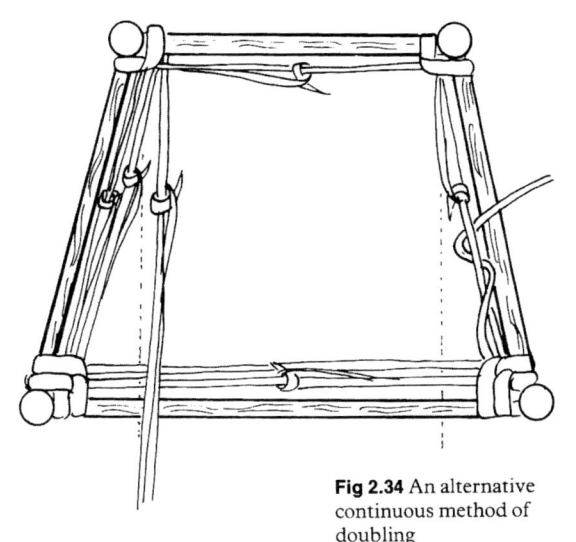

Fig 2.35a Front corners only method of doubling

Fig 2.35b Weaver's knot

Fig 2.35c Simple hitch

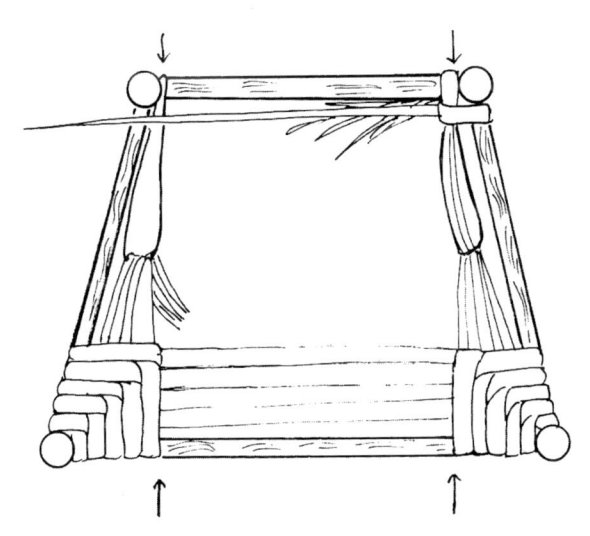

Fig 2.36 Front corners only doubling completed

2. Go back over the left front rail, and then back over left side rail.
3. Cross to the right front corner and repeat Steps 1 and 2.
4. Complete the two back corners in the usual way.
5. Work a plain round.
6. Repeat Steps 1 to 5 until the gaps on the front and back rails are equal.
   Note: Be very careful to keep the front corners square. This method is best reserved for chairs with only a small difference in length between front and back rails. Too many rounds worked this way could pull the two front corners out of shape.

FRONT CORNER ONLY METHODS

These all entail working on the front corners only until the gaps on front and back rails are equal in length.

Method 1

This is Kay's favourite method, quick, and easy to understand. It gives good tension over the front corners.

1. Measure the front and back rails, and mark the amount of extra space to fill on each side, on the front rail.
2. Tie loops of string or rush over the back rail at each corner.
3. Knot enough rushes to make a coil to the left-hand loop, work the front corners, and tie off to the right-hand loop (Fig. 2.35a).
4. Repeat until the marked spaces are filled.
5. Knot one more coil to the left-hand loop, and then work the seat as usual.
   Note: For the first coil, use a weaver's knot (Fig. 2.35b) for security. For subsequent coils, bring the rushes under the string, up through the loop, and then down between themselves and the old coil. This will hold well (Fig. 2.35c). Work until the marked spaces on the front rail are filled. If you wish, the first coil over the side rail on the right back corner can catch in all the rushes from the loop, and press them tightly against the back rail. Cut off the long ends (Fig. 2.36). Alternatively, trim off the ends below the loop, and press them towards the back rail with subsequent coils.

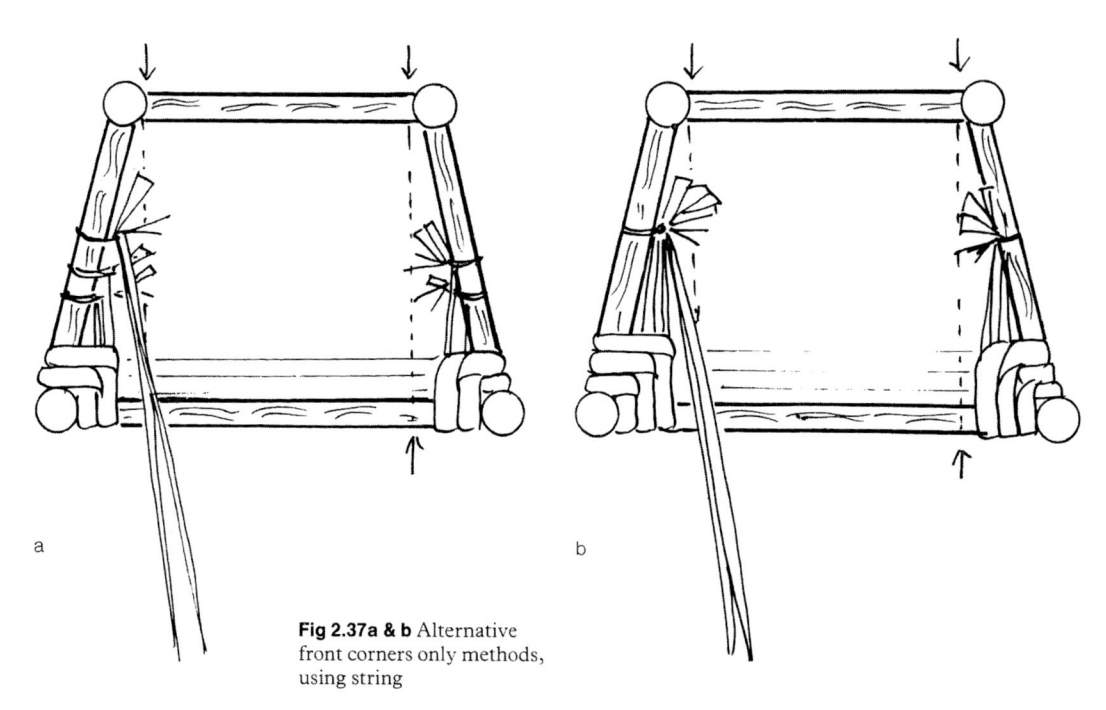

Fig 2.37a & b Alternative front corners only methods, using string

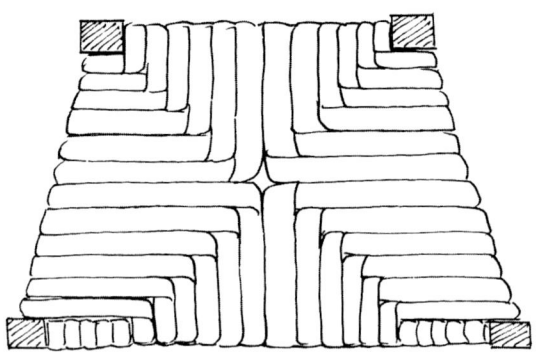

Method 2
This is a good method for a chair with thick coils which will hide the string (Fig. 2.37a).

1. Mark the space to be filled on the front rail on each side.
2. Tie enough rushes to make a coil to the left-hand side rail with thin string.
3. Work the two front corners, and tie the coil to the right side rail.
4. Repeat until the extra space is filled.
5. Tie on one more coil, and work the rest of the seat as usual.
   Note: The string will be covered up by subsequent coils, so make sure it is fine.

Method 3
This method uses a single tie of string over the side rails on each side (Fig. 2.37b).

1. Mark the space to be filled on the front rail on each side.
2. Tie a good bunch of rushes to the left side rail with fine string.
3. Take enough rushes from the bunch to make a coil, and work the two front corners.
4. Tie off to the right side rail.
5. Repeat till the extra space is filled.
6. Use one more coil from the bunch, and work round the seat as usual.
   Note: Use a long piece of string on the right side rail, and knot each coil with this. Add more rushes on the left if necessary. If there are more than you need, just cut them off. It is possible to estimate the amount you need by deciding on the number of coils to the inch, and the number of rushes in a coil, but it will only be a rough estimate.

Fig 2.38 Special method of doubling

Special method (Fig. 2.38)
This is an unusual method I found on an antique chair, and have never seen anywhere else. It looks attractive and is quick once you have grasped how it works. It involves filling in the extra space on the front rail by wrapping a coil round and round it at each corner, before starting to rush the seat in the usual way. This takes the place of doubling, so if the side rails are longer than the back rail, a special technique must be used (explained on page 99, in the section *Extra long side rails*).

The front legs of the chair must have narrow tops. If the tops are too wide, there will be an obvious gap between the coils round the front rail and the first coil over the side rails.

1. Mark the extra space to be filled on each side of the front rail.
2. Tie a loop of string over the left back rail, long enough to reach about three quarters of the way to the front. Tie the butt of a long rush to the loop.

Fig 2.39a Starting to wrap the front rail

Fig 2.39b Wrapping the front rail, steps d and e

Fig 2.40 Special method of doubling completed

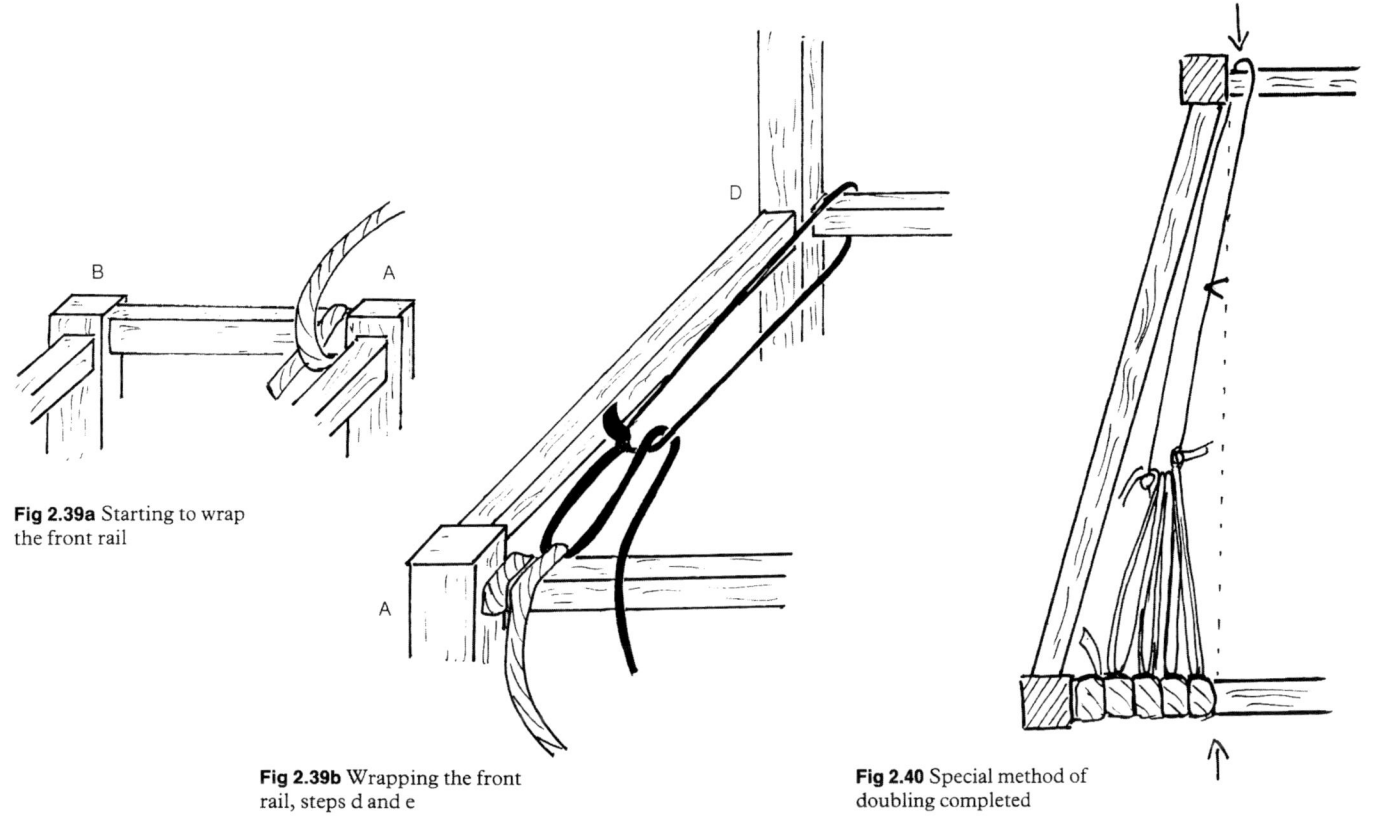

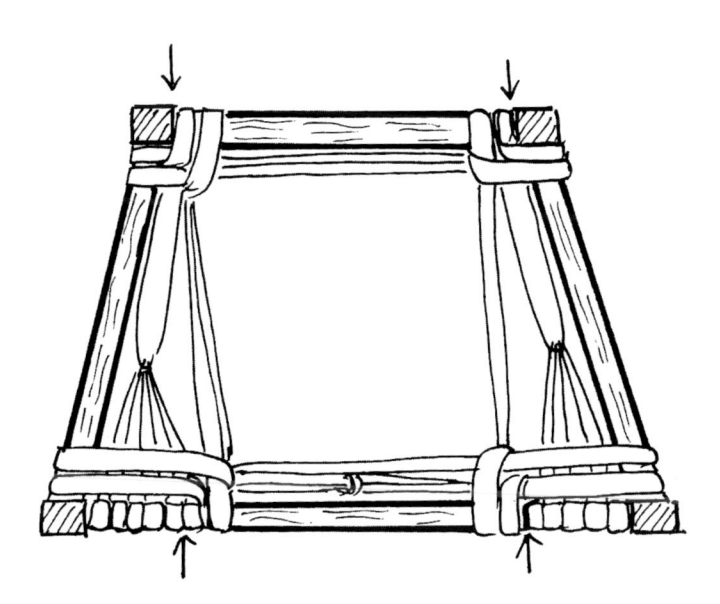

Fig 2.41 Special method with two rounds of work in place

3. Take enough rushes to make a coil, twist them, and start to wrap them round the front rail at the left corner, securing the coil by wrapping it over its own tail on the inside of the rail (Fig. 2.39a).
4. After one wrap round the rail, bring the coil up, catching in the single rush attached to the loop of string. Make the next wrap (Fig. 2.39b).
5. Take the single rush backwards through the loop of string, before bringing it forward again and under the next wrap over the rail.
6. Repeat until the gap is filled, adding rushes to the coil or the strand from the loop where necessary.
7. Tie off all rushes to the loop (Fig. 2.40).
8. Repeat on the right-hand side.

Work as usual from now on, starting by looping a new coil onto the string on the left (Fig. 2.41).

Note: Bringing the single rush forward from the loop each time, and catching it in with the coils, prevents a slit forming behind the wraps on the front rail. If the corner post is too wide, the single rush would be visible in front of the first wrap on the side rail.

English style drop-in seats (Photo 2.22)

These are designed to drop into the chair frame. They have polished wooden corners against which the coils rest. They are worked using any of the above methods for the appropriate shape. Great care must be taken to use a suitable size of coil, so that the seat fits neatly back into the frame. Check very carefully when you start work, and make sure you keep the size of coil even.

11. Continental methods

Different sequences of coiling, and methods which differ from the English traditional ones, are used on many Continental and Scandinavian chairs. I have used the general term 'Continental' to cover all of these. Wrapping the coils in a figure of eight over the rails in blocks of two, three, four or more can result in a variety of patterns. This is generally done over the side rails at the front, in combination with a single coil over the front rail (Fig. 2.42). The lines running towards the centre lie closer to the side rail, and the angle varies with the number of side coils in the block (Fig. 2.43a, b and c).

The side rails fill up quickly with this method, resulting in a wide bridge. In their country of origin these seats are generally worked with the coils twisted in one direction only for a straight across finish, and the twist continues underneath as well as on top. This is often necessary to hold the material together when fine materials such as straw, thin sedges, rushes or reedmace are used.

These patterns give a very long coil from the bridge to the front of the chair, and unless they are tightly worked and well stuffed they can grow loose and wear out quickly. The coils lie side by side underneath instead of bedding into one another, and do not hold the stuffing so well, which also reduces the life of the seat. Where possible, I always prefer to leave the underneath coils untwisted.

On trapezium shapes the blocks of coils are often worked on the front corners only, to fill up the extra space on the front rail. The single pattern is reverted to for the rest of the seat. This is another front corners only doubling method, in fact. They can be used to great effect to create different patterns on the seat. I once saw a beautiful Normandy chair with a curved back rail, which started with two side coils in a block and changed to singles just before the bridge, giving a curve exactly matching the curve of the chair frame (Fig. 2.44).

Photo 2.6 Pine kitchen chair seated with reedmace in a Continental pattern, four coils to a block

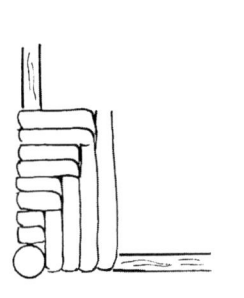

Fig 2.42 Continental patterns

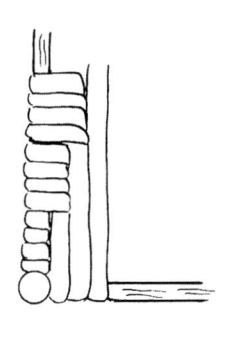

Fig 2.43a Lines formed by corner angles with two coils in a block

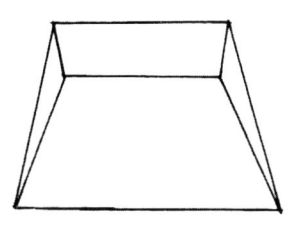

Fig 2.43b Four coils in a block

Fig 2.44 Lines formed on chair with curved back, two coils changing to one

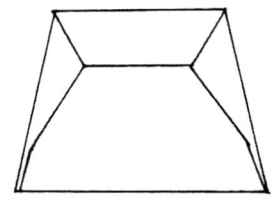

Fig 2.43c Four coils, changing to two

Methods of working

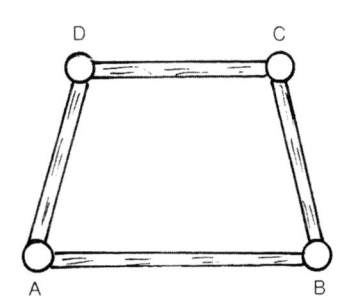

Fig 2.45a Corners labelled for Continental method

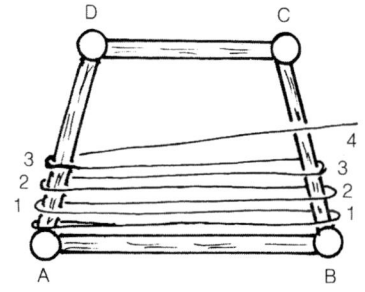

Fig 2.45b Steps 1 to 3 of the front corner Continental method

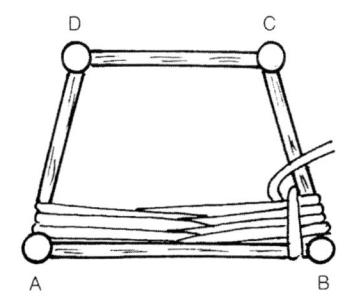

Fig 2.45c Steps 4 and 5

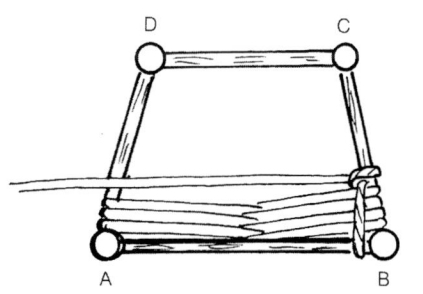

Fig 2.46a Step 6 of front corners only Continental method

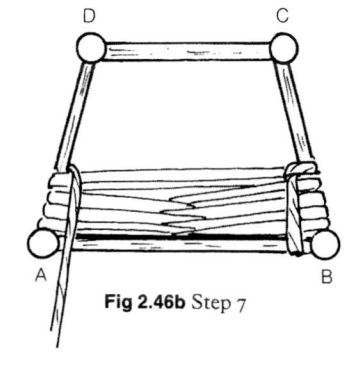

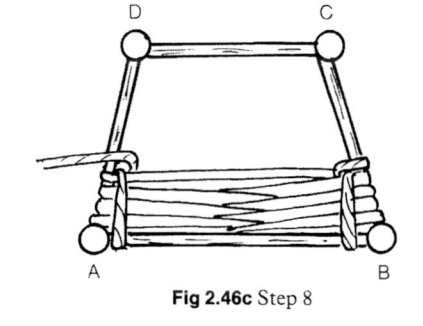

Fig 2.46b Step 7

Fig 2.46c Step 8

'FRONT CORNERS ONLY' METHOD, FOR A TRAPEZIUM SHAPE

Label the corners **A**, **B**, **C**, **D** (Fig. 2.45a) and decide how many coils you want in the blocks.

1. Loop a rush over the front side rail at **A**, and make up to size.
2. Lay the coil over the front side rail at **B**.
3. Figure of eight, coming up in the centre and out over the side rails each time until you have the correct number of coils on the **B** side. There will be one fewer at **A** (Fig. 2.45b).

   Note: The initial loop is hidden by the first coil at **A**.
4. Bring the coil up in the centre and over the front rail at **B**.
5. Up in the centre and back over the side rail at **B** (Fig. 2.45c).
6. Up in the centre and over the side rail at **A** to complete the number of coils in that block (Fig. 2.46a).
7. Up in the centre and over the front rail at **A** (Fig. 2.46b).
8. Up in the centre and back over the side rail at **A** (Fig. 2.46c). Both sides should now look the same.

Repeat steps 2 to 8 until the gaps on the front and back rails are equal.

To continue normal working around the seat
After step 8 cross to side rail **B** and continue to work each corner in turn as in the *basic method* (page 75). This gives an extra single corner on the right at **B**, unnoticeable on the finished seat.

Fig 2.47a Continuous method for Continental pattern, steps 1 to 6

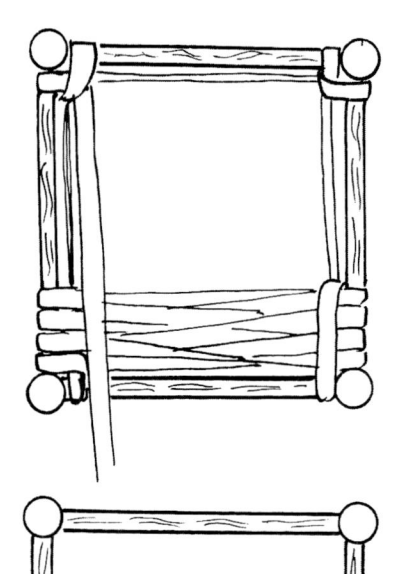

Fig 2.47b Avoiding an extra coil over the front rail

Variations

Photo 2.7 Child's chair in double Continental pattern, four coils to a block. It has a rush panel on the back

CONTINUOUS METHOD

This could be used on a square seat to create a bridge.

1. Loop a rush over the back rail at **D** and make up to size.
2. Complete corner **A** as usual.
3. Up in the centre and over the side rail at **B**.
4. Figure of eight until you have as many coils in the block as you want, finishing at **B**.
5. Up in the centre and over the front rail at **B**.
6. Complete the back corners as usual (Fig. 2.47a).
7. Repeat steps 2 to 6 until there are as many blocks as you want.
8. Complete the seat as usual.
   Note: This method gives one initial odd coil over the front rail at **A**, but this does not spoil the finished seat. It could be avoided by looping the rush over the side rail at **B** and laying the first coil over the side rail at **A** (Fig. 2.47b).

Doubling for a trapezium shape

After step 5, tie the working coil to the side rail, or hitch it over the back rail.

Hitch on enough rushes to make a new coil between **D** and **A**, and repeat steps 2 to 5.

Combine the two coils for the back corners, as in the *Basic method* (pages 83, 84). Repeat until the gaps on the front and back rails are equal, then work normally.

DOUBLE CONTINENTAL

Here the continuous method is used on both front and back of the seat, giving a very long bridge, and a modern look to the seat, which must be square, or rectangular with longer side rails. This child's chair also has a rush panel on the back (see page 93).

1. Work steps 1 to 5 of the continuous method.
2. Work the back as for the front, steps 2 to 5.
3. Work in this way until the side rails are very tightly filled, and then fill in the bridge with a figure of eight, finishing over the back rail.
   Note: Mark the centres of the side rail. It may be necessary to have fewer side-coils in the last block on both front and back of the chair, to reach the centre exactly. It would be perfectly all right to let the blocks for the front half go over the centre mark if this would fill in the gap exactly (Fig. 2.48a). The figure of eight could then be worked from right to left, and the bridge would be nearer the back (Fig. 2.48b).

Pack the coils very tightly on the side rails to avoid a wedge-shaped gap in the centre at each end of the bridge. This chair had to have two extra side coils added because it had not been worked tightly enough.

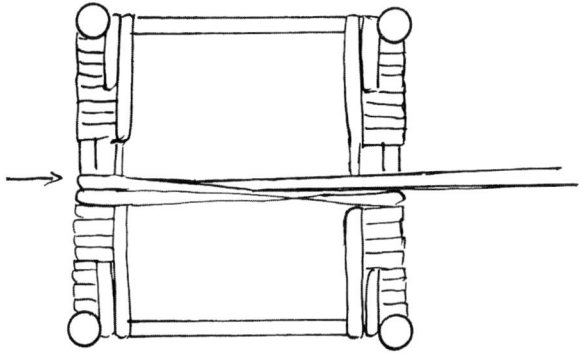

Fig 2.48a Double Continental pattern, filling in the centre

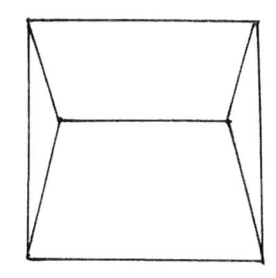

Fig 2.48b Lines formed on completed seat

FRENCH PATTERN (Photo 2.8)
This is a delightful pattern found by Mary on a chair in a French farmhouse. It shows one of the many variations to be found in France, and makes a most ingenious use of the figure of eight.

I have guessed at the way the pattern was worked, as a result of studying the photo with a magnifying glass. It seems to have been done in a semi-continuous manner.

1. Loop a rush over the back rail and make it up to size.
2. Work corner **A** as usual.
3. Figure of eight over front side rails for 9 coils, finishing over **B**.
4. Over the front rail at **B**.
5. Figure of eight over the back and front rails at **C** and **B** until there are 6 coils on the back rail and 13 on the front (including the one from step 4).
   Note: Use the continuous doubling method.
6. Finish over the front rail and tie off the coil in the centre to the interior coils.
7. Hitch a coil on the interior rushes between **D** and **A**, and figure of eight between the front and back rails until there are 5 on the back and 13 on the front, including the one from step 2, and finishing over the front. Use the continuous doubling method.
8. Tie off the coil to the interior coils in the centre.
9. Loop a rush over the side rail at **D** and make up to size.
10. Figure of eight 13 times over side rails at **C** and **D**, finishing at **D**.
11. Up in the centre and over the back rail.
12. Complete the seat in the usual way.
    Note: Extra wraps have been used in the centre of the side rails before working the bridge (see page 83).

This pattern could certainly be worked continuously, but the numbers of coils in each block would be slightly different.

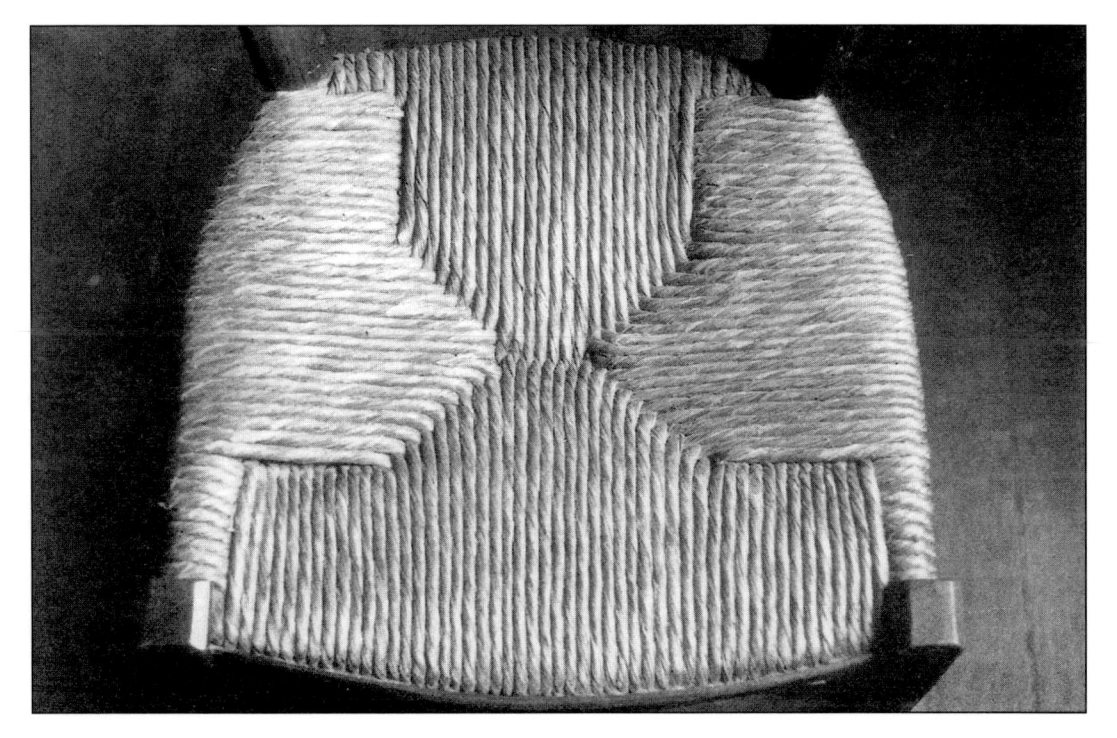

Photo 2.8 French farmhouse chair with patterned seat

Continuous method

Work to step 5 as above, finishing over the front rail at **B**.

6. Work the two back corners as usual.
7. Figure of eight between **A** and **D** until there are 13 coils on the front rail, including the one from step 2. Finish over the back rail.
8. Out over the side rail at **D**, then figure of eight between **C** and **D** 13 times, finishing at **D**.
9. Complete corner **D**, and then work the rest of the seat as usual.

BLOCKS ON EVERY RAIL FOR A SQUARE STOOL, WITH WRAPPED, ROUNDED CORNERS

This square stool has blocks of coils on both sides of every corner. This is achieved by wrapping the coils in a figure of eight over opposite rails on both sides of every corner (Fig. 2.49). In the stool shown in Photo 2.9 the rounded corners have first been wrapped individually (see page 97).

1. Loop a rush round side rail at **B** and make up to size.
2. Coil over side rail at **A**, up in the centre, and over side rail at **B**.
3. Figure of eight the required number of times, finishing over **B**. There will be the same number of coils on both rails.
4. Up in the centre and over the front rail at **B**, up in the centre and over the back rail at **C**.
5. Figure of eight the required number of times, finishing at **C**.
6. Repeat this sequence of moves for each corner until the seat is completed.
   Note: The end of one complete round of this method will be over the front rail at **A**, after the required number of figures of eight. Pack the coils tightly on the rails, and adjust the number of figures of eight in the last round to fill in the centre exactly.

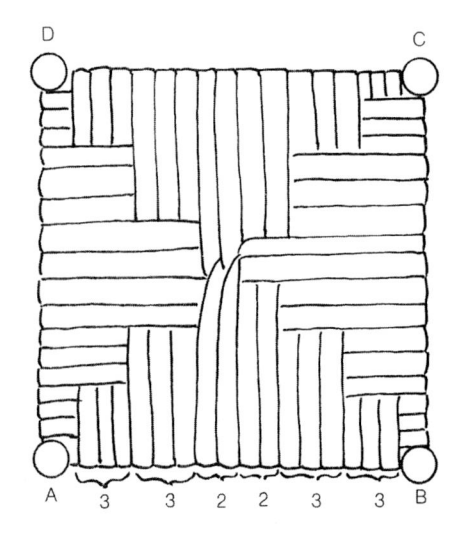

Fig 2.49 Blocks of coils on all four rails on a square stool

The pattern does not work out in the centre like an ordinary square seat. The last block of coils runs from front to back as for a bridge, and the two centre blocks on the left side rail will look like a double-sized block.

Photo 2.9 Metal-framed square stool with blocks of pattern on each rail, and curved corners

Chair backs

Continental and Scandinavian chairs often have decorative rushed panels on the chair back.

Sometimes this is a simple matter of a figure of eight over two rails, as in Photo 2.7. Sometimes it is worked over the uprights as well, and this would be worked in whatever pattern has been used for the seat. For these, the uprights on the back of the chair would either be indented or have decorative knobs to hold the coils in place.

REPAIRS TO CHAIR BACKS

These must obviously be worked in the same way as the original, and may have to be coiled on the back (the reverse side) as well as the front. If the back is coiled, new rushes must be twisted into the coil as invisibly as possible, and any butts or tips showing after completion must be tucked away. If used, an uncoiled back panel must be just as neat on both sides.

Tension
The work must be extremely tight, and the coils tightly packed together. If the bridge is a long one, take great care to get it straight.

Starting and finishing
Start with a loop over the back or top rail as usual, and make sure that this loop is completely hidden along the whole of its length to the bridge. To finish, tuck away the final coil as neatly as possible, with no knot.

STUFFING

If the work is a figure of eight over two flat rails, stuffing may not be necessary, as the pockets will not be very deep. If the work is over uprights as well, or there are deeper pockets, then stuffing may be necessary to prevent sagging after a period of use. Stuff either during or after the work, whichever you prefer.

If the back is coiled as well as the front, take great care not to let the stuffing show through the coils.

Drop-in seats, Continental style

Photo 2.10 Scandinavian chair with drop-in seat and curved cut-away corners. The pattern has two coils to a block

There are a number of different types of Continental and Scandinavian chairs which have a removable seat, designed to be lifted out of the chair frame and rushed separately. They generally have corners covered with rush, either squared-off, rounded, or cut away in a variety of shapes. Sometimes they drop into the chair frame, as in Photo 2.10; sometimes they are fixed to a sub-frame with screws or clips, with the coils showing on the edge of the seat.

SQUARE CUT-AWAY CORNERS

These seats are square or rectangular, and they usually have a small rim nailed to the inside of the corners to stop the coils slipping

Photo 2.11 Square drop-in seat with cut-away corners, from the underneath

off. A nail or wooden peg is sometimes driven into the underside of the corner to hold the coils in position or to slot into the sub-frame (Fig. 2.50). The frame is wide and flat, and the first few rounds of coiling must be laid on in a special way to cover this, before the usual method can be used.

1. Mark the corners on the inside of the rim **A**, **B**, **C** and **D**, so that you don't get muddled. The front left corner is **A**.
2. Loop a rush over the left back rail, or nail to the inside of the frame, and make up to size.
3. Lay the coil over the front rail close beside the front left corner, take it under the rail, behind the nail and rim, and up again on the outside of the side rail, still coiling in the same direction (Fig. 2.51a).
4. Lay the coil up and over the side rail from the outside, and cross to **B**, the second corner (front right).
   Note: The first coil will tend to slip away from the corner because it runs at an angle from the initial loop or nail. Keep it close to the corner.
5. In the same way, complete the next corner and then the two back corners (Fig. 2.51b).
6. Continue round the chair in this way, until the width of the flat rail is completely covered, and it is possible to bring the coil up in the centre and make a right angle for the corner in the usual way (Fig. 2.52a).
7. Complete the seat as usual.
8. Knock the nail backwards over the coils behind it, to hold them in place. If there is no nail, the rim will hold them.

This pattern can be worked with blocks of two coils in the early stages by wrapping twice round the frame before passing the coil behind the nail each time (Fig. 2.52b).

CURVED CUT-AWAY CORNERS

These are designed for chair frames with circular legs, and the seats may be square, rectangular, or trapezoid. The seat drops down on a sub-frame, and is held in place with screws, clips, or bars, or drop down into the frame, as in Photo 2.10.

There are two distinct types (Fig. 2.53). **A** has a shorter curve than **B**, and part of the flat rails must be covered before ordinary rushing can begin. This is shown by the dotted lines. Each corner is dealt with separately. If you take old seats apart, you will see that a staple gun has been used to fix short lengths of coil to cover this area. This gives a neat finish and is quite secure.

*For seat **A** (Stapled method) (Photo 2.12)*
1. Secure enough short lengths of coil to wrap over and cover the width of the dotted area on one side rail, by stapling the ends above and below the rail (Fig. 2.54a).

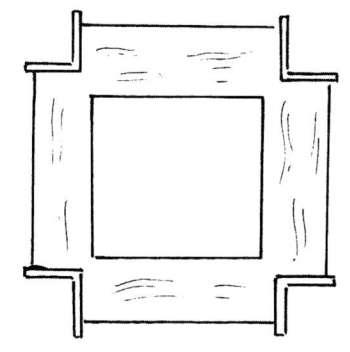

Fig 2.50a Top of a drop-in seat with square cut-away corners

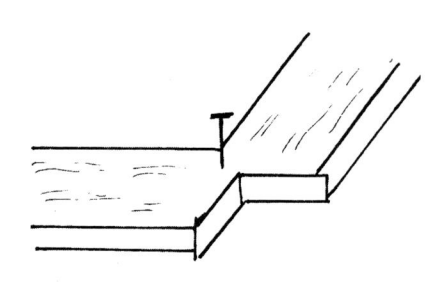

Fig 2.50b Underneath the seat

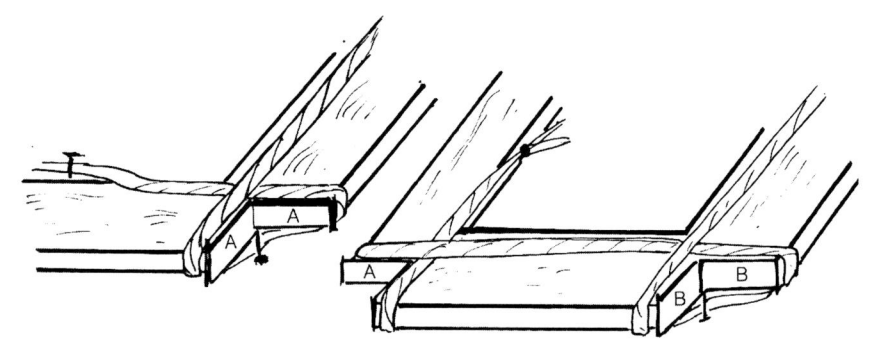

Fig 2.51a Cut-away corners, steps 1 to 3

Fig 2.51b Step 5

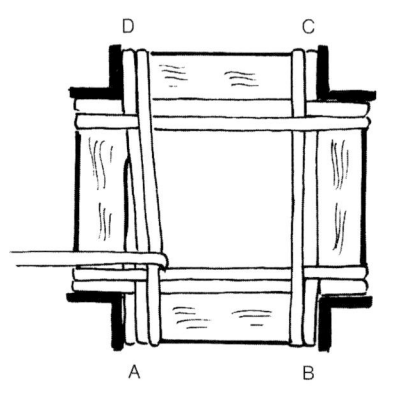

Fig 2.52a Cut-away corner, step 6

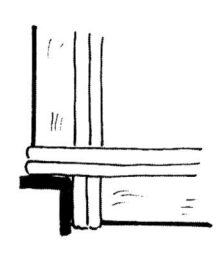

Fig 2.52b Blocks of two coils

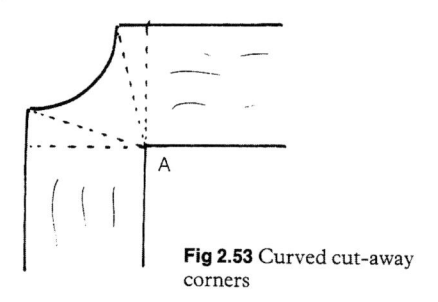

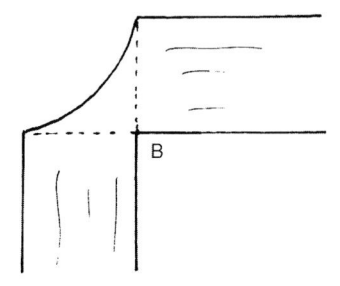

Fig 2.53 Curved cut-away corners

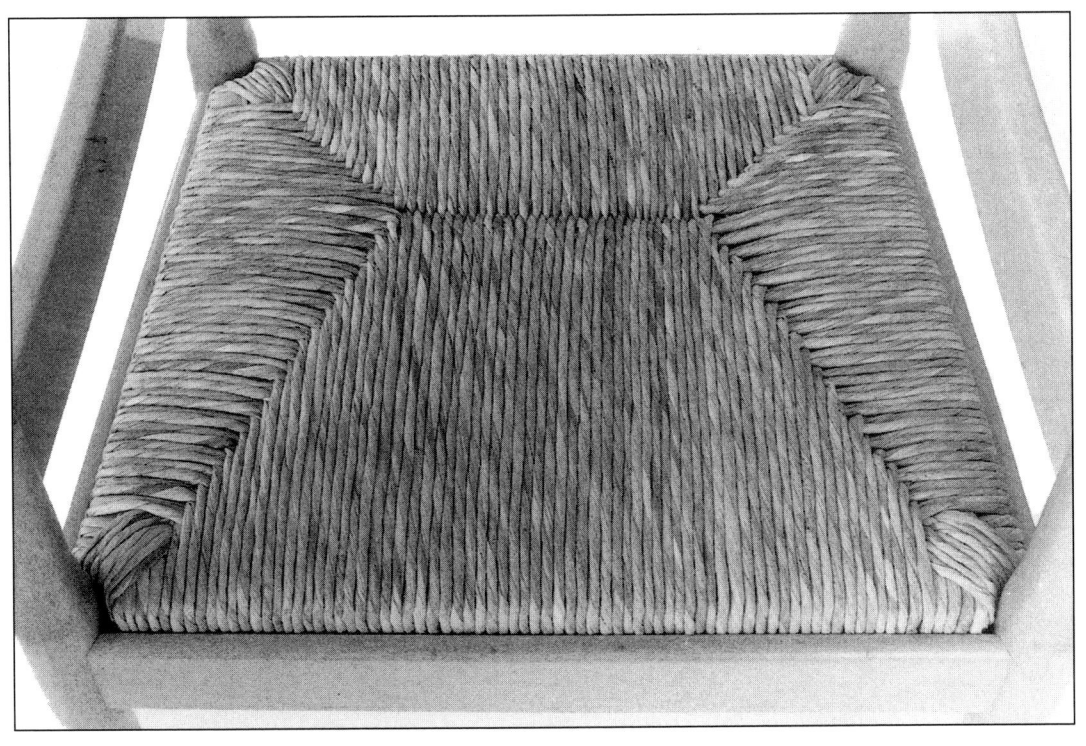

Photo 2.12 Close-up of Scandinavian chair, showing curved cut-away corner **A**

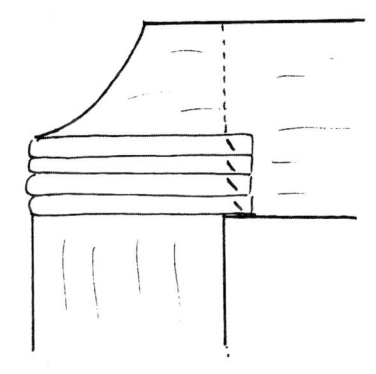

Fig 2.54a Corner A, step 1

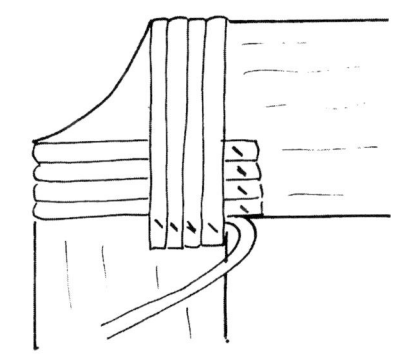

Fig 2.54b Corner A, step 2

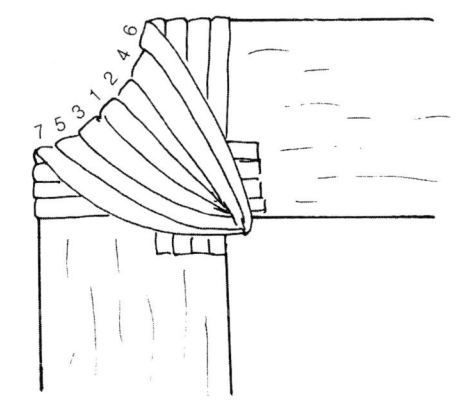

Fig 2.55 Cut-away corner, step 4

2. Cover the other side of the corner in a similar way, crossing the first coils (Fig. 2.54b).
   Note: Keep the end of the coils well in towards the inside of the rails, or they will be visible when you start the ordinary rushing.
3. Make the last coil a long one and bring it up in the centre of the corner.
4. Starting in the centre of the curved area, working first to the right and then to the left, wrap with coils to cover it completely, twisting in new rushes as needed (Fig. 2.55).
5. Secure the end with a staple on the inside of the frame.
6. Repeat for each corner.
7. Loop a rush over the back rail, and work the seat in the usual way.

*For seat **B***
1. Staple or tack a coil to the inside of the frame on a corner.
2. Cover the curved area as in steps 4 to 6 above.
3. Secure the end with a staple or tack.
4. Repeat for each corner.

95

Continuous method

The whole of corner type **A** can be wrapped with a continuous coil, though this can be rather bulky. Start at the front left corner.

1. Lay the coil over the front rail on the right of the corner.
2. Wrap it round the rail, trapping its own tail, until the dotted area is covered (Fig. 2.56a).
3. Bring the coil up in the centre, and wrap the left side of the corner in the same way (Fig. 2.56b).
4. Cover the curved area as before.
5. Carry the coil on to the next corner and cover in the same way.
6. Work the two remaining corners and carry the coil on to start the main part of the work.
Note: Twist in new rushes where needed.

Another continuous method

I found this method used in fine reedmace on a type **A** seat, and it gives a much flatter curve. It needs a nail for the underside of each corner.

1. Wrap the curved area with a reedmace leaf or split and flattened rush, securing the start and finish with a nail driven in under the corner (Fig. 2.57a).
2. Use the method for the seat with square cut-away corners (page 94) to cover the wide part of the frame, passing the coil behind the nail each time (Fig. 2.57b).
3. When the frame on the corners is covered, revert to the usual method.
4. Knock the nail backwards over the coils to allow the seat to fit into the frame.

SHARP COVERED CORNERS
(square, rectangular, or trapezoid)

Method 1

Staple on short lengths of coil around the corners as in curved cut-away corner, seat **A**, covering the dotted areas (Fig. 2.58).

Work each corner separately before starting the main part of the work.

Method 2

As for Method 1, but staple the coils on each side of the corner alternately to give the appearance of right-angled crossings (Fig. 2.59).

Method 3

Starting in the centre, lay on a continuous wrap in a figure of eight, from side to side, until a square has been created. This can be rather bulky, and the coils inside the corner must be very flat.

1. Lay the coil on the right side of the corner against the point.
2. Bring it up in the centre, and over the rail to the left of the corner, trapping its own tail to

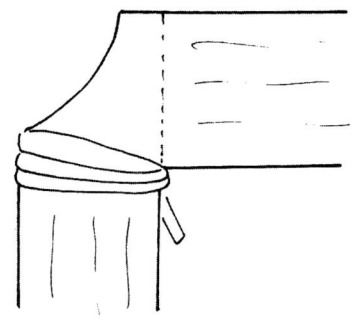

Fig 2.56a Corner B, steps 1 and 2

Fig 2.56b Steps 3 and 4

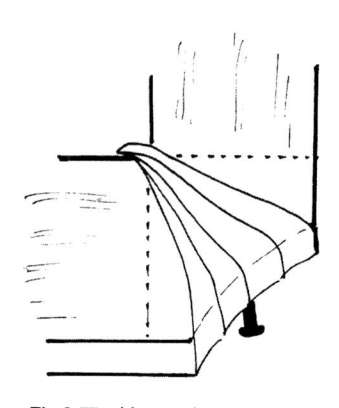

Fig 2.57a Alternative method, step 1

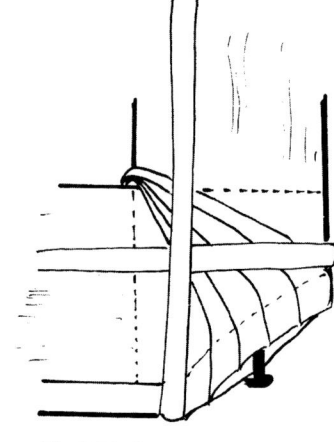

Fig 2.57b Step 2

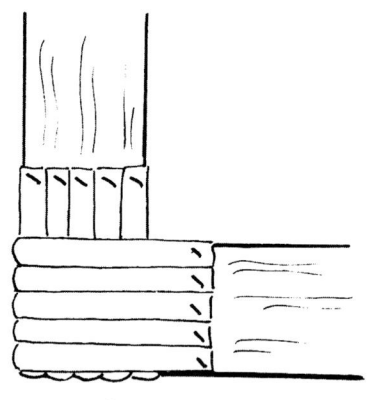

Fig 2.58 Sharp covered corner, Method 1

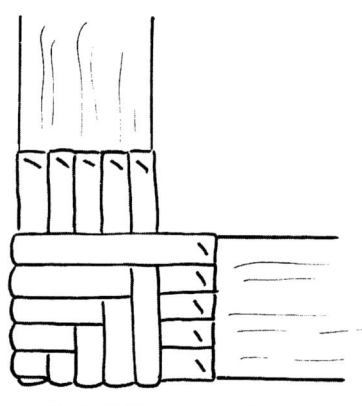

Fig 2.59 Sharp covered corner, Method 2

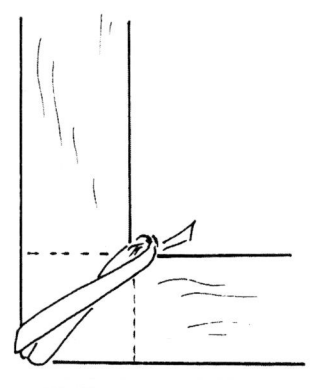

Fig 2.60a Method 3, steps 1 and 2

Fig 2.60b Method 3, step 3

secure it. It must cross the first coil as near to the point as possible (Fig. 2.60a).

3. Repeat steps 1 and 2 until the coils cross at right angles, and a square has been formed (Fig. 2.60b).
   Note: The coils cross each other a little further from the point each time. Secure the end by tucking it away, or using a staple.

Method 4
This is elaborate and tricky and must be done with fine rush to avoid bulk, but it does avoid the use of staples.

Corners **B** and **C** are worked together, then corners **D** and **A**.

First drive a nail in under each corner (Fig. 2.61).

1. Starting at **B**, lay the coil over the side-rail, and wrap it round the rail at **x**. Up in the centre, and over its own tail, to secure it.
2. Over the front rail right on the corner at **y**, and up in the centre (Fig. 2.62a).
   Note: These two wraps hold the coil in place on the side-rail.
3. Wrap the coil round the side rail until area **x** to **y** is covered (Fig. 2.62b).
4. Take the coil behind the nail and along the side-rail to corner **C**.
5. Up in the centre, and over the corner point on the back rail at **b** (Fig. 2.63a).
6. Up in the centre and over the side rail at **a**.
7. Cover the side rail from **a** to **b**.
8. Behind the nail, and back to corner **B** under the seat.
9. Now wrap from corner to corner right around front and back rails, filling in the space from the corners to the dotted lines (Fig. 2.63b), finishing over the back rail at **C**.
10. Take the coil on to corner **D**, first going behind the nail at **C**.
11. Work corners **D** and **A** in the same way, finishing over the front rail at **A**.
12. Carry the coil on over the side rail at **A** to complete the first right angle.
    Note: Twist in new rushes where needed. Complete the seat as usual.

ROUNDED COVERED CORNERS

These can be covered by wrapping a coil of rush round the corner from one side to the other. Secure with staples, or trap the starting end and tuck away the final end (Fig. 2.64 a and b).

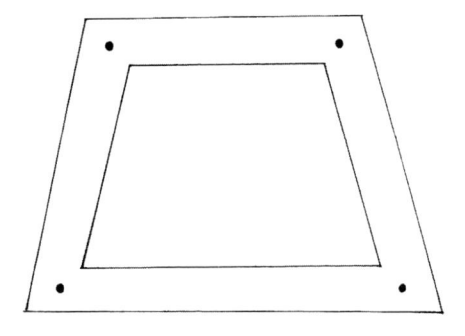

Fig 2.61 Frame for method 4

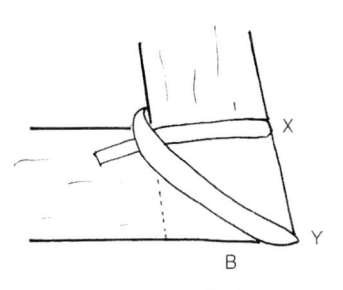

Fig 2.62a Method 4, steps 1 and 2

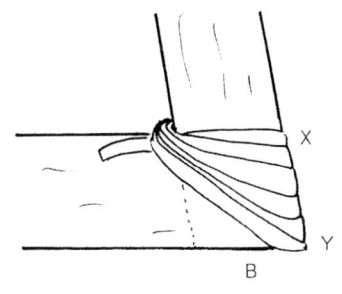

Fig 2.62b Method 4, step 3

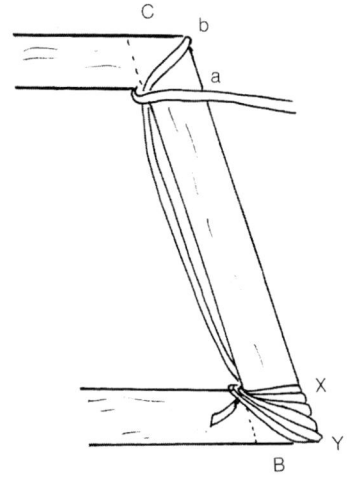

Fig 2.63a Method 4, steps 4 and 5

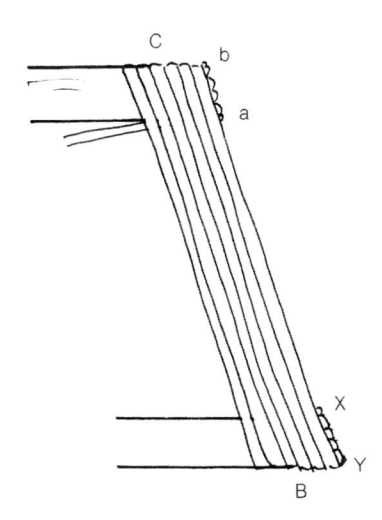

Fig 2.63b Method 4, step 9

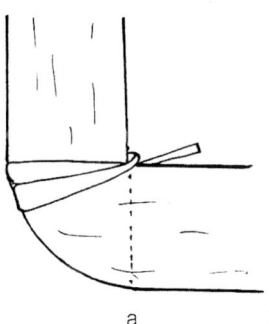

Fig 2.64 Curved corners

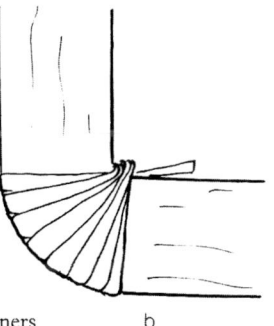

12.
Problem shapes

Chairs with long side rails

Some chairs have extra long side rails, and if these are rushed in the usual way, the bridge will run from front to back instead of from side to side (Fig. 2.65). Some chairs were designed this way, like those designed by the architect C. F. A. Voysey in the 1890s, and on these the front to back bridge looks right. On others, however, it can look clumsy and is not at all comfortable to sit on.

The Chapel chair in the photograph, possibly made by Skull's of High Wycombe in the 1860s, has long side rails, and would be uncomfortable if the bridge ran this way. To avoid this, the extra space on the side rails was filled up by laying a block of coils in a figure of eight over them at the back of the chair. It is less noticeable here than at the front, and looks better.

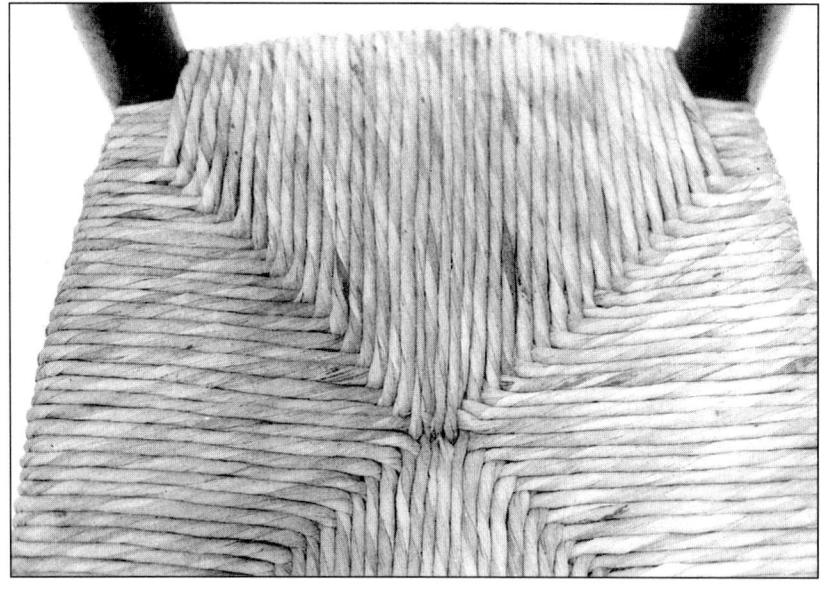

Photo 2.13 Chapel chair with extra-long side rails

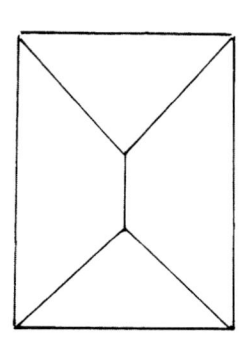

Fig 2.65 Patterns formed by extra-long side rails

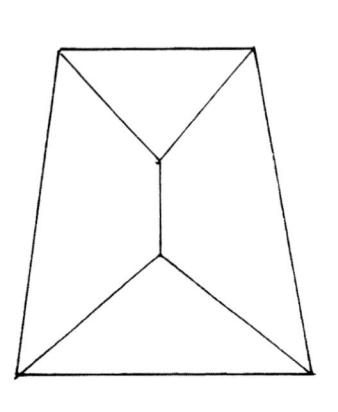

HOW TO DETECT EXTRA-LONG SIDE RAILS

Add together the measurements of the front and back rails, and divide the result by two. If this figure is less than the length of the side rail, you will need extra coils on the side rails.

METHOD

1. Loop a rush round the left side rail at the back. If you work from the back of the chair, which is easier at this stage, this rail will now be on your right.
2. Make the coil up to size, and lay it over the right side rail at **C**. Bring it up in the centre.
3. Lay the coil over the left side rail, covering the initial loop, and bring it up in the centre.
4. Repeat steps 2 and 3 until you have as many coils as you need on the side rails. See below for how to estimate (Fig. 2.66).
5. Complete the left back corner, and continue round the chair in the usual way, doubling if necessary.

   Note: This gives one extra coil over the left back rail, which will not show on the finished seat. There will be no coil on the right back rail until the next round.

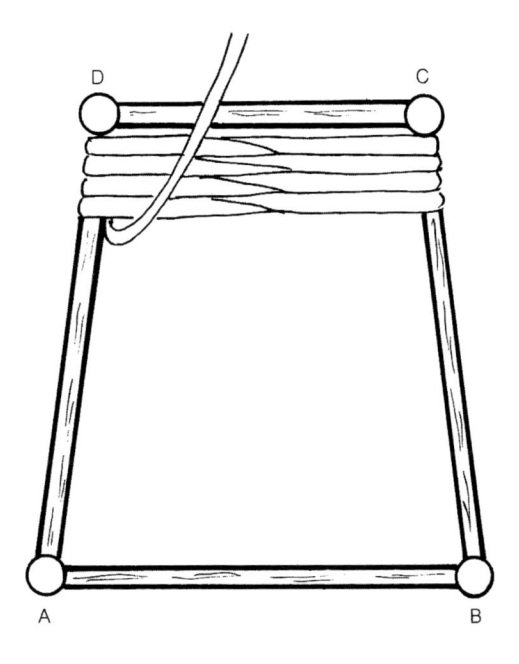

Fig 2.66 Filling in extra space on the side rails at the back

HOW TO ESTIMATE THE NUMBER OF COILS NEEDED

A) Rectangular seats

These are longer from front to back, but not trapezoid. Mark the extra length on the side rail at the back, and work figure of eight coils to fill the space. Then work as usual for a square seat.

B) Trapezium shapes

Front corners only doubling methods

It is much simpler to use these methods for chairs of this type, as the number of figure of eight coils can be estimated accurately.

1. Using any of the front corner doubling methods work till the extra space on the front rail is filled.
2. Measure the gaps on the side rails. If these are still longer than the gap on the front and back rails, mark and fill in the extra space with figure of eight coils (Fig. 2.67).
3. Work the rest of the seat as usual.

Continuous doubling methods

Here the figures of eight are done before the doubling, and the doubling causes the rails to fill up at different rates. Each round adds four coils to the front, three to the sides and two to the back.

If the side rail is about 2.5 cm (1 in) longer than the average length of the front and back rails, you will need to add at least a similar measurement of figure of eight coils. A couple

Fig 2.67 Doubling on a trapezoid chair with extra-long side rails, showing equal gaps on all rails

of extra coils would be safer, but remember that more than 6 or 7 coils can look clumsy, depending on the thickness. Work the figures of eight before using whichever continuous doubling method you prefer.

Note: Check the gaps after doubling. If the side rail gaps are still longer, it is possible to cheat a little by increasing slightly the size of coils over the side rails. This must be done as unobtrusively as possible.

These methods can be used to ensure that the seat finishes with a bridge. Some chair seaters would prefer always to have a seat finishing in a bridge, rather than at the centre, for both looks and comfort.

Widely-curved rails

Photo 2.14 Low chair with widely curved rails

On chairs with widely-curved rails, the coils have a great tendency to slip back towards the corners. This causes them to bulge and overlap on the top of the seat when you try to push them straight (Fig. 2.68). This can also happen on the back corners of very wide trapezoid chairs.

To prevent this, pull the coils very tightly before you lay them in place each time, and pack in towards the corners in the early stages, pressing the coils straight. This will help prevent bulges and overlaps later. Take care to keep good right angles. Avoid packing towards the corners too much in the later stages.

In many chairs of this shape, when you take off the old rush you will find that small notches have been cut on the top outer edge of the rail, to hold the coils in place. This is a great help, so if there are no notches, you could make some. Use a file or knife to cut shallow notches, with the straight edge nearest the corner. The coils rest against the straight edge to stop them slipping back towards the corners. One every 2 cm ($\frac{3}{4}$ in) should be plenty. Make sure they are smooth, and not too deep (Fig. 2.69).

Note: On bow-fronted chairs, it can be a great help to do one extra set of doubling when dealing with the wider front. This helps to prevent the tendency for the back rail to become crowded and the coils to pile up.

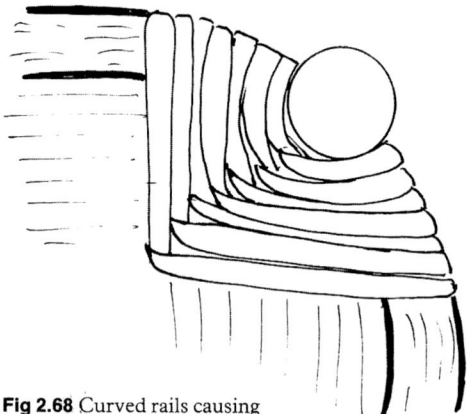

Fig 2.68 Curved rails causing piling up of coils

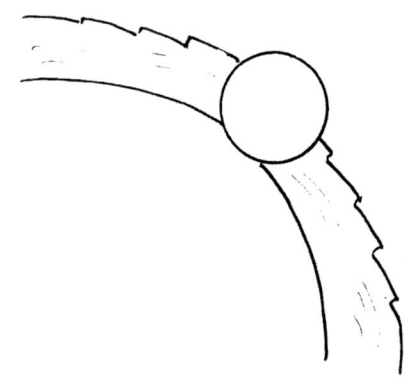

Fig 2.69 Notches on curved rails

Awkward arms

Several types of elbow chair have arms running down through or against the side rails, instead of down on to the front legs.

HOLES IN THE SIDE RAILS

Chairs of the William Morris type have arm-supports which run down through a hole in the side rail, finishing against a stretcher bar under the seat (Fig. 2.70).

Unless the arm is removed, and the hole dealt with in a special way, there will be an unsightly pile-up of coils on either side of the arm, and a gap on the side rail on the outside of the arm. You do see chairs in museums which show these gaps, but if you can dismantle the arm, and wrap the outside of the hole separately, it will look much better. (See page 102 for method of dismantling the arms.)

There are two methods of working the holes.

Photo 2.15 William Morris chair, with protective slats in place

Photo 2.16 William Morris chair, with close-up view of the arm

Method 1
With this method, the outside of the hole is wrapped before starting the main part of the seat.

1. Lay a coil over the outside edge of the hole, around the rail, and bring it up through the hole, securing its own tail (Fig. 2.71a).
2. Wrap around the frame and up through the hole until the outside edge of the hole is covered (Fig. 2.71b).
3. Finish by tucking the end away underneath, or fasten with a tack or staple.
4. Repeat with the other hole.
   Note: Keep the coil as flat as possible on the inside of the hole, to allow the arm support to fit back in place.

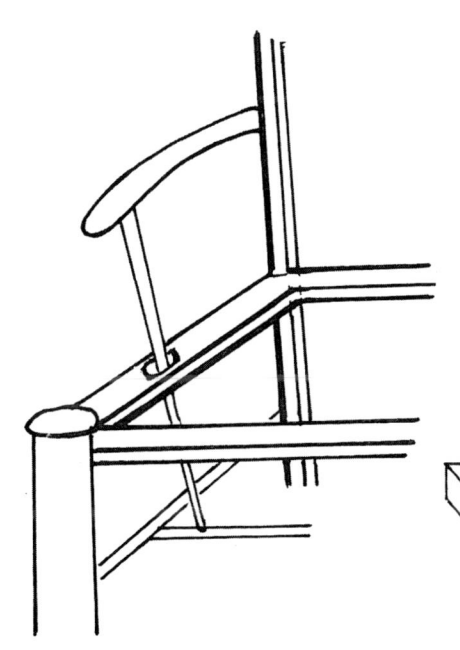

Fig 2.70 William Morris style arms

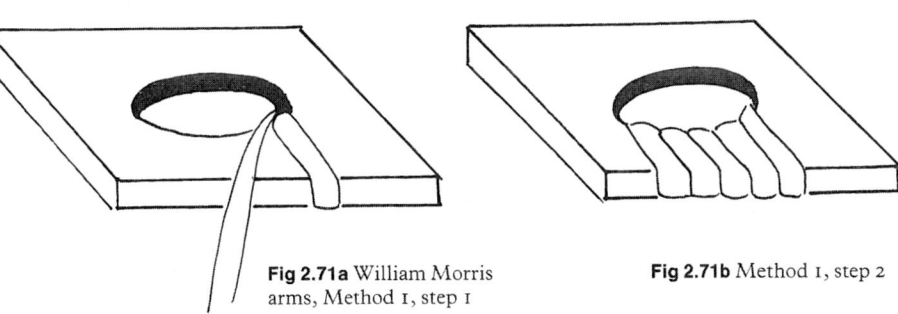

Fig 2.71a William Morris arms, Method 1, step 1

Fig 2.71b Method 1, step 2

Fig 2.72 Completed arm-hole

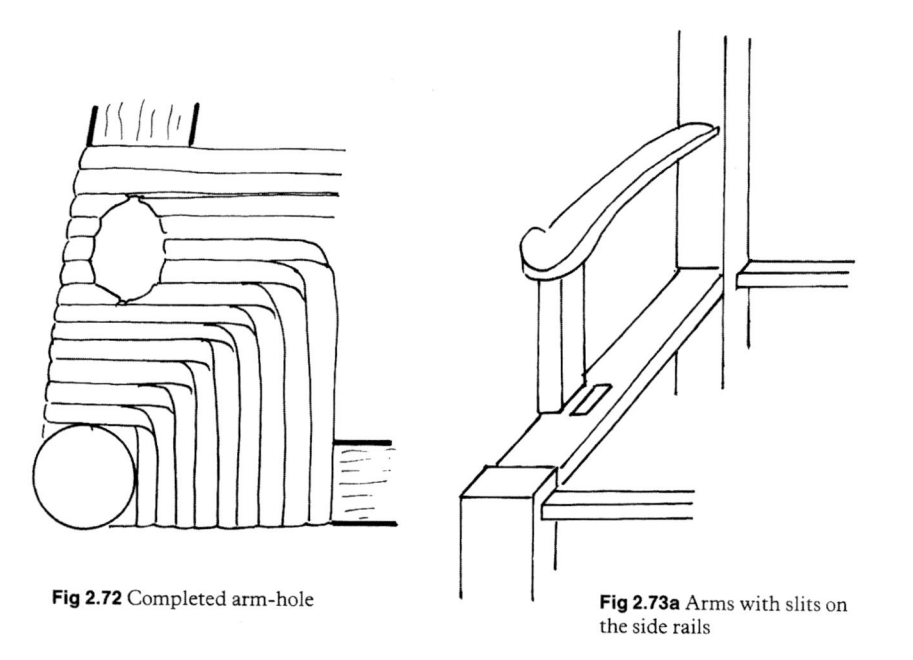

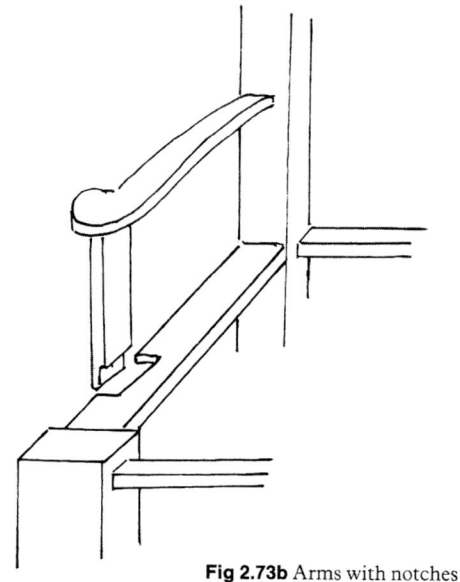

Fig 2.73a Arms with slits on the side rails

Fig 2.73b Arms with notches on the side rails

When working the main part of the seat, the continuous coil goes through the hole and over the inside edge (Fig. 2.72). Keep the coils flat on the inside as before.

Put the arm supports back in the hole while the coils are still damp, to compress them if they are rather too fat. The arms can be properly re-assembled later.

Method 2
With this method, the outside of the hole is covered at the same time as working the main seat. Work until the coil you are laying over the side rail is against the edge of the hole.

1. Divide the coil in two as it goes under the chair.
2. Bring one half of the coil up through the hole and use it to wrap the outer edge, making it up to size. Leave the end hanging down once the area is covered.
4. Use the other half of the coil to continue working normally.
5. Continue round the chair, going down into the hole each time you reach it, until the inside is covered.
6. When you go past the hole on the next round, pick up the free end from the outside, and take both coils back under the chair together.

Note: Treat both arms in the same way. Keep the coils flat on the inside of the hole.

SLITS IN THE SIDE RAIL
Some chairs have arm-supports resting against the edge of the rail, with a long slit in the rail alongside them (Fig. 2.73a). The coils of rush go down through the slit. This leaves a small, unavoidable gap between the coils and the arm support.

NOTCHED RAILS
Some chairs have arm-supports attached to the outside of the seat rails which fit into a notch. The arms must be removed, and the coils go into the notch, to be covered by the arm-support. Keep the coils flat on the outside of the notch (Fig. 2.73b).

It can be helpful to put a block of wood into the notch after working it and while you work the rest of the seat, to stop the coils on either side from sliding off.

DISMANTLING CHAIR ARMS
When the arm-support goes down through a hole in the side rail it generally comes to rest against a stretcher bar. It may be slotted into, glued, or screwed to this bar, and this joint needs to be separated first. Then the arm-rest joint is loosened by tapping gently upwards with a mallet padded with cloth to protect the wood. Gentle wiggling sideways will help to loosen the joint where the arm-support meets the chair-back, and then the whole arm can be dismantled.

Arm-supports which fit into a notch on the side-rail may be glued or screwed in, with a plug over the screw in some cases. This joint must be dismantled before the arm can be moved sideways away from the rail.

Snags
Glues and wood adhesives do not always respond to this treatment, especially if a modern adhesive has been used fairly recently. Damp cloths wrapped around the joints help to loosen old glue, and gentle persistence often achieves marvels. If, however, you are inexperienced in furniture restoration, and the joint appears immoveable, don't go on with it yourself: take it to an expert.

Triangular seats

You may sometimes find a triangular stool, or an antique chair like the cockfighting chair in the photograph. This was intended to be sat on back to front, with one's arms resting on the back while watching the unfortunate birds attacking each other. It is much more comfortable than any chair designed for such a horrid purpose has a right to be! The triangle is an equilateral one; that is, the seat rails are all equal in length.

Photo 2.18 Close-up view of triangular seat

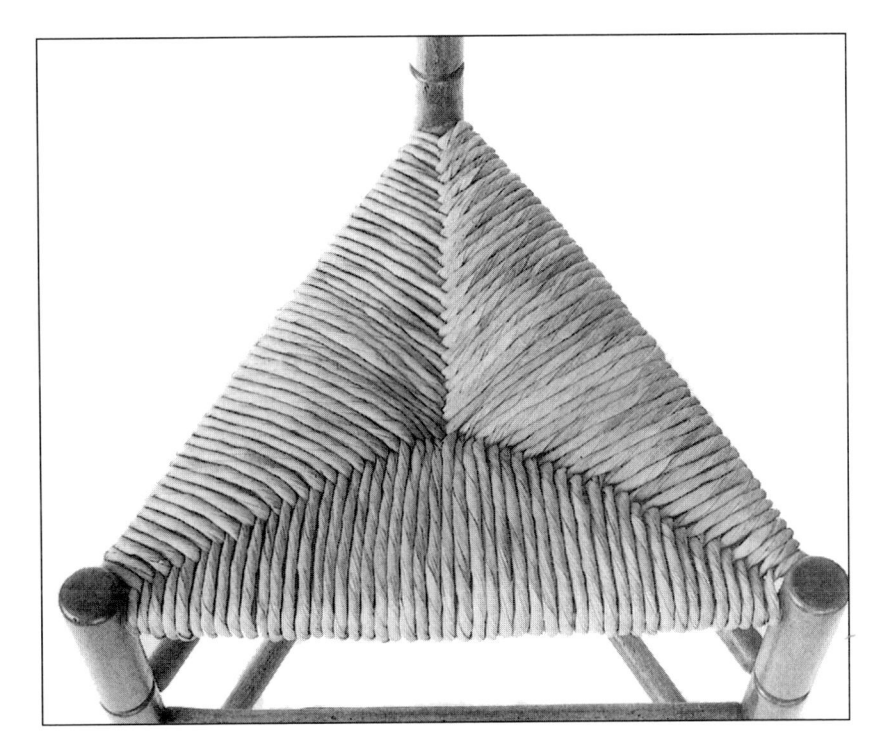

Photo 2.17 Early nineteenth-century cock fighting chair, with triangular seat

METHOD

When rushing a triangle, as with all shapes, it is essential that the coils cross the rails at right angles, in order to fill in the rails and the centre gap at the same rate. To do this with a triangle, you must ignore two of the important techniques used in other work. First, the angle at which the coils cross each other on the corners must be obtuse throughout. This is essential if the coils are to cross the rails at right angles (Fig. 2.74). Second, to make these obtuse

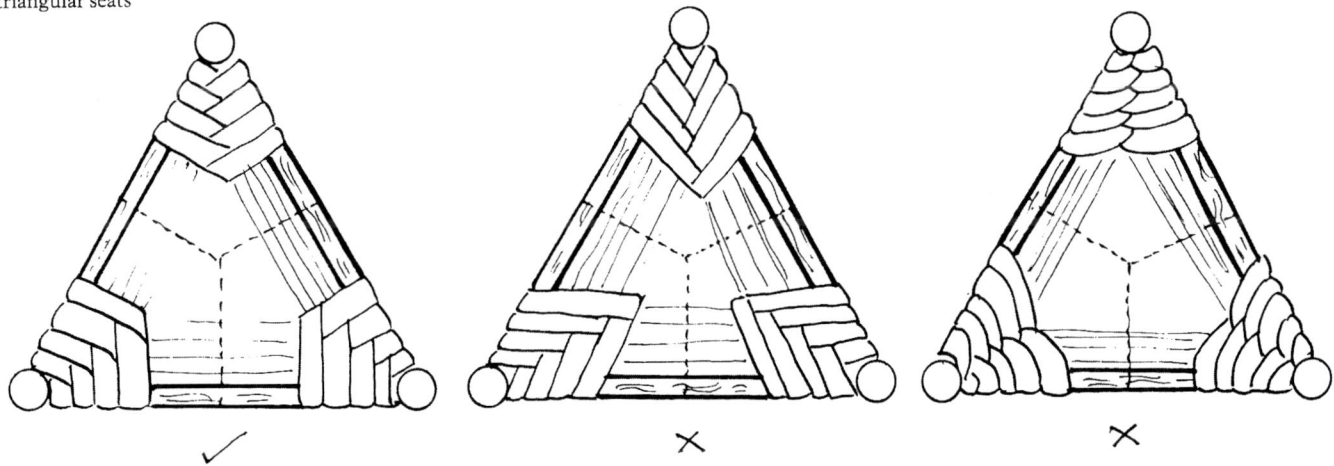

Fig 2.74 Correct and incorrect angles for triangular seats

103

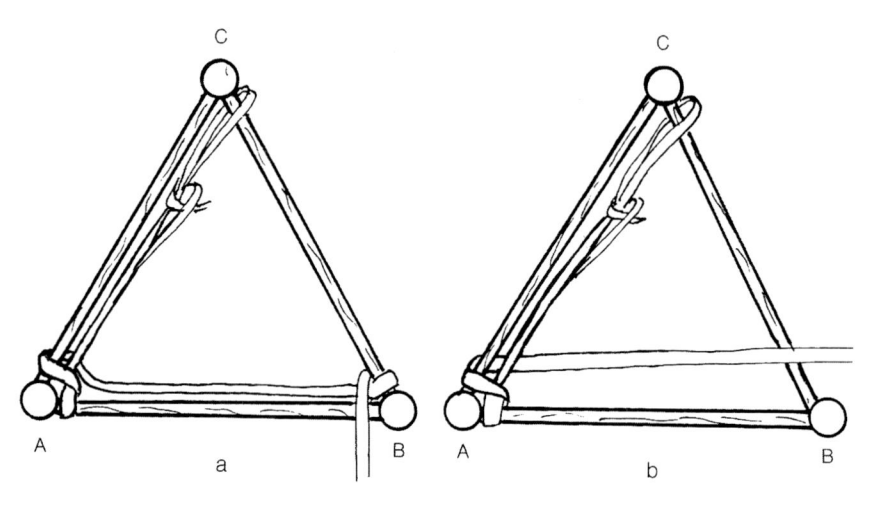

Fig 2.75 Correct and incorrect tension for triangular seats

angles possible, the coils must be left slack as they pass under the chair. This is so that they can be pulled in at both the next corner (to allow the obtuse angle to be formed), and the previous corner when you get back to it in the next round (Fig. 2.75a). If the coil is pulled tight, its natural path from side rail to side rail will be well out into the middle and away from the corner (Fig. 2.75b).

1. Loop a rush over the right side rail at the back corner **C**, and make up to size.
2. Lay the coil moderately loosely over the front rail at **A**, and bring it up in the centre.
3. Coil over the left side rail at **A**, pulling in very hard to make the obtuse angle. Make sure both coils cross the rails at right angles.
4. Up in the centre, and over the right side rail at **B**. It must be loose enough not only to pull it in for the obtuse angle at **B**, but also for the next obtuse angle at **A** in the following round (Fig. 2.75a).

   Note: To prevent the natural straight lie from side to side shown in Fig. 2.75b, hold the coil close in against the front rail at **A** with the left hand. The right hand lays the coil over the right side rail at **B**, loosely enough for it to turn away from the front rail, and cross the side rail at a right angle. Follow this procedure for each corner.
5. Up in the centre and over the front rail at **B**, pulling it in very tightly for the obtuse angle, and crossing the rail at a right angle.

   Note: Make sure that at **A** the interior coil is still loose enough to be pressed back against the completed corner (Fig. 2.75a).
6. Work the back corner **C** in the same way, hiding the initial loop of rush. Continue in this way, pressing the coils tightly together, until you are ready to stuff. Stuff as usual, lodging extra rush into the gaps between pockets. (If you prefer, the stuffing can all be done at the end.)

To finish, work until the gaps on the rails are tightly filled, finishing over the back corner at **C**.

Note: If the centre seems to be filling up too rapidly, you can try to enlarge it by pressing outwards firmly all round with the stuffing stick. You can also put in new rushes by the tips as you reach the centre, to give more bulk on the rail and less in the middle.

Both these measures can result in a crowded-looking centre if you are not careful.

Circular stools

A circular frame for a rush stool generally has deep notches cut in to the inside of the rail to make the four corners, with the legs attached at points about half-way between each notch. The legs are driven into holes on the underside of the frame/rail (Fig. 2.76). Each notch is wrapped in a figure of eight, until a right angle is created, to form the corners. The coils must pass on either side of the legs, and this causes a gap on the outside of the frame, which must be as small as possible. The circular frame causes the coils to pile up on one another (see *curved rails*). Notches can be cut if necessary.

There are two methods of working the seat.

METHOD 1
This is done leaving the legs in place. (They are set in at an angle, and cannot always be moved.)

1. Mark the stool to indicate the first corner. It is easy to lose your way later.
2. At corner **A**, lay the coil over the rail just to the right of centre of the notch.
3. Bring it up in the centre of the notch,

Photo 2.19 Circular stool, showing the first method of dealing with the legs

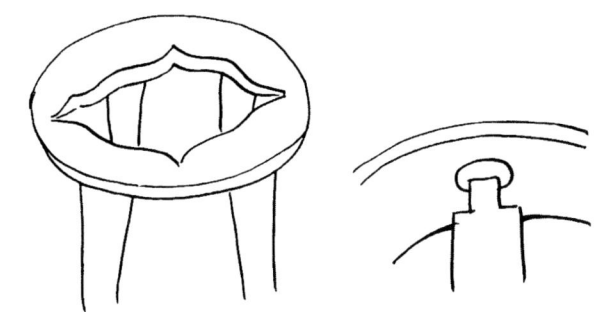

Fig 2.76 Circular stool frame and leg fitting

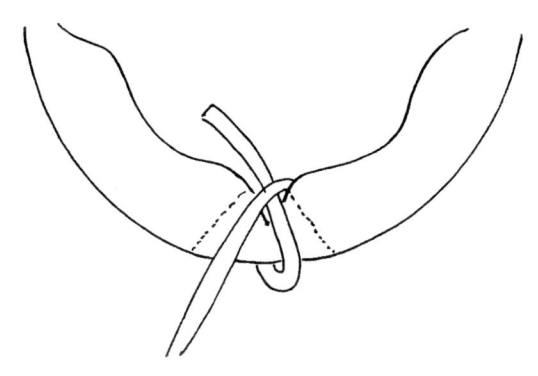

Fig 2.77a Circular stool, first corner, steps 2 and 3

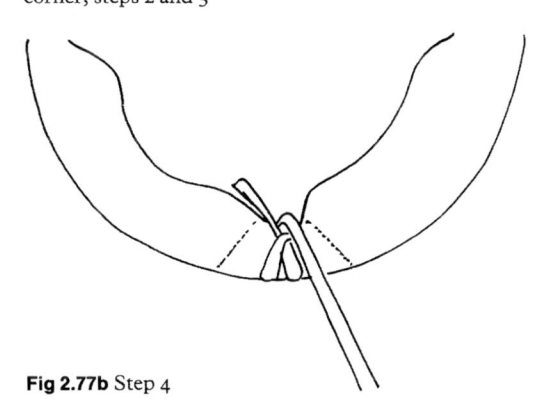

Fig 2.77b Step 4

securing its own tail, and lay it over the rail just to the left (Fig. 2.77a). The coils should cross as near to the outer edge as possible, at a very acute angle. They must hide the rail completely.

4. Repeat stages 2 and 3, crossing the coils a little further away from the edge, and at a less acute angle (Fig. 2.77b). To prevent a bulge, keep the coils as flat as possible inside the notch.
5. Repeat the crossings until the work forms a right angle, finishing over the left-hand rail (Fig. 2.78).
6. Take the coil on to the next corner, and work it in the same way.
7. Work the two remaining corners; the gaps on the rails should now be equal, and the coils running parallel in both directions (Fig. 2.79).
8. Work round the stool until you reach the legs.

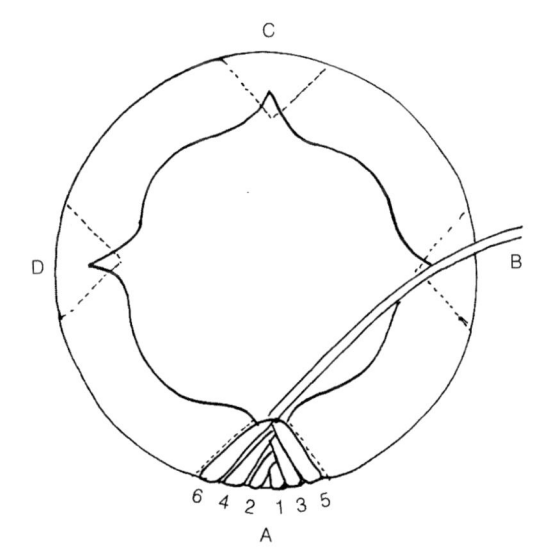

Fig 2.78 Circular stool, step 5

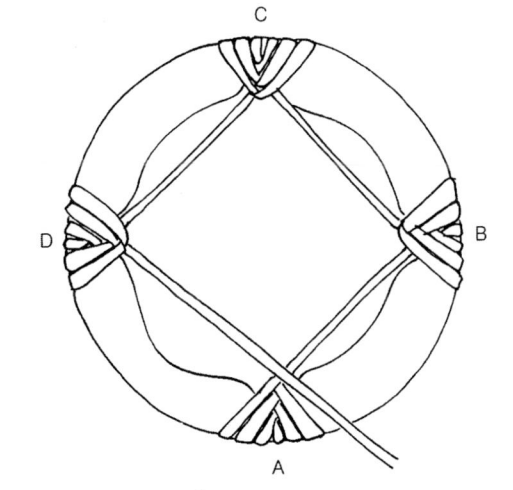

Fig 2.79 Circular stool, steps 6 and 7

To work the legs
These are not always in the same place on each 'side', so you may not reach them all in the same round.

1. Take the coil over the rail and down the side of the frame, turning it sideways a little to lie against the left side of the leg. Take it under the seat over the previous coil.
2. Repeat this each time you reach the leg until you reach the central point above it. The coils will pile up on each other against the leg. They must be pushed into a curve to cover the side of the rail (Fig. 2.80a).
3. In the next round, lay the coil to the right of the leg. Don't pull it too tight, but push it sideways to meet the previous coils.
4. Continue round the stool, laying the coils close to one another round the legs. Let them cover each other under the seat (Fig. 2.80b).
5. Once you are past the legs, finish the stool as usual.

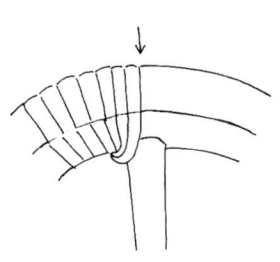

Fig 2.80a Circular stool leg, steps 1 and 2

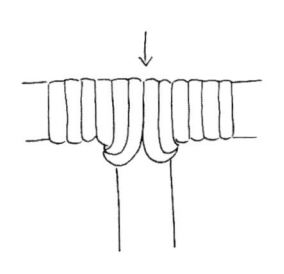

Fig 2.80b Steps 3 and 4

METHOD 2

Use this when it is possible to remove the legs. (The angle at which they are driven in can make this difficult.)

1. Work the stool top as above, but allowing the coils under the stool to cover up the leg holes.
2. When the seat is complete, force the rushes apart to allow the legs to be driven back in. You may need to hold them back on each side of the holes with a temporary nail.
3. Replace the legs, making sure that no coils are trapped under the legs, as they may be damaged or broken.

STUFFING

It is easier to stuff these stools after they have been completed.

Sofas

Very long sofas are quite a major task, as there is such a great distance from one end to the other. The seat must be rushed in the usual way. The result would not be strong enough if the two ends were worked separately with the front corners only techniques, and then the long rails worked in a figure of eight. It must have the internal coils from end to end for strength. The stuffing of the figure of eight must be very firm, and the coils packed tightly.

Some sofas are designed to be rushed in two or three sections. The simplest kind has separate seat frames which can be rushed independently (Fig. 2.81). Coils are stapled on to cover the plain areas on the frame.

Some have two or three panels which share dividing rails from front to back. They can be worked using the method for the long stool in the photo. The plain areas at the end of the dividing rails are first covered with coils which are stapled on (Fig. 2.82).

Photo 2.20 Long stool with interlocking panels over a central support rail

METHOD

This gives twice as many coils over the central rail as over the two side rails, because the two sections are rushed separately, using the same central rail. If you keep them smallish and not too tightly twisted, they can be packed to take up the same amount of room as the coils on the side rails. This hides the rail where they interlock, and forms a diamond pattern in the centre of the seat.

1. Loop a rush over the back rail at **D** and make it up to size.
2. Work a complete round on the left-hand section, and tuck the coil away between **D** and **A**. Keep the coils thinnish over the central rail.
3. Loop a rush over the back rail at **Z** and make it up to size.
4. Work a complete round on the right hand section. Tuck away the end between **Z** and **W**.

Fig 2.81 Sofa with separate seat sections

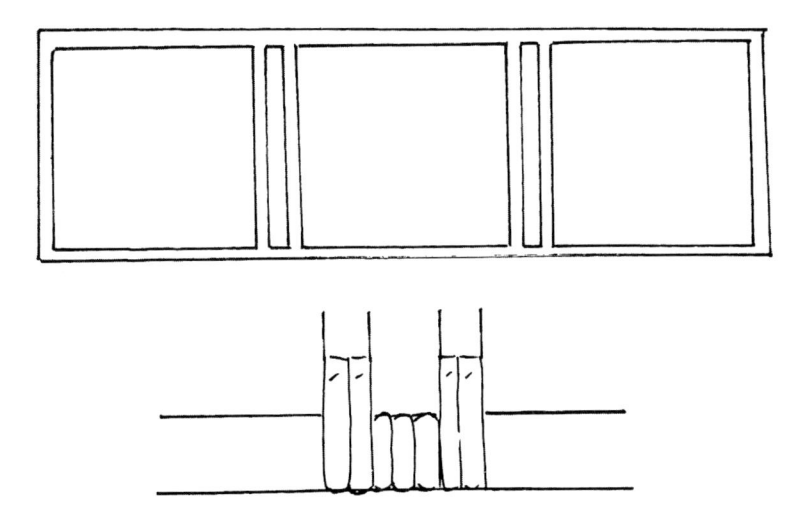

Fig 2.82 Stool with shared central support rail

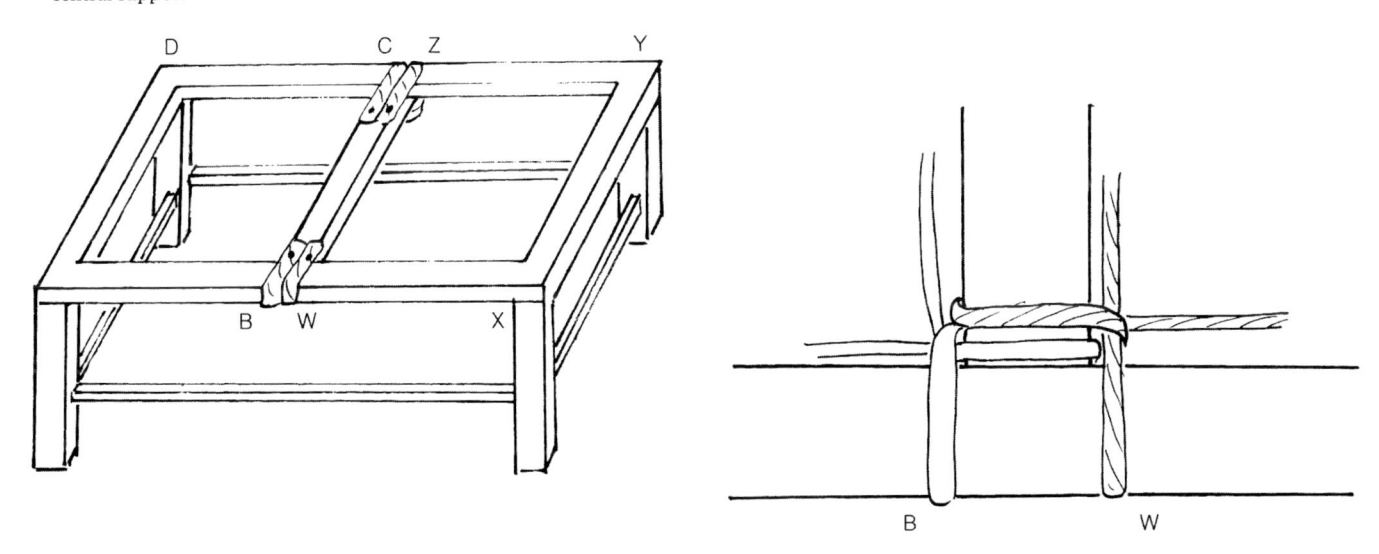

Fig 2.83 Working over shared support rail

Note: Where the coils cross the central rail, they must go down between the rail and the coil from the left-hand section. Keep them quite small (Fig. 2.83).

5. Continue to work complete rounds on each section in turn. All the coils which cross the central rail must go down between the rail and the interior coils which lie against it.
6. Continue until the separate sections are filled, leaving room for one more round on each.

Note: On each round, push the central section really tightly towards the front and back rails, to make room for the extra number of coils. Keep checking that the work is building up evenly.

TO FINISH

In order to make the coils over the central rail come alternately from each side, where the stool finishes in the centre, it is necessary to miss out the last corner, **Z**, on the final round on the right-hand section (see Fig. 2.82). If this is not done, there will be two coils from the right-hand section lying side by side over the centre of the central rail, which would spoil the pattern.

1. Complete the left hand section by finishing the final round over corner **D** as usual.
2. Complete the right hand section by finishing the final round over corner **Y**, and omit corner **Z** altogether.
3. Finish off both seats underneath.

Note: Adjust the size of the coils towards the end of the right hand section, to make sure that the omission of the final corner **Y** does not leave a gap.

STUFFING

It is much easier to stuff the seat after it is completed. Any overcrowding on the central rail can be worked down and ironed out after stuffing.

13. Straw-wrapped rush seating

Photo 2.21 Nineteenth-century chair with drop-in seat in straw-wrapped coils of crimson and gold

The fashion in England for rush seats with the coils overwrapped in straw seems to have started in the High Wycombe area, in the late nineteenth or early twentieth century. It was called 'straw matting', and was used as a way of adding colour and pattern to a rush seat. The coils of rush were overwrapped with split and flattened straw, which resulted in a hard, shiny surface, extremely resistant to wear. Sometimes the straws were used in their own natural golden colour; sometimes they were dyed in bright shades of blue, green or red. The coloured coils were alternated with natural straw for a striped pattern, and occasionally more than one colour was used on a coil, to give a striped barber's-pole effect.

This type of work was in general use in France, and a great many straw-seated chairs can be found there, particularly in churches. The split straw was wrapped over coils of fine rush or sedge, or over a coil of straw prepared in advance. Chairs are still seated by this method in France, where 'matters' can be seen at work in the market places of towns and villages. Today, however, many of them use an artificial coil, often coloured golden orange to resemble the colour of natural straw. I believe it is also possible to buy straw ready-dyed.

In England, straw seating is now done very rarely, but you may well have such a chair to restore, and it is worth taking the time and trouble to do it properly.

The aniline dyes which were originally used faded quite rapidly, and sometimes the only way to tell the colour of the straw is by looking underneath, where the ends can be seen protruding from the centre, and at the sides. The overwrapping extends from the top of the seat down over the rail, and for about 4 cm (1½ in) underneath.

The newly restored chair in the photograph is a lovely example, where the stripes of crimson and gold could clearly be seen on the edges of the drop-in seat, and underneath. The history of the chair is not known in detail, but if, as seems possible, it dates from the first half of the nineteenth century, it could well be French. If it is an English chair, then the striped seat may not have been the original one. Its owner was naturally anxious to have it restored to its stripes of crimson and gold, and by using modern dyes we were were able to match the colours almost exactly.

Materials

RUSHES

You need fairly fine rushes, as the straw adds considerably to the thickness of the coil, and the overall appearance must not be clumsy.

STRAW

Wheat seems to have been used in England in the early days, but I have used rye very successfully. It is extremely hard-wearing, and long stemmed. You can get the straw from a supplier of corn for corn dollies in order to get the long straw which you need. One of these sheaves should be sufficient for a chair.

DYES

Aniline commercial dyes came into use in the 1850s, and would have been used for this work originally, as they also were for the straw plaits used in the hat trade. I have experimented successfully with *Dylon*, which comes in a huge range of shades, and works very well on straw and cane. It is simple to obtain and use, but I have as yet no first-hand evidence on how the colours fade.

Preparation of straw

TRIMMING THE STRAW

You can use both the length of straw between the ear and the first joint, and the length between the first and second joints, depending on how long and how thick it is. Long straws are needed for the middle part of the seat, as the straw will only cover a coil of half its own length. The early straw matters appear to have used short lengths and joined them on the coil, but with long straws this should not be necessary. Too narrow a split straw makes it difficult to cover the coil; too wide and it will not coil so smoothly. A width of about 1 cm ($\frac{1}{3}$ in) at the wide end works well.

1. Go through the bundle, cutting off all the stems just above the first joint and slide off the leaf, or sheath.
2. Trim off all the ears, and put the stalks on one side.
3. Trim off all the first joints from the rest of the stalks, and then cut them all off above the second joint.

DYEING THE STRAW

Basic proportions for using *Dylon* are:
- 1 container of dye
- 1 tablespoon of salt
- 3 pints boiling water.

I use a long plastic plant trough, and make up two batches of dye at once, to give sufficient depth to cover the straws. Plunge the straws into the boiling dye and leave them there till the required depth of colour is reached. If it is not deep enough after an hour or so, repeat with a new dye-bath. If you can find a long metal container and boil the straw on the stove, it is easier to obtain darker shades.

Colours

Experiment carefully to get the colour you want. You can use a second dye-bath of a different colour, or mix two dyes in one batch, but keep a record of what you do, in case you need to repeat it. Red and green shades are not difficult to obtain, but there can be problems in getting a really dark blue, as the corn has a tendency to turn blue to green. Use dark shades in an extra strong mix. After dyeing, rinse the straw very thoroughly in cold water, till the water runs clear.

SPLITTING THE STRAW

The original English matters used their straw dry, but it is less likely to crack if it is mellowed. To do this, pour a kettle of boiling water over it and wrap it in a damp cloth for five minutes. Alternatively, soak it in cold water for ten minutes and wrap it in a damp cloth for half an hour.

Split each straw by running your thumbnail up it, and then open it out flat by pulling it between finger and thumb. You can flatten it still further by pulling it to and fro over the edge of the table. Keep it wrapped in a damp cloth to prevent it drying out while working.

Note: The dye may 'bleed' a little on the cloth. Try not to damp more straw than you need for a work session, although it can be dried out and re-damped successfully.

Method for overwrapping rush coils with straw

First select the longest straws and put them to one side for the later stages, where the coils are longer. Decide whether it is to be an arrowhead or straight across finish.

1. Start the rush coil as usual and coil enough to go over the front rail.
2. Still holding the end of the coil, undo a small area of twist a little way back from the corner, or make a hole in it with a pointed tool (Fig. 2.84a).
3. Tuck the narrow, tip end of a straw into this hole, and wrap it closely round the coil, shiny side outwards, and slanting towards the front of the chair, in the same direction as the coil (Fig. 2.84b).

Fig 2.84a Straw-wrapped coil, step 2

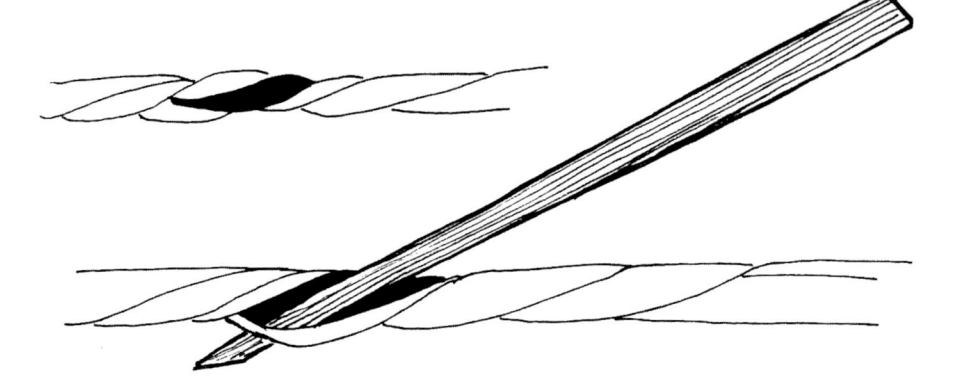

Fig 2.84b Step 3

Fig 2.84c Steps 4 and 5

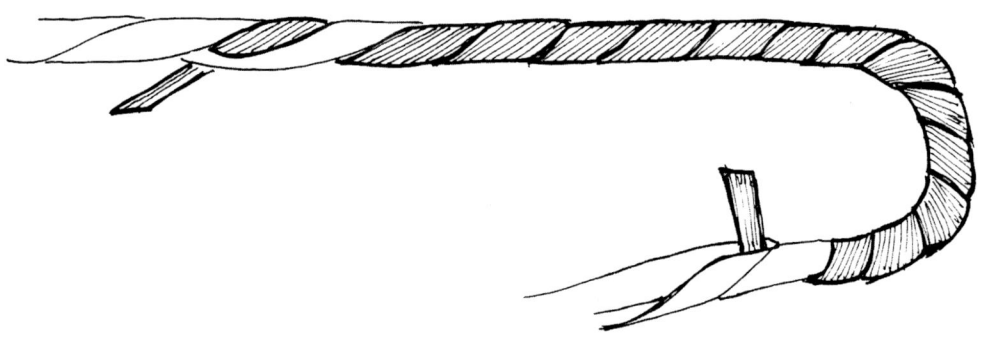

Fig 2.85a Second half of corner, straight across finish

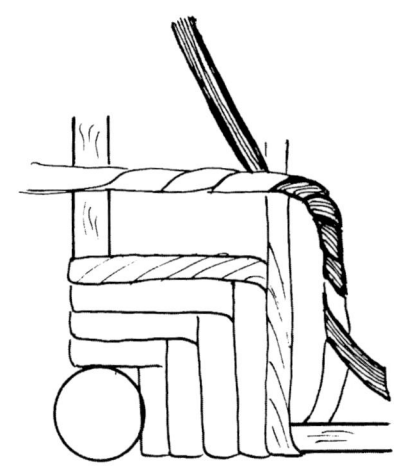

Fig 2.85b Second half of corner, arrowhead finish

4. Overwrap enough of the coil to go over the front rail, down the side, and underneath for about 4 cm (1½ in). The coil must be completely covered by the straw.
5. Trap the end of the straw between the rushes in the coil, and leave it sticking out under the chair (Fig. 2.84c).
6. Bring the coil up in the centre, and twist enough to go over the left side rail.
7. Make a hole to secure the tip of a new straw, or simply wrap the tip around the coil, well before it emerges in the centre.
   Note: For a straight across finish, coil and wrap towards the corner (Fig. 2.85a). For an arrowhead finish, coil and wrap away from the corner (Fig. 2.85b).
8. Overwrap enough of the coil to go over the side rail and under the seat.
   Note: The coil must be completely hidden, and must not show through where the right angle forms, so push the straw wrap down the coil if necessary.
9. Trap the end of the straw between the rushes in the coil and leave it sticking out under the seat.
10. Take the coil across to the opposite rail, and repeat steps 2 to 9.
11. Work round the chair in this way, doubling if necessary.
    Note: On the first two rounds, the straws may be long enough to complete both halves of the corner with a single straw.

Fig 2.86 Wrapping the coil

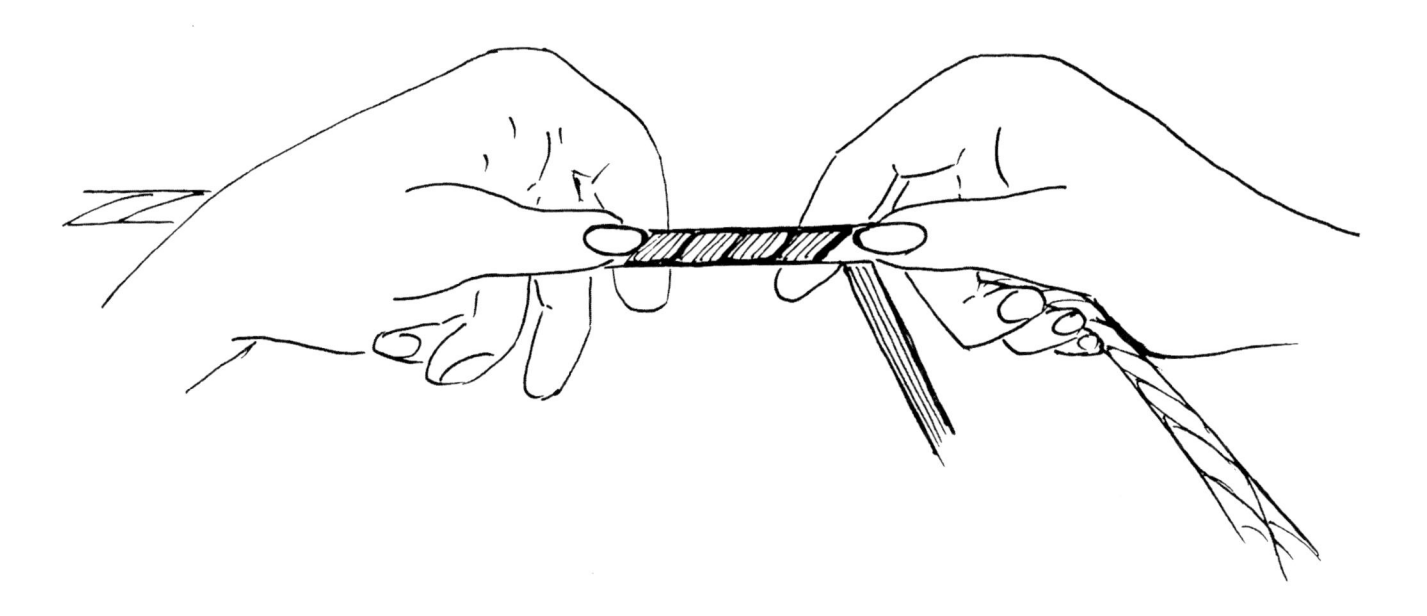

POINTS FOR A SUCCESSFUL FINISH
The work must be very tight. Tension, smoothness and even working are vital. The rush coil has a tendency to unwind as you wrap the straw over it. Hold it securely with your middle, ring, and little fingers, while forefinger and thumb work with the fingers of your other hand to manipulate the straw (Fig. 2.86). Trim off or tuck away any long ends of straw under the seat.

STRIPED PATTERNS
If you are using a striped pattern of two colours, you must decide whether or not you want to have two coils of the same colour in the centre of the rails. (A final complete round on a square seat would give this effect on each rail). If you want the stripes to alternate throughout, you must do a little cheating with the coiling sequence. This will not show if the colour pattern works out right.

For a square seat
Make sure the coils are tightly packed. Then, on the last round:

1. Coil over the front rail.
2. Over the left side rail.
3. Over the right side rail.
4. Coil over the back rail, and knot off underneath.
   Note: After step 3, come up behind the coil you have just laid in place before going over the back rail. This is where the cheating comes in, and if you do it neatly it will be very unobtrusive.

For rectangular or trapezium shapes
For alternate stripes throughout, on the last round before closing up the side rails do the 'extra wrap' method on page 83, using the correct colour. Make sure you finish the bridge with the correct colour stripe.

BARBER'S POLE STRIPES
These are a little more difficult to handle, as two or three straws are used at once on a single coil. Use narrower straws to make the wrapping easier, and insert them all at once, keeping them in the correct order throughout.
Note: These multi-stripes were generally only used on an occasional coil on the seat, to add interest to the pattern.

FRENCH METHODS AND PATTERNS
A great many different patterns of coiling are found in France, and that shown in Photo 2.8 and described on page 91 is just one example. There are also many different methods of wrapping. Some chairs are worked with an unwrapped straw coil. Some have the coil overwrapped with straw. Sometimes the coil is twisted and wrapped in long lengths before it is laid round the chair frame. None of the core shows at all. When the end of each split straw is reached, it is tucked down between the straws or rushes in the coil, and a new piece is inserted in the same place. With this method the core is not always twisted: sometimes it is left straight. The English method, described above, is also used.

The synthetic coil now in use has the appearance of a straw-wrapped coil.

14. Orkney chairs

Photo 2.22 Child's Orkney chair, with drop-in seat in rush. The top rows of straw have been restored

These chairs, unique to the islands of Orkney, use a very simple design, evolved centuries ago to make use of inexpensive and locally available materials. Modern versions are still made using traditional techniques.

In its earliest form, the Orkney chair was a low circular stool, covered with straw, and without a back. This developed into a low chair with a straw back and a circular seat, still covered in straw. Later still, a hood was sometimes added to give greater protection from draughts.

At about the end of the eighteenth century, when imported timber became more readily available, the chairs were made square with wooden seats. Straw coil attached to wooden uprights formed a comfortable curved back. In very old chairs, the size and shape depended on the materials available, and the skill of the worker to make the best use of what he had. Towards the end of the nineteenth century, the design became more standardised as the chairs were produced commercially. Sometimes the chairs also had wooden drawers beneath the seat.

The traditional materials were oat straw for the coiled back, (less brittle than wheat and easier to bend) and 'bent', a type of long grass twisted into thin rope for stitching the coils. (Sisal string is now used for this.) A thinner, harder twine is used for tying the coils to the uprights.

Until about 1920 wooden seats were still common. The first inset seats were originally seated in *coyer* (or *coir*), a coarse brown cord. Seagrass is now used for the seats, but the child's chair shown is seated with rush. Modern chairs are sometimes stitched with chair cane.

The modern chair seater may face the task of repairing an Orkney chair with some of the rows of straw coil broken away. It will therefore be helpful to look at the way in which the chairs were made.

Construction

The wooden chair frame has two uprights, one on each side. These are placed about 12.5 cm (5 in) from the back of the seat, and are about 90 cm (35 in) tall. The coils are tied to these, and the arms protrude from them, supported by two shorter uprights at the front of the seat. The main uprights have a groove at the back to take the straw coil. Holes are drilled through the back of the uprights 1.2 cm ($\frac{1}{2}$ in) in from the edge, and about 2.7 cm ($1\frac{1}{8}$ in) apart. The holes are about 4 mm ($\frac{1}{8}$ in) in diameter, with grooves on both sides running to the edge of the upright. The holes are stepped, with one side starting about 1.4 cm ($\frac{5}{8}$ in) up from the bottom, and the other 2.7 cm ($1\frac{1}{8}$ in) up (Fig. 2.87).

The rows of straw coil are stitched one above the other with sisal, to build up the back. They run from one side of the chair back to the other, are tied in with twine through the holes in the upright, and then bent over to run back to the other side. The topmost row is completely bound with sisal to form a rigid edge. The back is given a curve to fit the human back, and the hood, if there is one, should be a continuation of the back, with the rows of straw going in the same direction as before, straight across. However, today some chairs are made with the hood coils running in semicircles from the top of the chair, fanning out as the work progresses (see Fig. 2.88a and b).

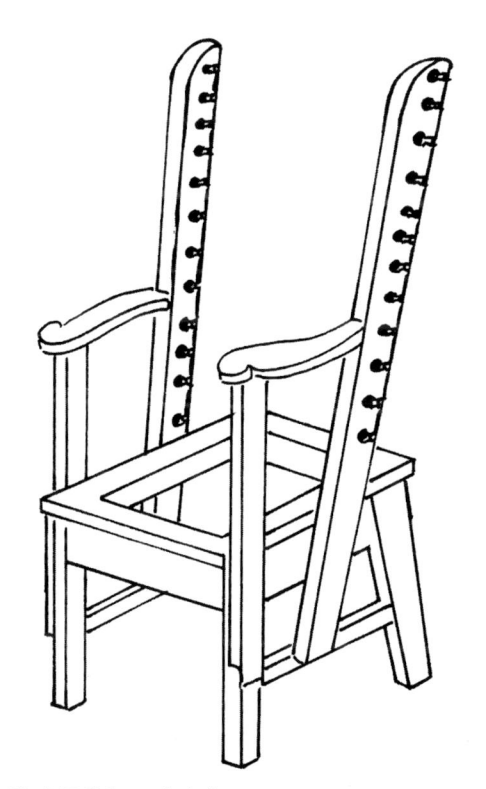

Fig 2.87 Orkney chair frame

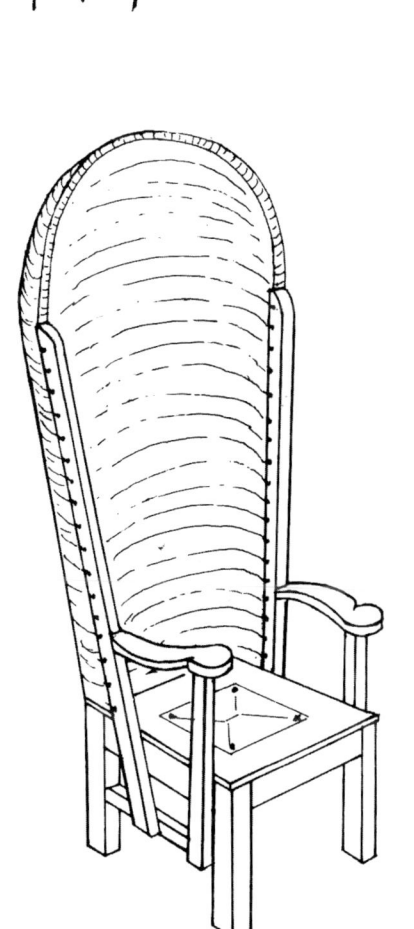

Fig 2.88 Orkney chairs with hoods

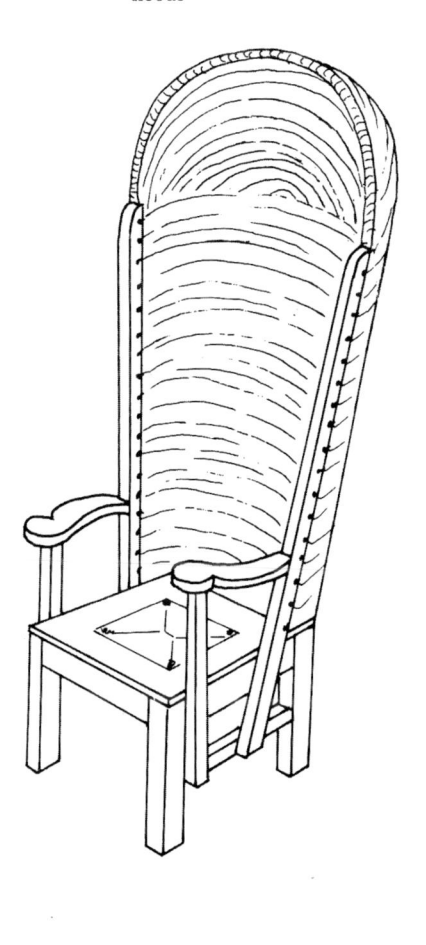

Basic stitching techniques

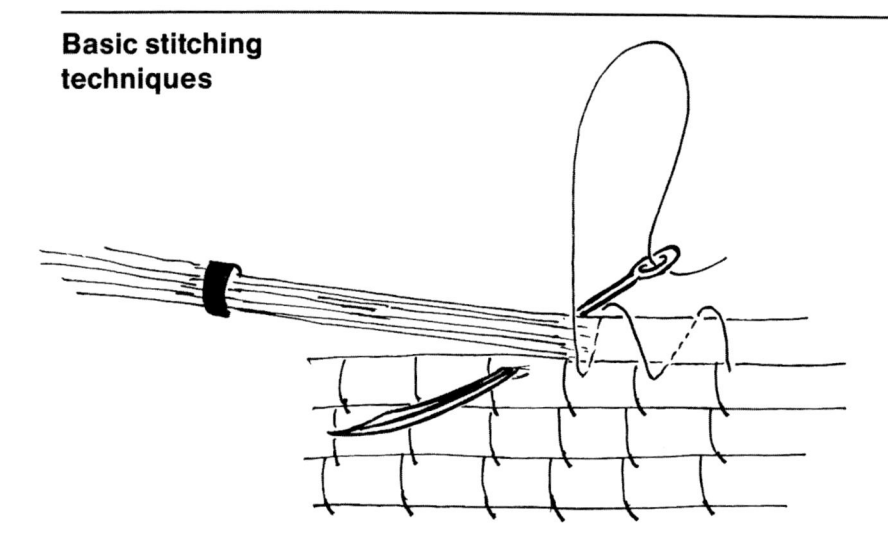

Fig 2.89 Method of stitching straw coils

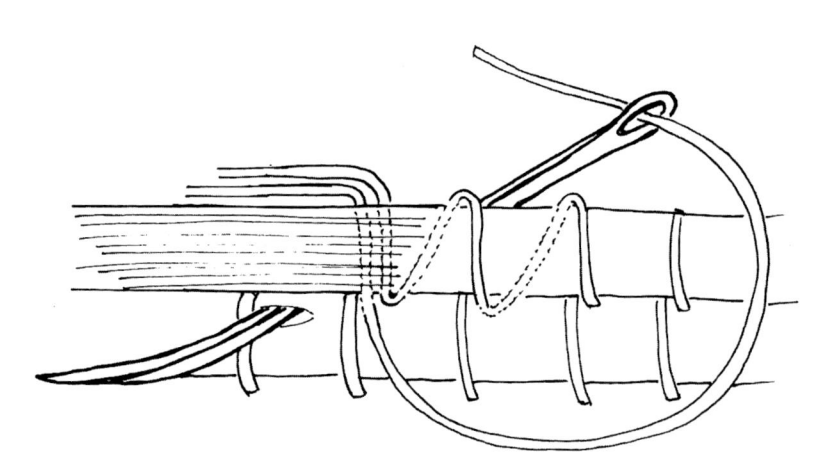

Fig 2.90 Joining in a new piece of sisal

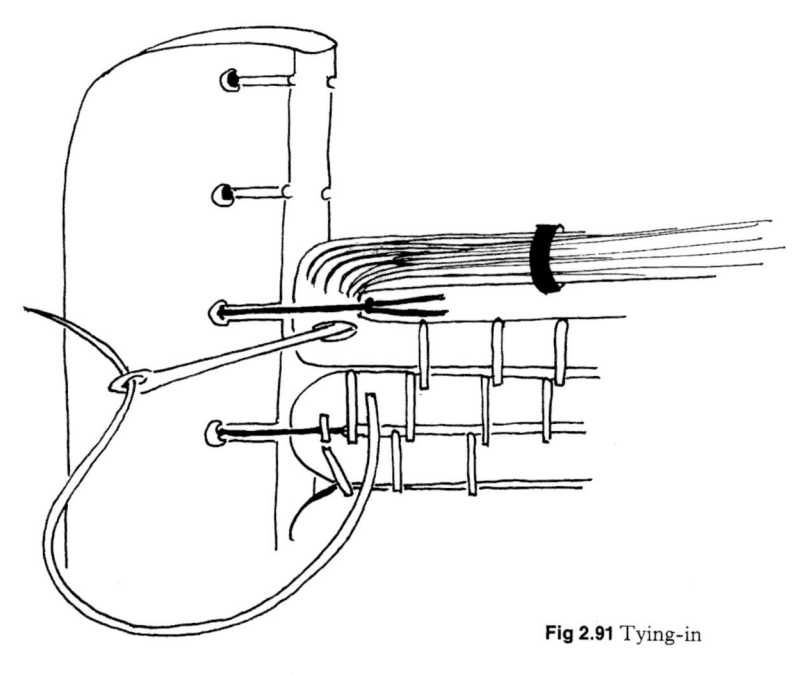

Fig 2.91 Tying-in

STITCHING THE COILS

The stitches are worked from right to left, about 1.5 cm (½ in) apart. They should be almost vertical. The needle goes through horizontally, taking in about a quarter of the thickness of the row below, but does not go through the top of the stitch on that row. Stitching is done alternately from the inside and outside of the chair, with the needle going in from the opposite side, and out towards the worker (Fig. 2.89).

TO JOIN THE SISAL (Fig. 2.90)

1. After completing a stitch, push the needle upwards through the centre of the coil, just in front of the last stitch. Leave a tail of about 15 cm (6 in), and pull tight.
2. With a new length of sisal, put in a stitch from the far side in exactly the same place as the last stitch, leaving a 15 cm (6 in) tail.
3. Put the tail up through the centre of the new coil with the old one.
4. Lay both tails flat and stitch over them with the new length of sisal. If done carefully, this does not show at all.

TYING IN (Fig. 2.91)

When the coil reaches the upright, it is bent upwards and tied securely with thin twine through the hole in the upright before being bent over to make the next row.

1. Complete the last stitch of the row and leave the needle hanging.
2. Thread a length of twine through the hole and tie it round the coil, using a slip knot pulled tight. Cut off the twine, leaving ends about 5 cm (2 in) long to be covered by the next row.
3. Bend the coil over.
4. Push the needle through the bottom coil below the tying-in string, and pull the sisal through.
5. From the other side, push the needle back through the coil, above the tying-in twine. Pull tight.
6. Push the needle through the bottom coil again below the tying-in twine, and pull tight.

The needle and sisal are now on the other side of the work, ready for you to reverse the chair and continue working the next row from right to left.

Note: An alternative method of tying in the sides can be found on page 117.

SHAPING

To make the back 'drop out', (curve outwards for the shoulders), the needle is put in at an angle, instead of horizontally. When working from the outside of the chair, the needle slopes downwards from the inside. When working on the inside, the needle slopes upwards from the outside. This sets each row slightly outside the one below.

Some workers use wooden moulds or templates to shape the back accurately, while others work without any aids to shaping. In repair work, it is not difficult to follow the shape set by the original maker.

To work a complete chair back, without a hood

You will need
4 or 5 sheaves of straw for a whole back, depending on size. If the sheaves are really large, one or two will be sufficient. Use oat straw if this is available; otherwise wheat or rye will work.
Tying in twine (hard string thin enough to go through the holes)
Sisal string (for stitching the coils)
Sacking needle
Broad-headed tacks, about 2.5 cm (1 in) long (for securing the bottom coil)
Hammer
Gauge for the coil (a brass ring, short length of pipe, or plastic funnel about 1.5 cm ($\frac{5}{8}$ in) diameter)

Prepare the straw by cutting off the ears and stripping off all the leaves. The full length of the straw is used (the joints help to stiffen the work). It is used dry.

BOTTOM COIL

1. Take enough straw, butt ends together, to fill the ring tightly, and with a good length of sisal make a clove hitch really close to the butt ends, leaving an 8 cm (3 in) tail. Pull tight (Fig. 2.92).
2. Turn the coil of straw with your left hand in a clockwise direction, so the sisal winds tightly round it, the wraps about 1.3 cm ($\frac{1}{2}$ in) apart. Make a coil long enough to go round the back of the seat, feeding in new straws by the butt. Conceal the tail of string in the coil.
   Note: Push new straws through the gauge into the centre of the coils, so that the ends do not show. Slide the gauge along as you work.
3. Nail the coil down on the back of the seat, butting the end right into the groove, and placing the tacks about 2.5 cm (1 in) apart. Make well defined angles on the corners.
   Note: Start at the side where the bottom hole in the upright is slightly higher.
4. Place the last nail close to the upright. Bend the coil upwards and tie in as described above, steps 1 to 3.
5. Make sure the sisal is lying in the correct position to complete steps 4 to 6 of *Tying in*. It should lie between the coil and the wooden frame.
   Note: If you nail the first coil from left to right, looking down on the chair from the front, then the second row will be worked from the front (the inside); if you nail from right to left, work the second row from the outside. That is, with you on the outside.

Remember all stitches are made towards you.

BUILDING UP THE BACK
Work about 13 or 14 rows, or about one third of the height of the back. The stitches must all follow the same pattern, and the angles on the corners should be well defined.

DROPPING OUT (Fig. 2.93)
Start to make the back drop out when you are working a row from the outside, slanting the needle downwards as described in *Shaping*. The needle slants up for the inside row.

Keep the back dropping out gradually until you reach the top of the uprights and only one hole remains unused.

Note: You may need to increase the number of stitches as the back gets wider, and the stitch pattern must be maintained as you do this. The curve should be gradual.

Fig 2.93 'Dropping out' the back

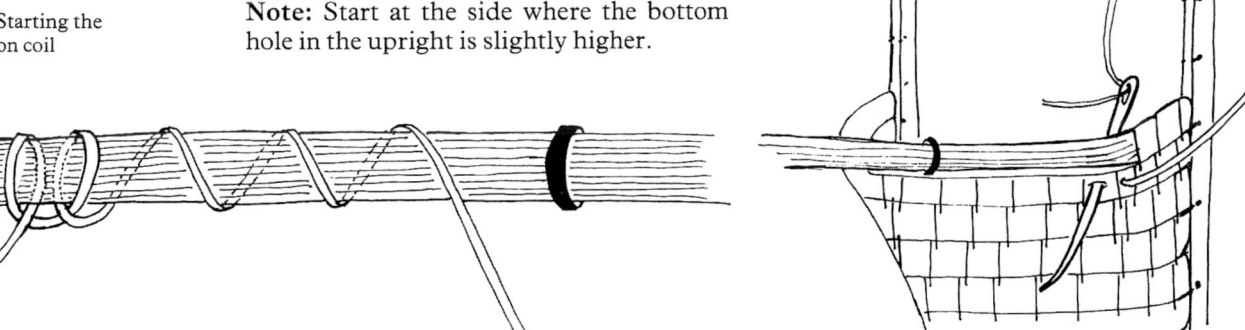

Fig 2.92 Starting the foundation coil

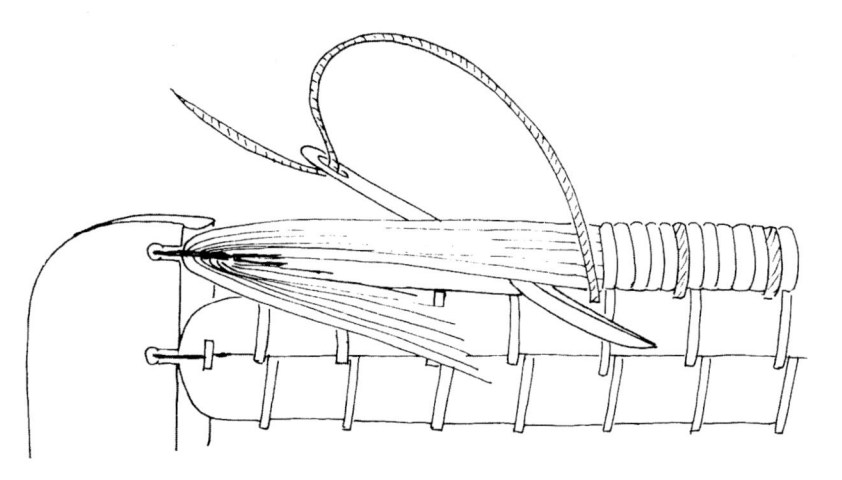

Fig 2.94 Finishing the top row

TOP ROW (Fig. 2.94)
This is reached when there is only one hole left unused, on one of the uprights. It is completely bound with sisal to make a rigid edge.

1. As you start the last row, wrap the coil several times between each stitch, pulling wraps and stitches really tight. Try to keep the number of wraps between stitches consistent, but the coil must be covered.
2. When you get within 18 cm (7 in) of the final hole, thin out the coil a little, and bend it over with the tips underneath. Butt the fold tightly against the upright, and tie it in, tucking the cut ends of twine into the coil.
3. Trim off the tips so that you can do the final stitches and wraps treating the doubled-over ends as part of the coil.
4. Pull the sisal through a couple of coils to secure it, and cut it off.
5. Trim off any visible ends of sisal or straw.

HOODED CHAIRS (These instructions are for Fig. 2.88a)
These are constructed in a similar way, but with taller uprights. The uprights have holes drilled vertically in the top to take the semi-circle of stout wire which will form the edge of the hood.

1. Work as for the hoodless chair until you reach the top of the uprights.
2. Push the wire semi-circle into the holes.
3. At the end of the next row, tie-in on the wire, using the same sisal with which you are stitching the coils.
4. Work straight for a few rows, tying in on the wire.
5. Begin to 'drop in' for the curve of the hood, angling the needle downwards towards the inside of the hood, and upwards towards the outside.

Note: The rows get shorter and shorter until you finish in the centre.

Stitched edge
This is a coil of straw stitched to the wire and the rows of straw. It is completely bound with sisal.

1. Using the ring gauge to keep the size, start by attaching a coil of straw to the outside of the right-hand upright. You could start by folding a thinner coil in half to give you something to stitch to, or simply by stitching several times over the end of the coil.
2. Stitch this coil to the wire over the tie-ins. Stitch over coil, wire, and through the tie-ins for several stitches, then just over the coil and the wire for several stitches.
3. Continue round the hood in this way, keeping the number of stitches in the blocks the same throughout.
4. Taper off the coil to finish as in the hoodless chair. Alternatively, simply cut off the ends of straw when you reach the left-hand upright, and stitch over the cut ends.

Repairs to Orkney chairs

It is very seldom that you will have to repair a complete back; it is much more likely that some of the rows along the top will be broken away, and the seat may need re-doing. The child's version in the photograph has had two or three top rows replaced, and the seat done in rush, instead of seagrass.

Although the straw is worked dry when new, an old chair is rather brittle and fragile where it is already damaged, and it might be best to damp it down with a spray bottle before beginning the unpicking. I always do this. Take careful note of the materials and techniques used, and match them up as well as you can. You may find the tying-in has been done with continuous lengths of twine running from hole to hole (see page 117 and Fig. 2.96). One chair I saw, which was stitched with chair cane, definitely had each stitch going through the loop of the one below.

The new coils can be stained with wood dye to blend with the old work. A supplier of straw for corn dolly makers should be able to provide the straw. If you cannot get oats, then use wheat or rye (see list of suppliers at the end of this book).

TO START THE REPAIRS
1. Damp down the broken portions.
2. Unpick until you reach a point where you have a sound lower coil, and a length of top coil which can be built up successfully with new straw.
3. If any ties are broken lower down than this, replace them and thread the ends of twine away into the coils with a needle.
4. Join in a new length of sisal as described on page 114.
5. Push new straws into the old coil to build it up. Work as described above until the top is

reached, and put on the final row.

Note: While you are still stitching into the old lower row, try and use the original holes to avoid breaking up the straw.

BROKEN STITCHES

You may find broken stitches on otherwise sound parts of the chair. If there are just one or two of these, they are best left alone. Where there is a big patch, however, particularly where the chair may have rubbed against a wall, they must be replaced.

1. Spray to dampen damaged portions.
2. Pick out any broken stitches.
3. Start by drawing the end of the sisal through a coil, leaving a tail (this is trimmed off later).
4. Re-stitch the area, matching the existing work carefully. If you get out of line it will show up badly.
5. Fasten off by drawing the sisal through a coil, pulling tight, and cutting off the ends.
6. Allow to dry well before colouring. Use a fine paintbrush for this.

CHAIR CANE STITCHING

Some modern chairs are stitched with chair cane, about No. 3 size. Dampen the cane slightly before use to make it easier to handle. Use it shiny side outwards, and join in new lengths as follows:

1. Complete a stitch and leave the end hanging down.
2. Slip the short end of a new length through in the same place, to the other side of the chair.
3. Fold both these ends over the lower row, and under the top one, in opposite directions (Fig. 2.95).
4. Make a stitch with the new length of cane. This holds the short ends in place, and they can be trimmed off later.

COLOURING REPAIRS

Wood dyes work well, but because of the way both sisal and straw absorb the dye, you have only one chance to get the right colour. It won't alter much with subsequent coats. Experiment on samples until you are satisfied. The sisal will soak up the dye quicker than the straw. Put on one coat, using cloth, sponge, or brush, and allow to dry. Put on a second coat, extending it slightly over the older portion to merge the join.

Note: If the chairback is dirty and dusty, give it a gentle clean first with water and a brush. Allow the straw to dry before colouring.

Sometimes a very shabby-looking back can be refreshed by including the whole surface in the final coat of stain, but not too heavy! The result must not look artificially new.

AN ALTERNATIVE METHOD OF TYING IN THE SIDES (Fig. 2.96)

This is done with a continuous length of twine on each side of the chair. A needle small enough to go through the holes and large enough to take the twine will speed up the work.

1. Take 2 lengths of twine at least twice the lengths of the upright, and thread one through each of the bottom holes on the uprights. Tie a knot leaving a long end, and a short end of about 12 cm (5 in).
2. For the bottom hole, tie in the coils as described on page 114, leaving the short end of twine to be covered by the next row. Bring the long end out between the old and new coils.
3. For subsequent holes, take the twine up and over the coil above it, and bring it back through the new fold.
4. Pass the twine through the hole, and back round the new fold again. Pull it tight as you bend the new coil down over it.
5. Leave the twine hanging for the next tie-in (Fig. 2.96).
6. On the final hole, tie a knot and thread the ends away into the coils.

Note: The tying-in twine must be kept very tight throughout, so you can knot it through itself inside the fold at step 4, or pass it twice through the holes in the frame.

HOODS

Hooded Orkney chairs are less common, and as the top edge is worked over stout wire, it is less likely to break up than the top of a hoodless chair. If you need to repair one, look very carefully at its construction, and try to copy it.

See page 116 for working the hood.

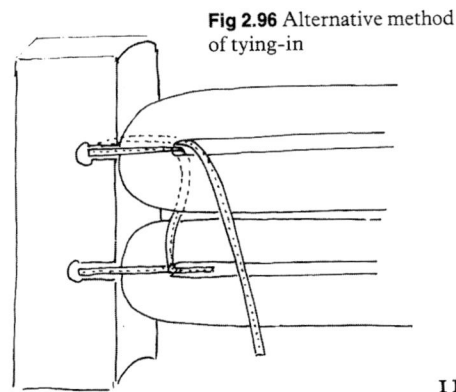

Fig 2.95 Joining chair cane

Fig 2.96 Alternative method of tying-in

15. Irish straw rope chairs

Photo 2.23 Irish hay rope chair showing restored coil

In Ireland very simple chairs seated with a rope twisted from straw, hay, or rye grass have been made since the eighteenth century. The frames were made with whatever wood was available, and had round or squared-off legs and back pillars, with round rails and stretcher bars. The joints were simple wedge-dowel, and the frames were often painted for protection.

The straw rope, or *súgán*, was made using a 'thraw-hook', (Fig. 2.97a). This was made of heavy wire or metal, with two loose wooden circular handles, which allowed the hook to be rotated with two hands. In England such ropes were used to hold down thatch, to tie bales of hay and straw and to secure loads, and the hook was called a 'whimmer' or 'whimble'. I have a very simple version, made for me by a farm worker out of hazel cut and bent into shape while green. It is fitted into a whittled socket bound with twine. The hook rotates in the socket, which is strapped to the waist on a belt (Fig. 2.97b). As late as 1970 straw ropes were being made by machine for a variety of uses, sometimes strengthened with a nylon thread.

The chair in the photo is probably eighteenth century, and has a seat made of rye grass. The frame has been stained and polished, but traces of green paint can be seen in the corners, and on the rope near the legs. Only a few coils needed replacing, and I was able to obtain rye grass for the purpose.

Fig 2.97a Thraw-hook or whimble

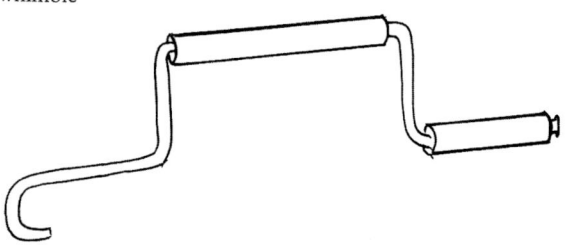

Fig 2.97b Hazel-twig whimble

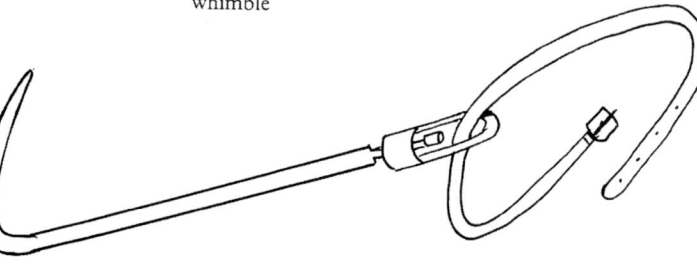

Photo 2.24 Close-up view of Hay Rope chair

To make the rope

Two people are needed, and the material is worked dry. Long, supple straw works best. The worker with the hook walks backwards, away from the other worker who stands still beside the bundle of straw, ready to feed it onto the hook.

1. A handful of straw is looped over the hook.
2. The worker with the hook walks backwards, twisting it as he goes. The second worker holds the rope that begins to form with one hand, and with the other feeds a handful of straw into the twist.
3. The second worker keeps a tension on the rope, and allows the twist to run through his hand as he feeds in the new straw with the other. It takes practice to produce an even rope of the required size.
4. As the rope becomes long and heavy, it must be kept clear of the ground so that the twist can keep running down its length.
5. When the rope is completed, wind it into a bundle to prevent the twist coming undone. (This can happen easily as there is only one twist, not two as in a ply yarn.)

Note: Keep the straw lying straight in the bundle, and feed in small quantities at a time. Feed in well behind the twist, so that the ends of the straws are included in the twist, and not left sticking out.

Method of seating the chair

The rope is wound on the frame in a very simple pattern. It is wound right round the frame from side to side, and then right round the frame from front to back over the top of the previous work. If the rope has to be joined, it is done by tucking the short ends into the previous work.

Note: The making of these chairs was a domestic task, done at harvest time. They were not expected to wear for many seasons. The winding of the rope on the frame was not done to any set pattern, and several variations can be found.

For a chair seat about 33×38 cm (13×15 in), about 30 m (33 yds) of rope will be needed. This will mean several joins in the work.

Fig 2.98a First layer of hay rope in progress

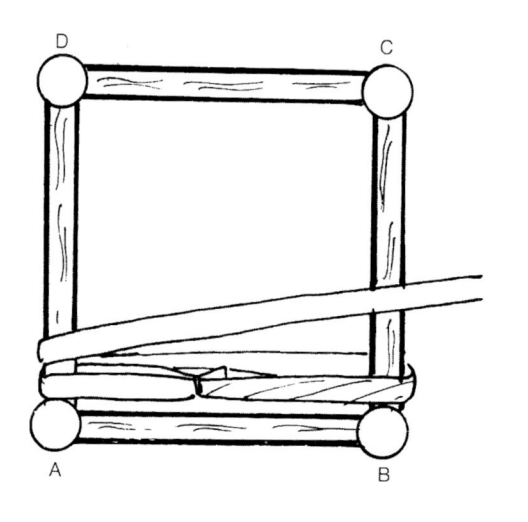

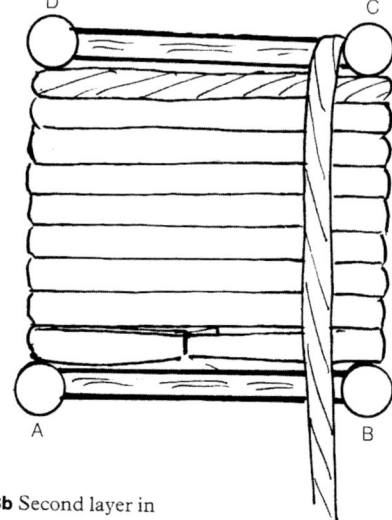

Fig 2.98b Second layer in progress

FOR A SQUARE SEAT

1. Loop the rope around the left side bar at **A**, and tie the short end to the long end to secure it. Make this knot halfway between **A** and **B**.
2. Lay the rope over the opposite side rail at **B**, under the frame, and back under the side rail at **A**.
3. Bring it up over the side rail from the outside, and back over the opposite side rail (Fig. 2.98a).
4. Continue to wrap the rope right round the frame over the side rails, filling them with closely packed coils until the back of the chair is reached, finishing over the right side rail at **C**.
   Note: Keep the rope at tension as you lay it on, to prevent it coming untwisted. Keep the joins on the underside, and in the centre of the seat, using soft string to knot it if you cannot make it secure without.
5. Take the last coil under the side rail, inside the leg, and up over the back rail from the outside at **C** (or start a new coil).
6. Bring the coil over the front rail at **B**, and underneath to **C** again.
7. Continue to wrap right round the frame, filling in the front and back rails with closely packed coils, until you reach the left side.
8. Finish over the front rail at **A**, and tuck the end in underneath.
   Note: Keep all joins underneath the chair. Tuck short ends into the previous work. The seat is not stuffed.

FOR A TRAPEZIUM SEAT

Mark the extra space on each end of the front rail, and simply leave this empty, as in the photograph.

Note: Sometimes a row of backstitches over several coils is made underneath, to hold the coils in place.

16.
Using artificial rush

There are a number of different types of artificial or fibre rush on the market, made of twisted paper and coloured to look like rush. It is an expensive material to buy in a craft shop, but if bought wholesale costs about the same per chair as rush. It is quicker to use, which cuts down the cost of the work, making it a cheap alternative to the real thing. It does not really look like rush, and would not be right for a chair of any quality, but for café, cheap kitchen or playroom chairs, it wears well. A coat of button polish or matt varnish will darken it a little and tone down the artificial appearance. It comes in several thicknesses.

It can be used in the same patterns as rush, but of course does not have to be joined nearly so often, and is laid straight on without any further twisting. It can be used dry or damp, but I find it best just to dip the ball in water and shake off any excess. This will dampen it enough to make it easy to handle and to pull really tight.

The size of the ball or spool with which you work is governed by the size of the gap between the stretcher bars and the seat rail. Use as big a ball as you can. If you are winding it on a spool or batten of wood take care not to let it either over-twist or undo itself. This also applies when working the chair.

Photo 2.25 Pine kitchen chair seated in artificial rush

Method

1. Knot the end of the coil and nail the knot to the inside of the left side rail. You could use string or a staple.
2. Wrap the coil round the chairframe in the usual sequence, pulling it very tight indeed, and packing the coils close to the corners.
   Note: If you find it easier, lay several complete rounds loosely on the chair, then go back and tighten up each corner in turn.
3. Repeat this sequence throughout, joining when necessary (see below).
4. Make all joins under the seat.
5. In the final stages, use as long a length of coil as you can, to have as few joins as possible in the centre.
6. Finish with a final knot.
   Note: To join synthetic rush, you can use a reef knot, but a much neater join can be made with a twist tie or a piece of wire or fine twine. If the short ends are turned upwards out of sight, the join can hardly be seen.

DOUBLING FOR A TRAPEZIUM SHAPE

Method 1
Use the front corners only method described on page 86, tying each separate length to the side rails with string, or fastening it with staples or tacks. A knot on each end of the piece of rush will stop it slipping.

Method 2
Use the repeated front corners method on pages 84 and 85, working round each front corner twice before going on to the next. Do this on alternate rounds.

STUFFING
You can do this as you go along, or at the end. If you press the coils really close together as you work, it should be possible to stuff with newspaper, brown paper, or even rags, without the stuffing showing through the coils on the underside. Many prefer to use corrugated cardboard, or ordinary thin card. Cut the material into triangles with the points cut off, and slip the pieces into place as you work the chair. The triangles should fit the pockets under the chair. Build up several layers (Fig. 2.99).

CONTINENTAL PATTERNS
These work very well in artificial rush, and can be used on rectangular or trapezium shapes. It should be possible to use artificial rush in any situation where you would use the real thing.

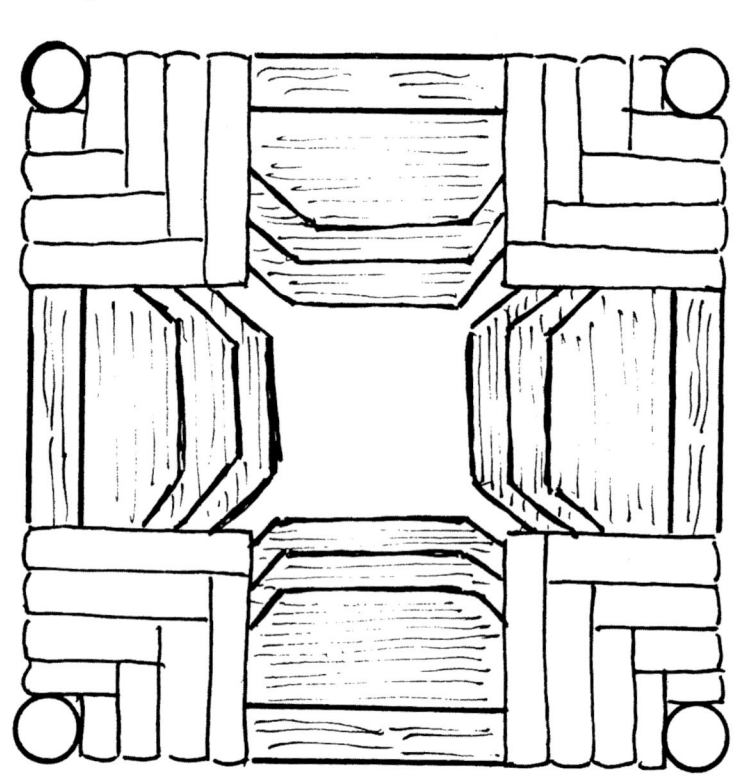

Fig 2.99 Stuffing an artificial rush seat with cardboard

Part III

WILLOW, CLOSE CANING AND CORDS

Willow seating   **124**
Whole willow seating   **126**
Skeined willow chairs   **137**
Close skeining   **140**
Open-skeined seats   **158**
Close caning   **168**
Danish cord chairs   **173**
Stools and seats in seagrass and cord   **177**

Mary Butcher

17. Willow seating

Willow and its preparation

The best willow for seating is *Salix triandra*, the almond-leaved willow. It is grown in Somerset as a commercial crop and can be bought in bundles, called bolts (see front cover), from a number of growers. Some addresses of growers are given on page 190. The bolts are usually made up of rods all of the same length but some growers now sell mixed bundles which might be useful for seating.

GROWTH AND PROCESSING

For more than a century willow for basket-making has been grown commercially in Somerset and Nottinghamshire. A willow bed is created by planting cuttings of about pencil thickness and about 23 cm (9 in) long. These are pushed into cleared ground in February. They are spaced 36 cm (14 in) apart one way and 70 cm (28 in) the other way. Each cutting produces a large number of shoots in late spring and these grow very quickly, as much as 2.5 cm (1 in) a day in warm, moist conditions, and can reach up to 2.5 m (8 feet) in a season. It is these one-year unbranched growths which are cut off close to their stumps when the sap is down, between November and March. Today much of the harvesting is by machine but traditionally growers used a bill hook, which, although it was slower, left the stumps more cleanly cut.

The crop is small for the first two or three years and the ground must be kept well weeded as willows respond badly to competition. As the crop increases, however, the shade produced inhibits weed growth. As they are susceptible to a number of pests and diseases, willows must be sprayed frequently throughout the summer. Willow plantations may last up to fifty years with regular cutting and the stumps gradually thicken to form a wide surface just above ground level. It is from this that the yearly growth emerges.

Two colours of willow are suitable for seating.

1. Buff willow

This is willow that has been cut and bundled, and then boiled for some hours in huge tanks. During this boiling, tannin from the bark penetrates the rod and dyes it a pale rusty brown. The bark is then peeled off.

For chairs woven of whole willow rods six foots and four foots would be needed. Skeins for close woven willow seats are made from six foots, or occasionally seven foots.

2. White willow

This has had the bark peeled without boiling the rods. It is a more labour-intensive process than peeling boiled bark, and so white willow is more expensive. Skein chairs are seated in white willow, although these darken with age to a deep honey colour, almost like a pale buff. Fine six foots are the best rods for making skeins. Whole white willow can be used for seating and looks very beautiful.

Before the bark can be removed to produce white rods the willow must be treated in one of two ways:

(a) part of the crop is left uncut until a short period in spring when the rising sap loosens the bark so that it can then be peeled.
(b) part of the crop is cut earlier, in autumn or winter, and stood in pits containing about 15 cm (6 in) of water. In spring, when the rods produce leaves, they can be peeled. This second method, 'pitting', means the rods do not all have to be peeled at the same time.

The peeling used to be done by pulling the rods through a pair of sprung metal arms called a 'brake'. (In willow-growing areas schools had holidays at this time so families could help.) Today, most white stuff is peeled using a mechanical peeler, a revolving drum with rotating blades into which first one end, and then the other, of a bunch of rods is pushed.

Fig 3.1 A willow rod
Two rods slyped in different ways

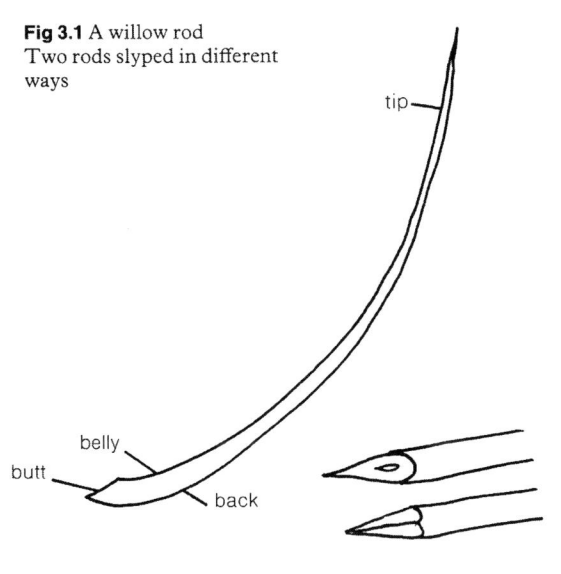

willow and with the temperature of the water. Cold water is best.

Soaking times

Length in feet	Time in hours
3	$\frac{1}{2}$–1
4	1–1$\frac{1}{2}$
5	1$\frac{1}{2}$–2
6	2–3
thick sticks	10–12

After soaking, the willow should be wrapped in a damp cloth and left for several hours to soften and mellow. Leave it in a cool place. The willow can be kept wet for one or two days in cool conditions, but after that it must be dried out. It can be resoaked for later use. If the surface becomes greasy from being damp for too long the willow can be washed in cold water and wiped.

Willow for skeining does not need to be soaked. The willow may be split when dry, after which it need only be dipped for processing further.

ROD STRUCTURE

Each rod has a natural curve, the outside of which is called the 'back' and the inside the 'belly'. The thick end is called the 'butt', and the thin end the 'tip' (Fig. 3.1).

PREPARATION OF THE WILLOW

Dry willow is brittle and will crack when bent, so it must be soaked before use. Soaking times vary with the length and thickness of the

PREPARATION OF THE CHAIR

All work on the chair frame, such as treating woodworm, mending rails, stripping and polishing, must be carried out before the seating is started. It is impossible to do a good job afterwards.

Tools

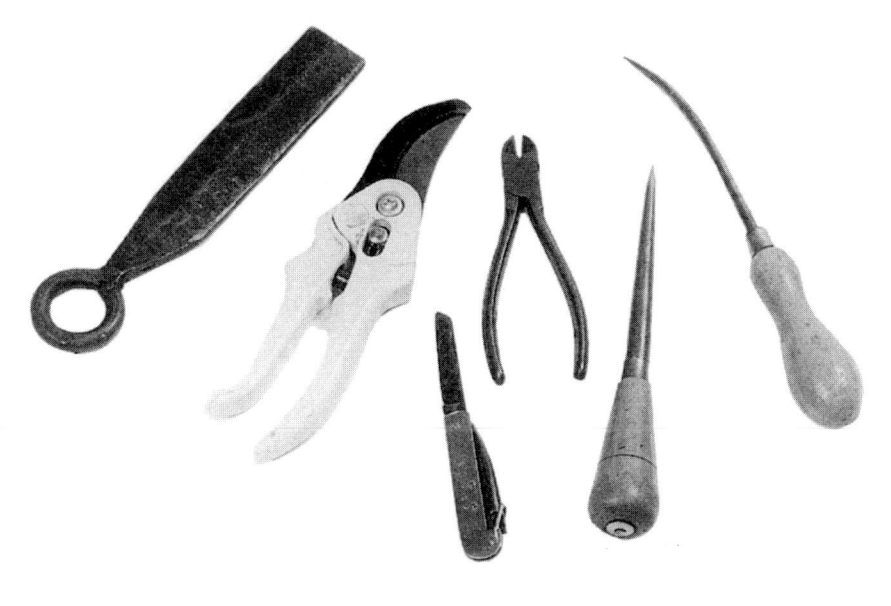

Photo 3.1 Willow tools. From left to right: rapping iron, secateurs, knife, side cutters, bodkin, curved bodkin

1. *Bodkins:* These tapering, pointed metal tools with wooden handles vary in size from large, which is useful for the whole willow chair, to the very fine curved awl, helpful when using skeined willow. They are used for making gaps in the work. The large bodkin in Photo 3.1 is 20 cm (8 in) long. The fine awl is about 13 cm (5 in) long. Metal skewers and curved tapestry needles are useful substitutes.

2. *Knives:* A very sharp knife is essential in willow work for cutting the ends of rods and trimming off the finished seat. Cobblers' shop-knives are available from shoe repairers, but a good pen-knife is fine. The traditional picking knife is now available from the Basketmakers' Association.

3. *Secateurs:* These are very useful for cutting and trimming of tough willow. They must be sharp enough not to squash the willow, as this leaves an unsightly end.

4. *Side cutters:* These plier-like tools with one flat side are useful for cutting skeins and for the tips of rods. The flat side ensures that they will cut really close to the work.

5. *Rapping iron:* This rectangular piece of iron which has one edge thicker than the other is used for tapping the rows of weaving to prevent gaps. A hammer can be used instead.

6. *Old cloths:* These are useful for soaking and wrapping round the prepared willow rods to keep them damp and flexible.

7. *A spray bottle:* Very useful for keeping the work damp.

18.
Whole willow seating

Photo 3.2 Tom Kealy's Somerset Carver and side chair

Very little information is available about the history of seats woven with willow rods. The techniques used are the same as those of basketmaking and the seating, probably done by basketmakers rather than by the rush 'matters' or chair-caners, was never common. Willow seats are now occasionally seen in churches, where an odd chair or two may have been given to a basketmaker to repair when a rush 'matter' was not available. Although I have contacted more than fifty museums, I have not been able to trace any of these seats, even in Somerset or the Trent area, where much of the English willow crop was grown in the nineteenth century. I was lucky enough to be given one that I spotted on an antique dealer's bonfire before it was lit. It is an attractive, black-stained beech chair, probably dating from about 1890, and is in good condition apart from having lost its arms. Members of the Basketmakers' Association have shown me other examples, all of which, with slight variations, are woven in the same basic way. One craftsman producing beautiful chairs of this kind today, using ash frames and willow seats, is Tom Kealy in Somerset (Photo 3.2). He learned his seating skills from the basketmaker David Drew.

Photo 3.3 Georgian High Chair with willow seat, loaned by R. Walton

Photo 3.4 Rows of chain waling were used at the back and front of this small 'Teddy Bear' chair

HOW TO RECOGNISE A CHAIR SUITABLE FOR A WHOLE WILLOW SEAT

A chair needing a whole willow seat is like a rush chair. It has raised corners which are properly polished. The legs are often rounded (Photo 3.3). Between the legs are rails which are unpolished and often roughly finished. These may be rounded or flat-topped. At the corners the rails fit into the legs to form a neat right angle at the inside edge (Fig. 3.2a, not b).

The chair first has a warp of willow rods put on from back to front. A weft of finer willow is then woven from side to side, starting at the back (Photo 3.4).

MATERIALS

About ten stout six-foot rods for the warp stakes
Twelve finer six foots for waling
About 1 kg of four foots for randing
A small number of fine six foots for skeining

The material may be buff or white. It must be prepared (see page 125) and it is important to keep the warp of willow rods damp so that the chair can be finished easily. If you have worked quickly and have a small chair, the willow may be damped down with a cloth before the final stages. If you have to leave the chair overnight, you will have to wrap the rods in a very damp cloth to keep them flexible. A large sheet of polythene under the wet rods will protect the chair.

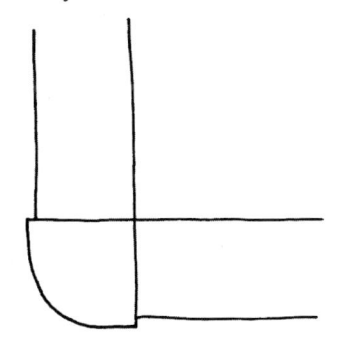

Fig 3.2a A chair corner suitable for willow seating

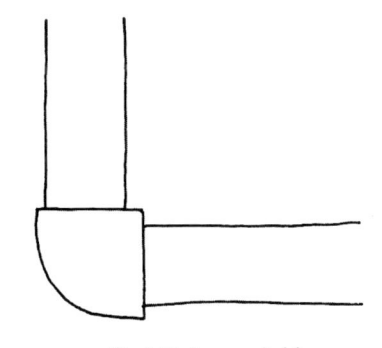

Fig 3.2b An unsuitable corner

Fig 3.2c Cross-section of rail

127

TERMS

Chain waling: Two rows of waling (see below), the second being the reverse weave of the first, giving a chain effect.

Randing: A weave using single rods worked alternately in front of and behind successive stakes.

Scalloming: A long tongue at the butt of a rod, made with a long, slanting cut.

Skeins: A fine ribbon of willow which has been prepared by splitting a rod, shaving off the insides and then making each piece even in width.

Slype: A long, slanting cut to the butt of a rod (Fig. 3.1)

Waling: A weave of three or more rods where each is used in turn over a number of stakes and behind one.

Wrapping the back rail

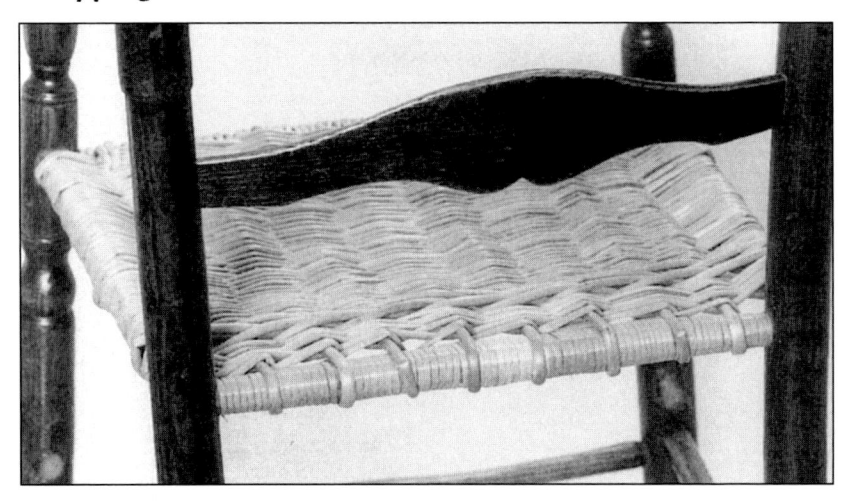

Photo 3.5 The back rail of a whole willow chair showing skein wrapping and scalloms

Fig 3.3 The underside of the back rail: beginning to bind it with a skein

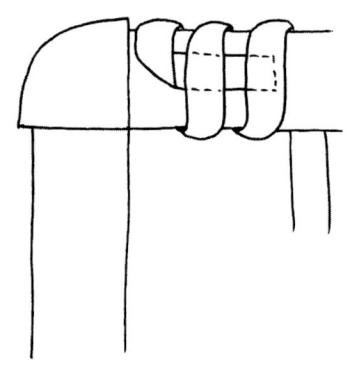

A small number of wide (5–6 mm or ¼ in) skeins must be prepared (see pages 137–9). They do not need to be exactly the same width all the way along so taking them once through the upright will be enough.

Take a skein and lay a short end under the back rail next to one leg (Fig. 3.3). Bend the end of the skein at a 45 degree angle at the chair leg and use it to wrap the back rail, taking it round and round, covering its own short end as you go. As this skein runs out, lay in another underneath the rail, with the rounded side touching. Wrap over this several times. Then turn the new skein at 45 degrees so it is in a position to continue wrapping (see Fig. 3.3). Turn the old end at 45 degrees so it lies in a position under the rail where it will now be wrapped. Continue wrapping, joining in again as necessary. When the rail is completely wrapped, the end of the last skein is turned and tucked under several wraps to secure it. Trim off this end, leaving about 2–3 mm (⅜ in).

Scalloming

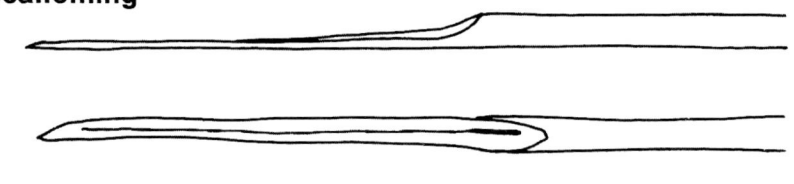

Fig 3.4 The butts of rods which have been scallomed

The six-foot rods to be used for the warp are attached to the back rail by the technique known as 'scalloming'.

Select enough of these six-foot rods to space them about 2.5–3 cm (1–1¼ in) apart across the back rail. The outside two will be set this distance in from the back legs. The rods should be straight and fairly thick. They must be carefully prepared by soaking and mellowing.

The butt ends must be made thinner to allow the rods to be wrapped round the back rail. These thinned butts are called *scalloms*.

At a point about 23 cm (9 in) from the butt, cut into the centre of the rod with a very sharp knife. Cut along the middle of the rod by bringing the knife blade round in a curve, cutting towards the butt. Once this cut is parallel with the length of the rod, lift the blade rather than continuing to cut and pull the two halves of the rod apart right to the butt. A long tongue, at most only half the thickness of the rod and at the end rather thinner, should be the result (Fig. 3.4). This tongue is a scallom. There will be a small amount of pith remaining along most of its length.

There are two ways in which the rod can be held to produce successful scalloms:

1. Hold the butt so that it rests on the fleshy

part of the left hand below the thumb, with the tip of the rod away from you. Push the blade in from above, about 22.5 cm (9 in) from the butt, until you are half-way through the rod. Bring the blade round towards you and then lift it to split the top section of rod away from the main section. Pull this top section away, tapering the scallom left behind. If the tip is too thick it can be cut away with the knife.

2. Sit on a chair with a pile of rods to be scallomed at your side, butts towards you. Pick one up and place the tip between your crossed feet to hold it. Curve the rod and place the butt on your chest bone with the back of the rod upwards. Support the curved butt underneath with your left thumb and cut in with the knife to half the depth of the rod. Lean forward slightly to curve the rod more and at the same time bring the knife blade towards you in a curving cut. The extra pressure on the rod will cause the top section to split away from the main rod and then the two sections can be pulled apart to leave the scallom on the rod.

Whichever method you use for holding the rod, make sure the initial cuts follow a smooth curve. A cut which turns at right angles in the centre of the rod will cause it to split towards the tip as well as towards the butt, and the scallom will be useless.

SCALLOMING ON THE RODS

1. Place the scalloms in water for five to ten minutes.
2. Place the chair with its back towards you.
3. Place a scallom over the skeins so that it projects over the back rail towards you on the right (as the chair is now) and about 2.5 cm (1 in) away from the corner (Fig. 3.5a). The curve of the scallom should sit on the inside top edge of the rail (Fig. 3.5b). Bend the scallom down over the back rail and carry it under and up again on

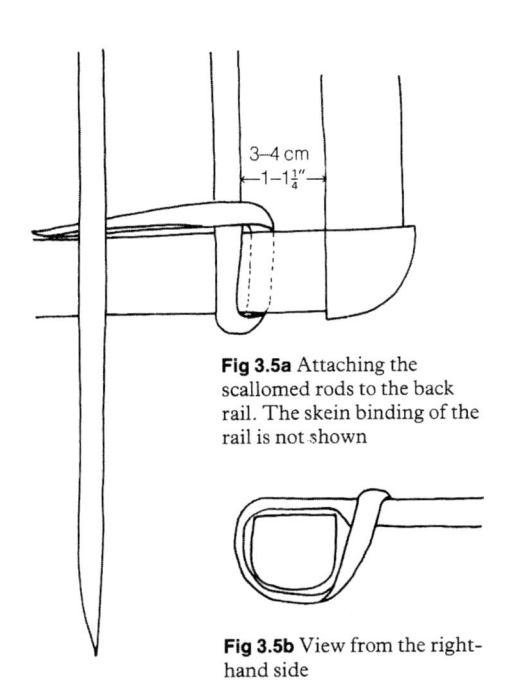

Fig 3.5a Attaching the scallomed rods to the back rail. The skein binding of the rail is not shown

Fig 3.5b View from the right-hand side

the right of its own rod. Bring it over itself and let it lie to the left, slightly below the top of the rail, with the cut surface against the rail. Do this as tightly as possible, really pulling on the scallom.

4. Place a second rod about 2.5–3 cm (1–1¼ in) to the left of the first (Fig. 3.5a) and repeat the movements with the scallom, holding down the butt of the first one as you place the rod in position. Continue to scallom on rods until you reach the left-hand side of the rail. The last scallom should be about 2.5 cm (1 in) away from the corner. The end of the last scallom should be tucked under the side rail of the chair. It will be held in position by the weaving.

All the rods should be tightly scallomed on to the rail (Photo 3.5). If each scallom is long enough it may be carried under two or three others as long as they sit neatly. The rods should lie across the top of the front rail and be evenly spaced. These rods form the warp on which the seat is woven, and are now referred to as 'stakes'.

Randing

Fig 3.6a Starting the rand; a join with tip to tip
Fig 3.6b A butt to tip join

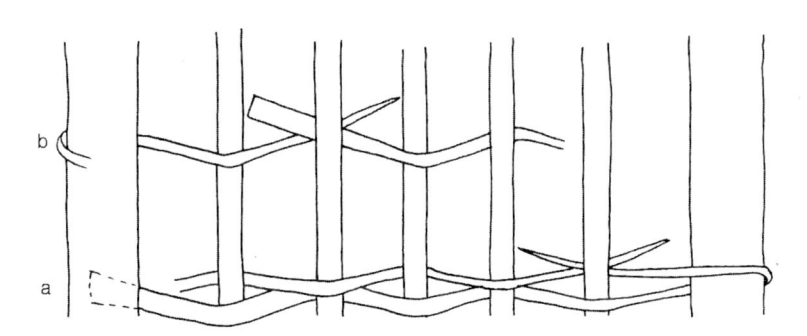

Four-foot rods are used next to weave over and under the warp stakes. This is called 'randing'. Start on the left with the back of the chair between your knees. It helps to tilt the chair towards you.

1. Place a butt below the side rail and carry the weaver over the first and under the second stake and so on until you reach the right-hand rail (Fig. 3.6a).
2. Carry the weaver round this and weave it back to the left going over the rods you previously went under.
3. Carry the weaver round the left-hand rail and continue weaving from side to side.

4. *Joining.* When the tip of the first weaver is reached it is left on the underside of the seat resting against a stake (Fig. 3.6a). A new tip is put in from the opposite side, resting against the same stake and the weaving is continued. When a butt is reached, join in a new butt in the same way. Join butts to butts and tips to tips.
5. Weave for about 5 cm (2 in) and finish with a tip. Make sure you have the same depth of weaving all the way across the chair.
6. Use a rapping iron or hammer to knock the weaving towards the back rail to keep the rows close together, and to even up the depth of weaving.

An alternative method of joining. You can start each new rod with a butt as you did with the first rod so the joins will all involve a new butt joining an old tip (Fig. 3.6b). Choose one join and use it throughout the randing.

Waling

Photo 3.6 Whole willow seat with two separated rows of waling at the back. The side rails are covered with full binds of willow between rows of randing. The final twisted rod on the left is woven away towards the right at the front

Fig 3.7a Starting the waling

Fig 3.7b Waling across the frame

The stakes tend to sink down during the randing and this must be avoided. One or two rows of a weave which is stronger than randing is put on to hold them up (Photo 3.6). This is called 'waling'.

1. Start by taking three fine six-foot rods, preferably thinner than the stakes.
2. Put the butt of one of these through to the underside between the left-hand rail (the back of the chair is still towards you) and the first stake, leaving about 20 cm (8 in) at the back. Bring the butt round on the outside of the rail, across it and the first stake, and behind to rest against the underside of the second stake from the left (Fig. 3.7a, rod **a**). Put the butt of a second rod to the underside between the first and second stakes leaving 3–4 cm (1½ in) at the back (Fig. 3.7a, rod **b**). Put in the third butt to the underside in the same way between the second and third stakes from the left (Fig. 3.7a, rod **c**). These two should be between the randing and the first butt. The rods should be angled so that the tips project towards the right.
3. You will now have three rods projecting from the top of the seat. Take the left-hand one of these (Fig. 3.7a, rod **a**), carry it over two stakes, behind the third and back to the front. Then take the new left-hand rod **b** in front of two stakes and behind one (Fig. 3.7b). Continue, always using the left-hand rod, until you reach the other edge of the seat. Hold the stakes horizontal as you weave and keep them evenly spaced, as they tend to dip down.
4. At the right-hand edge continue waling until the right-hand weaver of the three is coming up in the second space from the right-hand rail. Take the left-hand weaver (Fig. 3.8, rod **a**) in front of two stakes and to the inside leaving it there. Take the new left-hand weaver **b** in front of two stakes and to the back and leave it. Take the remaining weaver **c** in front of one stake and the rail, round behind the rail and then use it for randing. Bring it back to the front, carry it in front of one stake, take it behind

130

the next and so on.

5. Trim the two waling rods at the back with diagonal cuts with a knife or secateurs. Make sure these rods rest against a stake so they cannot push through to the top of the seat.

Fig 3.8 Finishing the row of waling; starting to rand again.
The randing rod can be cut off at **t** if a second row of waling is to be put on

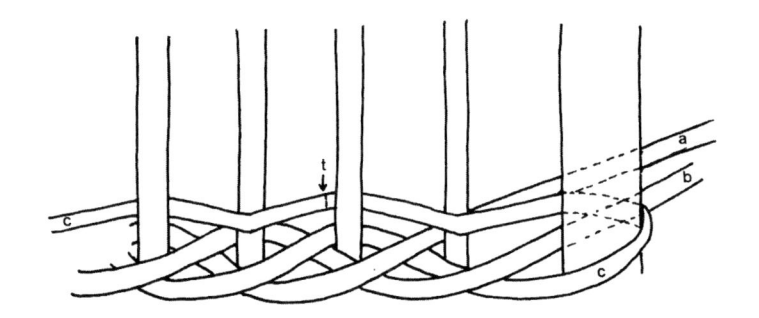

Alternative methods of waling

EXTRA ROWS

On large seats strength can be added by weaving on a second row of waling in exactly the same way as the first and immediately after it (Photo 3.7), in which case the rod of the first row which would otherwise be used for randing can be brought forward, taken down over one stake and trimmed underneath (Fig. 3.8, rod **c**). This will hardly show between the two rows of waling.

Sometimes 2.5 cm (1 in) of randing is woven between two rows of waling. This gives a striped effect. However, the rows of waling should remain towards the back of the seat as they make ridges which would be uncomfortable to sit on.

Note: The pattern at the back of the chair is normally repeated at the front to hold the stakes in position before they are finished off.

CHAIN WALING

Occasionally a second row of waling is put on immediately after the first, using the same rods (Photo 3.4) and working from right to left.

1. Start as described above (page 130) and work until the right-hand weaver is one space away from the right-hand rail. The left-hand weaver (Fig. 3.9, rod **a**) is now taken in front of two stakes and to the back where it is cut off, resting against a stake.
2. The new left-hand weaver, **b**, is taken in front of two stakes behind the rail as tightly as possible, round it and forward, in front of the rail and one stake (travelling from right to left now), behind the next stake (the second from the right-hand rail) and back to the front.
3. The third weaver, **c**, is now taken in front of a stake and the rail, down and under this right-hand rail and the stake next to the rail and up to the front again. Weavers **b** and **c** will cross on the underside of the rail.
4. Now take the cut-off section of the first rod used, **a**, and push its butt in from above so that it just rests against the underside of the rail (Fig. 3.10).

Photo 3.7 Whole willow seat with the second row of waling put on immediately after the first

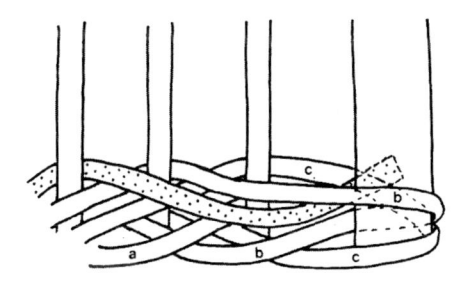

Fig 3.9 Starting the second row of a chain wale

Fig 3.10 Putting in the third weaving rod

131

Fig 3.11 Finishing the chain wale on the right-hand side

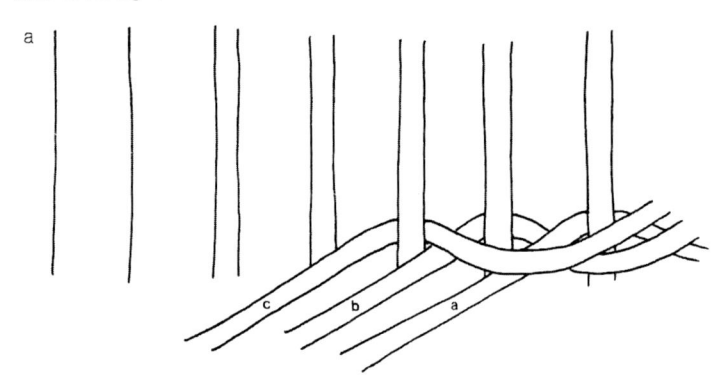

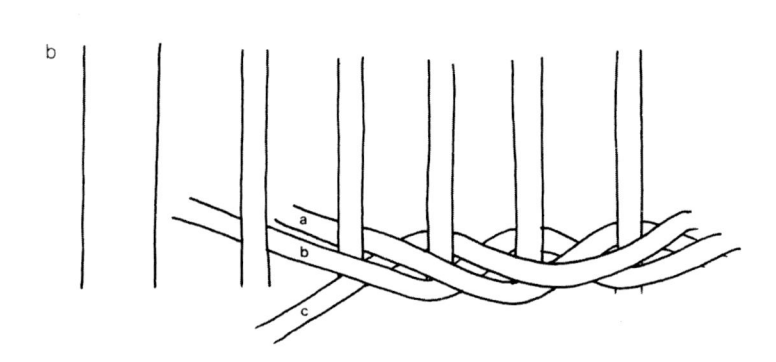

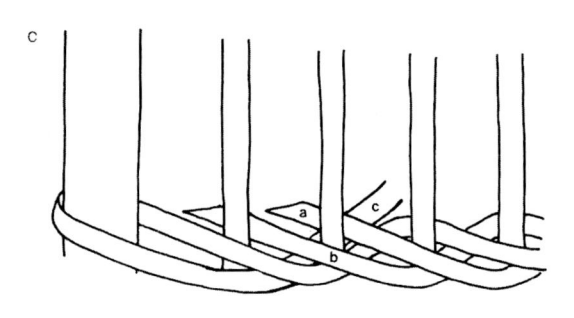

5. Use the three tips you have projecting to the left to wale to the left-hand rail. For each stroke take the right-hand weaver in front of two stakes, behind one and back to the front. This gives a chain effect with the first row.
6. At the left-hand side work until the left-hand weaver of the three is resting against the second stake from the left-hand rail with all three weavers projecting forwards to the left (Fig. 3.11a).
7. Take the right-hand one (Fig. 3.11b, rod **a**) in front of two stakes, and to the back so it is resting under the second stake from the left.
8. Take the new right-hand weaver (Fig. 3.11b, rod **b**) in front of two stakes and to the back to rest against the first stake from the left.
9. Take the remaining weaver (Fig. 3.11c, rod **c**) in front of two stakes and to the back. Bring it out under the rail, up over the rail and the first stake from the left, and take it through to the back by tucking it underneath itself. It should rest against the second stake from the left and be projecting to the right. Trim it against a stake.

There are a number of ways of producing this chain waling effect, but it is important to avoid leaving ends on the top of the seat, which could catch on clothes.

CONTINUING TO RAND

1. Starting with a butt, rand forwards and backwards across the seat, rapping the weaving close every few rows. As you weave over the rails keep the weavers tightly against the wood and take them round in the smoothest curve possible. The best curve is achieved by pulling the weaver to maintain constant tension.
2. Keep the stakes as straight as possible and, if the front of the seat is wider than the back, fan the stakes out a little so they are still evenly spaced at the front.

Points to watch out for

1. The two stakes nearest the side rails have a tendency to sink. Make sure you keep them up each time you rand round them. Also keep them parallel to the side rails.
2. The side rails will not normally be completely covered with weaving, and so you will be able to see very small sections of the wooden rails. This does not matter, but if you want to avoid it wrap each side rail completely by taking the willow weaver for one full turn round the rail between two rows of randing (Fig. 3.12 and Photo 3.6). Repeat this each side, after every 2.5 cm (1 in) of weaving.
3. Always rap the weaving close and take the weavers round the rails in the smoothest possible curve. Avoid kinks if possible.
4. As you rand make sure you wet the stakes with a cloth or a spray bottle at intervals, as the surface tends to dry very quickly.

Fig 3.12 Taking the randing rods round the rail for a full turn between rows

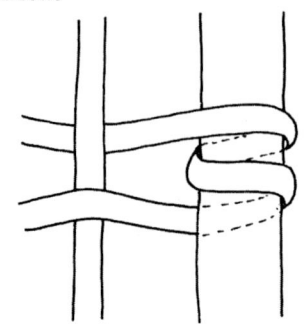

Front waling

1. When you reach the front of the chair a row of waling is put on in exactly the same way as at the back. The position of this row (or rows if you have used one of the alternatives) depends on the chair and will normally be arranged to match the back. Measure from the back of the back rail to the front edge of the waling. Measure back the same distance from the front edge of the front rail and have your waling at this point.

2. Put in your row or rows of waling.

At the front

1. Rand until the side rails are full and only one more weaving rod can be fitted round them.
2. Put in one more randing rod, which should be rather thicker than the others. Start it with the tip on the right (still with the back of the chair towards you) and weave it to the left, round the left-hand rail and up into the small space just inside the front leg. When the chair is turned round for the next stage this becomes the right front corner (Fig. 3.13a).

WRAPPING THE FRONT RAIL WITH THE STAKES

1. Before the front is completed the stakes, if they have not been kept damp, must be well soaked by tipping the chair and making sure the length of stake right up to the front rail is under water. If you have worked quickly and the stakes still have some pliability, this will not take long. If they have dried out completely they will need as long as they did when the willow was originally prepared. Protect the wood of the chair as far as possible, as water marks are difficult to remove.
2. *Twisting the willow.* Before using the stakes to wrap the front rail they must be twisted so they become rope-like. They will then take the correct curves necessary without cracking. This is a useful technique, as it breaks up the fibres to make a rope-like twist, and allows the willow to travel round tight curves without any danger of kinking. Producing a good twist is a knack and will need practice. Try first with some spare prepared rods, holding them securely in a vice or even pushed into soil. The tip of the rod is taken between the first finger and thumb of the right hand and rolled away from you to break up the rod. You will see splits appearing. Then the left hand holds the willow rather loosely about 12 cm (5 in) down. After the initial twist the tip is held firmly and the rod is moved clockwise as though you were turning a handle. This movement involves the right wrist moving round in a circle, which will become larger as the twist moves down the rod. At the same time the left-hand first finger and thumb roll the rod away between them to assist the twist and gradually move it down the rod. Move the left hand down too to keep pace with the twist. Do not grip tightly with the left hand. If the rod is a long one you can let go of the tip and move the right hand lower down. The tip will unravel but will twist up again easily later. Twist the whole rod as far as the butt.

   If you find that the willow splits into two or three sections along its length, it probably means you have not been cranking the tip round in large enough circles.

   When you have practised and managed to achieve a good twist down the length of a rod, you are ready to twist the stakes on the chair.

   Note: If you find it difficult to twist the willow in the way described, try this method: hold the tip on your right and, using both hands, roll it away from you until the fibres break up. Move your hands down to twist the next section.

3. *The first wrapping.* Start on the right with the front of the chair towards you. Take the end of the randing rod at the front right-hand corner, twist it up, then bring it forward over the front rail touching the corner, down under the rail and up into the space inside the front rail. Continue using it to wrap the front rail until you reach the first stake (Fig. 3.13b). This will normally only be two or three wraps. Keep it tightly twisted. If it unravels it can be twisted again.

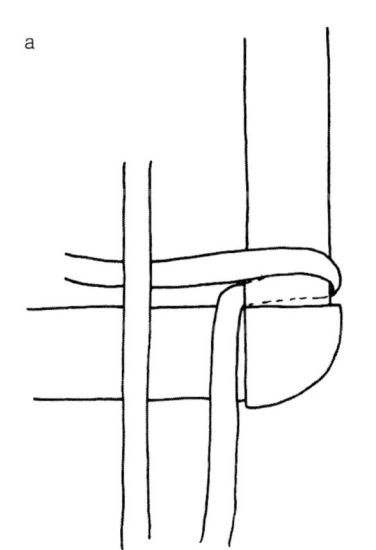

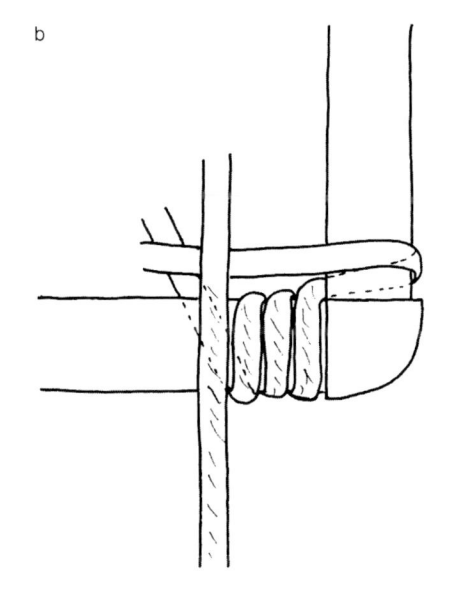

Fig 3.13a Bringing a randing rod into position for wrapping the first part of the front rail

Fig 3.13b Wrapping the first part of the rail with a twisted rod

Photo 3.8 The front of a whole willow chair. Twisted rods have been used to cover the front rail

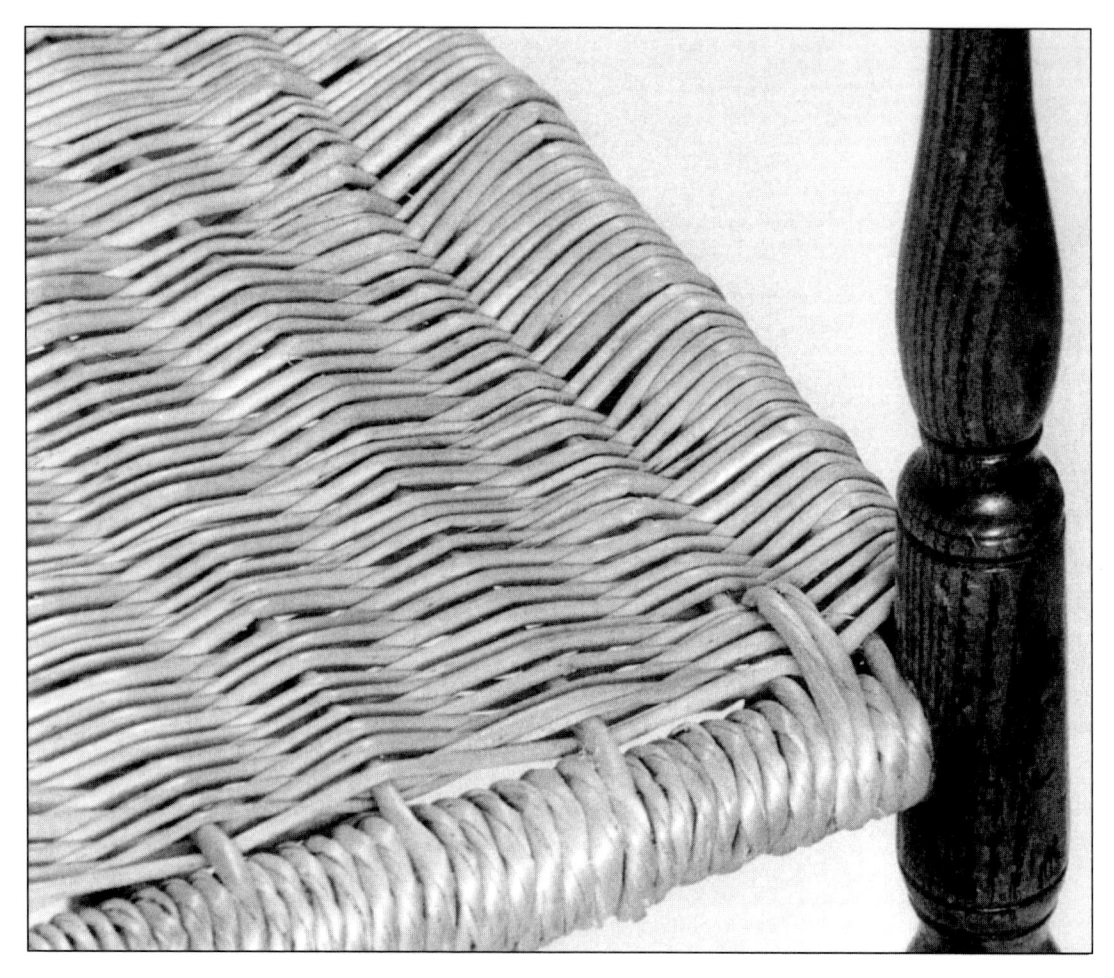

4. *Completing the front rail.*
   (a) Now twist up the first stake (Fig. 3.13c) and use it to wrap the next section of front rail. Keep it tightly twisted or re-twist if necessary. With the first wrap, catch in the twisted randing rod which has been used for the first section of the front rail. It should lie to the left underneath the seat and be held very firmly (Photo 3.8).
   (b) Take the next stake and twist it up and repeat the wrapping, catching in the previous one on the underside. Each stake will be used to fill in the space between itself and the next stake. Keep the wraps close together.
   (c) When you have used all the stakes and wrapped the whole of the front rail, the end of the last stake must be held firmly. Carry it up behind the front rail, over the side rail, back up into the same space and over the first stake on the left. Take the end down in the next space (Fig. 3.14).
   This wrapping can be difficult to get tight and neat. It is important to twist the willow really tightly and maintain this twist as you wrap. Make sure the space between the stakes is completely filled.
   Emergency measures: If a stake breaks, cut it off close to the randing and push in another matching rod (page 135). Slype a whole rod and push it in.

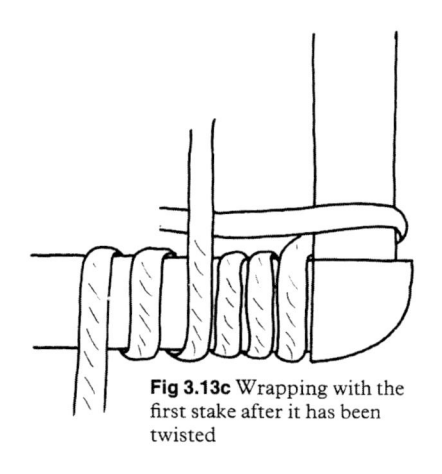

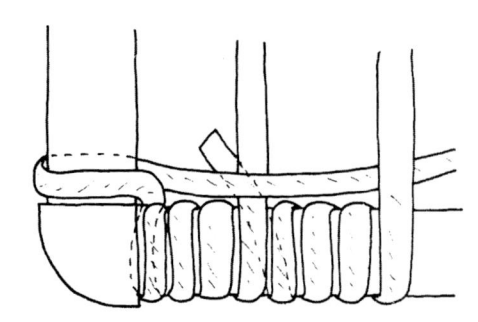

Fig 3.13c Wrapping with the first stake after it has been twisted

Fig 3.14 Finishing the wrapping by weaving the last stake away

Trimming

Fig 3.15 Trimming the randing against a stake so the ends cannot push through to the top of the seat

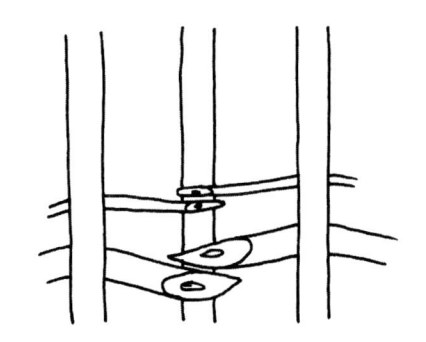

All the ends of the stakes should be cut off underneath as neatly as possible but leaving a short end so they do not come undone.

All the ends from the randing must be trimmed with diagonal cuts, making sure the ends rest against a stake and cannot push through to the top (Fig. 3.15).

Alternative finish to the front rail

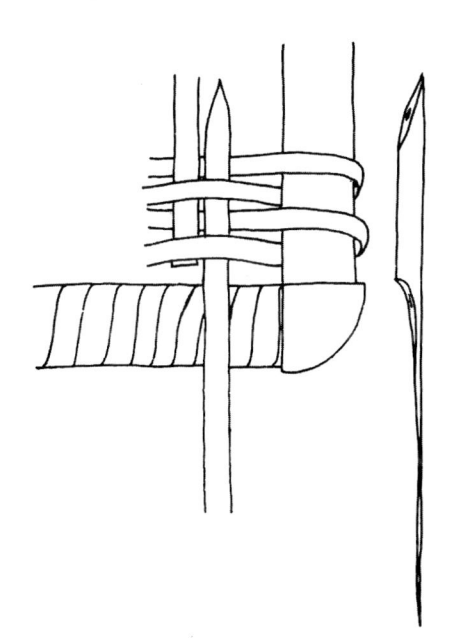

Fig 3.16 Replacement of a damaged stake. A new slyped rod is pushed in as far as possible beside the broken one. The broken one is then cut close to the randing. Side view of the new stake scallomed at one end and slyped at the other

1. When the randing is completed but *before* you put on the front waling wrap the front rail with skeins in the same way as the back (see Photo 3.7). This is easier to do before the waling holds the stakes too firmly.
2. Next scallom all the stakes. The easiest way to do this is to turn the chair on its back so the rods are up in the air and make the cut into each rod at the point where the rod meets the inside edge of the front rail. Cut in a curve and use the knife to lift the cut section off the rod and peel it back to leave a tongue about 25 cm (9–10 in) long.
   Note: Take great care, as cutting right through a stake presents problems! If this should happen, cut off the broken stake as close as possible to the randing. Then scallom a rod of the same thickness and slype it about 10 cm (4 in) beyond the scallom on the same side. Push in the slyped end of the rod beside the broken one (Fig. 3.16). Turn the slype downwards, leaving the curve of the scallom in the correct position on the front inner edge of the front rail.
3. When you have scallomed all the stakes, complete the front waling and the randing in front of it.
4. Soak the scalloms if necessary. They will only need 5 minutes at most.
5. Take the right-hand scallom (the chair should now be facing you) over the front rail, underneath and up on the right of itself. Pull it tight, take it over itself to the left and under the next two stakes to the left. Repeat with the stake to the left and work until you have a row of scalloms across the front. For security each should be held by two subsequent scalloms.
6. The final scallom on the left of the chair may be tucked under the side-rail, provided it is held tightly by the randing as well. Alternatively, it may be taken under the rail, over and down to the *left* of itself (Fig. 3.17a), or the end may be tucked into the loop of the scallom (Fig. 3.17b).

This method may look neater than the other twisted stake method but it is difficult to get the scalloms held really securely. Once the scalloms are prepared it is impossible to go back to the twisted rod method.

Fig 3.17 Two methods of finishing the final scallom

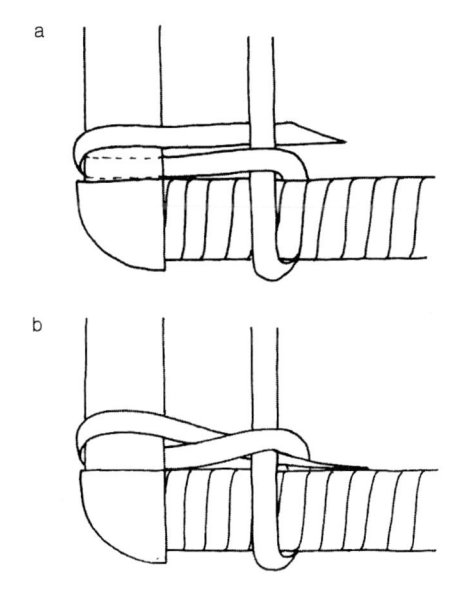

a

b

Chairs which present problems

It is difficult to put willow seats on chairs which have legs or back supports protruding into the centre of the chair. Chairs with rounded legs often present this problem.

If the scalloms take up the width **a** in Fig. 3.18a the seat may be woven as usual but the outer stakes on each side will need to be placed next to the legs so that the gap between them and the side rails is not too great.

If the scalloms do not fill up this width **a**, a few rows of randing will have to be put on to fill it. These rows will not be able to go round the side rails as the leg will be in the way. The outer stakes should be arranged about 1 cm ($\frac{1}{4}$ in) in from the legs and the randing will turn round these stakes (Fig. 3.18b). Carry this randing on as far as the end of the leg to fill up width **a**. Then the waling may be put on as before. These shorter rows of randing may also have to be repeated at the front of the chair.

For a really regular and neatly woven chair it is important to keep the stakes as straight as possible and to position them so that the seat does not sag in the middle. Careful waling towards the back helps prevent sagging. Also make sure that the stakes next to the side-rails remain parallel to them, as this greatly improves the seat's appearance.

These strong seats have a fine, smooth regularity which will last many years. There is no need for any treatment in the way of polish or varnish, as the willow will develop a sheen with regular use.

Fig 3.18a If the width **a** is filled with the scalloms the seat may be woven as usual

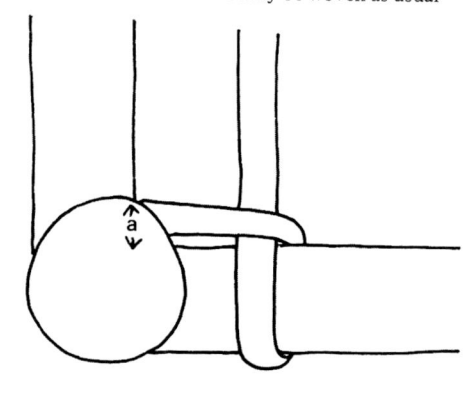

Fig 3.18b If the scalloms do not fill width **a** the first rows of randing must be taken round the outer stakes and not toward the rails

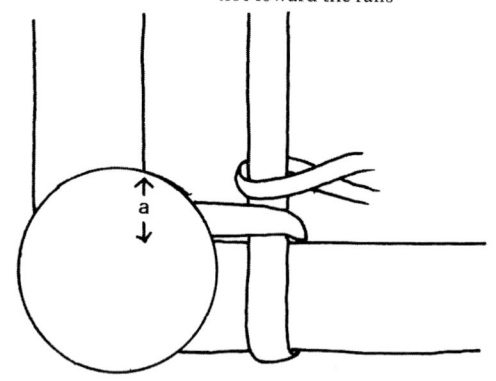

19.
Skeined willow chairs

A skein is a fine ribbon of willow which has been prepared by splitting a rod, shaving off the insides and then making each piece even in width. Seats made of these skeins are woven in a different way from the whole willow seats already described. In the first stage each skein is knotted to the chair frame and provides the warp by being passed from one side of the frame to the other. The second stage is worked from front to back and involves weaving skeins, in patterns, through those of the first stage. Many patterns can be woven in and the resulting seats are fine and delicate in appearance.

How to recognise a chair for skeining

A chair for a willow-skeined seat has features seen in both rush and caned chairs. It has raised, normally square, wooden corners, which have been polished and stained to match the chair back and legs. These may be raised as much as 1 cm ($\frac{3}{8}$ in) above the rails. Between the corners are rails which are normally well smoothed off and not as rough as those on a rush chair. These rails will have a horizontal top edge but may be rounded on the underside.

A unique feature of skeined chairs is the series of holes drilled through all four rails. These are similar in size to those on caned chairs and go vertically through the rails, but are much more widely spaced, usually about 2.5 cm (1 in) apart. The row of holes does not go right up to the corners; they are used for the foundation canes.

If you see polished raised corners and a series of caning holes, widely spaced, the seat has been prepared for skeining. Chair backs for skeining do not always have holes as no foundation caning is needed. As far as I know, skeined back panels are only found on chairs which also have skeined seats. Such chairs are mostly of the folding type.

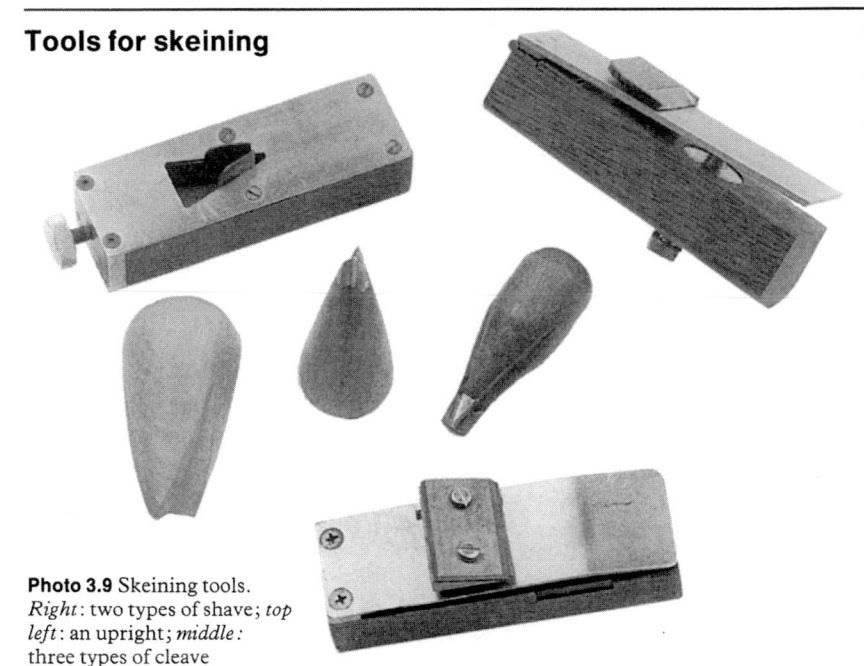

Tools for skeining

Photo 3.9 Skeining tools. *Right*: two types of shave; *top left*: an upright; *middle*: three types of cleave

Three special tools are needed for splitting and preparing willow skeins (Photo 3.9).

The cleave: Used for splitting dry willow rods. This is an egg-shaped tool about 8 cm (3 in) long, tapering at one end. It is traditionally made of boxwood. The pointed end has three or four vanes cut into it which have sharp straight edges. Sometimes these vanes have metal blades attached but wooden ones work well provided a good hard wood has been used. Three-way cleaves are most suitable for the size of skeins needed for seating. Four-way versions are suitable for heavier willow.

The shave: Used for taking the inside pith away from the split willow. It has a rectangular wooden base about 12 cm × 4 cm ($4\frac{1}{2} × 1\frac{1}{2}$ in) with a metal plate on its upper surface. This plate is hinged at one end but its position can be changed by turning a screw underneath which raises and lowers it. A sharp knife-blade is set above this plate. The skein is pulled through between the blade and the plate to remove the pith.

The upright: Willow which has had its pith removed is pulled between the blades of the upright to make it an even width.

This also has a rectangular wooden base, this time with a fixed metal plate on its upper surface. Set into this is a pair of vertical knife blades arranged in a V-shape. A screw at one end of the base allows the two blades to be moved closer together or further apart.

How to make willow skeins

A skein is a fine piece of the outer part of a peeled willow rod. For basketmaking and wrapping handles these are often left uneven in width, but for chair seating they must be uniform.

Selecting the rods: Rods for skeining must be of the highest quality without any knots or blemishes. It is worth taking time to choose them carefully. The best rods are six foots, which are fairly thin at the butt. They may be buff or white, though traditionally white is used.

Cleaving the willow: The rods are used dry. First make a long diagonal cut or slype with a sharp knife about 6 cm (2½ in) down from the tips of a bundle of rods (Fig. 3.19a). Then turn the bundle round and slype all the butts to remove any discoloured parts and any thick ends ('codgels') (Fig. 3.19b).

Next take one tip in your left hand and place your thumb and first finger of your right hand to the front and back of the rod and bend it backwards sharply to break the willow (Fig. 3.19c and d). It should split parallel with your thumb-nail, from one side to the other.

Take the cleave in your right hand and arrange it so that one vane points forwards and the other two slip into the break you have just made (Fig. 3.19e). Grip the willow in your left hand about 10 cm (4 in) below this and push it upwards. Do it gently at first, and if necessary wiggle the cleave a little to get the splits started. Then continue pushing the willow up with the left hand as evenly as possible and the rod will split into three pieces. Sometimes one piece will be fatter than the others and it is possible to move the cleave slightly towards this section to thin it down again. Continue the splits until the butt is reached (Photo 3.10).

Fig 3.19 Stages in cleaving
a Taking off the tip
b Slyping the butt
c & d Breaking the willow
e Position of the cleave prior to splitting the willow

Cleaving is a knack which, once acquired, seems very easy. At first you may find the willow breaks soon after the splitting has begun. This may be because you are pushing down too hard on the cleave rather than using the left hand to slide the willow upwards. Remember the cleave is a splitting tool, not a cutting tool.

For a whole chair cleave at least seventy rods. A small bedroom chair may take about two hundred skeins.

Shaving the willow: This can be done on dry cleaved rods, but you may find it easier to work with material that has been dipped in water. The pieces of willow are pulled between the metal plate and the knife blade, pith side upwards, starting with the tip. At first the plate must be set so that the butts have only a little pith cut off them. The screw must be adjusted for this.

1. The cleaved rods are placed on your right side, tips towards you. Hold the shave in your left hand so the blade faces away from you. The thumb should be along the left side and the first two fingers rest on either side of the screw underneath. This gives a firm grip. The edge of the hand and the corner of the shave nearest you are held in against the left leg to brace it.
2. One cleaved rod is taken, pith upwards, and placed so that the butt end is away from you and tip is between the blade and the metal plate. Grip the tip firmly with the right hand and pull it through with a strong even pull. Use your left thumb to guide the willow through and prevent it moving sideways (Fig. 3.20). At first only pith will be removed. Repeat this with all the remaining cleaved rods (Photo 3.11).

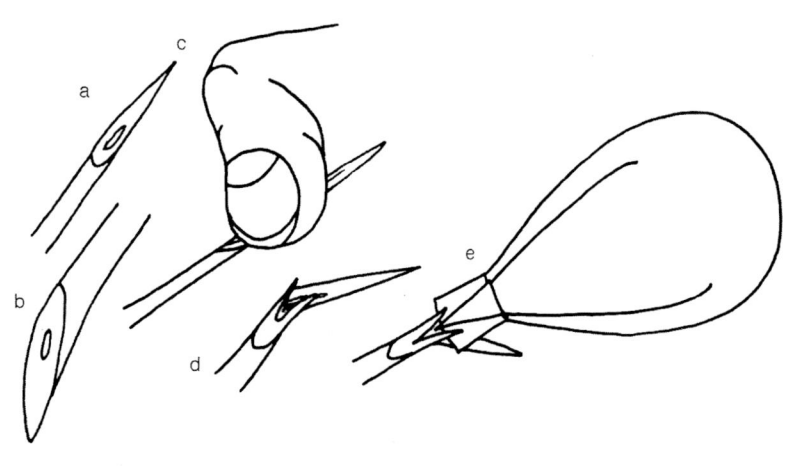

Fig 3.20 Shaving a piece of split willow with pith side uppermost

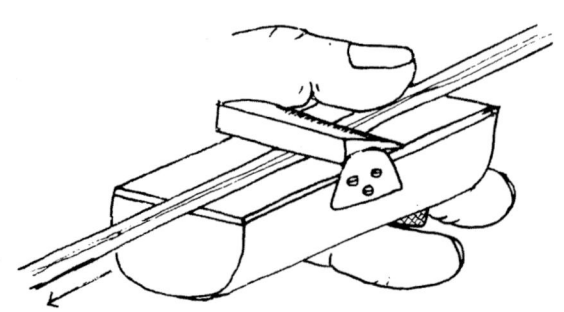

Photo 3.10 Leslie Maltby cleaving willow

Photo 3.11 Leslie Maltby shaving willow

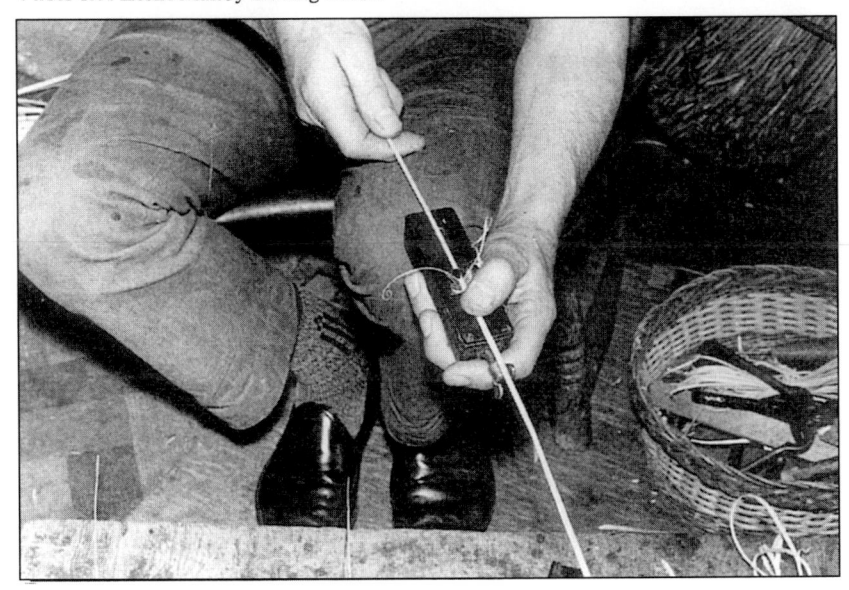

Photo 3.12 Leslie Maltby pulling the skein through an upright

3. Then tighten the screw a little to raise the plate closer to the knife blade and repeat the process with all the skeins to make them finer. Wet or lick the fingers of the right hand so you can grip the skein firmly.

   Note: It is much quicker to take all the rods through on one setting of the shave rather than preparing one skein completely and then having to alter the shave several times for the next one. Each piece must be taken through the shave about three times to remove the inner part of the willow completely. A fine piece of the outside, with its slightly curved silky surface, is left. Work to a system: take all the pieces through, alter the shave, take all the pieces through again, and so on. At this stage the skeins are wider at the butt.

Uprighting the willow: Again this can be done using dry or damped willow. Try some both ways, to see which you find easier. This is the final stage in preparing skeins.

The upright is held in the same way as the shave, with the sharpened blades away from you. The knife blades are adjusted to take off part of the outer edge to make the skein an even width. Start with a gap a little smaller than most of the skein butts.

1. Put a tip, pith side downwards this time, between the blades and hold the rest of the skein steady with the left thumb as before (Fig. 3.21). Pull steadily with a firm grip, keeping the skein straight (Photo 3.12). Pass all the skeins through this blade setting.
2. Then tighten the screw to bring the blades a little closer together and take all the skeins through again.
3. If necessary repeat a third time.

   Note: The skeins for seating should be 2–4 mm ($\frac{1}{8}$–$\frac{3}{8}$ in) wide along their length. The tips may need to be discarded but do this only when you start to use the skeins.

   The main difficulty when uprighting is that the skeins tend to move sideways and get cut in half. Use the left thumb to control this. A glove or leather thumb guard on the left hand may be useful.

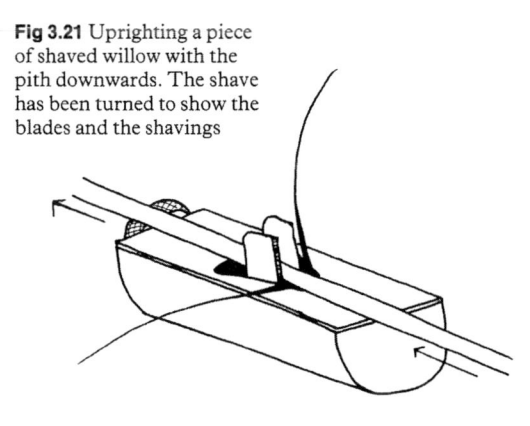

Fig 3.21 Uprighting a piece of shaved willow with the pith downwards. The shave has been turned to show the blades and the shavings

20. Close skeining

This type of seating involves the interweaving of skeins to form a solid, closely-woven seat. In the first stage, warp skeins are stretched across the seat from one side to the other and are knotted to the side rails. In close skeining these warp skeins touch each other to form a complete covering. The second stage involves weaving skeins between the warps to form a pattern and then attaching them with knots to the front and back rails. These skeins also form an entire covering of the seat, so it is covered with two complete layers.

Skeined chairs of this type were probably mainly produced in France and Germany, but from the late 1840s began to be made in quantity in Britain. Walter Skull, the chair-making company in High Wycombe, produced a hand-drawn and painted catalogue in 1849 which has about ten designs for willow-skeined seats, many using coloured skeins and elaborate designs. They were the first company in Britain to produce willow-seated chairs on a large scale. Almost all were bedroom chairs, which were then introduced by other companies in their catalogues. Benjamin North's catalogue of about 1860 shows five types. Wm. Collins and Son show 21 delicate bedroom chairs with elaborately carved backs and willow-skeined seats, and Glenister and Gibbons' catalogue of 1875 shows even more. All these firms operated in High Wycombe, making use of the beech woods of the Chil-

Photo 3.13 Skeined stool woven by Barbara Maynard

terns for the chair frames.

It seems that the frames were made at the factory and then delivered to outworkers, who put on the skeined seats. Dorothy Wright records one large family in High Wycombe in the 1860s, the Youens, who were basketmakers and also skeined-chair-seaters. One member of this family was still practising the craft into the 1930s. Leslie Maltby, who worked many of the seats shown here from the Museum of English Rural Life at Reading, is a descendant of this family.

Today these seats are rare. They can occasionally be found on chairs in antique shops, but the seating does not last more than fifteen to twenty years and so will often have been replaced by rush or seagrass. Many of the chairs shown in the catalogues were not robust and may not have survived in large numbers.

The craft has been revived by members of the Basketmakers' Association, notably by the late Barbara Maynard, who has produced some beautiful skein work (Photo 3.13).

I have come across two methods of close skeining, the main difference between them being the formation of the knots. Both are described below. The first method uses the most commonly-found form of knot, but the second method is quicker to work and just as neat and secure.

Method 1: The traditional method

MATERIALS

A bundle of skeins long enough to go across the chair plus 40–50 cm (16–20 in). You will need about 100 for a narrow panel, 200 for a bedroom chair

A six-foot willow rod, soaked and mellowed (page 125), *or* a piece of soaked No. 15 round cane long enough to fit round the inside of the seat frame. This will form the liner (see below)

Some No. 2 or No. 3 chair cane, about 10 lengths. The cane must not be wider than the skeins

String or masking tape

A tension stick of hardwood about 2.5 × 1 cm (1 in × ¼ in) and long enough to lay across the top of the chair frame from front to back

STARTING THE CHAIR

First prepare the skeins. The number needed will depend on the chair. If you are replacing a small panel as on a 'Campaign' chair (Photo 3.14) many of your skeins can be cut to provide two short ones. For a small bedroom chair you may need as many as 200 skeins.

Fig 3.22 The back right corner of the frame

Fig 3.22a Positioning and taping the liner

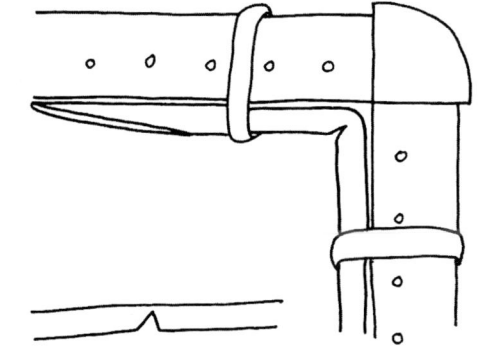

Fig 3.22b How to cut the liner to aid bending it into the corner of the frame

Fig 3.22c Joining the liner. The direction of the join does not matter

THE LINER

This is a willow rod or piece of round cane tied round the chair against the inside of the frame, just below the top of the rails. The skeins are knotted over it and are held firmly by it.

1. Use either the six-foot prepared willow rod or the piece of No. 15 cane, soaked for about half an hour. Make a long diagonal cut of about 10 cm (4 in) at the butt of the willow rod or one end of the cane (Fig. 3.22a).
2. Place the uncut edge on the inside of the back rail of the chair in the centre and hold firmly in place with either string or masking tape.
3. Carry the liner along to the corner and bend it exactly, making sure it will go right into the corner. It may help to use a penknife to cut a narrow notch in the liner to ease the bending (Fig. 3.22b). Hold it firmly in position with string or tape on either side of this corner.
4. Carry it along to the next corner and repeat, making sure it is just below the top of the rails. Repeat with the remaining two corners. It should fit tightly into all four.
5. At the back cut away the liner carefully with a diagonal cut to match the butt end. When the two are together they should overlap to form a neat join (Fig. 3.22c).
6. Tie them to the back rail. If you prefer, the liner may be nailed permanently to the rails with panel pins; pin it right through to the rail. Two pins will probably be needed on each rail to hold it firmly.

Alternative method: You may find it easier to bend the rod to fit tightly at the corners, without tying it in first. Leave a long overlap at the back, and make sure you hold it right into the corner before bending it.

1. Hold it firmly in the first corner with one hand while you find the position of the next.
2. Bend it at all four corners cutting notches if necessary.
3. Take the liner from the chair and slype the butt.

Photo 3.14 A Campaign chair with open-skeined seat and back

although those at the front may be further apart.
2. Put in canes passing from side to side weaving them over and under the first canes to form a mesh, unlike those in chair caning. A simple weave over one cane, under the next, over the third is used.
3. Peg all the holes (see page 33). Make sure the pegs are sunk slightly below the top edge of each rail.

Alternative method: On large seats a four-strand mesh may be put on with two canes in each direction in every hole in exactly the same way as the settings and weavings of the six-way caning pattern (page 17). This method can cause raised skeins in the seat later on.

THE FIRST STAGE
Individual skeins are attached across the chair from side to side. Start at the back left-hand corner as you face the chair. The chair back will be on the far side. All the instructions below refer to the chair in this position even after it is suggested you move the chair round.

Photo 3.15 Chair for skeining showing the arrangement of holes, the liner and the foundation caning

4. Measure the inside of the back rail carefully and overlap the two ends of the liner until they have exactly the same measurement along the back.
5. Mark the beginning and end of the slype on the uncut end. These will show you exactly where the second slype should be. Cut this carefully. Now tie or pin this liner to all four rails, keeping the join at the centre back.

THE FOUNDATION
A support for the willow skeins must first be woven. This is provided by a mesh of chair cane (Photo. 3.15) using the holes in the frame. It used to be known as 'Johnny save all'! Willow seats reputedly give way all at once and this canework prevents someone falling right through! The term is a nautical one, used to describe the nets under rigging. Use No. 3 or No. 4 cane. It should *not be wider* than the skeins.

1. Start by laying in lengths of cane from front to back as shown on page 17, joining as described if necessary. There are usually the same number of holes along the two rails

The left-hand side

1. First wrap the corner section of the frame. Here the thickness of the liner prevents the use of the knotting which covers the rest of the rail. Take a skein, dip it in water for one or two minutes and push it down in the back left corner between the chair frame and the liner, leaving a few centimetres hanging underneath (Fig. 3.23). Carry the skein over the top of the frame to the outside, under the frame and up into the centre of the chair, keeping the smooth side outwards. Now carry it over the top of the liner and frame to the outside and underneath again. Bring it over the liner and tuck it in between the liner and the frame, leaving a short end hanging down. Try and bind in the end you started with on the underside.

2. *The leaders.* Next the leaders must be put in. These are lengths of skein as long as the rails. They are laid on the horizontal surface of the rail to stop the loops of skeins moving sideways. Some of the skeins to be knotted (see below) go over the leaders; others go underneath them, producing a pattern on the top surface of the rails.

    For a simple pattern four leaders are used on each rail. Place all four, side by side, on top of the rail with the ends against the back of the chair. Make sure they are in the centre of the rail (Fig. 3.24). Tuck them under the wraps just put on. For security these four tips may be glued to the wood of the back corner with wood glue. Only glue them at the back of the rail, however, otherwise you will be in difficulties!

3. *The knot.* Make sure the skeins have been soaked and wrapped, or dip them in water just before using.

    Lengths of skein are tied on to the left-hand rail with the simple knot described below. The skeins must be close together, just touching each other so the wood is completely covered. The first ones will cover and hide all four leaders.

    (a) Place a length of skein over the left-hand rail leaving the long end to the right and with about 20 cm (8 in) projecting beyond the rail to the left. Also, leave at least 25 cm (10 in) beyond the rail on the right.

    (b) Fold this left-hand end down and under the left-hand rail and bring it up inside the chair to the back of the length of skein (Fig. 3.25a).

    (c) Bring this end towards you over the length of skein leaving a loop underneath.

    (d) Now take it down again, this time between the liner and the rail. Thread it towards the back of the chair through its own loop on the underside (Fig. 3.25b). Pull it until it is tight.

Note: On the upper surface there will be a small slanting knot holding the length of skein.

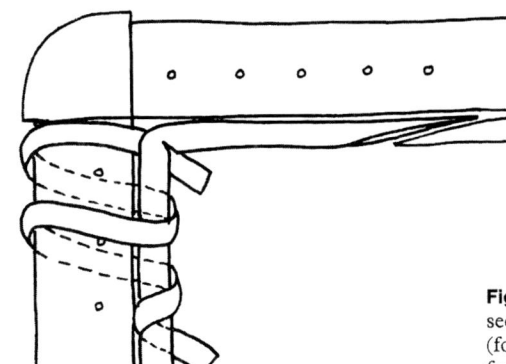

Fig 3.23 Wrapping the back section of the left-hand rail (foundation canes omitted for clarity)

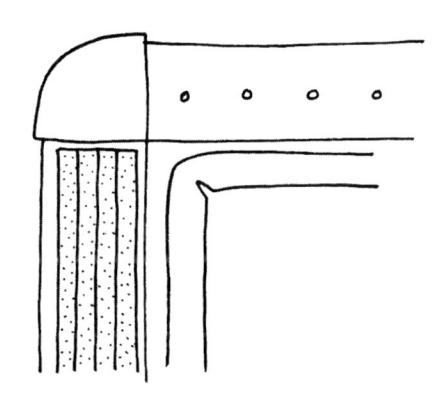

Fig 3.24 The position of the four leaders

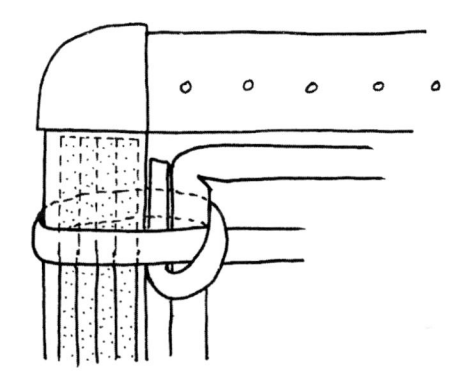

Fig 3.25a The first knot over the liner and the leaders. The first wraps are omitted for clarity and would cover the leaders

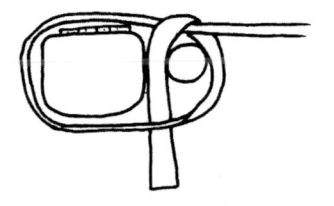

Fig 3.25b Section through rail showing the knot from the front

(e) Knot on three more skeins in this way (Fig. 3.26, skeins **a, b, c**). Each new skein may be knotted on a little way in front of the previous ones and then is slid up close to them. This gives more space for tying the knot.

Note: A fine curved bodkin may be used to help tighten the knots. It is placed with the tip along the length of skein, above and touching it just where the knot is to be on the inside edge of the top of the rail (Fig. 3.27). It is lifted slightly as the knot is first pulled tight, to help achieve a good angle of slant on the knot. It is withdrawn as the knot is pulled tight.

4. Lift the free ends of the well-damped central pair of leaders so that they are not covered by new skeins which will go underneath them (Fig. 3.26). Knot on four more lengths of skein carrying them under the central pair of leaders. Push all the skeins towards the back of the chair so they are really close together. Lift the outer two leaders away from the rail, but bring the central two down on it again.
5. Knot on four more skeins. This group will pass under the two outer leaders, but over the centre two.
6. Lift the centre two leaders away, bring the outer two down on to the rail. Knot on four more skeins, passing over the outer two leaders but under the central pair. The pattern created by the leaders is shown in Photo 3.16.

Fig 3.26 The first group of four knotted skeins pass over the central leaders, the next will pass under them

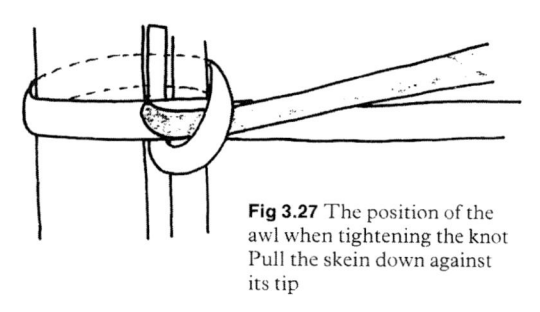

Fig 3.27 The position of the awl when tightening the knot Pull the skein down against its tip

Photo 3.16 Skeined seat showing how to soak the skeins before knotting

7. When a foundation cane is reached, knot it in with the skein.

Stages 5 and 6 are repeated until the left-hand rail is almost covered.

Note: The constant pulling down of the knots may pull the liner down too. It should remain just below the top of the rail, so adjust it if necessary.

Push the skeins close together and re-damp the leaders with a wet cloth as necessary. They will crack if allowed to dry out.

8. *The Front.* When you are about nine skein widths from the front corner, tie in four more skeins, lifting away the centre two leaders.
9. Knot on the last four skeins covering all the leaders. Try to create the same pattern at the front and back of this rail.
10. Two wraps must be placed round the liner and rail using a short skein, to cover all the leaders and the corner, as you did at the beginning (Fig. 3.23). Instead of using a fresh skein, it is possible to leave a much longer end than usual below the last skein to be knotted on. Bring this up to the outside of the chair and use it for two

wraps, finishing by tucking the end through the wraps on the underside.

The right-hand side

Before starting to knot on the other side, up-end the chair and carefully put all the long loose ends of the skeins in a large bowl of water (Photo 3.16). Make sure the parts which will have to be used for knotting on the right-hand rail are submerged. Leave them for about five minutes so they are thoroughly flexible. (The sections across the centre of the seat do not need to be wet.)

1. Place or glue the tips of four leaders on top of the rail in the centre as on the left (Fig. 3.24).
2. Wrap the back corner with a short length of skein in the same way as for the left back corner (Fig. 3.23), but as a mirror image.
3. *The tension stick.* This is a firm hardwood or dowel rod placed under the skeins of the first stage. It provides enough slack in the skeins to allow for the weaving of the second stage. Its size will vary with the size of the chair but for a small bedroom chair 1.5 cm ($\frac{1}{2}$ in) square should be suitable. Until you are experienced it is important that inflexible hardwood is used so the pressure of skeins above it will not cause it to bow downwards.

   Place it across the centre of the seat from front to back and tie it on to the front and back rails (Fig. 3.30t).
4. *Knotting.* Start knotting at the back of the right-hand rail. Rewet the skeins when necessary. If you find the loose skeins are in the way, tie them into a bundle and fold them towards the left of the chair (Photo 3.17). Withdraw one at a time for knotting.
   (a) Bring the first skein over the tension stick from the left, carry it round the rail and to the back of the length of skein.
   (b) Carry it forwards over the section of skein which lies across the chair, leaving a loop underneath.
   (c) Take it down between the liner and the frame and through its own loop underneath (Fig. 3.28). The end will project towards the back of the chair (Fig. 3.28b).
   (d) Pull it tight to give the diagonal knot, using a bodkin as before.
5. Continue knotting, adding leaders and keeping the leader pattern as before (pages 143–4) and pushing the skeins close so the frame is covered. At the front of the chair, match the wrapping and leader pattern of the left-hand side.

   Note: Many chairs have curved fronts and backs. At this stage there may be gaps between the skeins and the curved rails at the front and back (Fig. 3.29). These will be filled in later.

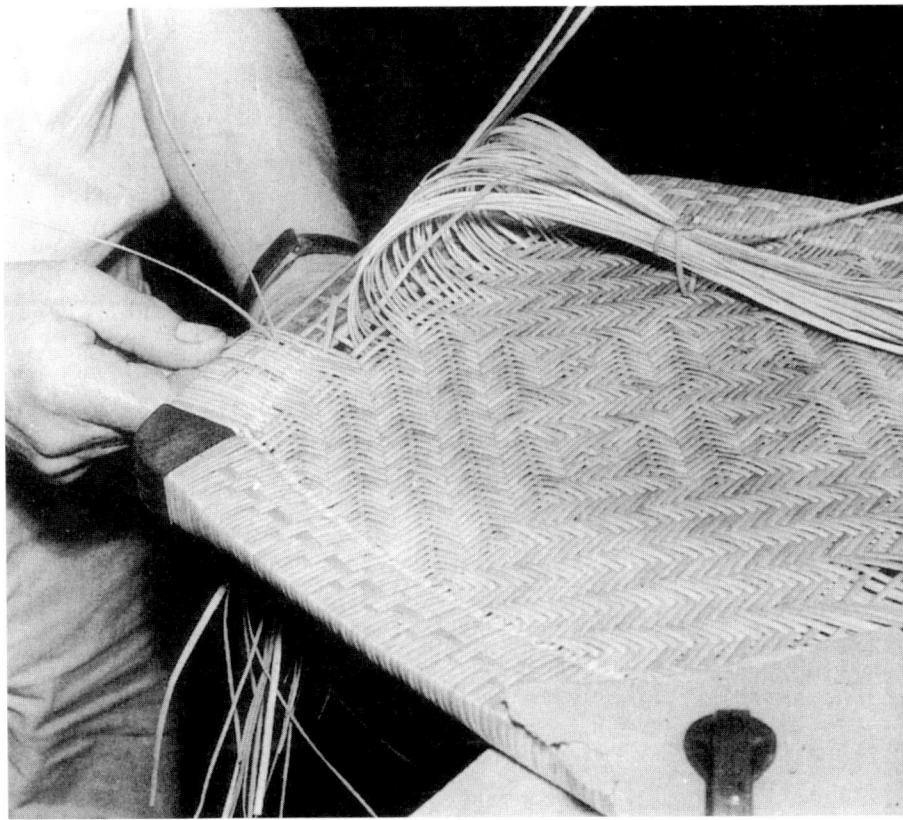

Photo 3.17 Showing the way in which skeins may be bundled to keep them out of the way. This may be done at any stage in the work. Here, the second stage knotting has been started.

Fig 3.28 Knotting on the right-hand rail

Fig 3.29 Gaps (shaded) may have to be filled in when the main body of the seat has been woven

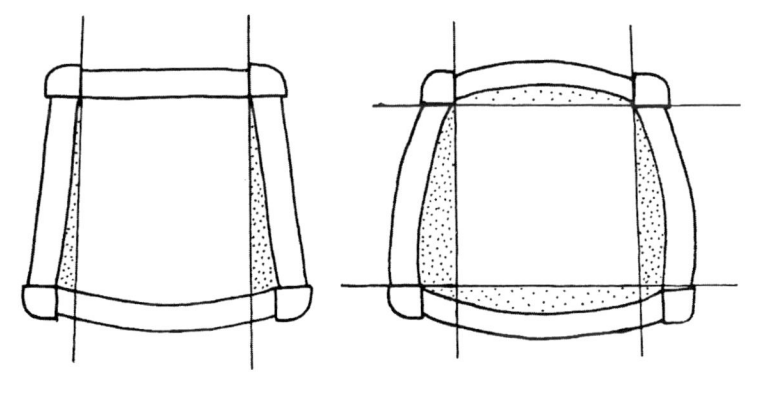

THE SECOND STAGE

This is worked from front to back. The skeins are woven in before being knotted (Photo 3.16).

A large number of different patterns can be woven into the seat at this stage. Many are damask patterns of diamonds, very elaborate and beautiful.

One of the simplest is a twill weave, carrying the skeins over three others, under three, over three and so on (Photo 3.30). Avoid closer weaves, such as over one and under one, which would need a much larger tension stick and would not give a comfortable flat seat. A *simple twill weave* is described here.

1. Soak and wrap a bundle of skeins. You will probably find it easier to turn the chair sideways, but try various positions and use whichever you find most comfortable.
2. Start at the back of the chair on the left. Take a damp skein and weave it *over* three, under three of the knotted skeins until you reach the front (Fig. 3.30 skein **a**). There may be less than three in the front group but this does not matter. If the chair is curved at the side this skein will leave an unwoven gap between itself and the left-hand frame. If the back rail is shorter than the front there will also be gaps at the front and the skein will not lie beside the front leg. These gaps will be filled in later.

   Leave at least 20 cm (8 in) of this woven skein projecting beyond the rail at both the back and front of the chair.
3. The woven pattern is continued as follows:
   (a) Weave the second skein to the right of the first taking it *over two* skeins, then under three and over three to the front (Fig. 3.30 skein **b**).
   (b) Start the third *over one*, then under three, over three (Fig. 3.30 skein **c**).
   (c) The fourth starts *under three*, over three, under three and so on (Fig. 3.30 skein **d**).
   (d) The fifth passes *under two*, over three, under three (Fig. 3.30 skein **e**).
   (e) The sixth *under one*, over three, under three to the front (Fig. 3.30 skein **f**).

These six weavings complete the pattern. The seventh would be the same as the first, starting over three skeins.

Continue to weave skeins in this pattern, pushing them as close together as possible at the back and keeping them at right angles to the front rail.

Note: A shell bodkin or small curved awl may help with this weaving. Push it down in the space you wish the skein to come up. Hold it on the diagonal and push the end of the skein into the groove of the bodkin. Draw up the bodkin and the skein should come with it. This avoids the need to have one hand underneath the chair and speeds up the work.

4. *Including the foundation.* On each side of the chair some foundation canes must be included in the second stage weaving to provide extra support to the seat. There does not have to be any particular pattern to this but if you are taking a skein under a group of three, when you meet a foundation cane pass under that cane as well. This is for extra strength and to prevent sag. These catchings of the foundation are kept to the area between the side rails and the second foundation cane in from the edge. It is done wherever you can in these side areas (Photo 3.18).
5. Push the tension stick to the right as you work and when you are about two-thirds across the back rail, take it out. Work until the back rail is filled. You should have a rectangular panel of weaving the width of the back rail.

Note: *What to do if the tension is wrong.* If you find that you have not used a large enough tension stick, use a wet cloth to

Fig 3.30 Starting the twill weave of the second stage. A dowel tension stick (**t**) has been used during the first stage. Foundation canes and leaders omitted.
The graph shows the complete twill pattern.
The second graph shows the pattern providing a twill with the opposite diagonal

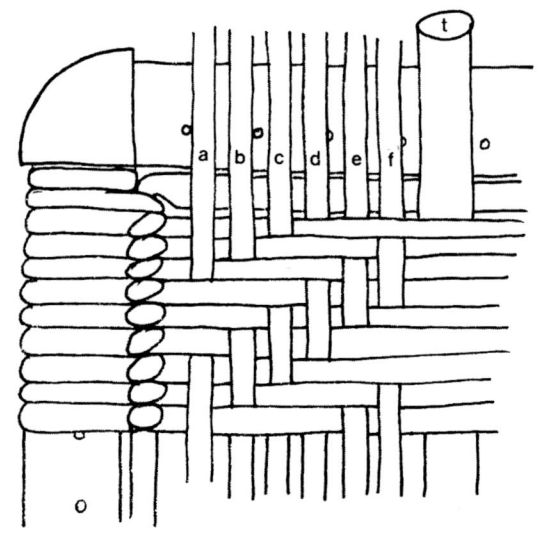

146

Fig 3.31 Filling in the gap by the side rail

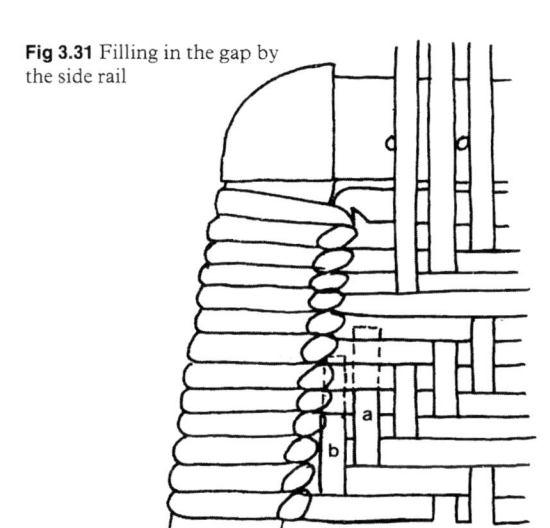

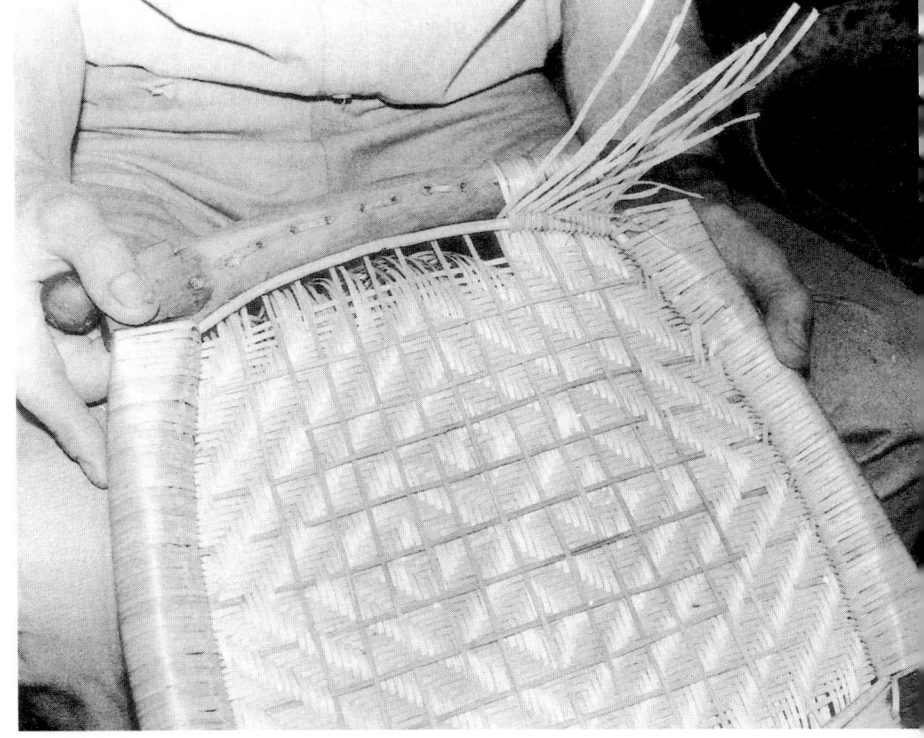

dampen all the knots on the right-hand side. Push up all these knots carefully to loosen them and allow for the final weavings of the second stage. When this is completely finished and the sides have been filled in, on shaped chairs, dampen the knots again and pull them tight using a fine tool to keep them at the correct angle.

6. *Filling in the sides* (Photo 3.18). The lengths of front rail on either side which still have no skeins over them must be filled in next. Skeins are woven in but will not be knotted until later.

(a) Start on one side towards the back at the narrowest point of the gap (Fig. 3.31). Push the end of a skein down between two of the knotted skeins, leaving an end 2–3 cm (1 in) long (Fig. 3.31, skein **a**). It must follow the twill pattern and must first come over a group of three skeins.

(b) Weave it to the front next to the panel of weaving and following the pattern.

(c) Leave an end of about 20 cm (8 in) hanging over the front rail.

(d) The next will be put in further forward than the last one at a point where it will again go over three skeins at the start (Fig. 3.31, skein **b**). It will be nearer the row of knots along the side rail and should completely fill in the remaining gap near the back of the chair. Use the curved bodkin to help the weaving.

(e) Continue putting in short pieces, starting each one nearer the front, until the front rail is completely covered. On most chairs this will also fill in the gap at the side of the chair.

Note: If the side rails have a pronounced curve there may still be a small gap along the side. Fill this in with short pieces of skein leaving both ends hanging underneath. These pieces will never be knotted.

Repeat to fill the gap on the other side.

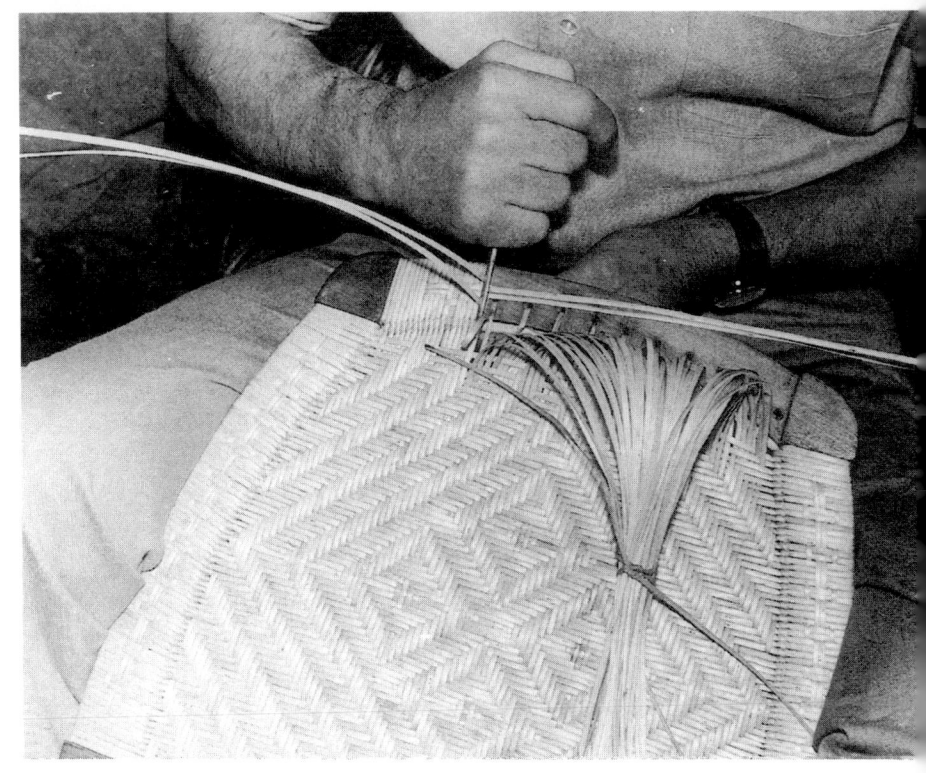

Many of these skeins may catch in the foundation canes.

7. *Knotting the back rail* (Photo 3.19). Leaders are used on the back rail to match those on the sides. You will probably not need to wrap the corners of the back rail as the knotted skeins will cover all the wood without difficulty. If you do need to wrap the first section of rail cover it with a short skein (Fig. 3.23).

Photo 3.18 Showing the inclusion of the foundation skeins when weaving
Photo 3.19 Knotting the back rail showing the use of the small bodkin or awl

To knot the back rail you may find it comfortable to sit with the back of the chair between your knees. Start knotting on the right-hand end of the rail as the chair is now.

(a) Soak all the skeins as before. Tie them all up in a bunch about half-way along their length and fold them forward (Photo 3.17). This keeps them out of the way and prevents them drying as quickly.

(b) Use four leaders. Glue their four ends to the top of the back rail on the left or tuck them in if you have had to wrap this first section of rail (Fig. 3.24).

(c) Pull out the skein nearest the left-hand corner, carry it over the top of the rail, underneath and up into the small gap in the corner between the rail and the first stage skeins (Fig. 3.32).

(d) Bring it over itself, leaving a loop underneath, then down between the frame and the liner and to the left through its own loop underneath. Pull it tight.

(e) Continue to knot more skeins in this way, pulling each skein out of the bunch as you need it.

(f) Weave over and under the four leaders as before, matching the pattern of the side rails.

(g) Continue knotting until you reach the other end of the rail. You may need to use a short skein to wrap the rail corner as you did at the beginning of the rail.

8. *Filling in at the back.* If the back rail is curved you will still have a gap which must be filled. Fill it with short pieces of skein as at the side, keeping the twill pattern. Both ends of these must be left underneath as they cannot be knotted (Photo 3.20). You

Photo 3.20 Short skeins have been woven in just in front of the back rail

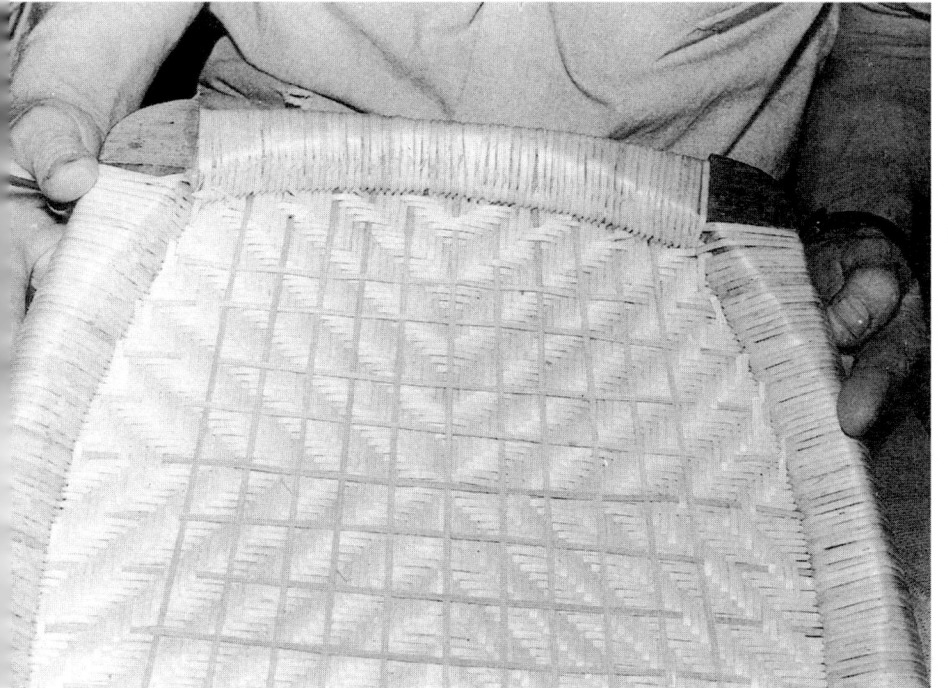

Fig 3.32 Knotting at the back (the wrapping of the first part of the back rail is not shown)

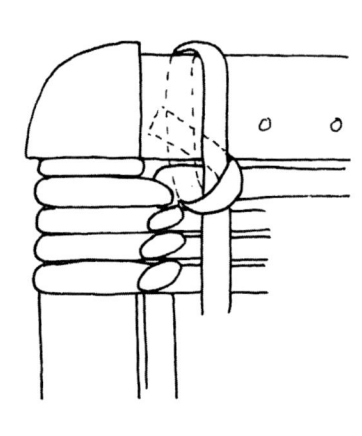

Fig 3.33 Knotting at the front. You may need to wrap the first part of the rail with a short length of skein

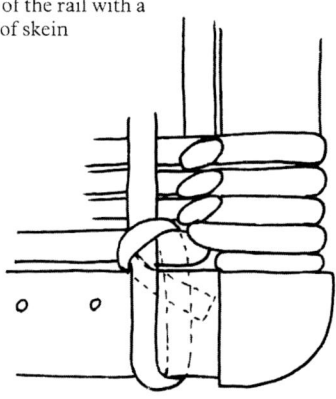

will find the easiest way to weave is to thread the end of the skein up and down vertically, step by step. Use a shell bodkin, or have one hand under the chair and one above. Catch in the foundation canes wherever necessary.

Alternatively, these short skeins may be laid in as you are knotting along the back. They may then lie flatter than if woven in afterwards, and it is quicker to do.

9. *Knotting at the front.* This is finished off in the same way as the back.

Note: There seems to be no rule about which way the knots should lie but if you want the diagonal of the front knots to match that at the back, start at the right-hand corner. You may find it easier to work with the chair back on your left. Use a short skein to cover the first part of the rail (page 143) if necessary.

(a) Wrap the first skein (probably one of the short ones from stage 6) over the rail, carry it underneath the rail and liner and up into the small space in the corner to the right and over itself leaving a loop underneath (Fig. 3.33).

Fig 3.34 Way of knotting so the end comes forwards

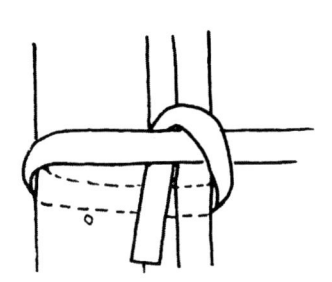

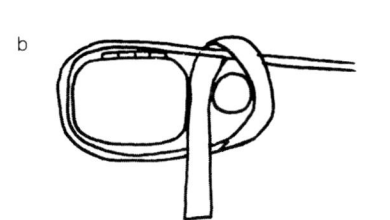

Fig 3.35 Knotting without threading the end through the loop underneath

ALTERNATIVE METHODS OF KNOTTING

These skeined seats were traditionally done by individual basketmakers and not by chair seaters. Many different patterns and knotting methods can be found on old chairs. The advantage of the method already described is that the ends of the skeins lie away from you as you work the next knot and do not get in the way.

Method 1. In some chairs the knots are put on in the reverse direction to that described and the end of the skein is bound in under the next two or three skeins and then cut. It is slower to work and does not add to the strength of the chair. There is a slight improvement in neatness underneath.

For this method tie all the knots on the side rails as follows:

1. Lay the skein over the rail and liner, carry it underneath and up into the centre of the chair, to the *front* of the long piece of skein this time. Carry it over itself, down between the liner and the frame and through its own loop underneath to point forwards (Fig. 3.34).
2. When knotting the next skein nearer the front of the chair bind in the end of the previous knot. Carry this end along the underside of the frame under three or four knots and then cut it off. Subsequent skeins also have their ends bound in so you will be carrying several pieces along the under side.

Method 2. Often the knots are not carried through their own loop underneath but are left hanging down after passing between the liner and the frame. The knots can be formed to slant in either direction (Fig. 3.35 a and b).

This method is a little quicker but the knots are not held so firmly. It presents difficulties on seats with complex patterns which have to be started in the middle as for one half of the chair the knots are not held by previous skeins.

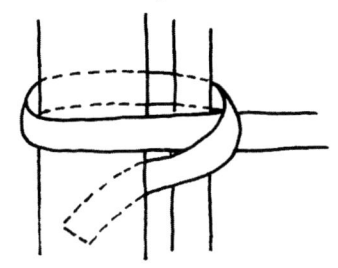

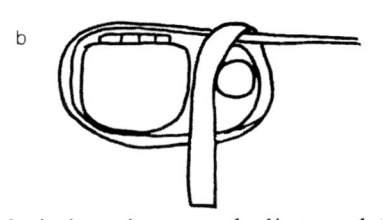

(b) Take it down between the liner and the frame and through its own loop underneath.
(c) Pull it tight using the bodkin to guide the knot.
(d) Continue to knot all the way along, putting in leaders as before.
Note: All the knotting on one rail follows the same direction.

10. *Filling in the front.* This is only necessary if the chair has a curved front rail. Again short pieces are woven in, following the twill pattern and leaving ends underneath to fill the space left by the curved front rail. Catch in the cane foundation as you did at the back. (Photo 3.20)
11. *Trimming underneath.* Each rail will have ends of skein hanging underneath. They are cut off only about 1mm ($\frac{1}{16}$ in) away from the rail using a sharp knife or scissors. Make sure they are cut horizontally or there will be sharp 'dragon's teeth' underneath, which can hurt when you pick up the chair.

Cut the short ends of the skeins used for filling gaps leaving $\frac{1}{2}$–1 cm ($\frac{1}{4}$ in) underneath for security.

Close skeining: Leslie Maltby's method

The seats shown in Photos 3.21–24 were all woven for the Museum of English Rural Life at Reading in 1966 by Leslie Maltby, a retired basketmaker who was formerly based in High Wycombe. They show variations on the method already described and are, perhaps, simpler and quicker to work. The method may also be used for close caning with cane rather than skeins. The instructions include details of a diamond pattern. Details of other patterns follow.

THE LINER

Here the butt lies inside the front rail, the slype being in the front right-hand corner. Notches are cut at the corners and the tip, still quite sturdy, lies along the right-hand rail into the front corner. Nail it or use tape as before (Fig. 3.36). There is no overlap of the ends of the liner here and the butt and tip may be trimmed after the liner is held by knotting the first stage on the left-hand side.

Photo 3.21 Weaving the second stage using two tension sticks. The end holes in the back and front rails have not been used for foundation canes

Fig 3.36 Leslie Maltby's method of putting in the liner

THE FOUNDATION CANES

Put in these as before, but do not use the holes in the frame next to the corners on either the front or back rails. Leave these empty for starting skeins later (Photo 3.21).

THE FIRST STAGE
The left-hand rail

1. Glue the ends of four leaders at the back left-hand corner so that they lie along the middle of the rail (Fig. 3.24).
2. Take a skein and push the end down into the first hole in the back rail and peg it from on top (Fig. 3.37).

    Take this skein down in the corner between the liner and the frame, under the left-hand rail, up on the outside, over the rail and leaders, down again between liner and rail, under the rail, up again and then carry the long end over to the right of the frame.
3. Start a new skein by tucking the end under the first wrap on the left-hand rail (Fig. 3.38). Push it in from above just inside the inner-edge of the rail. Bring the skein forward over the long end from stage 2, then take it down over the liner to form a diagonal knot. Take it under the liner and rail, up on the outside, over the rail, and across to the right-hand rail.
4. Start a new skein by pushing its end under two wraps (**a** has just been knotted) on the inside top edge of the left-hand frame (Fig. 3.39). Bring it forward over the long skein from stage 3 above, down over the liner, underneath the rail, up outside the rail, over the rail and leaders and across to the right-hand rail.
5. Continue to add new skeins in this way (Photo 3.22). As you move away from the corner the new ends tuck in on top of the liner. Each end of about 1 cm (½ in) should go under three knotted skeins that are already in position but need not go further. Each will tuck in underneath two ends from the previous two skeins so there will be three thicknesses of tucked-in skeins above the liner.

Fig 3.37 Putting on the first skein

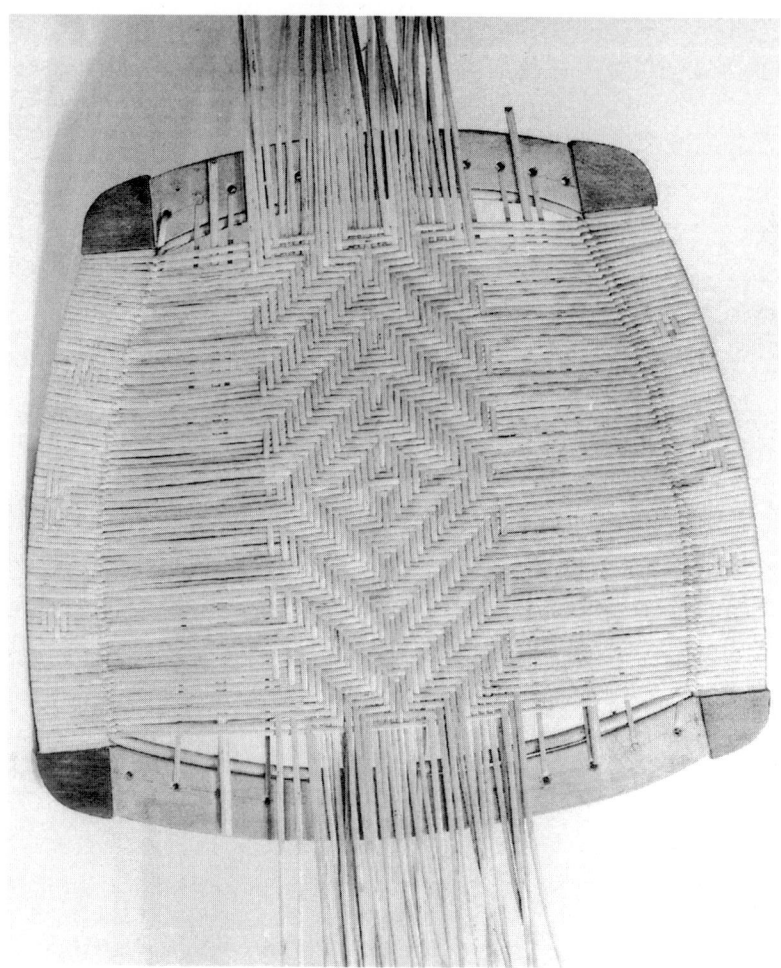

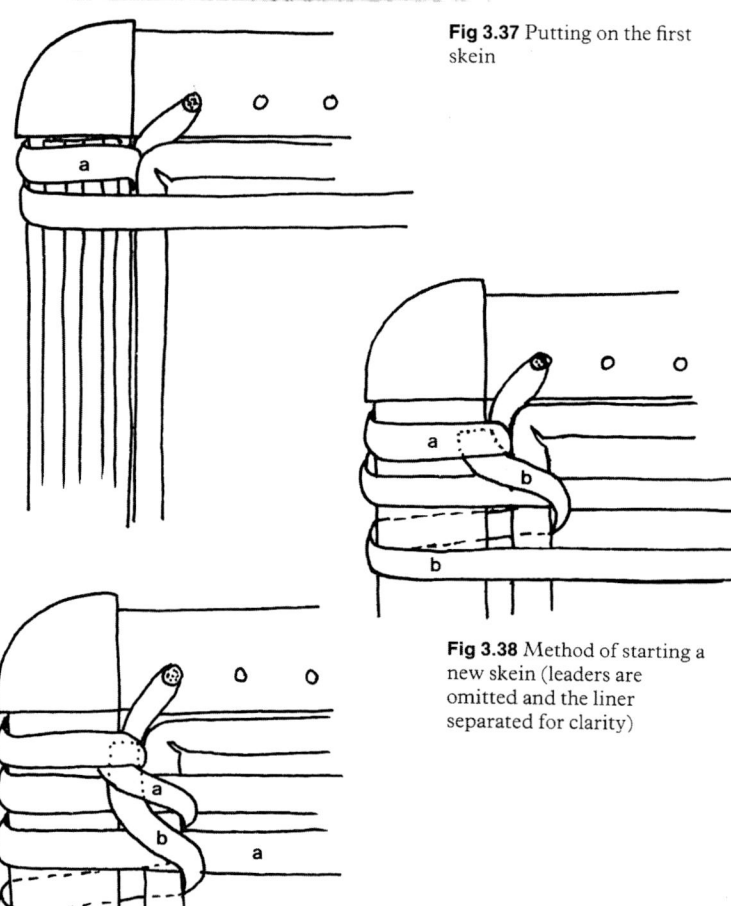

Fig 3.38 Method of starting a new skein (leaders are omitted and the liner separated for clarity)

Fig 3.39 The second skein being put in

150

Photo 3.22 Leslie Maltby knotting skeins along the left-hand rail, starting at the back

Fig 3.40 Finishing the row of knotting on the left-hand rail

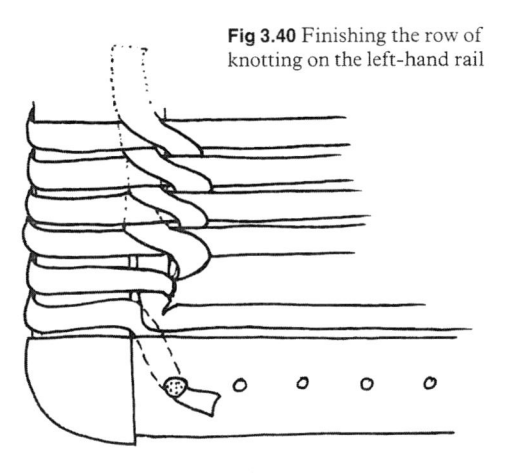

Fig 3.41 The first knot on the right-hand rail

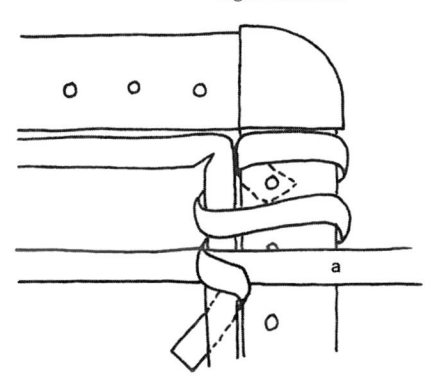

Fig 3.42 The method of knotting on the right-hand rail (each skein knots the skein to the front of it)

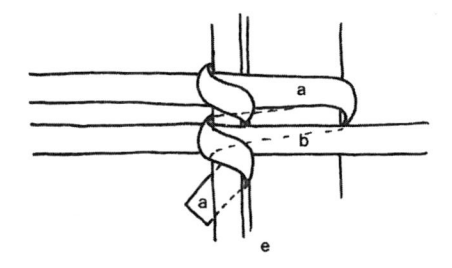

6. Use the leaders for any pattern you like (Photos 3.19, 3.21. 3.23). Keep them well damped so they do not crack.
7. Knot over the foundation canes as well as the skeins across the chair where you meet them. Make sure the skein is immediately above the cane to hide it. These knots tend to be pulled out of position by the foundation canes, and so appear a little higher than those either side. This does not matter.
8. At the end of the left-hand rail make a final knot (Fig. 3.40). Take the end down inside the liner, underneath the rail, over the rail and leaders and down between the liner and the frame. Cut off the leaders. Wrap the rail a second time between the liner and the frame, covering the ends of the leaders, and take the end underneath on to the front rail, tuck it up into the hole nearest the corner, and put in a peg from underneath. Cut off the skein end.

The right-hand rail

1. Glue the tips of four leaders to the top of the rail in the middle at the back corner (Fig. 3.24).
2. Put two tension sticks of hardwood about 1 cm (½ in) square (or use one wider one). When you have had some experience the butts of five-foot rods may be used across the frame from front to back (Photo 3.21).
3. Each skein knots the one in front of it. All the long skeins from the left should be lying across the right rail at this stage. Tuck the end of a short piece of skein down between the liner and the frame leaving 2–3 cm (1 in) underneath (Fig. 3.41). Bring the longer end over the top of the rail to the outside, down and under the rail, tucking in the 2–3 cm, then up in the centre and round the rail and liner again. Take the same end forward over the liner and the first long skein from the left to knot it and then take it down between the liner and the frame.
4. Now use the first long skein from the left (Fig. 3.42, skein a). Take it over the liner, rail and leaders, down and under the rail and liner, up between itself and the second skein across from the left, forwards over this second long skein and down between the liner and the frame. Pull tight.

151

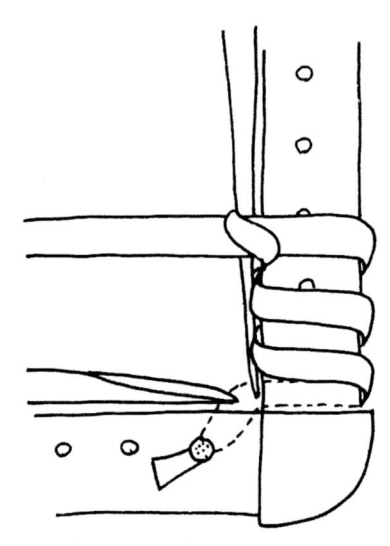

Fig 3.43 The final wraps of the right-hand rail

5. Continue in this way, each long skein being used to knot the one in front of it. Push all the skeins towards the back of the rail after knotting so the wood is closely covered.
6. Use the leaders to match the pattern on the left-hand rail.
7. At the front of the right-hand rail the last long skein is knotted by the previous one (Fig. 3.43). Take the end of this last long skein over the liner and rail, down and under the rail, up between the liner and the rail, then at the corner, wrap just the rail once and then a second time. Take the end across underneath on to the front rail and tuck it up through the hole nearest the corner and peg this hole from underneath.

THE SECOND STAGE

1. Push the two tension sticks apart towards the side rails. If you have only used one push it to one side.
2. Find the first stage skein which lies at the exact centres of the side rails and mark it with string or a loop of skein.
3. *Weaving the second stage: the Diamond pattern* (Photo 3.21). The weaving starts in the centre of the chair, and then is carried out each side of this central skein so that the woven section expands towards each side rail at the same time.
    (a) The central skein of the second stage is taken under the five central skeins of the first stage, then goes over five, under five etc., on both sides of it, until the front and back rails are reached (Fig. 3.44, skein **a**).
    (b) The two skeins either side of this central one pass under the centre three of the first stage, over five, under five, and so on to the edges of the chair (Fig. 3.44, skein **b**). Work outwards both ways from the middle.

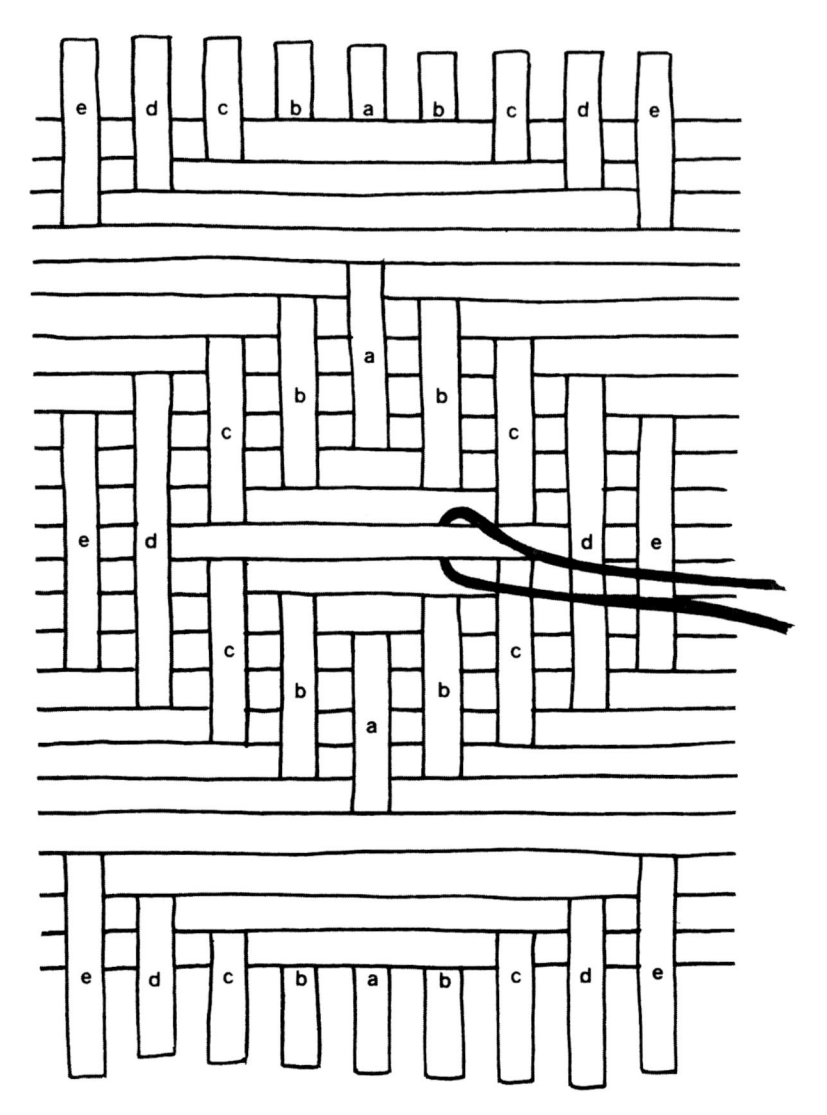

Leave long ends front and back as before.
(c) The next two skeins, one either side of the three so far in place, pass under the central one, over five, under five etc. (skein **c**).
(d) The next pair go over the central nine, under five, over five etc. (skein **d**).
(e) Then over seven, under five, over five etc. (skein **e**).
(f) Over five, under five, etc.
(g) Over three, under five, over five, etc.
(h) Over one, under five, over five, etc.
(i) Under the central nine, over five, under five, etc.
(j) Under seven, over five, under five, etc.
(k) Under five, over five, under five, etc.
(l) Under three, over five, under five, etc.
(m) Under one, over five, under five, etc.
Don't forget you work two skeins for each step above. You will have woven a block in the centre of the seat, adding one skein each side of this block at each of the stages (b) to (m).

Now repeat stage (d) to (m) to create the pattern as far as the rails (Figs 3.44 and 3.45).

Fig 3.44 The central block of pattern (the skeins of the second stage are separated for clarity). The loop of skein marks the central skein of the first stage

Fig 3.45 The complete pattern of the close skeined seat shown in Photo 3.21. It is counted in fives

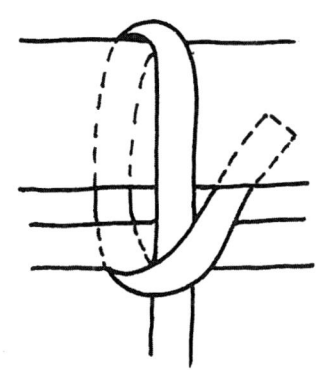

Fig 3.46 Knotting at the back

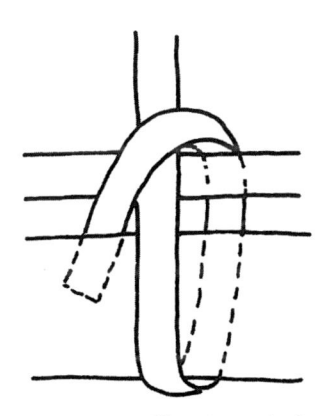

Fig 3.47 Knotting at the front

As you work outwards on each side, you will have to push the tension sticks further over and finally remove them completely.
Note: If you find working out each side from the middle confusing, work one side first, then go back to the centre and work out the other side.

4. Fill in the sides as on page 147, following the diamond pattern. (If you need to adjust the tension of the first stage skeins, see p.146.
5. *Knotting the second stage skeins.* Here each skein knots itself.
Damp and tie up the skeins.
At the back. Here each skein goes over the top of the rail, down underneath the rail and liners, up to the left, over itself to the right and down between the liner and frame (Fig. 3.46).
Note: The end of the skein does not go through its own loop underneath here when forming the knot. Pull tight.

Start at the right back corner and work along to the left. Push the knotted skeins to the right to keep them close together.
At the front. Prepare the skeins by soaking them.
If the diagonal of the knots is to match those at the back, start at the left-hand corner. Take the skein over the front rail, down, under the rail and liner, up to the right, forward over itself and down between liner and frame (Fig. 3.47). Pull tight.
Work along to the right-hand corner.

6. *Filling in at front and back.* Weave in short lengths of skein (page 148) leaving the ends underneath and continuing the pattern of weaving. The number of short lengths needed will vary with the curvature of the rails. The ends can be held in place on the underside with small amounts of wood glue.
7. Trim off all the ends underneath (page 149).

ALTERNATIVE PATTERNS OF WEAVING

It is the weaving of the second stage that can give different patterns to the seat.

1. *The diagonal cross* (Fig. 3.48 and Photo 3.23).

    (a) The central skein passes *over* the central skein of the first stage, then under five, over five to the rails. Start in the centre with the centre of a skein and weave one end forward to the front rail, the other backward to the back rail. The front and back groups may be less than five. This does not matter.
    (b) The skeins each side of the central one pass over three in the centre, then under five, over five, etc.
    (c) The next two go over five, under five, over five, etc.
    (d) Over seven, under five, over five, etc.
    (e) Over nine, under five, over five, etc.
    (f) Under one, over five, under five, etc.
    (g) Under three, over five, under five, etc.
    (h) Under five, over five, under five, etc.
    (i) Under seven, over five, under five, etc.
    (j) Under nine, over five, under five, etc.

    This sequence is repeated to the edge of the seat. The sides, back and front are filled in as before if the rails are curved.

2. *Squares pattern* (Fig. 3.49 and Photo 3.24).

    (a) The central skein passes over the central one of the first stage, then under six, over six on each side to the back and front.
    (b) The two each side of (a) go over three, under six, over six, etc.
    (c) Over five, under six, over six, etc.
    (d) Over seven, under six, over six, etc.
    (e) Over nine, under six, over six, etc.
    (f) Over eleven, under six, over six, etc.
    (g) Under one, over six, under six, etc.
    (h) Under three, over six, under six, etc.
    (i) Under five, over six, under six, etc.
    (j) Under seven, over six, under six, etc.
    (k) Under nine, over six, under six, etc.
    (l) Under eleven, over six, under six, etc.
    Repeat stages (a) to (l) until you reach the edges of the back rail.

3. *Pattern with three diamonds*

    The diamond pattern described above (Fig. 3.45, page 153) has a central diamond and then a plainer pattern carried to the edges of the chair. It is possible to weave in a diamond either side of this central one (Fig. 3.50). Work as follows using the instructions above. For each stage weave in one skein *each side* of the central block.

    Work stages (a)-(m), stages (d)-(h). These produce the central diamond. Then stages (g)-(d), (m)-(i), (h)-(d), (m)-(k). This (k) is the central skein of the side diamonds.

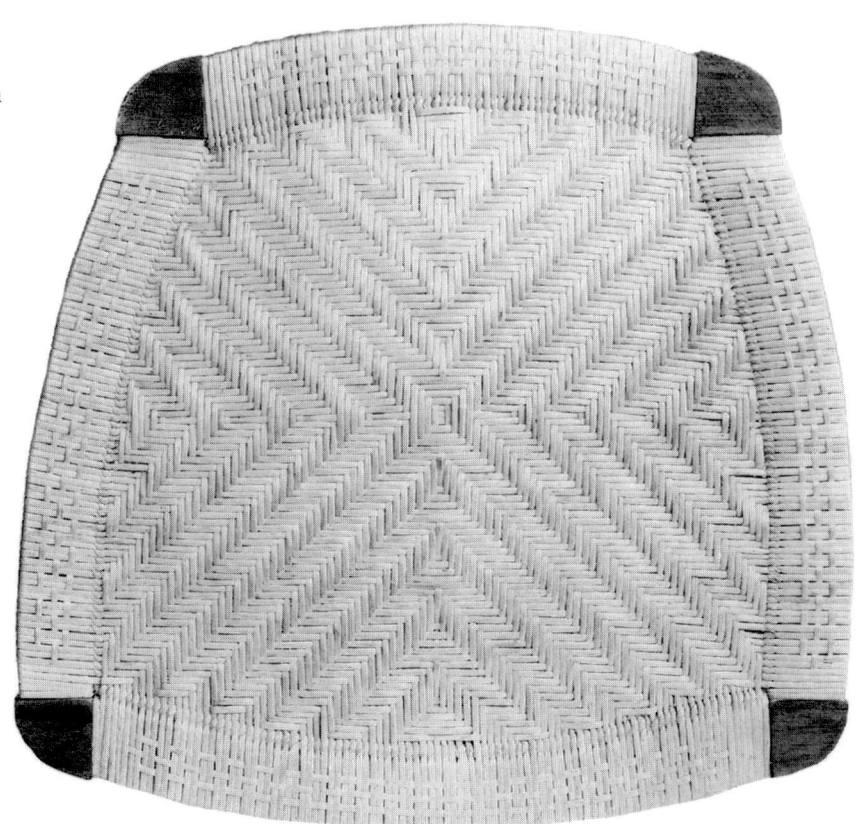

Photo 3.23 A close-skeined seat with the diagonal cross pattern

Fig 3.48 The diagonal cross pattern, counted in fives

154

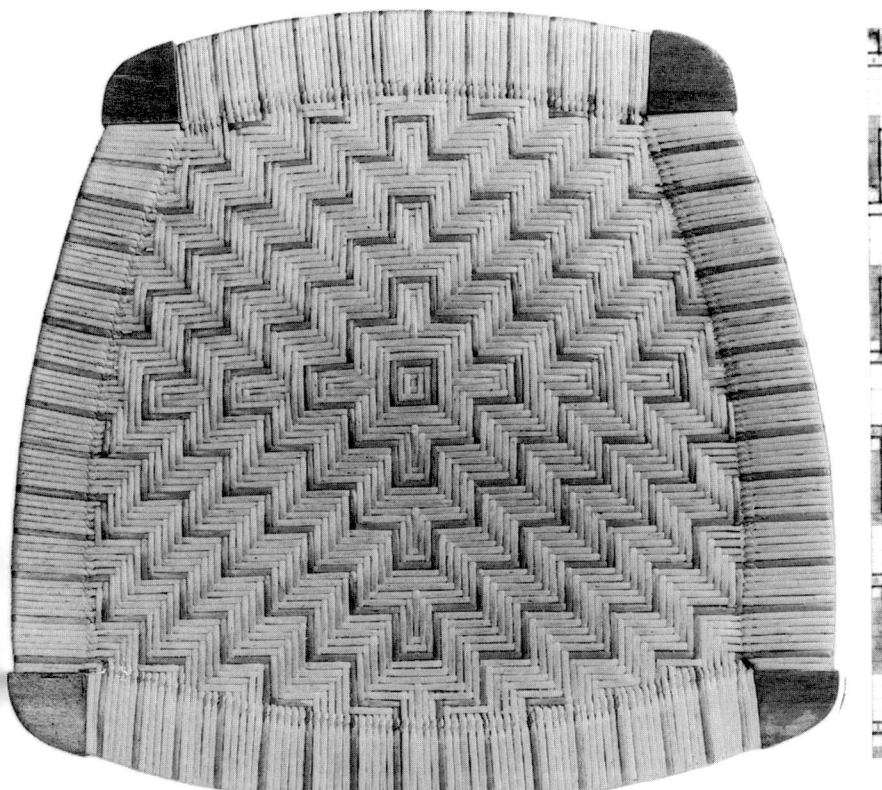

Photo 3.24 The 'Squares' pattern, close skeined

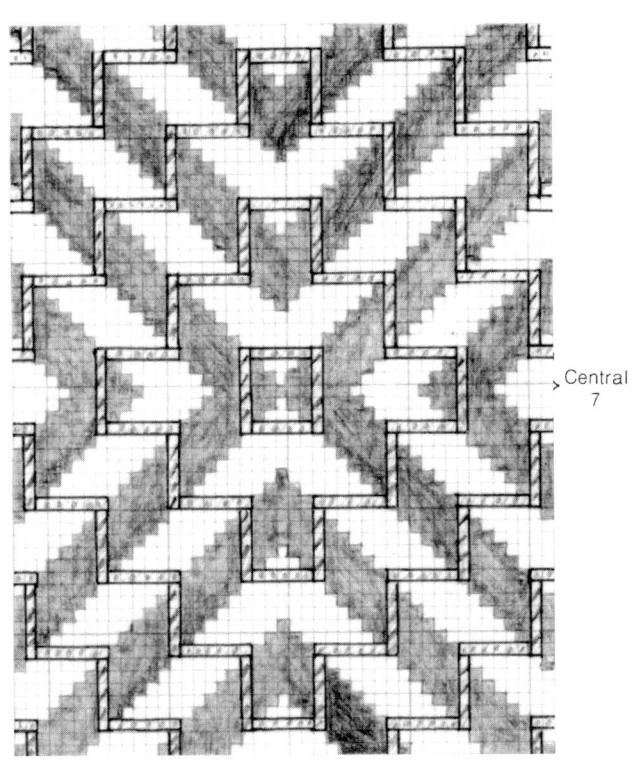

Fig 3.49 The squares pattern. This pattern is counted in sixes

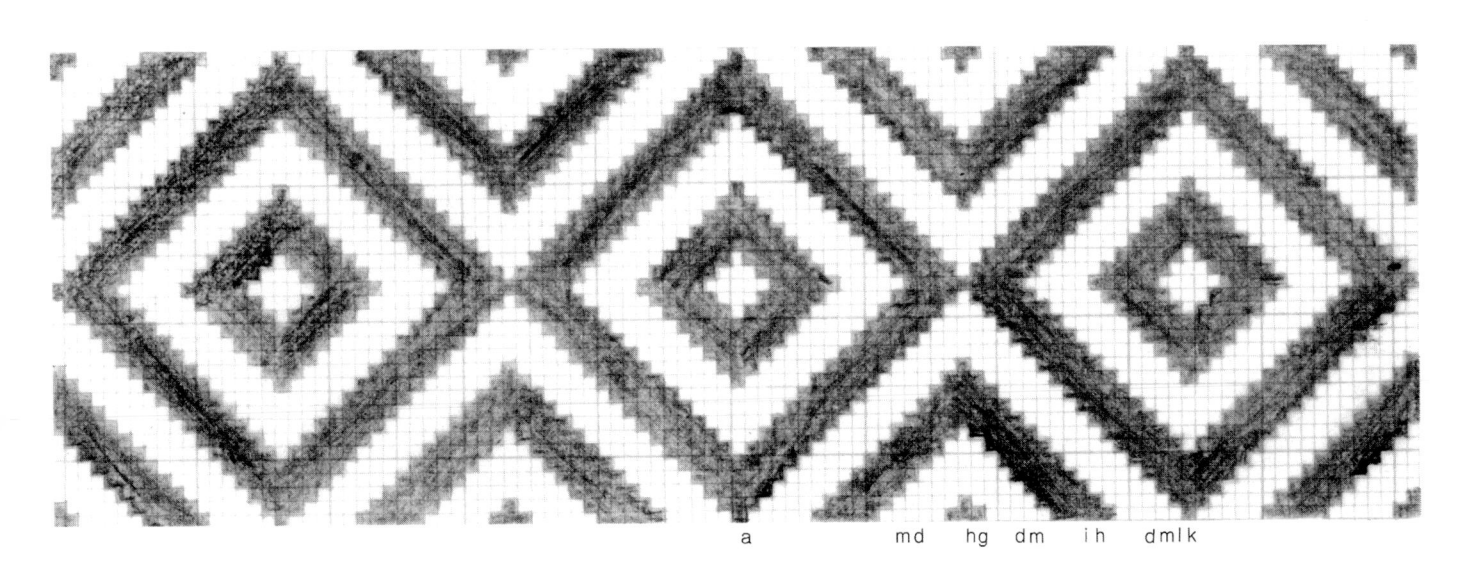

Central 7

a   m d   h g   d m   i h   d m l k

Fig 3.50 Three diamond pattern

155

Following the graph (Fig. 3.50), weave in the other halves of the outer diamonds. You may not be able to complete these before you reach the side rails. This does not matter. Behind and in front of the three diamonds, weave in a simple pattern of V-shapes and diagonals.

Introducing colour patterns

This pattern can include coloured skeins very successfully. They can be dyed with either cold or hot Dylon dyes following the instructions on the packet. Alternatively, buff and white skeins can be used to produce a subtle contrast.

The first stage. Put five skeins between each coloured one. In Photo 3.24 the first coloured skein at the back is pale turquoise, the next magenta and these two colours alternate. The seat is worked following the second basic method already described, but the knotting of these coloured skeins cannot be done in the usual sequence as each must knot to itself rather than the one in front in order to keep the colours together. Each coloured skein should have a coloured knot holding it.

1. Lay a coloured skein (**c**) over the left-hand rail leaving the long end across the whole frame (Fig. 3.51a). Take the shorter end (20 cm or 8 in) across the left-hand rail, down under the rail and liner, and up in front of the coloured long end. The short end is then tucked under the previous two skeins, one of which is still unknotted. Pull the long end to tighten the knot.
2. The next new skein (Fig. 3.51b, skein **a**) tucks in above the long unknotted skein behind the coloured one, is taken over this undyed skein and down inside the liner, and then underneath the liner and rail (Fig. 3.51b). Here on the underside it is brought forward across the coloured skein. Bring it up outside the rail, over the top and across to the right-hand rail.

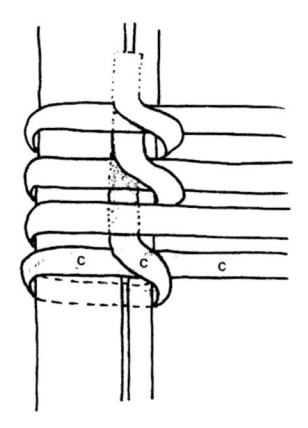

Fig 3.51a The first step in knotting the coloured skein

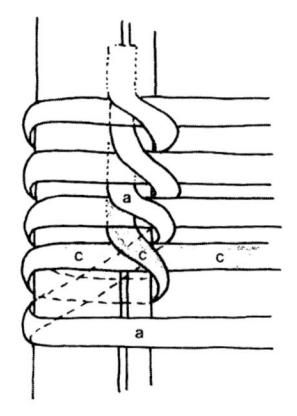

Fig 3.51b Putting in the white skein next to the coloured one

Fig 3.52 A pattern of small checks which is very effective

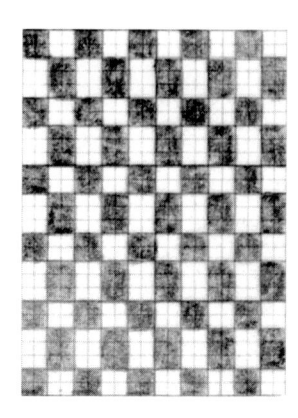

Fig 3.53 Four diamonds may be fitted onto a bedroom chair if the skeins are fine

Repeat (1) and (2) every time you need to lay in a coloured skein (here, every sixth skein). Each coloured skein has five white ones between it and the next one. Leaders may be used for a pattern as before or may be omitted as illustrated (Photo 3.24). Coloured leaders may also be inserted.

3. On the right-hand rail the coloured skeins must knot themselves in the same way.

The second stage. Weave in skeins following the pattern. On the back and front rails each skein knots over itself so knotting is as already described on page 143.

In this square pattern (Fig. 3.49) the coloured skeins must be put in wherever the weaving of that skein starts in the centre by going either *over seven skeins* of the first stage, or *under seven*. This will allow for five white skeins between coloured ones as in the first stage.

156

Other patterns

Many other patterns are possible. Any counted thread design such as those used in embroidery is suitable, but usually designs found on old seats are geometrical. I did hear from Joy Viall, President of the Basketmakers' Association, of a person who wove some desert scenes into a bedhead for King Farouk, so seats with motifs for the user are possible. The thought of flowers for gardeners, or instruments for musicians, is delightful.

All designs must be planned on graph paper first, at least by the inexperienced. Designs found on old seats are shown in Figs 3.52–3.55. Parts of old seats were kindly loaned to me by Joy Viall, who has done much research on the subject of willow-skeined seats. She was given them by Mr Mayes, former Curator of the High Wycombe Chair Museum, who also has a great interest in the subject.

Fig 3.54 A continuous diamond pattern counted in sixes

Fig 3.55 Another diamond variation, counted in fives

21.
Open-skeined seats

These seats have a more open weave than those so far described and are often found as narrow panels on the seats and backs of folding 'Campaign' chairs. The method is called 'open' skeining because pairs of skeins are taken across the frame. Each pair is separated by wraps on the side rails. The pairs of skeins are used as the basis for the weaving of knotted skeins from front to back as in the previous method. Bedroom chairs, because they usually have little wear, are often skeined in this way. Three methods are described. All can also be used for open caning.

MATERIALS

A bundle of skeins. The number depends on the chair but you will need about 120
A thick willow rod (six foot) or piece of No. 15 round cane for the liner
No. 4 chair cane for the foundation
Masking tape for holding skeins

There are at least three methods of working these seats. The final effect is the same but the working of the first stage is very different. For all three methods you will need to start in the same way.

THE LINER
Put this in as described on page 141 or pages 149–50.

THE FOUNDATION
Put in the base caning as described on page 142, using all the holes for methods 1 and 2, leaving out the ones nearest the corners on front and back rails for method 3. This is omitted on narrow chair backs where less strength is needed.

Photo 3.25 A Campaign chair open skeined (Method 1). Notice the row of pairing inside the rails of the back

Method 1: Barbara Maynard's method

This is first described in detail and then summarised (Photo 3.25).

In this method the strands which pass from one side to the other are put on the seat first. Start them at the back and work forwards, fixing them at both sides as you work, not on the left rail first as already described for close skeining. *Liner* and *Foundation canes* are put on.

THE FIRST STAGE
Start at the left back corner of the chair.

Leaders
Glue the tips of four leaders to each side rail at the back keeping them in the centre (Fig. 3.24).

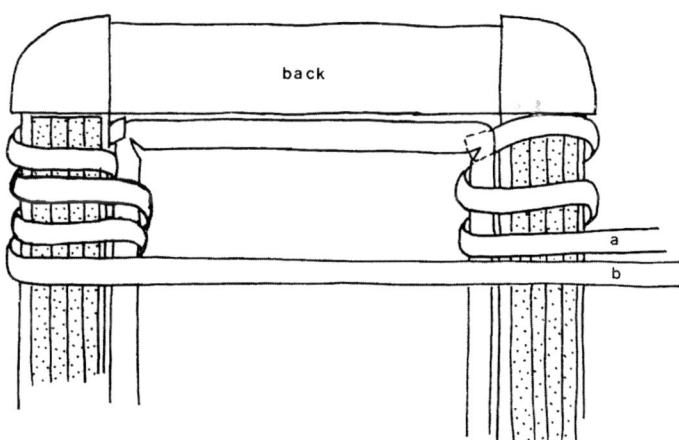

Fig 3.56 Starting the first stage of open skeining at the back of the chair. A skein is started on the right (**a**) and a second long one on the left (**b**)

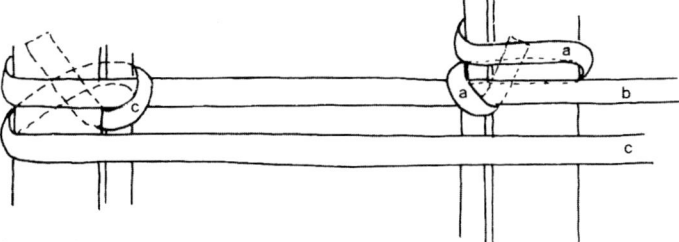

Fig 3.57 Knotting the first long skein on both sides

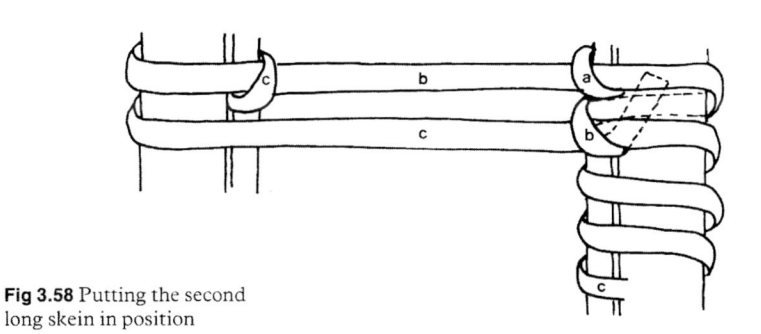

Fig 3.58 Putting the second long skein in position

Before starting the four processes which make up the first stage of open skeining a small part of the rail on the *right* must be covered.

On the Right
Push a short piece of skein down between rail and liner, at the back right-hand corner. Using the longer end, take it over the rail and use it to wrap round the liner and rail twice (Fig. 3.56, skein **a**). Make sure the upper surface of the skein remains on the outside. These wrappings will cover the leaders. Hold the long end (**a**) to the top of the rail with masking tape or string. It will be used again next in (1) below. Alternatively, attach it to the chair stretcher below the seat with a bulldog clip.

On the left

1. Take a long piece of skein and push one end up from below about 1 cm ($\frac{3}{8}$ in) between liner and rail. Bring the long end underneath to the left of the chair, up over the top and down between the liner and the rail, under again and up round the rail and liner twice (Fig. 3.56, skein **b**). Instead of wrapping it a third time carry the skein over to the right of the chair and hold it on top of the rail with tape (**b**).

   Now take the long end remaining from the wrapping on the right (**a**) and use it to knot the long end (**b**) as follows: take it under the rail and liner, leaving a loop underneath, and bring the end up between the back rail and the long skein (**b**). Carry it over this long one, down between liner and rail and through the loop. Pull it tight (Fig. 3.57). Use a fine bodkin to help the knot (page 144) if you wish.

2. Start a new skein on the *left*. Use it to form a knot over the long skein from (1) as follows: place it across the frame just in front of the previous long skein with about 20 cm (8 in) projecting to the left and the long end (**c**) on the right rail (Fig. 3.57 skein **c**). Take the short end under the rail and liner on the left, leaving a loop, and up behind the first long skein from (1). Bring it forward, down between the liner and the frame, through the loop underneath. Pull it tight.

   On the right, use the other end of this skein (**c**) to wrap round the liner and rail twice and hold it with tape (Fig. 3.58) or use a bulldog clip on the stretcher below.

   Also on the right use the long end (**b**) to knot the long section of (**c**) (Fig. 3.58). Bring the end up on the inside of the frame to the back of (**c**); bring it forward over (**c**) leaving a loop underneath, then take it down between the liner and the frame and through its own loop underneath. Pull it tight.

159

Fig 3.59 Knotting the second long skein on the left; knotting and wrapping on the right-hand rail

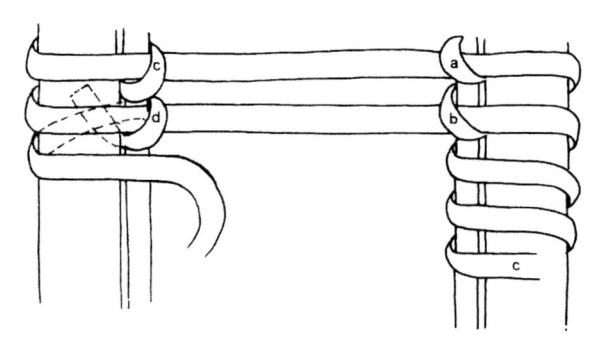

Fig 3.60 Wrapping the left-hand rail and knotting the same skein on the right

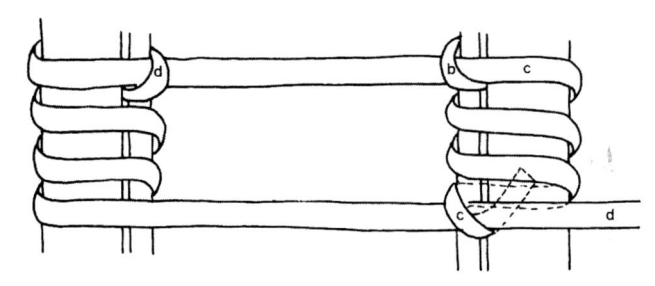

3. Again a new skein (**d**) is started on the left (Fig. 3.59). Use it to knot the previous long one as described at the start of stage 2. Wrap it twice round the liner and frame (Fig. 3.60) and then, instead of completing a third wrap, take it right over to the right-hand side. Hold it in position with a knot using the skein (**c**) previously held with tape (Fig. 3.60). Make sure the knot takes the same diagonal as all the rest.
4. Another new skein is now started on the left by using it to knot the previous one into position as described in stage 2. This skein then goes across the top of the chair to the right, and wraps round the frame and liner twice and is held with tape or clip.
   It is knotted in position on the right by the end of the skein used in stage 3.
5. *Leader patterns*. Knot skeins over and under the leaders to form a pattern as before (pages 143–4).
6. Repeat stages 3 and 4 until the front of the chair is reached. Remember that all wraps are clockwise on both rails, and that all knots on one rail take one diagonal, but those on the other rail take the opposite diagonal.

The upper surface of each skein must be the one that shows.
Note: Here the knotting described leaves the long ends of skeins projecting backwards underneath. This keeps them clear of the worker. Make sure the skein wraps covering the rails are as close to each other as possible to cover the liner and the frame. Keep the leader patterns regular if you have decided to put in leaders.

At the front of the chair try to finish on the right with stage 4 pushing the end down between liner and rail to hold it after the two wraps. It may be necessary to wrap the rails three times to cover them. This does not matter. On the left there will be a small gap at the front.

Use a short piece of skein to knot the remaining unknotted long skein. Wrap this twice round liner and frame and anchor it either by pushing it up between liner and frame and cutting it off or by tucking it underneath some of the previous wraps on the underside of the rail.

Summary (Fig. 3.61)
Cover the first piece of right-hand rail before starting.
1. On the left: wrap rail and liner, wrap again, then take it over to right. Knot it with the end of the short skein.
2. On the left: knot new skein over (1), take it under rail and liner and over the top to the right, wrap twice on the right. Knot it with the skein from (1).
3. Knot (2) skein on left with a new skein. Wrap twice round left-hand rail and liner and carry it over to right-hand rail. On the right: knot it with (2) skein.
4. On the left: knot a new skein over (3), carry it over to right and wrap twice round liner and rail. Knot it on this side with (3). When you are a few centimetres from the back on each rail and the rhythm is established, use the following jingle to help you:

   Knot, over, wrap, wrap.
   Knot, wrap, wrap, over.

Fig 3.61 Showing all the stages involved in the first stage of open skeining, Method 1

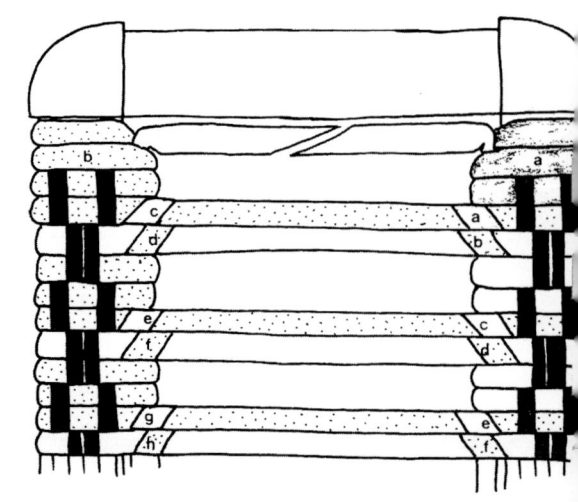

160

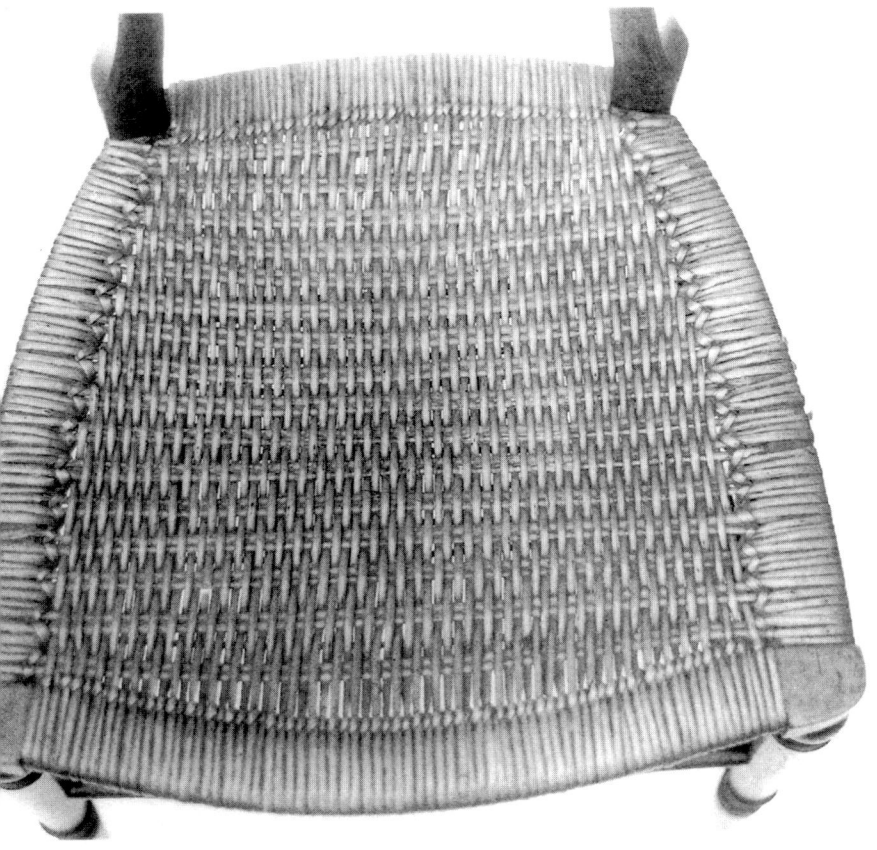

Photo 3.26 An open skeined chair with a interesting knotting pattern

ALTERNATIVE METHODS OF KNOTTING

Method 1. The knots may be put on the other way round so that the final ends on the underside project forwards, but I find these tend to get in the way.

Method 2. Knotting may be done on alternate diagonals. This gives attractive 'V' shapes down each side of the chair. In the example shown (Photo 3.26) the first knot is as follows: the skein comes over behind the long skein, forwards over it and down between the liner and the frame. This is the same on both rails, left and right.

The second knots travel the other way. The skein comes up in front of the long skein and backwards over it and down between the liner and the frame.

Method three. Knots on both sides may take up the same diagonal. This would involve leaving ends on one side projecting backwards and those on the other side projecting forwards.

These alternatives can be chosen for their appearance.

The second stage

This is worked from the front to the back of the chair. It follows the knotting technique of the close skeined chair in that all the skeins are knotted over themselves at either end.

Weaving. The weaving for this stage is normally very simple, as the pairs of skeins which lie across the chair are treated as one. As with the previous technique, it is easier and quicker to complete all the weaving of this stage before doing the knots.

1. Start at the left-hand back corner and weave forwards. Take a skein and carry it over the first pair of skeins, under the next pair, over the next and so on to the front. This skein will lie next to the corner at the back, but if the chair is wider at the front there will be a gap between this skein and the left-hand front leg. Leave at least 20 cm (8 in) of skein at both the front and back for knotting.

   The second skein is put in beside the first and goes under the first pair, over the second pair, under the third pair, and so on to the front.

   Continue to put in skeins, keeping the weaving pattern correct, until the whole of the back rail is covered. You should have a rectangle of woven skeins.

2. *Filling in the sides.* The triangular areas at the front on either side of this rectangle will need to be filled on all but rectangular or square frames. Follow the directions on page 147, making sure the weaving pattern is correct.

3. *Knotting across the back.* Damp all the ends of the skeins (page 144). Knot all the back skeins, starting at one side and working systematically to the other. It is easier to knot in a direction which leaves the long end underneath and pointing away from you as you work (page 143).

4. *Knotting across the front.* Again soak all the ends of the skeins. Start knotting at one corner. This time it looks best if the knots follow the same diagonal as those at the back so arrange to start whichever side will allow this and leave the ends underneath turned away from you. Knot each strand over itself and pull the knots tight.

   When you reach the rectangle of strands which have been knotted at the back, pull each one gently before knotting, to keep the tension even. Knot right across to the opposite corner.

5. *Filling in gaps at the front and sides.* There may still be small gaps at the sides of the chair if the rails bow out a lot. There may also be gaps at the front and back. Fill these in with short lengths of skein as described on page 147.

6. *Trimming underneath.* All the ends underneath should be cut off very short with either scissors or a knife (page 149).

Method 2: The Campaign chair method

I have seen an old 'Campaign' chair worked in a slightly different way (Photo 3.27). On this chair the panels to be filled were very narrow. The back panel was rectangular and flat and the seat rectangular but curved. The following method is not suitable for seats that are wider at the front than at the back or for very wide rectangles (over 25 cm or 10 in). The other two methods can be successfully used on Campaign chairs.

Fig 3.62 Wrapping the back rail and liner, open skeining Method 2

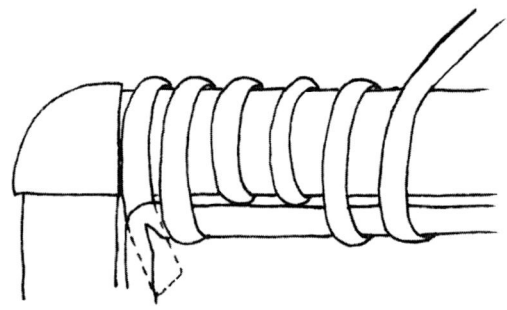

Fig 3.63 Joining at the back or underside of the rail. When wrapping with skeins, **n** is the new end, **o** is the old one

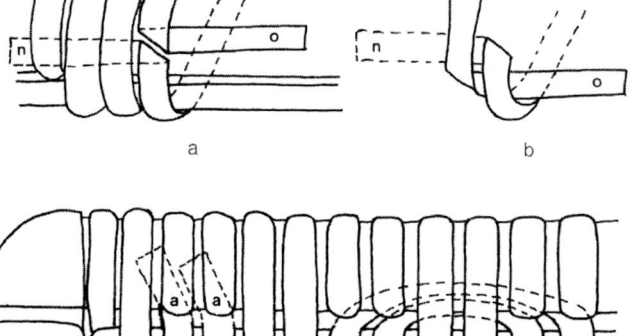

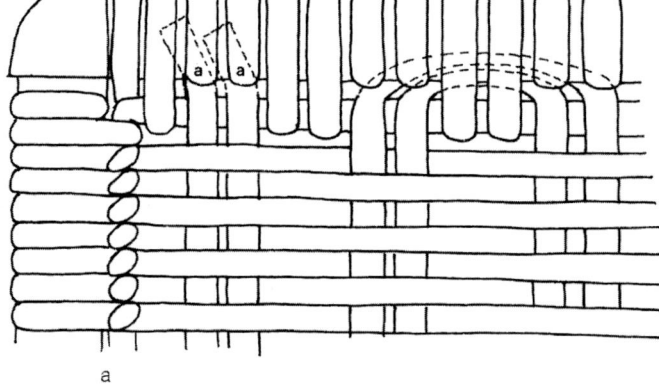

Fig 3.64 Starting the second stage, taking the skeins behind the wrapping to start a new row. The first stage skeins are shown touching but the second stage ones are spaced for clarity

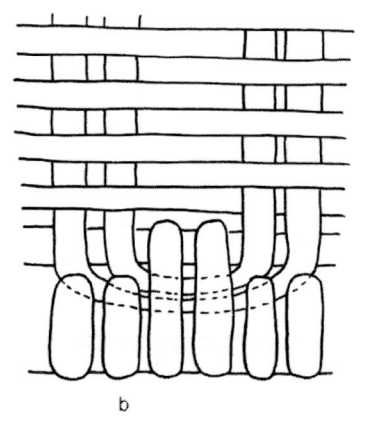

MATERIALS
A bundle of wide skeins, about 4 mm ($\frac{1}{8}$ in). About 90 will be needed for each small panel in the seat and back
Willow rods (six foots) for liners
No. 4 chair cane for the foundation caning on the seat.

THE LINER
This is put in as before (pages 141, 149–50).

FOUNDATION CANING
This is put on the seat (page 142) using all the holes. It is not normally put on chair backs as there are unlikely to be suitable holes.

WRAPPING THE FRONT AND BACK RAILS
In this method these rails (the front and back rails on the seat but the top and bottom rails on the back of the chair) are wrapped, leaders being incorporated into the wrapping.

1. Tuck a skein down between the liner and the frame in the back left-hand corner (Fig. 3.62). Take it over the rail to the outside, round the rail and liner once, and then twice round the rail alone by threading it up between the liner and the rail (Fig. 3.62).
2. Continue in this way, wrapping twice round both rail and liner, and then twice round the rail alone. At the same time put in a simple leader pattern.
3. *To join:* turn the old end at 45 degrees and lay it along the uncovered section of rail on the underside (Fig. 3.63a). Tuck a new end in as far under the wrapping on the rail as possible with the right side of the skein next to the wood of the rail. Turn this at 45 degrees so that it fits against the turned old end. Use the new skein to continue wrapping and secure the old end. A more secure join could be made by wrapping the old and new ends round each other as you turn them (Fig. 3.63b).

THE FIRST STAGE
This stage is worked from side to side and uses separate skeins, each of which needs to be knotted. The skeins are wide ones, about 4 mm ($\frac{3}{8}$ in square), or the butt of a six-foot rod ($\frac{1}{8}$ in). If the chair is a wide rectangle, i.e. more than 20 cm (8 in), you will need a small tension stick laid from front to back of the frame. Use one that is about 1 cm ($\frac{3}{8}$ in square), or the butt of a six-foot rod.

1. The sections of the rail and liner nearest the legs on both right and left and back and front must be filled with two wrappings as described on page 143 (Fig. 3.64a).
2. Then, starting at the back, knot on skeins round the liner on both sides. On a curved

seat this will maintain the curve of the wooden rails. Continue the leader pattern as you go. The method is the first described for close skeining (pages 143–4).

THE SECOND STAGE

Damp some long skeins. The pairs of skeins are woven together from front to back through the skeins of the first stage in a simple over and under pattern and are tucked between liner and frame and then behind the wrappings on the front and back rails. They are not knotted (Fig. 3.64).

1. Start on the left of the seat at the back by tucking two ends down between the rail and the liner in position **a** (Fig. 3.64), leaving about 10 cm (4 in) on the underside. Weave the long ends of these two skeins through the knotted skeins of the first stage, starting by going over one. Weave to the front of the seat (Photo 3.27).
2. Thread the two skeins down between the liner and the rail in the gap. They do not go round the rail, but are taken sideways to the right under the two wraps of the front rail (Fig. 3.64b). Then they are threaded up again between the liner and the rail to the upper surface of the chair.
3. Weave them towards the back, going over the skeins the previous row of weaving went under.
4. At the back again thread the two skeins down between the liner and the rail, round to the right over two wraps and up between the liner and the rail (Fig. 3.64, Photo 3.28).
5. Weave them back to the front again. Continue until the right-hand edge is reached. This may only be about nine rows in a narrow seat.

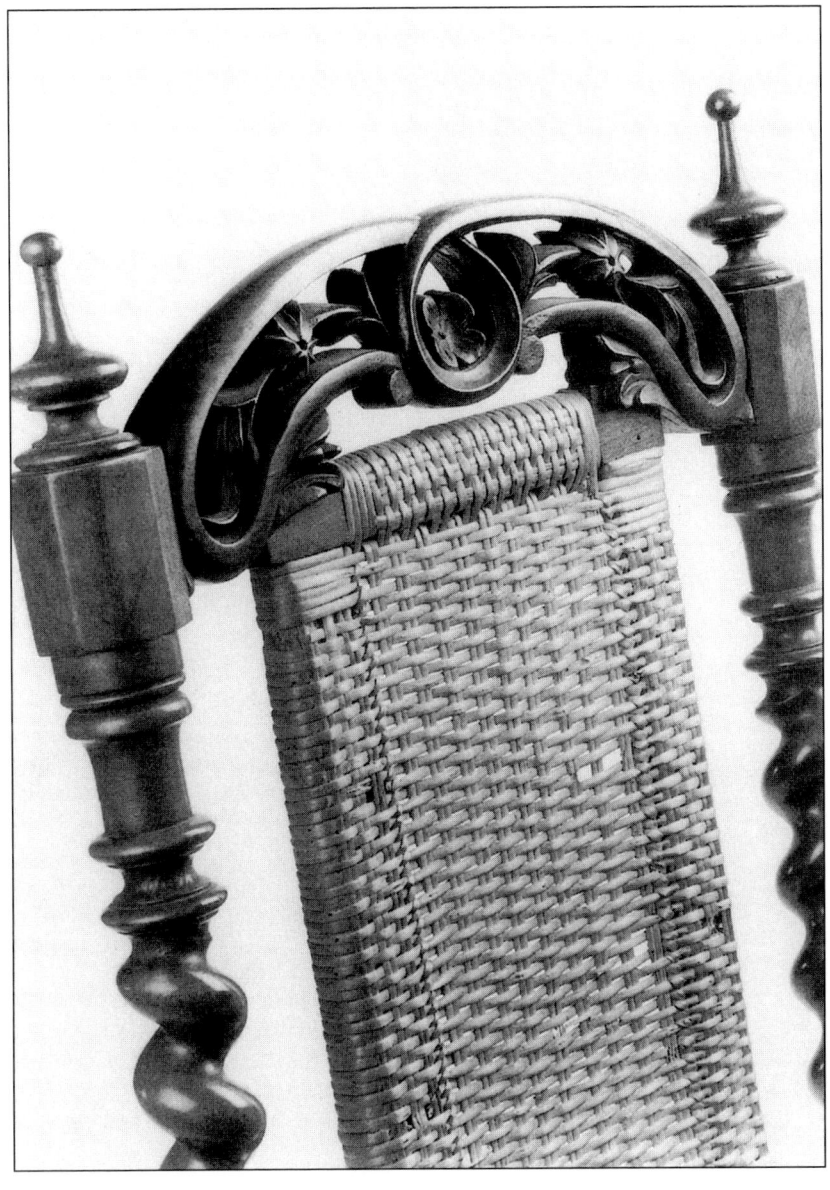

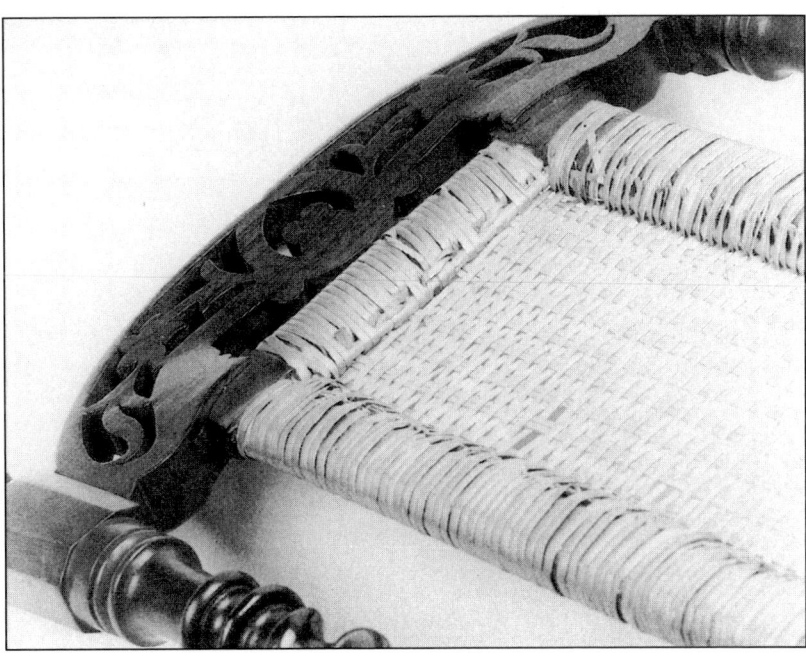

Photo 3.27 The back panel of a Campaign chair open skeined using Method 2. The top rail is wrapped with skeins first

Photo 3.28 Back view showing how the woven skeins of the second stage are taken behind the wrapping of the rail

163

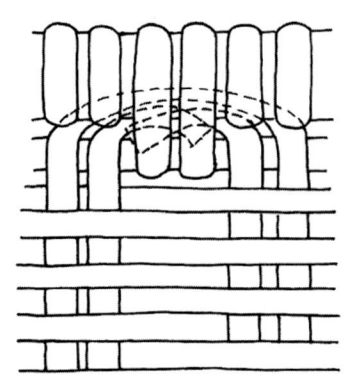

Fig 3.65a The join in the second stage skeins seen from the front or top. There is one continuous skein. The old end of the other overlaps a new end

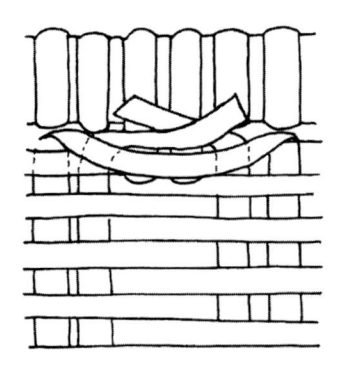

Fig 3.65b The join from the back or underside showing the overlapping ends before they are tucked in

6. *To join:* Try not to join both skeins in the same place. Joins are always kept to the underside of the rail and are never made in the centre of the chair.

   The old skein is cut short to about 1 cm ($\frac{1}{4}$ in) and this is held under the second skein as it loops round the wraps (Fig. 3.65a). The end of the new skein is brought down from above between the liner and the rail and overlapped with the old end. Both are held in place by the second skein when its loop is pulled tight (Fig. 3.65b).

7. *To finish:* push the ends of the two weaving skeins down through the gap between the liner and the rail and either cut them off or push them under one or two wraps on the underside of the rail.

   This finish may be at the back or the front of the chairs. It depends on whether there is an odd or even number of rows of weaving.

Method 3: Leslie Maltby's method

This is shown on a seat commissioned by Dorothy Wright for the Museum of English Rural Life at Reading (Photo 3.29). It was done by Leslie Maltby. It involves working the full length of the left-hand rail before starting any knotting on the right-hand rail. It is a less laborious method than the first one described in this chapter and, unlike the second method, is suitable for seats which are wider at the front.

Photo 3.29 A seat open skeined by Leslie Maltby

MATERIALS
A bundle of skeins 3–4 mm wide; they may be heavier than those used for close skeining. You will need about 90 for a panel, and up to 200 for a bedroom chair

A liner, as before

No. 4 round cane for the foundation

No tension stick is needed

LINER
Put this round the frame in any of the ways previously described (pages 141, 150).

FOUNDATION CANES
Weave these on the frame as before (page 142). The holes nearest the corners on each rail are left empty.

THE FIRST STAGE
This is worked across the chair from one side of the frame to the other. All the skeins are knotted to the left-hand rail first, although it would be possible to knot each skein first on the left and then on the right.

The left-hand rail

1. Glue the tips of leaders on to the rail (Fig. 3.24).
2. The end of a skein is brought up between the liner and the *back* rail to anchor it. Push it down into the first hole on the back rail and peg (Fig. 3.66).

   Bring it under the left-hand rail, over the top from the outside and down between the liner and the rail in the corner. Use it to wrap the rail and liner twice. Carry it under the rail again, over the top and across the frame to the right-hand side. Lay it over the right-hand rail (Fig. 3.66, skein a).

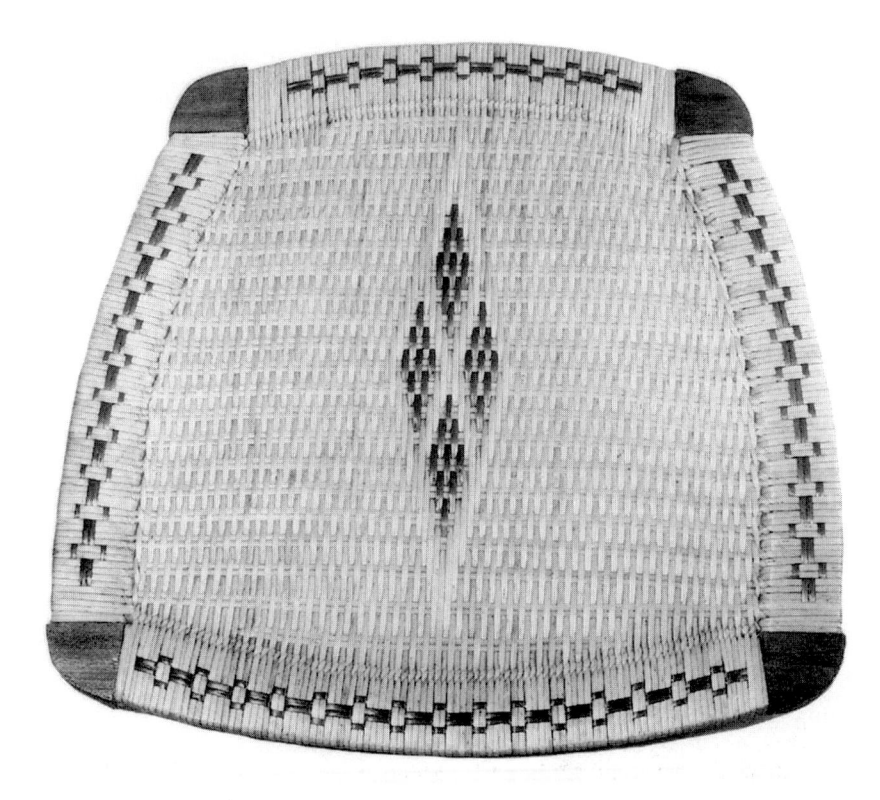

Fig 3.66 Knotting on the left-hand rail in Method 3, Leslie Maltby's open skeining

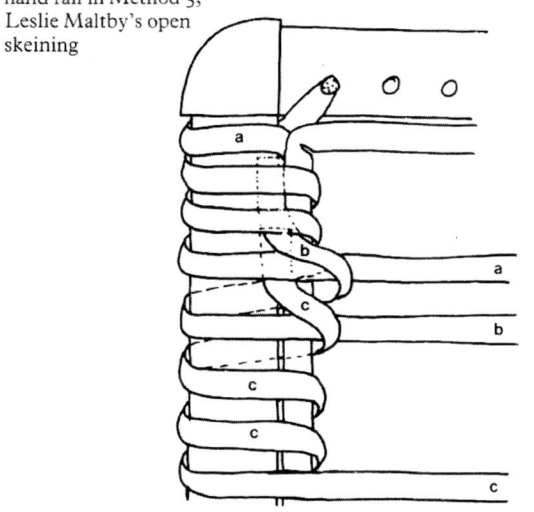

Fig 3.67 The Leslie Maltby method: knotting on the right-hand rail
a Wrapping the first part of the rail and the first knot
b Using the first long skein to knot the second
c Using the second long skein to wrap the rail and knot the third
d The third long skein from the left used to knot the fourth from the left

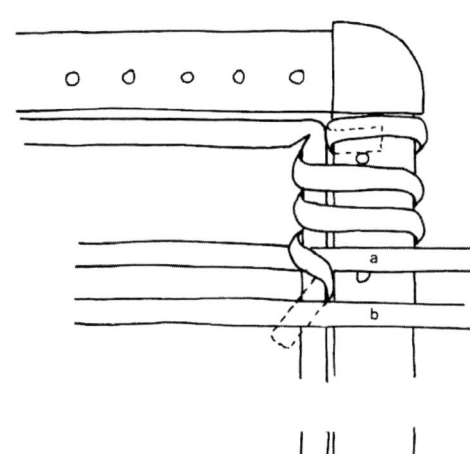

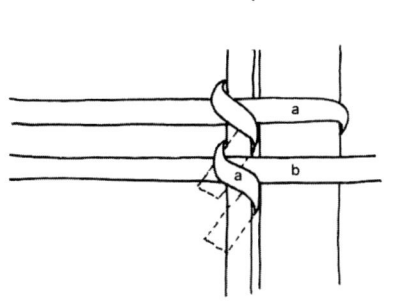

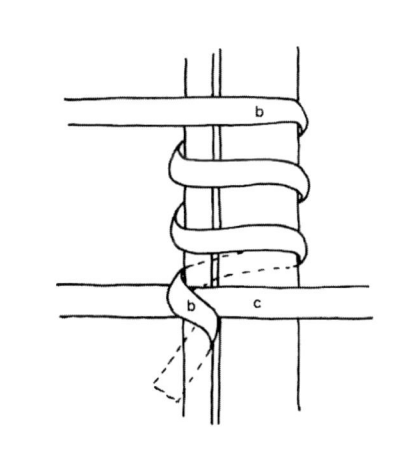

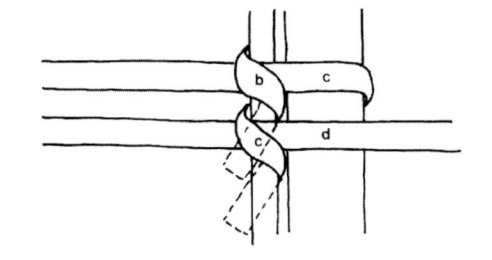

3. Take the end of a new skein and tuck the end under the wraps on top of the rail, near the inner edge, over the gap between the liner and the rail. Bring it forward and over the long skein across the frame and over the liner, down into the centre of the chair, under the liner and left rail, up over the rail and across to the right-hand rail (Fig. 3.66, skein **b**).
4. Start using the leaders to make a pattern.
5. Take a new skein and tuck the end under two or three skeins on the upper surface of the left-hand rail over the gap between rail and liner. Bring it forwards over the long skein from (2), take it down into the centre of the chair, carry it under the rail and liner, up and over the rail and liner, wrap right round rail and liner again and then over to the right hand side of the frame (Fig. 3.66, skein **c**).
6. The stages with skeins **b** and **c** (stages 3 and 5 above) are repeated alternately until the front of the rail is reached. Each skein knots the previous one. Finish with a wrap round the rail only and peg the end of the last skein in the first hole on the front rail to match the back.

The right-hand rail
A tension stick is not required for this stage.

1. Soak all the ends of the skeins (page 144).
2. Take the end of a new skein down between the liner and rail in the back corner (Fig. 3.67 skein **a**). Wrap the long end over the rail, down and under it and up inside the rail and liner, catching in the end on the underside. Wrap the rail and liner twice and bring the skein up in the centre of the chair. Bring it forward and to the right over the first long skein from the left and down between the liner and the rail. Pull it tight to form the knot over this first long skein. Use an awl to help position the knot (page 144).
3. Now use the first long skein from the left (Fig. 3.67 skein **a**). Take it over the rail, down on the outside, under rail and liner, up in the centre, forward and to the right over the second long skein from the left (Fig. 3.67b), and down between the liner and the frame. Pull the knot tight.
4. The second long skein from the left (**b**) is now wrapped twice round rail and liner and is then used to knot the third long skein from the left (**c**), the knot coming forward over it (Fig. 3.67c).

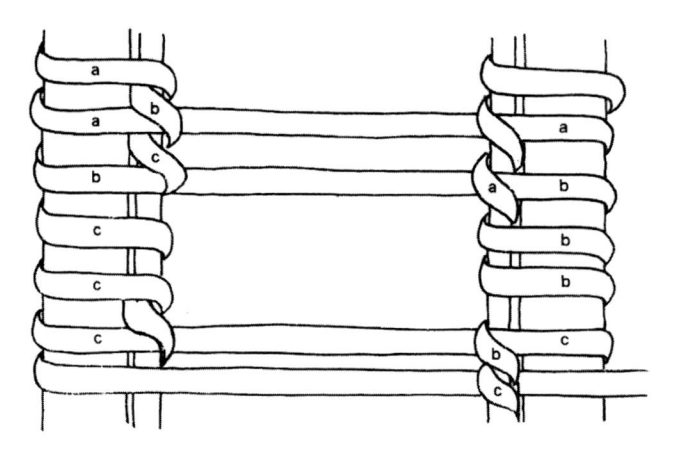

Fig 3.68 The full pattern of knotting for open skeining, Method 3

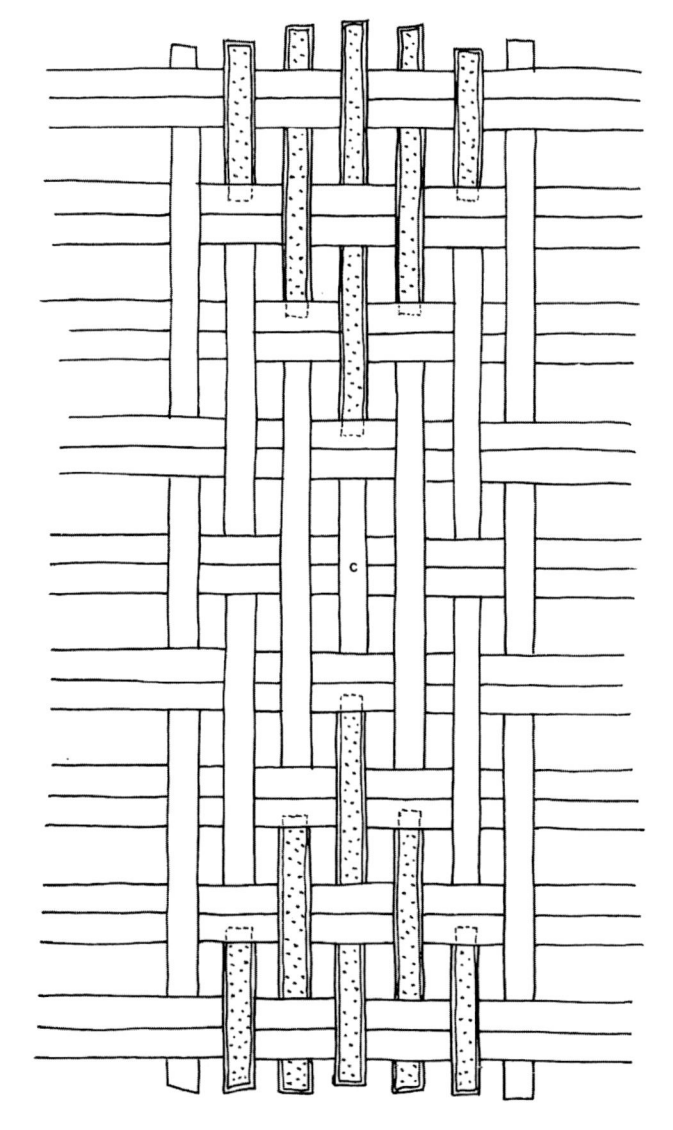

Fig 3.69 The central section of the diamond pattern showing the way the coloured skeins are laid above the full-length ones. **C** marks the centre of the seat

5. The end of this third skein from the left (**c**) is brought up behind the fourth long skein from the left, forward over it to form a knot and down between the liner and the frame (Fig. 3.67d).
6. The fourth from the left is then used to wrap rail and liner twice and then knots the fifth from the left. Stages 5 and 6 are repeated (Fig. 3.68).

At the front on the left you will have to cover the last pieces of rail and liner with a short skein (page 143).

THE SECOND STAGE

The skeins are all woven with long ends left at the front and back for knotting later. The weave is often a basic one, running over one pair of skeins from the first stage, then under the second pair, but it is possible to put in a pattern of diamonds (Photo 3.29).

1. *The diamond pattern*

Find the centres of all four rails and mark them on the upper surface. Pencil marks can be rubbed off skeins later.

(a) The centre skein from front to back is woven in first. Start weaving with it in the centre of the seat and work out towards the rails. It passes over the pair of skeins which is at the centre of the side rails (Fig. 3.69). Weave both ends under the next pair, over the next, etc., until the skein has been over three pairs on either side of the centre. Carry each end under the next pair and then over three pairs. This may reach the rails, depending on the size of your chair. You may find that you are only able to carry it over two pairs, in which case the third pair is woven in later when the curve of the rails is filled in.

Note: For all the subsequent stages described below, weave in one skein either side in the same pattern so that the centre panel of weaving increases towards both rails (Fig. 3.70).

(b) The skeins on either side of this central one are woven over the three central pairs, under one pair, over one pair, under one pair, over one pair, under one pair, then over three pairs. If this does not bring you to the seat edge, finish by weaving under one, over one to the rails.

(c) The next two, one on either side of the group of three, pass under the central pair of the first stage, over two pairs, under one pair, over one pair, under one pair, and over three pairs. Finish with the usual weave.

(d) The next two weavers pass over the central pair of the first stage, under one pair, over two pairs, under one pair, then over three pairs. Carry them to the edges under one pair, over one pair.

166

(e) These two pass under the central pair, over one pair, under one pair, over four pairs, then as usual.

(f) These are woven over the central pair, under one pair, over one pair, under one pair, over two pairs, and then as usual.

(g) Weave these under the central pair, over one pair, under one pair, over two pairs, then back to the basic pattern.

(h) Weave these over the central pair, under the next pair each side, over the next two pairs, and back to the basic weave.

(i) These two pass under the central pair, over two pairs, and then follow the basic weave to the edge.

(j) The final two skeins which form the outer edge of the diamond pattern pass over the central three pairs, under one pair, over one pair, etc.

(k) Continue to weave in skeins following the basic pattern of over one pair, under the next, until you have a block of weaving the same width as the back rail.

2. *Filling in the sides.* Fill in the sides as on page 147. Near the back you may find it necessary to start two short skeins in one space to fill up the gap properly (Fig. 3.71).

3. *Pairing.* The sides are often finished with a row of pairing which fills up any small gap between the knots on the side rail and the weaving.

(a) Take two skeins and tuck the ends down into two consecutive spaces at the front of the left-hand rail (Fig. 3.72).

(b) Take the skein nearest the front over one pair of skeins of the first stage, thread it down next to the rail and up under the next pair of skeins.

(c) Repeat (b) with the skein now nearest the front and continue pairing until the back corner is reached. The two ends are left underneath and trimmed. They may be held with a drop of wood glue.

(d) Repeat on the right-hand side, this time starting at the back and working forwards.

4. *Knotting.* Knot the skeins on the front and back rails as on page 148, introducing leaders.

5. *Filling in at the front and back.* Pairs of short skeins are woven in (Photo 3.29). Only one pair will probably be needed at the front and one at the back. Using the shell bodkin to help you, weave in one skein at a time, starting with the longest one. It looks best if the one nearest the rail is shortest.

6. Trim underneath (page 149).

INTRODUCING COLOUR

Short coloured skeins can be laid over the skeins of the second stage to introduce blocks of colour to the seat. Dylon dyes can be used successfully (page 156). Here they are laid on the sections forming the centres of the diamonds where the weaving is tight (Fig. 3.69). They cannot be used successfully for long strokes of the pattern, as they may become loose and pull away. The ends are cut so that they just rest under a pair of skeins of the first stage.

If the dyes used on the skeins are water-soluble and not colour-fast, the seat may have to be varnished with a clear matt varnish. Anything too glossy, however, will detract from the sheen of the skeins.

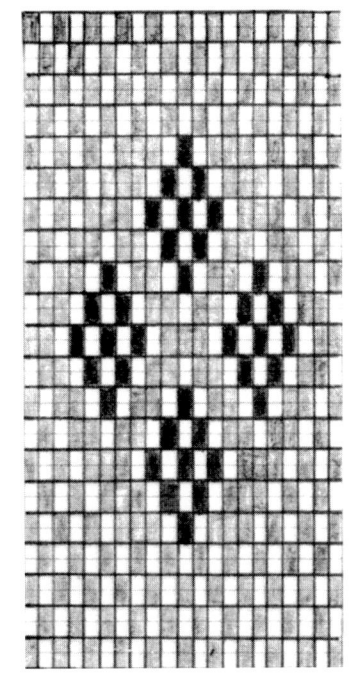

Fig 3.70 Graph to show the complete diamond pattern. The gaps between the pairs of skeins of the first stage are not shown. Each square represents one skein, white squares show where the second stage skeins pass under those of the first stage

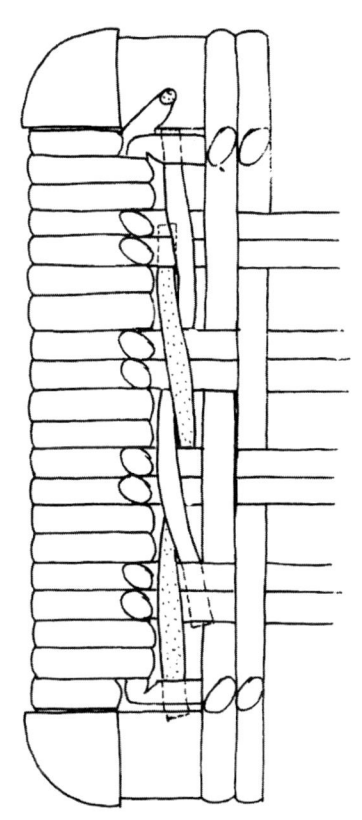

Fig 3.72 A row of pairing between the knots on the side rail and second stage skeins. See also the Campaign chair in the cover photograph

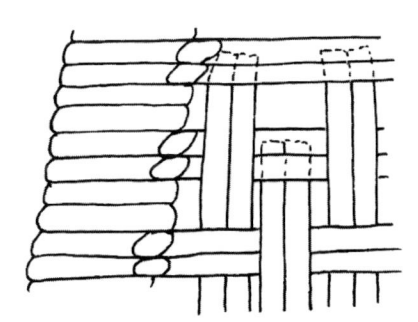

Fig 3.71 A way of filling up the gap between the side rails and the woven skeins of the second stage

22.
Close caning

Photo 3.30 A chair close-caned in a twill pattern

Photo 3.31a Nancy Furlong's close caned bedroom chair

Photo 3.31b Close caning techniques were also used on chairs with wide cane or willow frames. This photograph, found in a junk shop, shows such chairs outside a café or pavilion. The clothes suggest it was taken in the late 1920s

Many chairs can be found which have closely woven seats of wide chair cane. The chair frames have the same features as those suitable for willow skeining, the rails having raised corners and widely-spaced holes. These chairs may be seated in any of the ways described for willow skeining, using either the closed or open methods.

Occasionally chairs with corners and rails suitable for either willow skeining or close caning are found without the drilled holes for the cane foundation always put on willow seats. This indicates that the chair would have been woven with cane, which is a stronger, more durable material than willow. Using cane saves the time needed to prepare the willow skeins and is useful if skeining tools are not available.

The cane used for weaving must normally be No. 3 or No. 4 for the close patterns, and No. 6 for the open method. The cane used for the foundation should be the same size or smaller than that used for weaving.

The chair in Photo 3.30 is close caned with No. 3 chair cane in the method described on pages 141–9. It uses the alternative twill pattern described there and each individual skein of both first and second stages is knotted at both ends.

The bedroom chair in Photo 3.31 has been close caned by Nancy Furlong, worked in the knotted way used above, but the knots are difficult to see. This is because no leaders have been used. Instead, the pattern of weaving used on the seat has been continued on and over the rails, giving a continuous pattern with small diamonds, one on each rail. No tension stick was used on this chair, which is in No. 2 cane, as the cane is fairly thin and has little bulk. The canes were all knotted over the front rail first and then each pulled tight at the back before knotting. Weaving was done mostly with the fingers, a needle being used for the final stages and for the weaving on the rail.

Chairs with drop-in seats

Some stools and seats are made with a frame which is finished and polished all round. Within this is a smaller frame which fits fairly closely and can be pushed up and taken out of the chair (Photo 3.32). It is usually rather shallow and is sometimes a solid piece of wood. If this inner frame has raised polished corners it was meant to be rushed (page 93) but if the corners are unpolished and there are no raised sections, it was designed for close caning.

MATERIALS
For a frame about 30 cm (12 in) square you will need about $\frac{1}{4}$ kg No. 6 chair cane. Soak it as needed (page 15).

METHOD
Cover the thin edge of the frame with a piece of chair cane, starting in the centre of one side where the join may be hidden (Fig. 3.73a). This cane is glued in position and is to cover the corners of the frame, which would otherwise show as the seat may be raised above the outer frame. If the frame is large, short pieces of cane can be glued on to cover only the corners (Fig. 3.73b). If the frame is deep you may have to use two pieces of No. 6 cane side by side.

169

Photo 3.32a A close-caned panel or drop-in seat showing the start and methods of joining

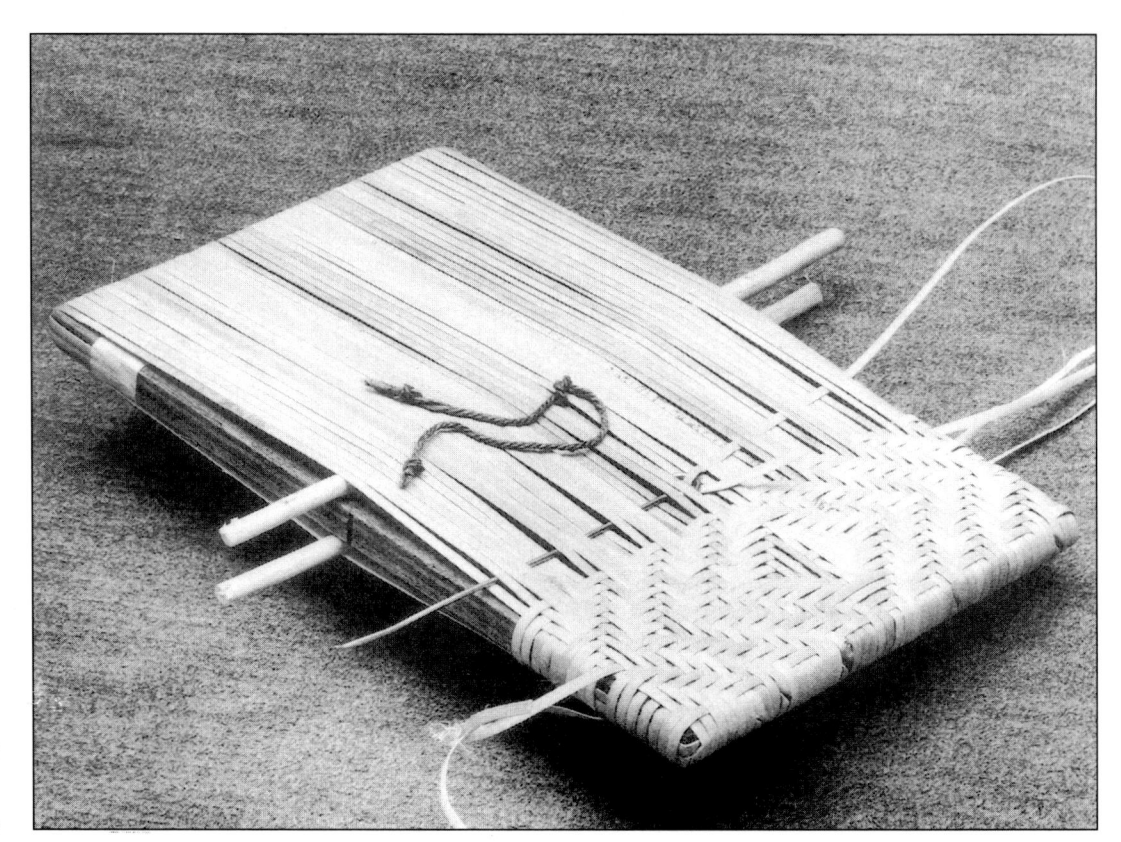

Photo 3.32b View of the end of the close caned panel showing the start and different methods of joining

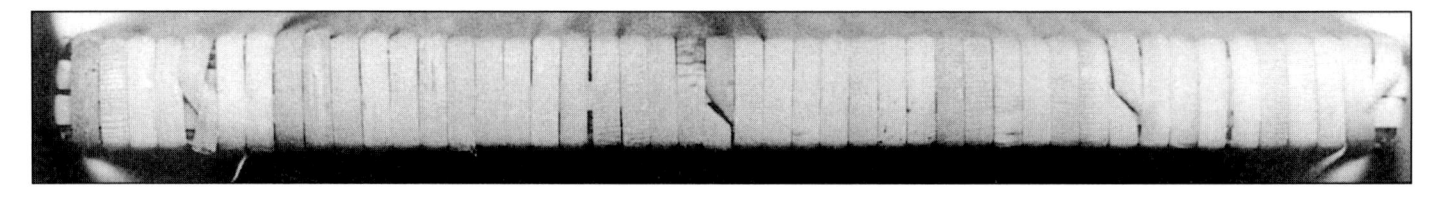

Fig 3.73 Methods of covering the edges of the frame of a drop-in seat

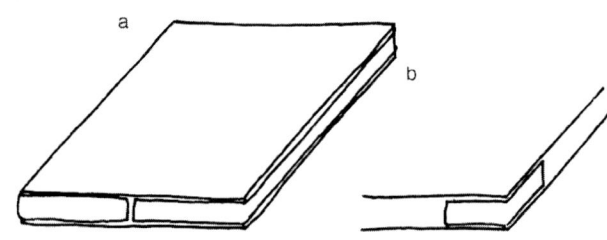

Fig 3.74 Close caning: starting the first stage. Note the tension sticks **t** and the tape holding the first wrap. **C** is the centre of the uncovered edge

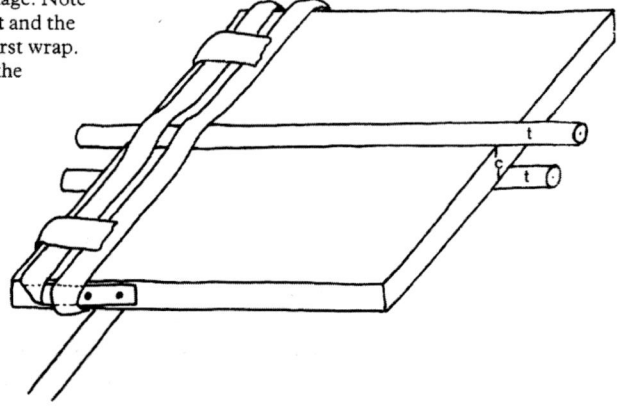

FIRST STAGE

This is best planned to go round the longer side of the rectangle, leaving the shorter rows for weaving.

1. Fold back 4 cm (1½ in) of one end of the cane at 45 degrees and lay this short end along one short edge (it does not matter which) of the frame with the long end at one corner (Fig. 3.74). Either glue this short end with wood glue or pin it with two small panel pins. This cane will be used to wrap round and round the frame.
2. Use two tension sticks about 1 cm (⅜ in) thick (they may be round or square) and tie them across the frame, one above and one below (Fig. 3.74). They should be at right angles to the wrapping of the first stage.
3. Now use the long length of cane across the top of the frame, glossy side up. Take it up, across the top of the frame and down again (Fig. 3.74). Wrap it round and round the frame, over the tension sticks, keeping the canes as close together as possible. You may find it helpful to tape across the frame and the first few wraps to hold them in position (Fig. 3.74). This tape can be taken off later.

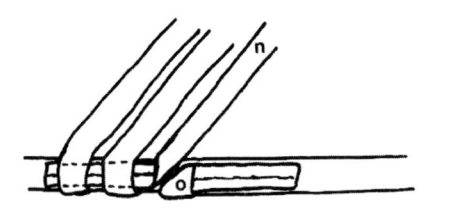

Fig 3.75 Joining the cane at the edge of the frame

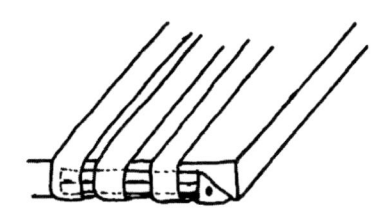

Fig 3.76 Finishing by tucking the end under several wraps. Canes are shown separated for clarity

4. *To join.* Thread the end of a new piece of cane under several wraps along the thin vertical edge of the frame (Fig. 3.75). The glossy side should be against the frame. Turn the new cane back at 45 degrees and continue to wrap the frame. Take the old end, turn it at 45 degrees glossy side down, to lie along the uncovered section of the frame. It will be secured by the next wrap. Hammer the join gently to flatten it. There should be a neat diagonal line to show the position of the join.
5. *Finishing.* At the end of the first stage there are two ways of finishing the work:
either
(a) turn the cane end back at 45 degrees and thread it under several wraps along one edge of the frame (Fig. 3.76) and put a panel pin in to hold it or
(b) leave a long end, fixed temporarily with tape, for weaving in at the end.

THE SECOND STAGE
This involves weaving in a pattern by threading the cane over and under strands of the first stage and round the whole frame. The canes will lie at right angles to those of the first stage. Any of the patterns described in the willow skeined sections can be used.

1. Mark the centres of the uncovered edges of the frame (Fig. 3.74). Mark the central cane of the first stage on both the top and bottom of the seat with a loop of string or cane if the pattern you would like to weave has a central motif.
2. Start weaving at the centre of one unwrapped rail, leaving a long unwoven end. A long wire seating needle (Photo 3.32a) is helpful for lifting the canes of the first stage but a packing needle or any curved tool will help to lift canes and make threading easier. Thread the end of the weaving cane through the eye of the needle and weave the needle and cane through the canes of the first stage.

    It is also possible to thread the needle, eye first, through from the end of the row, then thread the cane through the eye and pull back the needle.
3. Turn the frame over and weave the cane across under the seat. It is usual to put different patterns on the opposite sides of the seat.
Note: A twill pattern (page 146) on one side is easy and effective and something more elaborate may be put on the other side. If the pattern has to be counted from the centre of each row you will have to mark the central cane of the first stage with a loop of cane or string (Fig. 3.44) and count back from the centre to the edge to make sure the needle goes in correctly at the start of the row.

    As you continue to cover the frame, bind in the end you started with along the edge of the frame after turning it at 45 degrees. Join in new canes where necessary.
3. As weaving progresses remove the tension sticks to give more slack in the first stage. This makes weaving much easier.
4. After completing the first half, go back to the centre. Tuck the end of a new cane in along the thin edge of the frame, glossy side against the wood, then turn the cane at 45 degrees to start the weaving (Fig. 3.75, Cane **n**). Use a small panel pin to secure the end if necessary.

Alternative method
Leave a second long end as you start weaving with a new cane. This will lie beside the first long end at the start of the second stage. When the weaving is complete these long ends can be woven in on top of other canes so there is an overlap of at least 6 cm (2½ in). These overlapping canes must follow the pattern of weaving and can be glued for extra security.

5. Work as close to the edges as you possibly can. Use a shell bodkin or a packing needle to lift the outer wraps of the first stage.
6. Tuck the final end in as far as possible after turning it at 45 degrees and secure this and all other ends with glue or panel pins.
Note: As you weave, push the strands close together, either with the threaded needle by pushing it sideways while it is woven into the first stage, or from above using a piece of wood or blunt tool. Do not use a sharp bodkin, as it will cut the canes.

Photo 3.33 A stool close caned by Nancy Furlong.
a) top surface b) underside

The close caned stool in Photo 3.33 is worked in the drop-in seat method but on an ordinary stool frame. There is no need to cover any part of the shallow edge of the frame, as it will all be concealed later by either the first or second stage. Different patterns are woven above and below the seat. All joining involves overlapping old and new canes for several centimetres and glueing them together. This removes the need for the join shown in Fig. 3.75 and no glue or panel pins are needed on the frame.

With these stools it is only experience which enables you to judge what size of tension stick, if any, is needed. If you are unsure, start work by leaving a long end and, when joining during the first stage, also leave long ends. It is then possible, with patience, to adjust the tension of the first stage. The canes can be pulled tight to take up any slack remaining at the end of the second stage. Spraying the canes as you adjust them will help to keep them in place.

23.
Danish cord chairs

These chairs are of a modern Scandinavian design (Photo 3.34) and have rows of L-shaped nails round the inside of the frame. They have two single side rails or two pairs of side rails, the rails in each pair arranged one above the other. The material used is made from treated brown paper twisted to form a strong cord with a smooth surface. The cord is only available in one width. If bought from the manufacturer (see list of suppliers), it is only available in rather large quantities. Craft shops, however, often sell smaller amounts.

MATERIALS AND TOOLS

Approximately 1 kg of Danish cord (about 400 feet) is needed for the average Danish dining chair with a seat about 40 × 46 cm (16 × 18 in), as well as some tacks and a hammer. Pliers may be useful for loosening the L-shaped nails.

PREPARATION

Before you start, carefully examine the existing seat on the chair. Count the numbers of pairs of cord strands from front to back on your chair. Count the number of wraps between these pairs at both the front and back of your chair. Record this information to help you later.

Pull all the L-shaped nails away from the frame a little to release the old cord and allow for the new strands. Cut away all the weaving of the old seat.

The cord itself needs no preparation.

THE FIRST STAGE

On these chairs this stage is worked from front to back. There are two methods of working this stage.

Method 1

1. Start at the front left-hand corner. Cut about 30 m (100 feet) off the coil. Wind it into a small ball. Tack one end of the cord to the inside of the front rail (Fig. 3.77). Bring

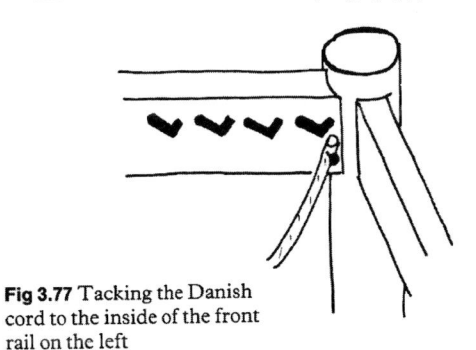

Photo 3.34 A chair seated in Danish cord. It has single side rails

Fig 3.77 Tacking the Danish cord to the inside of the front rail on the left

173

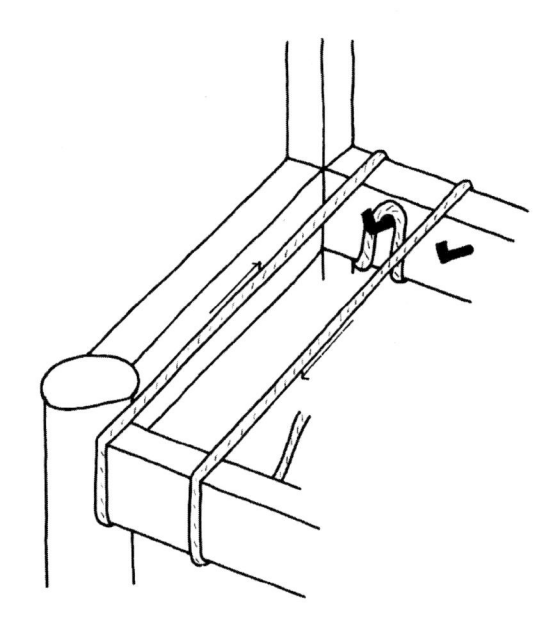

Fig 3.78 Starting the first stage, using the first nail on the back rail on the left. The cord is shown away from the back leg but will be pushed up to it when working

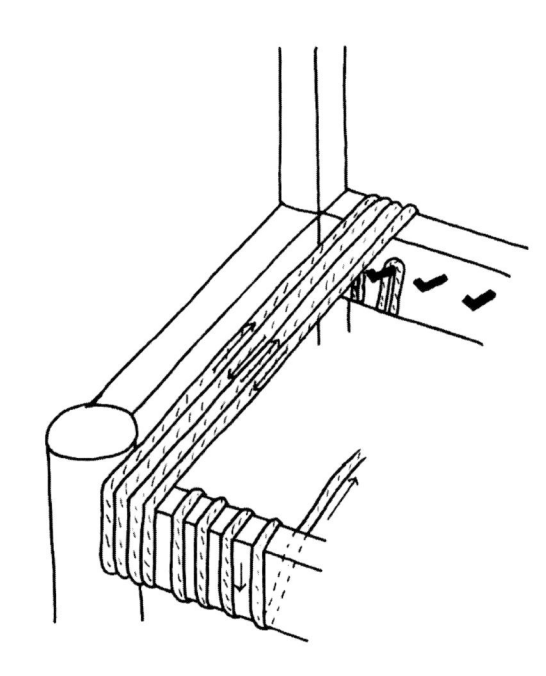

Fig 3.79 The wrapping of the front rail after putting on four strands from front to back of the frame

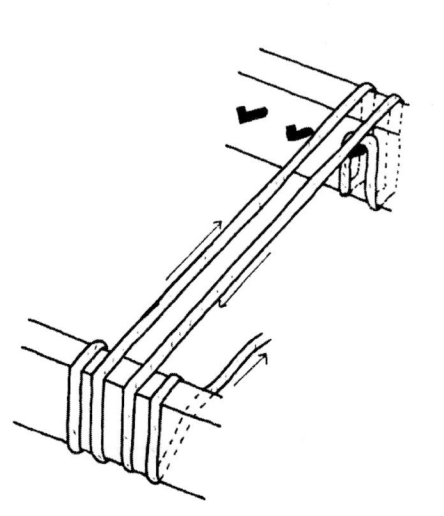

Fig 3.80 Two strands from front rail to back

the cord to the outside under the rail, up over the front rail, across to the back, down outside the back rail and under it to hook the cord round the first L-shaped nail (Fig. 3.78). Then bring the cord back outside the back rail and over to the front. Pass the cord outside the front rail and take it to the inside to hook it round a nail. Take the cord back to the outside and over to the back again. Lay the cord across the chair each time without leaving it slack or pulling it tight.

Repeat these stages until four strands lie over the seat finishing with the cord at the front.

2. Now wrap the front rail tightly by carrying the cord round and round it (Fig. 3.79). The number of wraps will vary with the chair, but is normally four. Tap the wraps close together with a hammer.

3. Now repeat stage one but only put two strands across the frame before putting another four wraps on the front rail (Fig. 3.80). Continue until you reach the right-hand side. Put four strands across the chair at the end to match those at the start. Finish by tacking the end to the inside of the front frame.

Note: Arrange to have an odd number of pairs of strands so that both sides match when weaving the second stage.

4. *The back rail* must now be wrapped. Cut a length of cord of about 12 m (40 feet) and tack one end to the inside of the back rail. Take the cord to the outside of the back rail and wrap to fill in the first gap on the rail (usually 3–5 wraps, depending on the chair), press or hammer the wraps close together, and when you reach the first cord held by a nail carry the wrapping cord across on the inside before wrapping the next section of rail.

Continue wrapping until the back rail is covered. Tack the end of the cord to the inside of the rail.

Method 2
In this method, the first stage involves putting on the strands from the front to the back of the frame using the cord still on the spool. The front and back rails are then wrapped separately with individual lengths of cord.

1. Start by cutting off two lengths of cord about 12 m (40 feet).
2. Tack the end of the cord to the inside of the front rail on the left of the chair (Fig. 3.77) and work Method 1, stage 1 (Figs 3.77 and 3.78).
3. After putting on four strands across the frame bring the cord over the second L-shaped nail *and* the third L-shaped nail on the left side of the inside of the front rail (Fig. 3.81a).

174

Fig 3.81a The arrangement of the cord over the rails on the inside of the front rail

Fig 3.81b The arrangement on the back rail, showing the direction of working

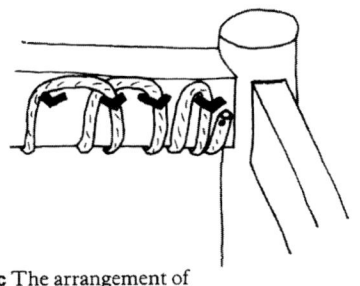

Fig 3.81c The arrangement of the inside of the front rail

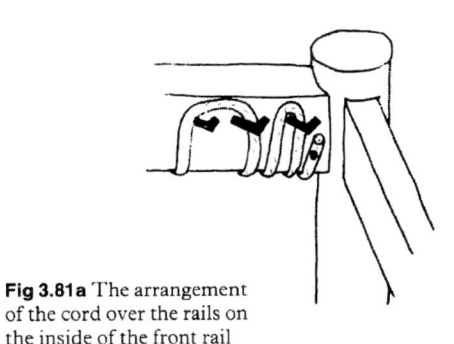

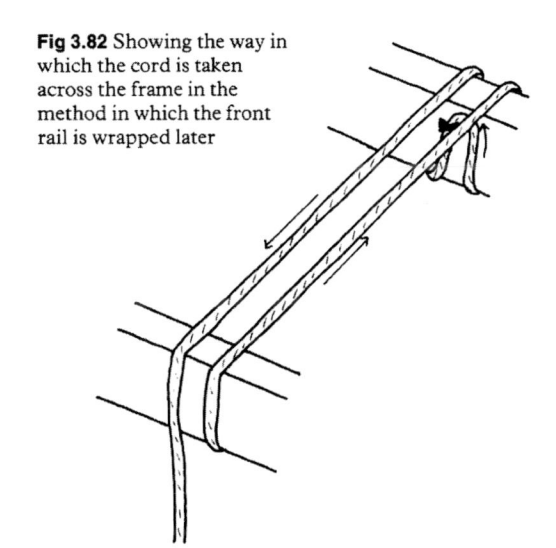

Fig 3.82 Showing the way in which the cord is taken across the frame in the method in which the front rail is wrapped later

4. Take the cord to the outside of the front rail, over to the back and hook it round the third nail from the left corner but this time from right to left (Fig. 3.81b). Bring the cord to the outside and bring it back to the front *on the left* of the cord last put in position (Fig. 3.82). Take the cord over the front rail and loop it over the third and fourth nails (Fig. 3.81c).
5. Continue in this way until you reach the right-hand side. Arrange to have an odd number of warp pairs and to have four strands across the section next to the right-hand rail. Do not cut off the cord.
6. *Wrapping front and back rails:* Use the 12 m (40 feet) lengths you cut off originally.

    Either wrap them as described in Method one, stage 5, or start by hooking the middle of each length of cord round the central nail of a rail and using the ends to wrap to the sides of the rails.

THE SECOND STAGE
This is woven through the cords now already on the seat and is the same whichever method you used for the first stage.

Single side rail chairs

1. Start at the front. Either tack the new end to the inside of the rail at the right front of the chair or use the cord left on the spool inside the right rail at the front corner and take it round the inside of the leg to the right side.
2. Pull out a loop of cord long enough to stretch across the seat and back again plus about 20 cm (8 in).
3. Form a loop of the cord by folding it in half. Take this loop over the right-hand rail from

Photo 3.35 Starting the second stage of a Danish cord chair

175

the outside and over the four strands next to the rail (Photo 3.35). Weave it under the next pair, over the third and so on to the right-hand rail. It should pass over the four strands next to the left-hand rail to match the weaving on the right.

4. Take the loop down on the outside of the right-hand rail and under it to loop round the L-shaped nail at the front of this rail. Now pull the loop tight from the right-hand side of the chair.
5. Now take the working strand on the right side of the chair under the rail, hook it round a nail on the underside and then pull out another long loop to weave through the strands of the first stage. This loop passes under those strands which the first loop went over.
6. Repeat until you reach the back of the chair. Tack the final end of cord on the inside of the rail. Push the side weavers close to each other with a wooden wedge or wide screwdriver and a hammer.

Note: There may be a double row of L-shaped nails on the inside of the side rails. A nail from each row is used alternately. This arrangement allows the weaving to be very close.

Double side rail chairs

1. Pull about 20 m (65 feet) of cord and cut it off the spool. Fold it in half and tack both cut ends to the inside of the left rail at the front (Fig. 3.83). Weave with the loop. Carry the loop to the outside of the left-hand rails, up over both rails and over the first four strands of the first stage. Weave the loop under the next pair, over the next and so on to the right-hand side. Pull through the whole length of cord.
2. Take the double strand down outside both right side rails (Fig. 3.84a), under the lower one and to the outside through the space between the two rails (Fig. 3.84b). Take it down again round the lower rail, out again through the gap between the two rails but this time carry it up over the top right rail and weave back to the left-hand side (Fig. 3.84c). Weave under the strands previously woven over. Pull all the cord through.
3. On the left take the double strand down outside the top rail through the gap to the inside, and down round the lower rail (Fig. 3.85). Completely wrap the lower rail again and then carry the double strand up outside both rails. The double strand is now ready to be woven across to the right as in stage 1.
4. The three stages above are repeated until the back of the seat is reached. Push the weaving close at intervals.
5. *To join:* tack the finished ends to the side rail on the inside. Tack on two new ones and weave with a loop forming a double strand as before.
6. Finish by tacking the two ends of cord to the frame. Trim off any surplus. Hammer all the nails tightly into place.

This cord does not need any treatment but you can darken it by staining with button polish. Wipe the button polish (available from ironmongers) over the seat with a soft cloth made into a firm pad.

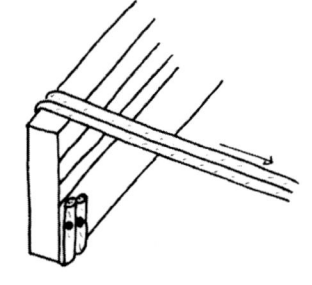

Fig 3.83 Attaching the cord when starting a chair with double side rails (the front left leg is omitted for clarity)

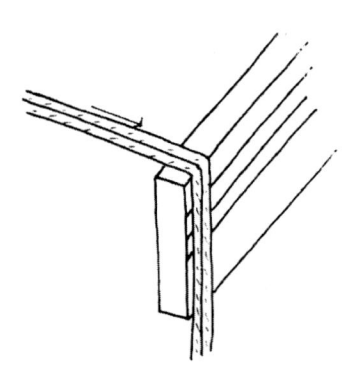

Fig 3.84a Take the loop of cord down outside the right side rail

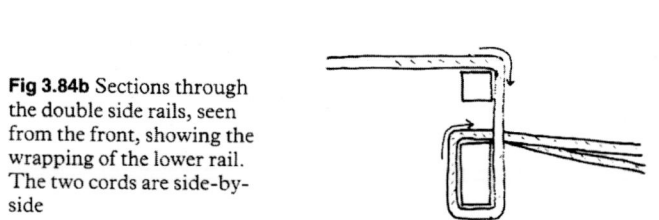

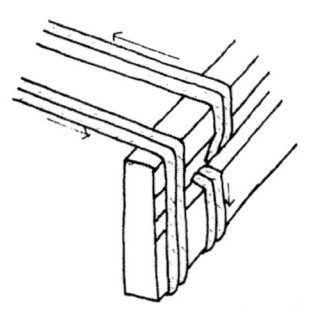

Fig 3.84c The full wrapping of the double rails on the right

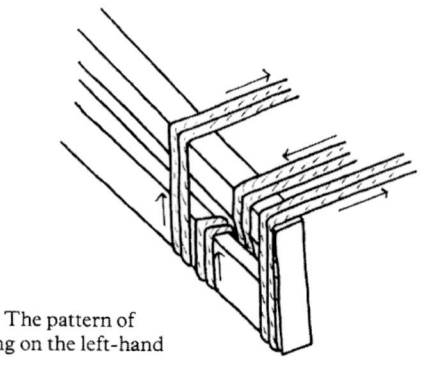

Fig 3.84b Sections through the double side rails, seen from the front, showing the wrapping of the lower rail. The two cords are side-by-side

Fig 3.85 The pattern of wrapping on the left-hand rail

24.
Stools and seats in seagrass and cord

Photo 3.36a Stool frames, tools and materials. From back to front and left to right: stool frame (JYW), parts of stool frame (JYW), ball of cotton string (D), reel of cotton stool cord (D), thick polychord (D), thin polycord (S), two fine bodkins, wooden seagrass needle (S), metal cord or rush needle (JYW), seagrass on spool, and in a hank (JYW). My thanks to Jacob, Young & Westbury, Smits, and Dryad for supplying materials.

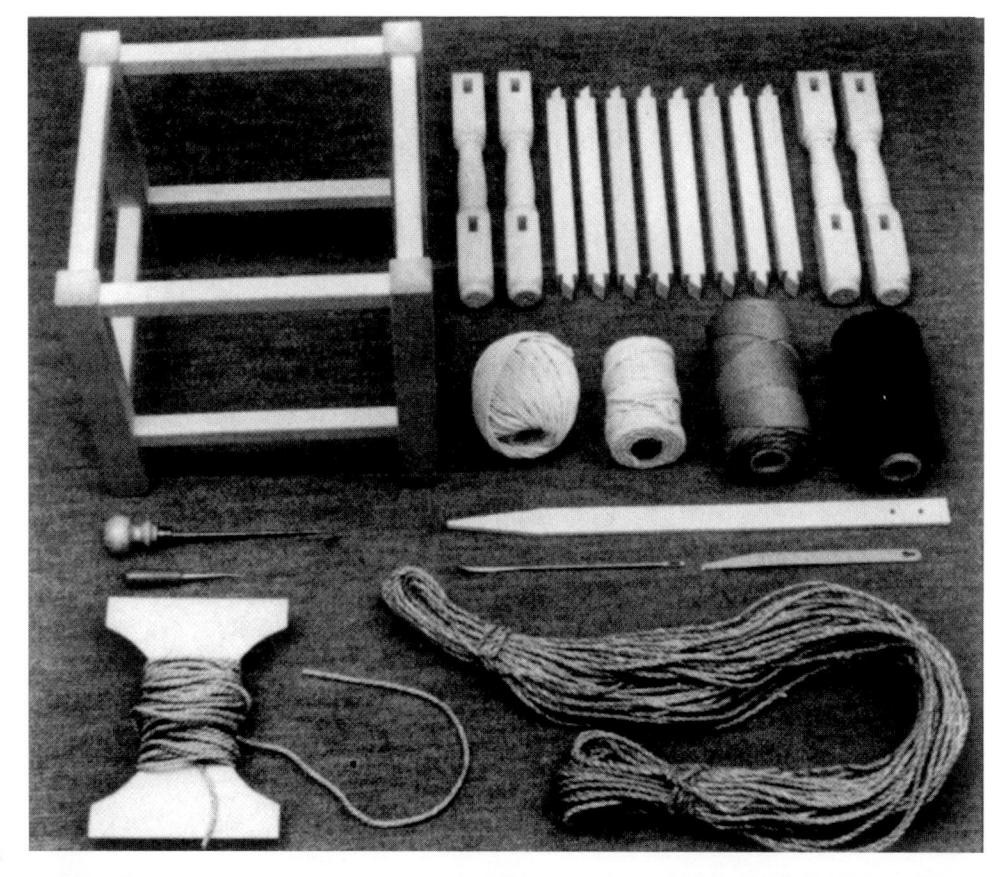

Photo 3.36b Three miniatures worked by Barbara Maynard. Left to right: using crochet thread, no. 0 chair cane, and sewing thread in the knotting method

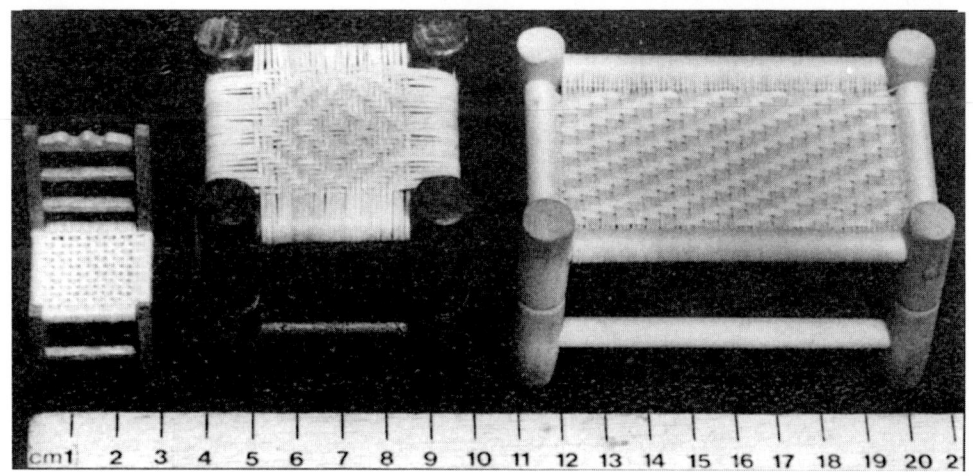

Photo 3.37 The maze pattern on a square stool

MATERIALS
A wide variety of materials are available today and the designs described can be carried out using any of these. They include seagrass from China, flax and hemp cord, polypropylene cords and twines and finer cotton string (Photo 3.36). The essential feature of the material must be that it is not too elastic or the seat will sag after only short use. Fine threads may be used successfully for miniature stools and chairs (Photo 3.36b).

TOOLS
side cutters
knife
scissors
padding stick
seating needle
long wooden seating needle
packing needles
seagrass spool
tacks
hammer or rapping iron

TERMS USED
strand: a single piece of seagrass

block: a group of single strands all woven in the same way across the frame

wrap: a single strand of seagrass carried right round the whole frame from one rail back to the same rail

bind: a length of seagrass taken right round one rail only

Woven methods

THE MAZE PATTERN
This is the simplest stool pattern and very effective. It can be done in any of the materials described above, but seagrass is particularly suitable. The pattern produces a comfortable seat which dips towards the centre. It is often seen on both chairs and chair-backs from Afghanistan and Spain (Photo 3.37).

The first stage
This is worked from front to back.

1. **Either:** tie a half knot and use a tack to fix this on the inside of the back left leg or to the inside of the rail as near to the leg as possible. It will be hidden by seagrass layers above and below it (Fig. 3.86a).
   Or: tie one end of the seagrass to the leg of the stool below the foot rail (Fig. 3.86b). This then becomes the back left leg for the following instructions.

2. Bring the seagrass over the back rail, across

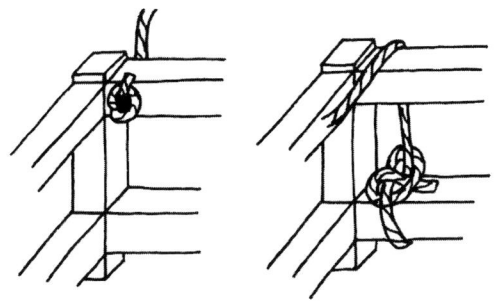

Fig 3.86a Tacking on a knot of seagrass

Fig 3.86b Tying the seagrass to the stretcher

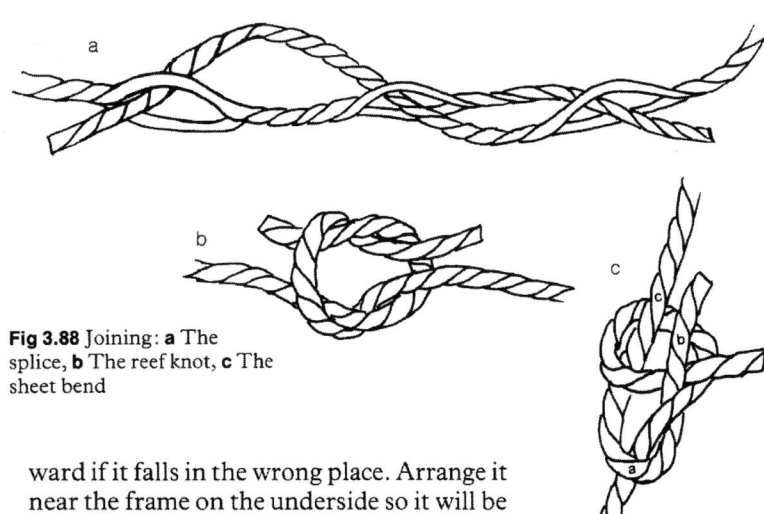

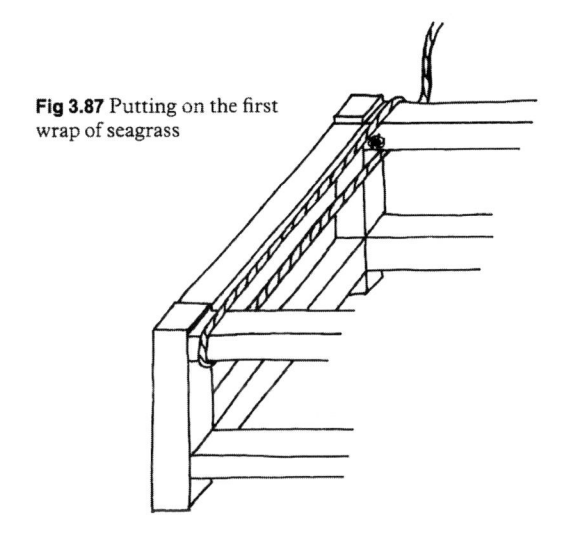

Fig 3.87 Putting on the first wrap of seagrass

Fig 3.88 Joining: **a** The splice, **b** The reef knot, **c** The sheet bend

the top, round the front rail, across on the underside of the seat and up over the outside of the back rail again (Fig. 3.87).

3. Continue this complete wrapping of the frame to the right-hand side of the stool.
   Note: Keep the seagrass tight and finish with the cord at the front of the seat on the right. Push the wrapping close together to make sure the frame is covered completely. If you have to stop before you have finished wrapping, just tie the seagrass temporarily to the foot rest of the stool.
4. *To join:* If you have to join before reaching the other side, splice the two ends on the underside of the stool (Fig. 3.88a).
   (a) Take the old end and untwist the two plies about 8 cm (3 in) from the end to create a small hole. Push the end of the new hank through this and pull through about 18 cm (7 in).
   (b) Then untwist the two plies of this new piece about 12 cm (4½ in) back from its end and push the old end through this.
   (c) Push the new end through the old piece about 12 cm (4½ in) from its end (Fig. 3.88a). Make sure you have at least 2 cm (¾ in) of each end projecting from the splice.
5. *An alternative join*
   The two ends can be joined with a reef knot (Fig. 3.88b). This can be bulky and awkward if it falls in the wrong place. Arrange it near the frame on the underside so it will be hidden later. Leave the long ends on the knot for later retying.

Joining slippery material
For polycord and similar twines a more secure knot must be used. A sheet bend is suitable (Fig. 3.88c). Form a loop first with the old end of the cord. Take the new end and carry it round the loop as shown. Its end will go under the loop at **a**, come up through the loop, take it behind **b** and **c**, over **c** and under itself and out over **b**. Pull the two pieces of cord to tighten the knot.

The second stage
This is worked from side to side and involves weaving. The underside will be woven here in the same pattern as the top.

1. Mark the centres of the empty side rails with pencil.
2. Bring the end of the seagrass from the first stage round on the inside of the front right-hand leg of the chair and up on the right. If necessary knot on a new piece here so the knot will be hidden behind the right leg.
   Thread the end of the seagrass through a needle to help the weaving.
3. Carry the seagrass under the first five strands of the first stage, over the rest and under the last five on the left of the stool (Fig. 3.89). Take the cord round the left rail and on the underside take it under the first five and the last five of the first stage strands.

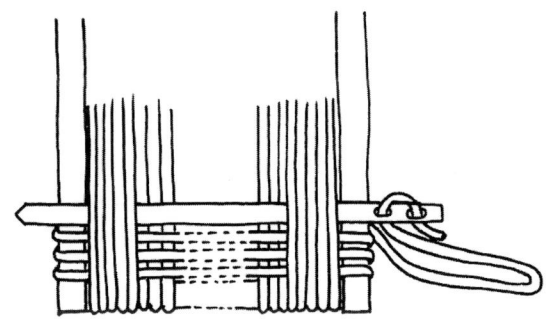

Fig 3.89 Weaving in the first block of the second stage. Two more strands are needed to complete the first block of five strands

179

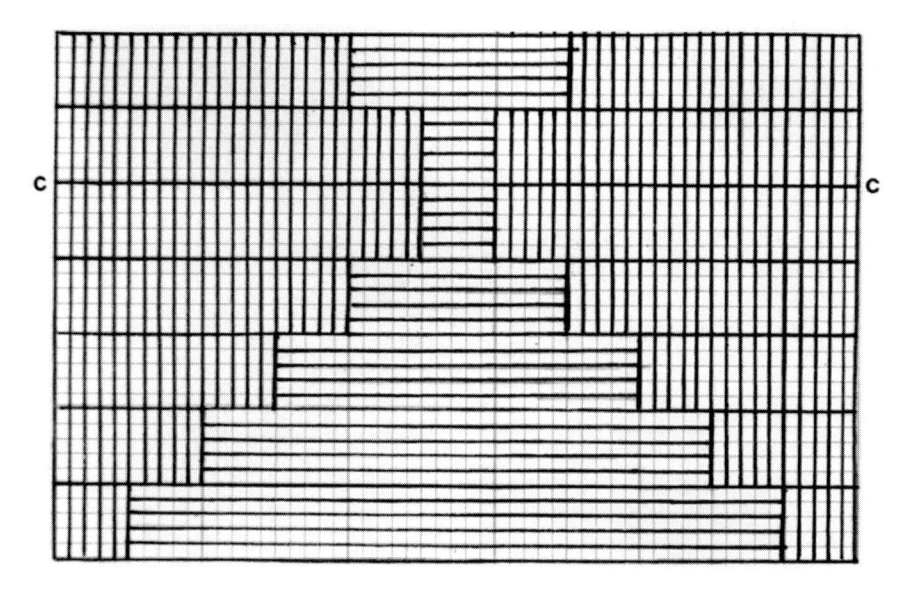

Fig 3.90 The second stage of the maze pattern put in from side to side. The blocks are marked across the strands of the first stage to help with counting. **C** is the centre of the side rails and the centre of the pattern. The first block (bottom of diagram) passes under the first and last five of the first stage

4. Continue until you have five wraps following this arrangement. This forms one block.
5. Then put on five more wraps passing them under the first and last 10 strands on the top and underneath the stool.
6. The next five wraps will pass under 15 strands on both sides of the top and underside.
7. The next five pass under 20 strands each time and the following group under 25 strands (Fig. 3.90).
   Note: By this time the wrapping will have almost reached the centre of the stool. Push the wraps closely together.
8. Continue to wrap, passing under 25 strands on each side, both top and bottom, until you reach the centre of the side rail (Fig. 3.90, c). Count the number of this group of wraps you have put on, and continue passing under 25 on each side until you have doubled this number.
9. The next five wraps pass under 20 strands, on each side of both the top and bottom; the next five under 15; the next five under 10; and lastly five wraps just pass under five in each place. The two sides of the stool should be mirror images.

Finishing
The end of the seagrass will be on the left. Untie the original end that was tied to the chair leg, and using either a reef knot or sheet bend, knot the two ends together and tuck them out of sight. If you nailed the first end, the final one may also be nailed underneath, inside the leg, as inconspicuously as possible.

Simple method for the underside
See pages 181–2. The underneath may be divided into two or three large blocks.

VARIATIONS
The underneath is woven in the same pattern as the top here.

First variation
The simplest involves altering the number of wraps on different parts of the stool when weaving the second stage. This alters the width of the blocks and so alters the appearance. For example the first five weavings could pass under five strands each side, as before. The next six could go under six strands each side, the next seven under seven strands each side and so on until you reach the centre of the stool. Then work out from the centre, reversing the pattern of the first half.

Second variation
A variation which eliminates the very long unwoven strands at the edges of the stool is worked as below (Photo 3.38, left).

Photo 3.38 Left: Second variation of the maze pattern in seagrass
Right: The maze pattern on a rectangular stool

First stage
As described above.

Second stage
Here blocks of four wraps are used. Mark the centres of the empty rails.

1. Loop a piece of string round the centre four wraps of the first stage. Do the same for the central 20 strands as in Fig. 3.44.
2. Start at one edge by weaving the first block of four wraps under the first four of the first stage, then under the central 20 and under the last four (Fig. 3.91).
3. Repeat this arrangement underneath the stool.
4. The next block of four strands passes under the first eight wraps, under the central 12 wraps of the first stage, and under the last eight wraps.
5. The third block of four strands passes under the first 12 wraps, under the central four wraps, and under the final 12 wraps of the first stage.
6. The seat is then worked by passing the next block of wraps under sixteen strands each side and over all the central ones.
7. Continue increasing by four each time the number of strands the wraps pass under each side until the centre of the side rails is reached.
8. Reverse the pattern for the second half. Finish as on page 180.

Third variation
This is the reverse of the patterns already described and you may find it easier to work.

First stage
Work the first stage as previously described. The strands should be divisible to give an odd number of blocks of weaving so that there is a central block.

Second stage
1. The first block of four strands is woven over four strands and then under all the others except the last four (Fig. 3.92).
2. The second block of four strands goes over eight strands at either side.
3. The third block is over twelve strands on either side.
4. Continue increasing by four the number of strands each block passes over on each side until the centre of the side rails is reached.
5. Reverse the pattern for the second half.
   Finish either by knotting the first and last ends together or with a knot and tack as appropriate (page 180).

Fourth variation
Coloured seagrass or cord may be used for the first stage and a different colour for the second stage. Different sections of each stage may be put on with contrasting colours to produce an effect of checks or stripes.

Note: Keep joins underneath and as close to the rails as possible.

Fifth variation: rectangular frames

The first stage:
This is worked from short rail to short rail (the longest distance possible). You may keep the same number of strands in each block but the centre section can be much longer than the other (Photo 3.38, right). Here five strands are used for each block.

If you would like this central section to be shorter, each block of wraps may include six or seven strands rather than the five shown. Each wrap will still pass under five strands of the first stage on each side and underneath. Here the finished stool will have wider blocks going across the short side than those along the length.

The underside may be woven in a much simpler way (page 182) by dividing it into three large blocks (Photo 3.39).

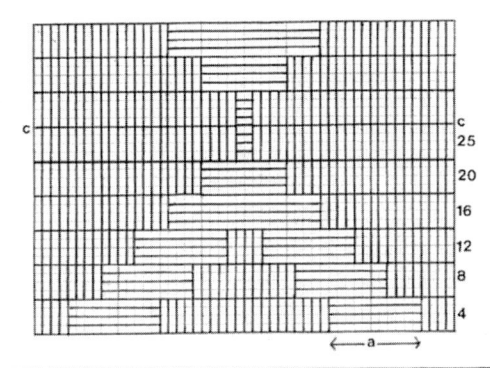

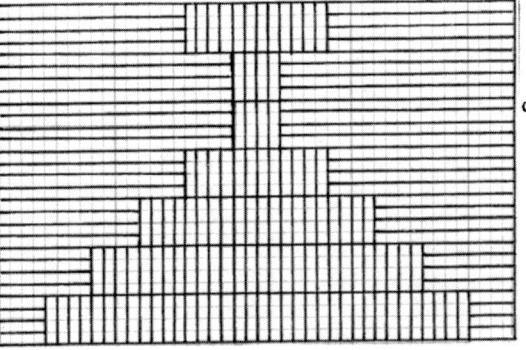

Fig 3.91 The second maze variation. The number of strands in length **a** will vary with the size of the stool. The first block passes under the first four strands, the central twenty and the last four of the first stage

Fig 3.92 The third maze variation. The second stage is worked from side to side as before. The first block (bottom of diagram) is carried over the first and last four strands of the first stage

Photo 3.39 Underside of seagrass stool showing the method of weaving in large blocks

Photo 3.40 *Left*: Check weave stool. *Right*: twill weave with seagrass

CLOSE WOVEN CHECK AND TWILL PATTERNS

These are suitable only for square and rectangular seats and stools.

THE CHECK PATTERN (Photo 3.40, left)

The first stage

The simplest method involves wrapping the seagrass right round the frame as described for the maze pattern, but this time a tension stick must be used for the first stage to ensure enough slack for the weaving of the second stage. The size will vary with the size of the stool but normally a piece of wood about 2.5 cm (1 in) square and about 36 cm (14 in) longer than the frame is suitable. If you wish to weave the same pattern on top and underside of the stool a second tension stick must be put in on the underside. If you want to use a simple weave underneath there is no need for the second stick.

Tie the ends of the tension sticks together with string or tie them to the side rails to hold them in place (Fig. 3.93). It is essential they are not made of any material which will bend.

Wrap the frame and tension sticks as for the maze pattern (Fig. 3.92), joining (page 179) as necessary. The total number of wraps should be divisible by four, five or six if the second stage is to work out.

The second stage

This is a woven stage. A long seating needle (easily made out of hardboard, Photo 3.36a) is useful for pulling the seagrass through, but you can also use your fingers. Seagrass is rough and fairly hard so you may find it helps to wear a thin glove (use an old one or a gardening glove) on your pulling hand.

1. Bring the seagrass from the first stage round behind the stool leg and up on the outside of the rail to begin the weaving. Thread the end of the seagrass through the end of the needle and take it over four strands if the total number of wraps at the first stage is divisible by four. Then weave it under four, over four, etc., right across. Carry it over five or six strands for a larger block. Take it round the outside of the rail and weave back across underneath in the same way if you have put in a tension stick here. If not, divide the wraps underneath into three equal groups and take the seagrass under the first group, over the second and under the third (Photo 3.39). Bring it up over the rail and repeat the top weaving. Carry on until you have four weavings (or five, or six) all the same, both top and bottom (Fig. 3.94).
2. Then for the next block of four start each by going under the first four, over the second four, etc., to give a check weave.
3. Continue across the seat, joining where necessary.

   Note: On the underside, if you have no tension stick, change the weaving pattern about a third of the way along, going under the groups you previously went over. After a further third change back to the original weaving. This will give three blocks of weaving.

   If you have a tension stick, continue to weave underneath in the pattern of the top.
4. Towards the end the wooden needle will not fit through the wraps of the first stage, so use either your fingers or the metal

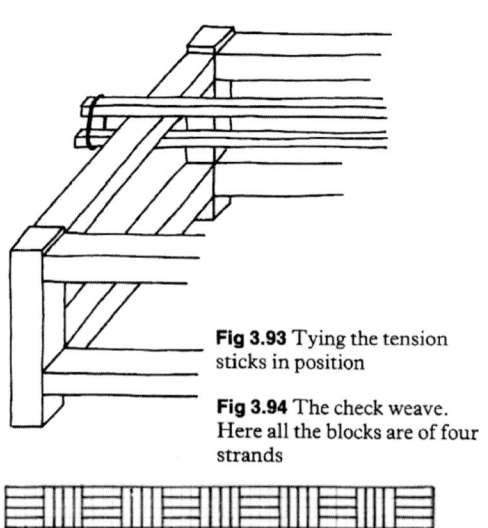

Fig 3.93 Tying the tension sticks in position

Fig 3.94 The check weave. Here all the blocks are of four strands

182

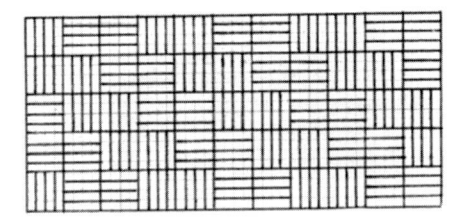

Fig 3.95 The twill weave variation. The instructions start from the right front corner (r)

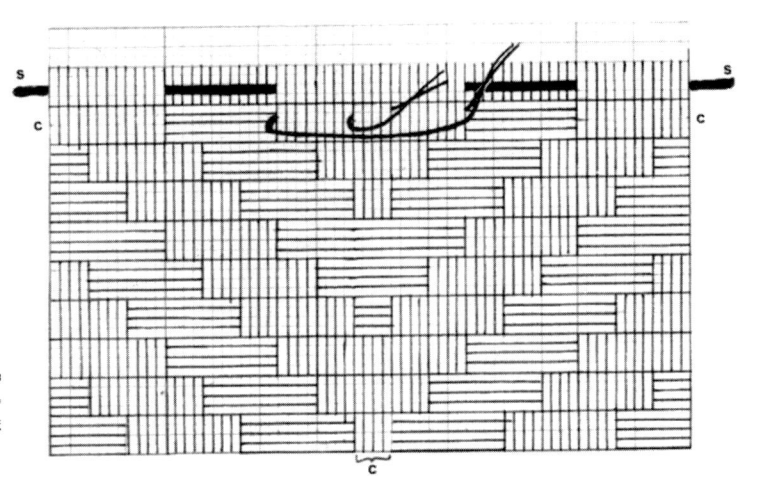

Fig 3.96 The diamond variation. A loop marks the central block. A short piece of seagrass **S** is put in to he with the pattern

needle. This is threaded back through the work, then the seagrass is threaded through the eye and pulled through. A knitting-needle head can be used in the same way and the seagrass tied to it before being pulled through.

Note: You will find that it is difficult to keep each weaving at right angles to the first stage, as they will tend to curve outwards. Overcome this by pushing the strands on the rails as close together as possible and use a bodkin or the edge of the needle to pull each block of weaving back towards the rail.

5. Make sure you finish with a block of four strands (or five or six) and either tie the final end to the starting piece or use a knot and tack as before.

Note: Don't weave with less than four strands together as the strands do not pack closely enough to fill the rails.

TWILL WEAVE VARIATION

This is worked as the previous example until the second stage. The number of wraps should be divisible by four. If your stool is rectangular the woven rows should be the shortest as the material is difficult to pull through long woven rows.

1. Start by weaving over eight strands, under eight, and so on across the stool. It does not matter if you finish over or under eight or four strands. Repeat four times (Fig. 3.95), using either the same pattern or the large block method underneath.
2. The next set of four weavings passes under four strands, then over eight, under eight, as before.
3. Start the next block by going under eight, then over eight, under eight.
4. The next block of four strands will start by going over four, then under eight, over eight all the way across.

These four blocks make up the pattern and form the twill weave. Continue them to complete the seat.

Note: The final block must be a block of four strands, but may be any of stages 1 to 4.
5. Finish as described above (page 180).

The twill pattern can be varied by including different numbers of strands in each block or by weaving the two stages in different colours.

DIAMOND VARIATION

This is a modified twill variation. It has a central diamond and chevrons on either side. The description involves using blocks of four strands as before but this can be varied.

First stage

Complete as described on page 178, making sure the number of strands divides by four and that there is an uneven number of blocks of strands to provide an odd one for the centre of the diamond. Remember that on a rectangular stool this stage is put on along the length of the stool, so that the weaving rows are short.

Second stage

1. The centre block of strands must be put in first so find the centre of the two uncovered side rails and the centre block of strands from the first stage. Loop a piece of string round the centre block of the first stage (Fig. 3.96). Move the string so it is in line with the centre marks on the uncovered side rails.
2. Start with a short piece of seagrass or string to map out the pattern. Take it under the central 20 strands (five blocks) over the 12 strands either side, under the next 12 and so on, to each side rail. You may have to go over or under four or eight strands near the rails.
3. Take a short end of a new skein of seagrass and thread it with needle or fingers in beside the short length you have put in (Fig. 3.96).
4. Tie it on the foot rail below the seat frame.
5. Thread the other end through a needle and take it under the stool and either weave the simple pattern underneath (pages 181–2) or

183

repeat the top pattern. Weave in four strands in this pattern and push them so that two strands are either side of the centre marks on the side rails.

6. Before starting the second block, put in another short length of seagrass or string, starting it in the centre, to make sure the diamond is right, and work it out to the rails. Weave in four strands following this short length (Fig. 3.96).
7. Continue to weave in blocks, maintaining the pattern on both surfaces, until you reach the rails. Finish with a complete block of four strands.
8. Start a new length of seagrass in the centre and work the second half of the stool to be the reverse of the first. Remember there is one central block.
9. To finish both ends, use a tack to anchor the last wrap as before leaving a length of seagrass at least 20 cm (8 in) long to be woven away inside.

VARIATIONS

A large number of patterns can be woven into these stools and they may be worked out on graph paper.

The first stage of weaving can be put on and the number of strands counted. If the stool is square the number of strands for the second stage will be the same. Mark off these numbers on graph paper, mark the centre block of the first stage to give you the centre of the weaving and decide how many strands you can fit into each block.

Some examples of charts are shown in Fig. 3.97. Each block has four strands, as already described, but this may be varied. Avoid having blocks of less than three strands as the patterns tend not to show well and the weaving becomes very tight unless you have used a very large tension stick. Larger blocks can be used, depending on the size of the stool.

Many patterns are possible using simple designs but introducing two colours of seagrass. The colour could be changed at intervals during either wrapping or weaving to give a striped effect, or during both stages which produces checks. On small stools use of more than two colours tends to look rather overpatterned.

OPEN WEAVING METHOD

This involves alternating the wrapping round the whole seat with the binding of the individual rails (see cover). It gives a more open weave, which is quicker to produce. This method and its variations may be used for seats which are wider at the front than the back.

The first stage

1. Put some seagrass on a spool (Photo 3.36a).
2. Put a tension stick of about 2.5 × 1.5 cm (1 × ½ in) across the top of the stool. Put another underneath if you are using the same pattern (Fig. 3.93).
3. Tie the seagrass to the back left leg or tack it in place (Fig. 3.86). Bring it up outside the back rail, over the top, forwards, over the front rail, and underneath to the back again. Repeat until you have four wraps round the frame (Fig. 3.98).

Now bind the front rail once and then carry the seagrass to the back rail on the underside of the stool. Take it outside the back rail, up and over the top and bind this

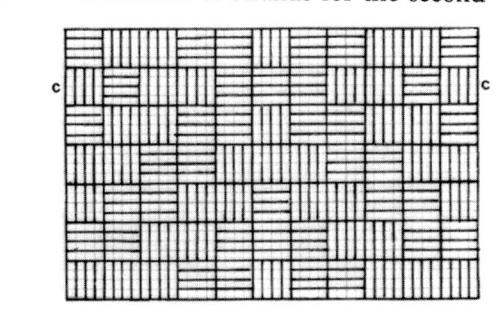

Fig 3.97a The large diagonal cross design

Fig 3.97b Chevrons

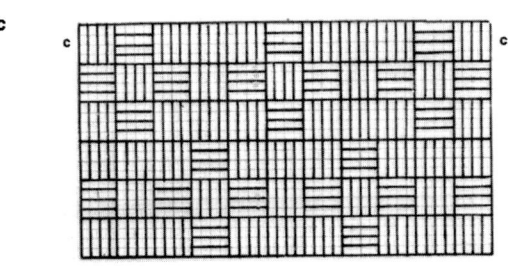

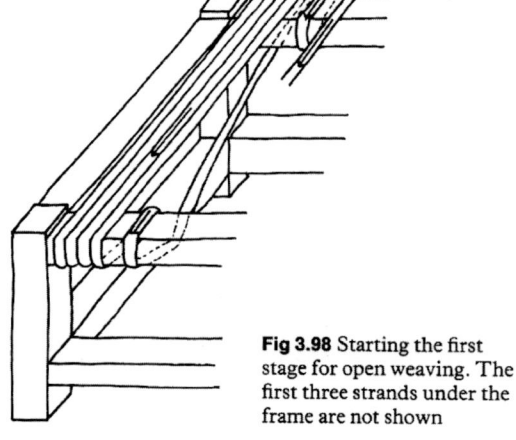

Fig 3.97c Small crosses (c marks the centre of each design)

Fig 3.98 Starting the first stage for open weaving. The first three strands under the frame are not shown

rail once. This will give a diagonal stroke underneath (Fig. 3.98).

4. Put on four more wraps round the whole frame, then bind the front rail once, carry the seagrass to the back and then bind the back rail.
5. Continue in this way until the wrapping is completed, finishing with a block of four strands on the front and back rails to match the start.

Join with a splice where necessary (Fig. 3.88). If you are using cord, leave long ends on the knot so it can be re-knotted at the end if it shows.

The second stage

This involves wrapping and binding in the same way as the first stage, but the two surfaces of the seat must be woven at the same time.

1. Start by joining in coloured seagrass at the front right leg or continue to use seagrass from the first stage.
2. Take it over the first block of four strands, under the second block, and so on.
3. Take it underneath and repeat the weave.
4. Put on three more strands to make the first four-strand block of the second stage.
5. Bind the left-hand rail once then weave through underneath, alternating the weave to begin a second block.
6. Wrap once round the right-hand rail (Fig. 3.99).
7. Now put on four more strands, this time starting each off by going under the first block, then over the second, to give a check weave.
8. Continue working round the frame with blocks of four strands separated by binds until you reach the back of the stool.

Note: As you work, take care to keep the wraps as straight as possible as you put them in. Use the needle to push the weaving towards the front of the stool. Finish as on page 180.

Variations

1. Colours can be used to give stripes and checks.
2. Two or even three binds can be put round each rail between blocks of wraps.
3. The number of strands in the blocks can vary. The blocks of the first stage may be much wider than those of the second stage.
4. Twill weave and other patterns can be woven instead of the check weave. Photo 3.40 (right) shows a stool which uses single strands, each separated by one bind on each rail. The second stage repeats this and uses a twill weave of over three and under three. A smaller tension stick is needed for the first stage here because of the extra binds. Un-

derneath either the same pattern is woven in, or wide blocks are used (Photo 3.39).

There are six parts to the pattern. Remember to bind each rail separately once, before weaving a strand across (Photo 3.40 and Fig. 3.100). Each block may contain any number of strands.

5. *The chevron pattern.* The first stage: as described in variation 4 above. The second stage: this has no binds between the wrapping strands as in Photo 3.41, but they could be put in as in the first stage (Fig. 3.101).

The entire pattern is made up of seventeen rows. When starting a second pattern, its first row, the eighteenth, will be the same as the last row of the previous pattern, so there will be two rows together that are the same.

This pattern shows best if different colours are used for the first and second stages.

Fig 3.99 The first two blocks of the second stage with one bind between each

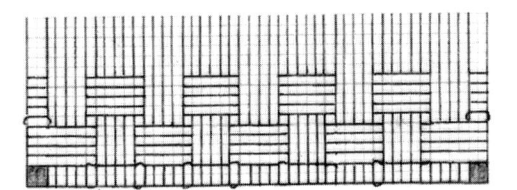

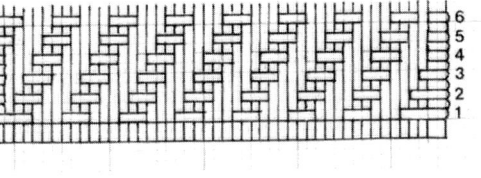

Fig 3.100 The six stages of the twill weave with one bind between each

Fig 3.101 The seventeen stages of the chevron pattern. No binds are shown between each

Photo 3.41 Chevron pattern woven in fine macramé twine

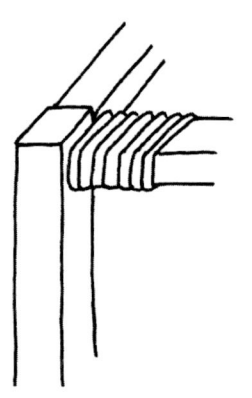

Fig 3.102 Binding the extra length on the front rail

SEATS WIDER AT THE FRONT
Measure the front and back rails and work out the difference between their lengths. The extra length at the front can be filled in various ways.

Method 1
If the difference in length is 5 cm (2 in) or less, it is possible to bind the front rail at each side with a single strand of seagrass or cord before starting to work the seat. Bind 2.5 cm (1 in) at the left and another 2.5 cm (1 in) at the right of the front rail. The ends of these binds may be secured under the rail with tacks (Fig. 3.102).

Method 2
This looks a bit daunting, but do not be put off!

1. Decide how many strands you are to have in the pattern and how many binds round the rail between each, say, 5 strands to a block with two binds between each, making 7.
2. Measure the width of this number of pieces of seagrass or cord placed side by side. Here 7 widths of seagrass make 2.5 cm (1 in) on average.
3. Calculate the extra length of the front rail. In our example this measures 10 cm (4 in).
4. The number of extra strands of seagrass needed across front (**B**) = the number of strands and binds in the pattern (**S**) multiplied by the extra length of the front rail (**F**) divided by the width of the strands and binds in the pattern (**W**),

   i.e. $B = S \times \dfrac{F}{W}$

   So in our example:

   $B = 7 \times \dfrac{10}{2.5}$

   $= 7 \times 4$
   $= 28$

   So here 28 extra widths of seagrass are needed across the front.

5. Next work out how many strands and binds you can fit across the back rail. Call this **N** in the formula below.

   Measure the back rail and divide its length (**R**) by the width of the strands and binds in the pattern (**W**)

   so $N = \dfrac{R}{W}$

   so if W = 2.5 cm and R = 30 cm

   $N = \dfrac{30}{2.5}$

   $= 12$

   So in this example 12 blocks of 5 strands with 2 binds between will be needed to cover the back rail.

6. Next divide **B** (see above) by **N**. The answer will be the number of extra binds which must be put on at the front between each block.

   Number of extra binds between blocks

   $= \dfrac{28}{12}$

   = 2 remainder 4

   You could put 2 extra binds between each block at the front using up 24 of the 28. The remaining 4 can be included by putting 2 extra binds at either end of the front rail next to the legs.

The rush pattern used on stools

The traditional rush pattern can be used with seagrass or cord but is very difficult to do well.

It is easier than using rush in that there is no twisting to do and very few joins, but it is difficult to keep good right angles as you work round the corners.

TO START A SQUARE STOOL

1. Tie a knot in one end of the cord or seagrass and tack this to the inside of the left side rail close to the back leg.
2. Wind the seagrass on to a spool.
3. The direction of working is described on page 75.
   Note: At all times, pull the seagrass as tight as possible or the seat will sag later.
   The right angles, formed where one strand crosses another, must be kept true. This can be difficult as seagrass tends to slip and does not keep right-angled bends easily. As the work gets closer to the centre only a small hank will pass through the central hole. For the last few rounds just pull a long end through.
4. If the stool is square, work until you reach the middle.
5. On the underside tie off the end round one of the opposite strands using a sheet bend (figure-eight knot) (Fig. 3.88c). Tuck away the end.

STUFFING (See *Artificial rush* (page 121) and Figs 2.18–2.19

Rectangular seats

1. If the seat is rectangular, work until the side rails are filled.
2. Work backwards and forwards in a figure of

eight until the spaces on the long rails are filled.

Note: The strands will cross in the stool centre and should form a straight line or bridge (page 73). Push them up very close to help keep this straight line and prevent the strands crossing at different places.

3. Finish with a knot as before.

Trapezium shapes

See instructions for artificial rush (page 121).

Variations

1. The continental rush patterns already described (Chapter 11) may all be followed using seagrass or cord.
2. Colour can be put in round each corner. Join in coloured seagrass after a few rounds and work five or six rounds in the colour before going back to the original seagrass. Stripes can be put in by joining and changing colour every few rounds. Make sure you have an equal number of strands in each group on each corner.

The false rush pattern

This is best kept for square seats. It looks like a variation of the rush pattern described above, but it involves taking the seagrass or cord backwards and forwards in a figure of eight to give two wraps on opposite rails before turning the corner. It is easier to maintain the right angles at the corners so the result may be neater than that using the normal rush method.

1. Wind the seagrass on to a spool or into a ball held with an elastic band.
2. Tack a knot of seagrass on to the inside of the back left leg.
3. Bring the seagrass up inside the frame, out over the back rail, up in the centre again and over the top of the front rail next to the front left leg.
4. Carry the seagrass under the front rail, up into the centre and out over the back rail.
5. Now take it over the back rail and back up into the centre, then out and over the front rail again (Fig. 3.103a).

    Note: Starting in this way gives the necessary two strands over both back and front rails.
6. Carry the seagrass to the right over the three strands and the left side rail at the front, keeping it close to the leg. Take it round the left rail and up into the centre.
7. Carry the spool over the right-hand rail and up into the centre again.
8. Repeat stages 3 to 7 to complete the next corner (Fig. 3.103b).
9. Work each corner round the seat in the same way until the rails are filled.
10. Finish underneath by knotting the seagrass round one or two strands from the opposite side of the chair.

Fig 3.103 Starting the false rush pattern with seagrass

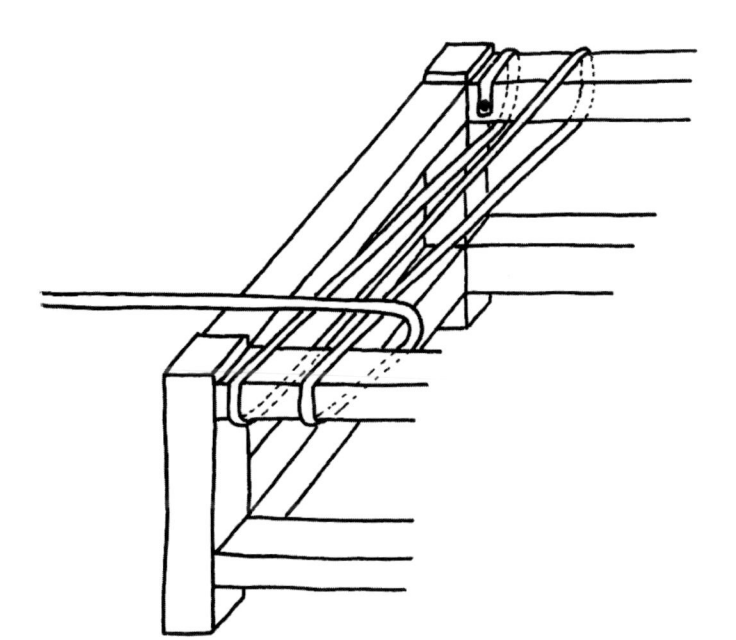

Fig 3.103a The first six steps of the instructions

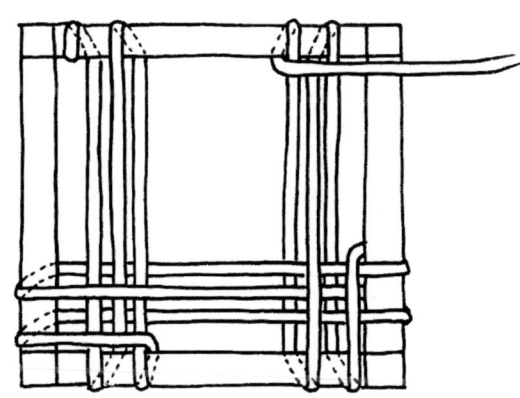

Fig 3.103b Viewed from above

Knotted seating

This method is not suitable for seagrass but is good with cotton string. Anything which will not stretch too much and is not too thick to tie knots easily will be suitable. Photo 3.42 uses cotton string, and macramé twine is very good.

In this method the stool is covered with one layer of cord. It takes longer than those previously described.

Use a tension stick of about 2.5 × 2.5 cm (1 in) square on top of the stool. Wind the string on to a spool or leave it loose for pulling through. Use long lengths to avoid joins as far as possible. Mark the centre of each rail.

The first stage

If the stool is rectangular this stage should go from short rail to short rail. This means there will be shorter rows of weaving in the second stage.

1. Start by tying the string on to the front of the stretcher bar on the left-hand side. Wrap this rail once (Fig. 3.104).
2. Take it from the top of the left rail, over to the right-hand rail, down the outside, up in the centre between the front rail and itself, over itself, then under the right-hand rail to the outside. Push the knot to the corner and pull it tight.
3. Take the string over the top from the outside and across to the left-hand rail, round the left-hand rail, and up between the front rail and the two strings across the seat. Pass it over the two strings, down behind them and under the left-hand rail to the outside. All knots from now on will be worked over two strands until the final (single) one.

Now repeat stages 2 and 3 above, pulling all the string taut and pushing the knots towards the start to make sure the rails are well covered. Each time bring the spool up between the knotted strings and the ones ready to be knotted. Arrange the knots so they all lie at the same angle.

At the end you may need to carry the thread under its own loop, making three strings in one loop on one side before putting on a bind round the rail on the other to match the start.

To join

Tie a reef knot in the middle of the seat and leave long ends so that, if necessary at the end, the knot can be undone and reworked in a position where it will be out of sight.

The second stage

1. Take out the tension stick and take the string off the spool. Continue to use the string from the first stage by passing it inside a leg on to a new side of the stool.
2. Pass it once right round the rail, as at the beginning, and work exactly as for the first stage but weaving it through the first stage each time it is taken across.

   Note: Any of the patterns already described could be used. A wooden seagrass needle may be useful when weaving, as you will have to pull longish lengths of string through.
3. Push the knots of the second stage really close to each other. If they will not push up, simple binds may be put on the rails at intervals. This may be necessary if the strands will not lie close to each other.
4. To finish, either knot each end and tack to the frame or tie ends round a strand on the underside and cut off neatly.

Photo 3.42 A stool seated by the knotting method, using cotton cord

Fig 3.104 The knotted seating method: the first knot passes over one string, all others except the last, over two

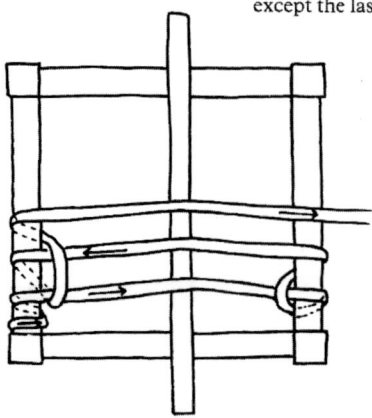

Recommended reading

GERMAINE BROTHERTON
Rush and Leafcraft, Batsford

MARGERY BROWN
Rush and Cane Chair Seating, Batsford

GEORGE BUCHANAN
Illustrated Handbook of Furniture and Restoration, Batsford

HILARY BURNS
Cane, Rush and Willow; Weaving with Natural Materials, Apple Press

BILL COTTON
Country Chairs, Antique Collectors' Club

Dryad Leaflet No. 16
Recaning a Stool or Chair Seat
Dryad Leaflet No. 524
Cord and Seagrass Seating

J. DUNWELL & M. KINGDOM
Chair Caning Method for Frames of all Types, Stool Seating Method in Cord, Seagrass and Rush, Dunwell & Kingdom

BILL FIMPLER
Danish Seat Cord for Chairs, Cane & Basket Supply Co.

NORAH FLORENCE
Rushwork, Bell

DESMOND GASTON
Care and Repair of Furniture, Collins

RICKY HOLDSTOCK
Seat Weaving in Rush, Cane or Cord. Guild of Master Craftsmen

LORRAINE JOHNSON
How to Restore and Repair Absolutely Everything, Michael Joseph

BARBARA MAYNARD
Cane, Rush and Straw, Excalibur
Cane Seating, Dryad Ltd
Rush Seating, Dryad Ltd

ROFFEY & CROSS
Rushwork, Pitman

IVAN SPARKES
English Country Chair, Spur

ROBERT TOWER
'Orkney Chair' (articles in *Practical Woodworking* magazine, May/June 1985)

JIM WIDNESS & BRUCE MILLER
The Caner's Handbook, Collins

DOROTHY WRIGHT
Complete Book of Baskets and Basketry, David & Charles

DOROTHY WRIGHT
'Repairing Victorian Willow Chair Seats' (article in *Antique Collector*, July 1983, pp. 70-2)

Suppliers

please always enclose a S.A.E. when requesting information.

Chair Cane & Centre Cane

Fred Aldous Limited: PO Box 135, 37 Lever Street, Manchester M60 1UX.
Telephone: 0161 236 2477
Cane and chair seating suppliers.

The Cane Store: 207 Blackstock Road, Islington, London N5 2LL.
Telephone: 0171 354 4210
Cane and imported willow supplies.

The Cane Workshop: The Gospel Hall, Westport, Langport, Somerset TA10 0BH.
Telephone: 01460 281636
Cane and imported rush suppliers.

Former Glory: 258 Station Road, West Moors, Ferndown, Dorset BH22 0JF.
Telephone: 01202 895859
Cane and chair seating cord suppliers.

Jacobs, Young & Westbury: Bridge Road, Haywards Heath, West Sussex HR16 1TZ.
Telephone: 01444 412411
Cane and imported willow suppliers, raffia, cords, rush and chair seating materials.

S.A.R.L. Cannage et Paillage: Zone Industrielle des Torrièrs, Route de Frebecourt, 88300 Neufchâteau, France.
Telephone: 29 06 16 46
Cane, paper, cord, rush, straw and raffia suppliers.

Smit and Company Limited: Unit 1, Eastern Road, Aldershot, Hampshire GU12 4TE.
Telephone: 01252 343626
Cane, plastic cane, chair seating cord and raffia suppliers.

The Woodworkers Superstore: Riverside Sawmills, Boroughbridge, North Yorkshire YO3 9LJ.
Telephone: 01423 322370
Cane and chair seating cord supplies.

English Rush

Felicity Irons: Keepers Lodge, Pound Lane, Kimbolton, Cambs. PE18 0HR.
Telephone: 01480 860819 (home), 01234 771980 (workshop), 0378 266386 (mobile)

County Chairmen: Home Farm, School Lane, Ardington, Near Wantage, Oxon. OX12 8PY
Telephone: 0123 5833 614 & 632

Imported Rush

Iain Brown: 58 Commercial Road, Hereford HR1 2BP.
Telephone: 01432 58895 (business)

John Excell: The Cane Workshop, The Gospel Hall, Westport, Langport, Nr. Ilminster, Somerset.
Telephone: 01460 281636

Susan Wright: (Dutch Freshwater)
Telephone: 01473 658324

M.R. Abbey: (Portuguese)
South Wind, The Street, Gooderstone, Kings Lynn, Norfolk.
Telephone: 03166 328711

Geoff Berry: Acadia, Swansbrook Lane, Horam, Heathfield, E. Sussex TN21 0LD.
Telephone: 014353 2383

Jacobs, Young & Westbury Ltd: JYW House, Bridge Road, Haywards Heath, West Sussex HR16 1TZ
Telephone: 01444 412411

The Cane Store: 207 Blackstock Road, Highbury Vale, London N5 2LL.
Telephone: 0171 354 4210

Iorweth Pritchard: 17 Heathcote Grove, Chingford, London E4 6RZ

J. Burdekin Ltd: Osset, West Yorkshire WF5 9AQ.
Telephone: 01924 273103 / 273515

English Willow - *large or small quantities*

Reg Hector: 18 Windmill Hill, North Curry, Near Taunton, Somerset. Telephone: 01823 490236

Andrew Basham: (Heavy 2 year & older willow sticks - white or brown) Church Barn, Ridlington, Norfolk NR28 9NR.
Telephone: 01692 650998

R. J. Moore
Telephone: 01493 700279

P. H. Coate & Son: Meare Green Court, Stoke St Gregory, Near Taunton, Somerset.
Telephone: 01823 490249

Stoke Willows: Dark Lane, Stoke St Gregory, Taunton, Somerset TA3 6EU
Telephone: 01823 480407 *Stephen Pearce/Helen Tyler*

Robert Goodwin: *(Brown Willow)* Ashmans Farm, Kelvedon, Nr Colchester, Essex CO5 7BT.
Telephone: 01621 815934

J. Burdekin Ltd: Osset, West Yorkshire WF5 9AQ.
Telephone: 01924 273103 / 273515

Earle Male: Brookside, Stembridge, Martock, Somerset TA12 6BB.
Telephone: 01460 240407

Dereham Bros.: Fosters Farm, North Curry, Taunton, Somerset TA3 6BB.
Telephone: 01823 480407

H. J. Lock: *(any amount supplied - buff, white, red, yellow, grey)* Lockleaze, Thorney Road, Kings Episcopi, Martock, Somerset TA12 6BQ.
Telephone: 01935 823338

Les Musgrove: 20 Lake Wall, Western Zoyland, Somerset TA7 0LP.
Telephone: 01278 691759

The Willow Bank (BA) Mail Order:
Catalogue and colour brochure, P.O. Box 17, Machynlleth, Powys, SY20 8WR.
Telephone: 01650 511395

G. A. Pipe: Frog Lane, Longport, Somerset TA10 0NE.
Telephone: 01458 253299

G. Butterworth: Bedfordshire.
Telephone: 01767 260682 Mobile: 0403 675010

Imported Willow

Jacobs, Young & Westbury Ltd: JYW House, Bridge Road, Haywards Heath, West Sussex HR16 1TZ
Telephone: 01444 412411

The Cane Store: 207 Blackstock Road, Highbury Vale, London N5 2LL.
Telephone: 0171 354 4210

Straw

Armitage: West Hall Farm, Sedgeford, Hunstanton, Norfolk.
Telephone: 01485 70941

Corn Craft: Monks Eleigh, Ipswich, Suffolk.
Telephone: 01449 740456

A. C. Castle & Son: Home Farm, Charlton, Wantage, Oxon OX12 7HE

Danish Cord

Iorweth Pritchard: 17 Heathcote Grove, Chingford, London E4 6RZ

Tools

John Excell: The Cane Workshop, The Gospel Hall, Westport, Langport, Nr. Ilminster, Somerset.
Telephone: 01460 281636

Geoff Berry: Acadia, Swansbrook Lane, Horam, Heathfield, E. Sussex TN21 0LD.
Telephone: 014353 2383

Mary Butcher: *(Bodkins, sidecutters, books by M. Butcher)* 6 Downs Road, Canterbury, Kent CT2 7AY
Telephone: 01227 766427

The Cane Store: 207 Blackstock Road, Islington, London N5 2LL.
Telephone: 0171 354 4210

Smit and Company Limited: Unit 1, Eastern Road, Aldershot, Hampshire GU12 4TE.
Telephone: 01252 343626

Jacobs, Young & Westbury: Bridge Road, Haywards Heath, West Sussex HR16 1TZ.
Telephone: 01444 412411

Former Glory: 258 Station Road, West Moors, Ferndown, Dorset BH22 0JF.
Telephone: 01202 895859

The Woodworkers Superstore: Riverside Sawmills, Boroughbridge, North Yorkshire YO3 9LJ.
Telephone: 01423 322370

For details of **The Basketmakers Association** please contact;
the Membership Secretary,
37 Mendip Road,
Cheltenham,
Glos. GL52 5EB
enclosing a S.A.E.

Index

acute angles on rush seats 77
arrowhead finish 73, 81, 82, 109, 110
artificial straw coil 108, 111
assessing your work 81
awl 144, 146, 147

back panels on a rush chair 90
batten 47, 48
beading 13, 15, 23, 24, 25, 26, 28, 55
beechwood chairs 29, 37
beeswax 15
bentwood chairs 37
bind 178
blind holes 13
block 178
blocks of coils, rush 88, 91, 92, 98
bodkins 124, 144
bolts, willow 124
bow-fronted chairs, rush 100
bridge on rush chairs 72, 81–4, 88, 98, 99
broken stitches on Orkney chairs 117
bulrush 70
butt,
    alternative methods 80
    corner joins, rush 76, 80
    rush 70

candlewax 15
cane,
    choice of 15, 16
    deterioration of 15
    diagonal lines 33
    foundation 53
    French 54
    hairpins of 28, 50
    imperfect 15
    interlocking 14
    jagged ends 25
    join, in close caning 170, 171
    joining 17, 26
    loops 18, 25, 26
    nodes of 15
    on Orkney chairs 117
    preparation 11, 15
    right way 18
    shiny side of 17
    sizes of 15
    soaking 15
    storing 15
    tails of 25
    tension of 18, 19
    three-in-a-bed 33
    twisted 17, 19
    webbing 59
    wrapping 171
    wrongly woven 20

centre cane 3, 59
chain waling 128, 131–2
chair, preparation of 125
chair backs, for skeining 137
check patterns, seagrass 181, 182
chevron pattern 184, 185
cleave 137
cleaving willow 138
clusters 21
coir/coyer 112
continental rush patterns with seagrass 187
cord, Danish 173
corner angles on rush seats 77, 103
corner holes 20, 27, 36, 38
corners, for whole willow 127
couching 15, 24, 25, 26, 28, 55
covered corners on rush seats 93–7
    curved cut-away 94–6
    rounded 97
    sharp 96–7
    square 93
crosses 21
crossings 13, 14, 20, 21, 26, 33–6
    in circular shapes 38–41
    in rising sun 44–6
curved front rails 145

Danish cord, joining 176
diagonal weaves 15
diamond pattern:
    close skeining 152
    open skein 166
    seagrass 183
dismantling chair arms 102
dolly (smoother) for rush seats 71
double diamond pattern 61
doubles 20, 33, 36
doubling for trapezoid rush seats 79, 83–7, 91
    continuous methods 79, 83–5, 90, 91
    front corner methods 85–7, 88, 89
dragon's teeth 23
drawing-through tool 12, 32
Drew, David 126
drop-in seats 169
dyes for straw 108–9, 117
dylon dyes 155–6, 167

extra long side rails on rush seats 86, 98–9

finishing methods
    for Orkney chairs 116
    for rope chairs 120
    for rush seats 78, 80, 82, 107, 121
    for straw seats 111
fisheye 20, 33

foundation canes 137, 142, 150, 158
    weaving in 146, 147, 149, 150, 151
French weaving 64
Furlong, Nancy 168, 172

gaps in the frame 22, 23
Garrick, David 68, 69
gauge for straw coil 115
golden rule 34, 37, 45
golf tees 12, 26
graph paper 184

hacksaw 13, 23
hairpins 28, 50
half hitch join 26
harvesting rushes 70
hay rope 119
High Wycombe 140, 141, 149, 157
holes
    in rails, for skeining 137
    uneven 31, 37
hoods for Orkney chairs 113, 116–17

Indonesia 11
interior rush coils 72, 73
interlocking
    canes 14
    rush panels 106, 107

Johnny save all 142
joining
    artificial rush 121, 122
    cane 17, 26
    chair cane for Orkney chairs 117
    cord 188
    hay and straw rope 119, 120
    in Medallion 48, 49
    in randing 129–30
    rushes 76, 77, 79
    sisal for Orkney chairs 114
    skeins, Campaign chair method 164
    straw coil 109, 115
    without knots 79

Kealey, Tom 126
kisses 21
knot
    clove hitch 115
    half hitch 75, 76, 79, 84
    reef 76, 78, 79
    skein 143–4, 145
    weavers' 85
knotting skeins
    alternative methods 149
    alternative methods for open skeining 161

at the back 147
at the front 148
Maltby's method 150, 151

lapping cane 27
leaders 143–4, 146, 151
leaf nodes 11, 15, 18
left-handed workers 73
liner 141–2, 149–50
lines of weaving 26
London–Liverpool 21
loose ends 24

Malaysia 11
Maltby, Leslie 141, 149, 164
Mayes, John 157
Maynard, Barbara 140, 141, 159, 177
marram grass 68
maze pattern 178–80
  variations 180–1
mellowing willow 124
misses 33
Morris, William 69, 100–2
Museum of English Rural Life 141, 149, 164

nails
  blunt 13, 23
  L-shaped 173
North, Benjamin 140
notches
  in liner 141, 149
  on curved rails 100, 104
Nottinghamshire 124, 126

obtuse angles on rush seats 77, 103–4
overcrowded rush coils 78, 82

packing needle 171, 178
padding stick 178
painted rush chairs 68, 118
pairing 167
patterns for rush seats
  Continental 88, 89
  Double Continental 90–1
  English 69, 77
  French 89, 91, 111
  straw 108, 111
pegs, for skeined seats 142
pegging 16, 19
plugs 12, 13, 15, 23, 24, 26
preparation
  of artificial rush 121
  of chair frame 74
  of rush 71
  of straw 109, 115
  of straw/hay rope 119

rails
  for skeined chair 137
  for whole willow seat 127
randing 128, 129, 132
rapping iron 124, 178
reedmace 70, 83, 88
repairs to chair frames 66, 75
rods for skeining 138
rush
  bottomers ('matters') 68, 126
  needle 178
  pattern on stools 186
rush coils
  in blocks 88, 91, 92, 98
  direction of 73, 79, 81
  to make 72, 75
  overwrapped with straw 109–10
  size 69, 72, 75, 87
rush seats
  building up 77
  to finish 78, 80
  to start 75, 79

Salix triandra 124
scalloming 128–9, 135
seagrass 112
  block weaving for underside 180, 181, 182
  finishing 180
  joining 179
  needle 178, 179, 188
  open weaving method 184–5
  stuffing 186
  on seats wider at the front 186
  spool 178, 184
  stool patterns 184
seat frames 72, 83, 93, 98, 101–4, 113
seating needle 171, 172, 178, 179, 182
seats, drop-in 169
sedges 72, 88
settings 13, 14, 17, 18
  adjustment of 19, 26
  alternative method 27
  short 31
shaping Orkney chairs 114
shave 137
shaving willow 138–9
shell bodkin 12, 19, 146, 171
Sheraton 58
side cutters 12, 124, 178
sisal 113–15
skein
  knot 143–4, 145, 146, 148, 149, 150, 151, 161
  patterns 152–7, 166–7
skeining
  colour patterns 155, 156
  filling in at front and back 145, 148, 149, 153, 167
  filling in at the sides, close skeining 147, 167
  filling in at the sides, open skeining 161
  tools 137
skeins 128, 137–9
  bundled while working 145, 148
  joining 164
  knotting 143–4, 145, 146, 148, 149, 150–1, 161
  soaking before knotting 144, 145
slats on rush seats 74
slype 125, 128, 135
soaking whole willow 124
Somerset 124, 126
spider weave pattern 60
splines, removal of 55
spool, for cord and seagrass 177, 184, 187
stake breakage 134
Star pattern 61
steamer 54, 64
stiletto 45
stool
  frames 178
  seats 16, 23, 51
storage of rushes 70
strand 178
straight across finish 73, 75, 81–2, 88, 109–10
strap, use of 52

straw coils for Orkney chairs 112–16
straw
  matters 68, 109
  rope 118–19
  to split 109
stuffing 72, 78, 80, 81, 93
stick 71, 78, 81

tacks 173, 178
tannin 124
tension
  adjustment 146, 172
  stick 141, 145, 146, 150, 151, 163, 169, 170, 172, 182, 184, 188
Thonet, Michael 37
thraw hook 118
threading tool 71, 78
thumb guard 139
tip of rush 70, 76, 78, 79, 80
toenail cutters 12, 23
trimming
  skeined seats 149
  skeins 149
  whole willow 135
tub chair 51
turpentine 12
twill pattern 146, 171, 182, 183, 185
twisting willow 133

upright 137, 138
uprighting willow 139

varnishing
  artificial rush 121
  rush seats 68, 69
Viall, Joy 157
Voysey, C.F.A. 69, 98

waling 128, 130, 133
weavings 13, 14, 17, 18, 26
  alternative method 27
  finishing 19
  short 31
webbing 59
wedges 49, 59
wedge-shaped gaps 82, 83, 90
whimble (whimmer) 119
wild iris 70
willow
  break 124
  buff 124
  butt 125
  growing 124
  mellowing 124
  peeling 124
  rod structure 125
  seat frame, recognition 127
  seats, difficult shapes 136
  trimming 135
  twisting 133
  white 124
wrap 178
wrapping
  front rail with whole willow 133
  with skeins for open skeining 162
  with skeins for whole willow seat 128
Wright, Dorothy 141, 164
Wycombe chair 34

Yeovil–York 21
Youens family 141